A Guide
to the Library of the
New England Historic
Genealogical Society

A Guide
to the Library of the
New England Historic
Genealogical Society

Maureen A. Taylor

Henry B. Hoff

Editors

New England Historic Genealogical Society
Boston, Massachusetts
2004

Cover design: Carolyn Sheppard Oakley
Back cover photos: Doug Sisko (1), Marieke Van Damme (2, 3)

Published and distributed by
New England Historic Genealogical Society
101 Newbury Street
Boston, Massachusetts 02116-3007

International Standard Book Number: 0-88082-159-0
Library of Congress Control Number: 2004114988

Printed in the United States of America.

Contents

SECTION 3

Rare Books and Manuscripts

SECTION 4

New England

SECTION 5

Beyond the Northeast

Preface

The idea of a guide to the library of the New England Historic Genealogical Society has been discussed for several years, but developing a concept for such a project was daunting. How could a single guide do justice to such an extensive and diverse library? We decided our goal was to provide readers with background information and research perspectives that would let them take full advantage of the general holdings at 101 Newbury Street — not necessarily to delve into the content of specific collections within the library. To that end, this book relies heavily on articles that have already appeared in print and online, which we have supplemented with original material as necessary. This book is divided into eight sections: a general introduction to the library, articles on genealogies and manuscripts, regional studies — New England, beyond the Northeast, Canada, and the British Isles and Ireland — and methodological articles on diverse topics.

Choosing articles for an anthology means making difficult decisions about what to include and leave out. There are inconsistencies in style and presentation among the articles because it is a compilation by different authors. For instance, not all pieces include call numbers for items owned by the Society. In the New England articles, call numbers are included except for items not held by the library.

Every project has lists of people to thank for their participation and this one is no different. Laura G. Prescott, Director of Marketing, sent us her files on an earlier version of this project. The contributors of reprinted articles — Lynn Betlock, Marie E. Daly, David Curtis Dearborn, Christopher Hartman, David Allen Lambert, Michael J. Leclerc, Julie Helen Otto, Gary Boyd Roberts, George F. Sanborn Jr., Timothy G. X. Salls, and Ruth Wellner — updated and revised their original works. Several individuals wrote new pieces for this anthology — Joseph C. Anderson II, Cherry Fletcher Bamberg, Scott Andrew Bartley, Sherry L. Gould, Julie Helen Otto, Joyce S. Pendery, George F. Sanborn Jr., Helen Schatvet Ullmann, and the two editors. The staff of the NEHGS library, especially David Curtis Dearborn, David Allen Lambert, Julie Helen Otto, Gary Boyd Roberts, and George F. Sanborn Jr., answered questions and verified sources. Four reviewers caught many small discrepancies that we had overlooked: Helen Ullmann and Michele Leinaweaver (who fact-checked and edited parts of the manuscript), Tom Kozachek (who copy edited the manuscript), and Eric Grundset (who prepared the index). Photographs and illustrations used in the text are from the NEHGS Library and Archives with the exception of the photographs of the library today, taken by Marieke Van Damme and Doug Sisko.

This book would not have been possible without the support of D. Brenton Simons, Assistant Executive Director, Gabrielle Stone, former Director of Publications, and Martha Bustin, her successor, who guided us from the proposal stage through publication.

We hope you enjoy learning about the library of the New England Historic Genealogical Society!

Maureen A. Taylor
Henry B. Hoff

Introduction

Great libraries start small. The New England Historic Genealogical Society library, which began in 1845 with just a few volumes, is now one of the country's finest research libraries, with over 200,000 volumes, two million manuscripts, rare books, and a staff of leading genealogical scholars and librarians. Initially an organization created by a few men interested in pursuing genealogical research, it now includes members from all over the world. Bricks and mortar librarianship combines with twenty-first-century technology in a website (*NewEnglandAncestors.org*) that increases access to the collections through an online card catalog, databases, and research articles.

The prominent founders of the New England Historic Genealogical Society — Charles Ewer, Lemuel Shattuck, John Wingate Thornton, Samuel G. Drake, and William H. Montague — were men of their times. In the late eighteenth and early nineteenth centuries, Americans became interested in preserving history — local, institutional, and familial. Across the country historical societies were established for just that purpose. In New England, the Massachusetts Historical Society (1791), the Rhode Island Historical Society (1822), the New Hampshire Historical Society (1823), and the Connecticut Historical Society (1825) all began collecting books and manuscripts about the history of the country and their particular regions. Spurred on by this notion of keeping the past for the future, the founders of the New England Historic Genealogical Society turned their efforts to the founding families. The NEHGS mission was "to collect, preserve and disseminate the local and general history of New England and the genealogy of New England families."[1]

Society President William Whiting called for the development of a comprehensive library in 1852. His presidential address, published in *The New England Historical and Genealogical Register* in 1853, invited members to donate materials. Those donations became the foundation for the library that grew to 3,294 volumes and 14,000 pamphlets by 1861, a mere nine years later. The library doubled in size by 1865, due to an expansion of the collection to include "local history, genealogical family histories, biographies, travels, journals, histories of corporations and military expeditions."[2] By 1903 President James Phinney Baxter began a book-buying campaign that would make the library the "centre of genealogical knowledge not only for New England, but for the whole country."[3] He intended to buy every American genealogy ever published.[4] While collecting material from all over the country and the world gave members incredible research opportunities, it created space concerns.

The collection grew so quickly that the NEHGS rapidly outgrew the three rooms in the City Building on Court Square No. 9 that the Society occupied from February 1846 to October 1847. From 1846 to 1964, the New England

Historic Genealogical Society moved six times before settling into its present location at 99/101 Newbury Street in 1964, formerly the New England Trust Company. Space considerations for library acquisitions and usage resulted in four floors being added to the building, and later renovations provided extra space for patrons and collections.

Research institutions are more than the materials that sit on their shelves waiting to be used. The New England Historic Genealogical Society staff includes prominent genealogists — individuals who base their career on understanding the nuances of genealogical research. Two librarians, George F. Sanborn Jr. and David Curtis Dearborn, hold the lifetime distinction of being named Fellows of the American Society of Genealogists (FASG). Each staff member has specific areas of interest and expertise that enhance the value of the library's holdings. Patrons consulting collections can meet with staff to discuss their research problems, thus making the staff as valuable a resource as the books and manuscripts.

A little over a hundred years ago, James Phinney Baxter and his staff had a goal for the library: they believed in "building not for our own day, but for the future" to create "a unique archive of family history." [5] They accomplished their dream: the library has an amazing collection of genealogical materials

View of 5 Tremont Row, home to the Society from 1851 to 1858.

The Seymour Morris Reading Room at 9 Ashburton Place, 1935. NEHGS was at this location from 1912 to 1964.

pertaining not just to New England families. Even though utilized by thousands of researchers every year, the library is still relatively undiscovered by many. With a broad range of geographical and historical materials, the library at NEHGS has much to offer researchers in a variety of disciplines.

This guide aims to help individuals understand how to make the most of the library's resources. The breadth of the collections, the expertise of the staff, and the history of the organization all make this library one of the outstanding research facilities in the country for those researching a family or a location.

Notes

1. John A. Schutz, *A Noble Pursuit: The Sesquicentennial History of the New England Historic Genealogical Society 1845–1995* (Boston: NEHGS, 1995), 36.

2. *Ibid.* 22.

3. *Ibid.* 78.

4. *Ibid.*

5. *Ibid.* 79.

Contributors

Joseph C. Anderson II, CG, FASG, is editor of *The Maine Genealogist* and a coeditor of *The American Genealogist*.

Cherry Fletcher Bamberg has written numerous books and articles on Rhode Island and is coeditor of *Rhode Island Roots*.

Scott Andrew Bartley, editor of *Vermont Genealogy* and the *Mayflower Descendant*, is the author of numerous articles on Vermont published on *NewEnglandAncestors.org*.

Lynn Betlock is the editorial manager of *New England Ancestors*. She has a M.A. in American History from the University of Delaware.

Marie E. Daly, director of library services at NEHGS, is past president and cofounder of TIARA (The Irish Ancestral Research Association) and has been researching, lecturing, and writing about Irish genealogy since 1976.

David Curtis Dearborn, FASG, is a reference librarian at NEHGS. David's interests include the Dearborn family (descendants of Godfrey, who arrived in New Hampshire by 1638); families of Essex County, Massachusetts, and Maine, New Hampshire, and Vermont; New York City and urban genealogy; twentieth-century genealogy; eighteenth-and nineteenth-century English and Scottish genealogy; Italian genealogy; and westward migration.

Sherry L. Gould is a professional genealogist and genealogy lecturer in New Hampshire. She is the author of numerous articles published in *New England Ancestors*, on *NewEnglandAncestors.org*, and in *Eastman's Newsletter*.

Christopher Hartman, major gifts officer for NEHGS, has been an editor and director of the Society's Newbury Street Press. He has worked extensively in the rare book trade, specializing in genealogy and printed and manuscript Americana.

Henry B. Hoff, CG, FASG, is editor of *The New England Historical and Genealogical Register*. He is the past editor of *The New York Genealogical and Biographical Record*.

David Allen Lambert is a reference librarian at NEHGS who specializes in New England and Atlantic Canadian records, military records, and Native American genealogical research in New England. David is the author of *A Guide to Cemeteries in Massachusetts* (NEHGS, 2002), and is involved in content development for the website and the Society's online genealogical service.

Michael J. Leclerc is director of special projects for NEHGS, writing and editing books for Newbury Street Press, working with Plimoth Plantation on the "Plymouth Ancestors" joint project, and involved with the planning of the Society's education programs and tours. Michael is a member of the board of directors of the Federation of Genealogical Societies and a past board member of the Association of Professional Genealogists.

Julie Helen Otto is a reference librarian at NEHGS who specializes in general New England genealogy; the Blackman/Blakeman, Tiffany, Everest, and Dunton families; and using material culture to uncover genealogical clues. She has worked extensively on matrilineal descents and onomastics (names and naming patterns) and has explored deaths by lightning in colonial and later New England.

Joyce S. Pendery, CG, a trustee of NEHGS, is the author of several articles on Connecticut published in *New England Ancestors* and on *NewEnglandAncestors.org*.

Gary Boyd Roberts, senior research scholar at NEHGS, specializes in royal descents; the ancestry of American presidents and many other notable figures; *Mayflower*, Rhode Island, and Connecticut families; the South; and printed sources for each. He has published extensively on all of these topics.

Timothy G. X. Salls has served as the NEHGS archivist since 1999. Tim has written numerous articles for *New England Ancestors* and edited *Guide to the Manuscript Collections at the New England Historic Genealogical Society*, published in 2002.

George F. Sanborn Jr., FASG, FSA Scot, is a reference librarian at NEHGS. His specialties include northern New England; the Canadian Maritime Provinces (particularly Highland Scots settlers of Prince Edward Island and Cape Breton Island); and the Hebrides of Scotland.

Maureen A. Taylor is the author of *Scrapbooking Your Family History* (Betterway, 2003), *Preserving Your Family Photographs* (Betterway, 2001), and *The Avery Family: The Ancestors and Descendants of Christopher Avery* (Newbury Street Press, 2003).

Helen Schatvet Ullmann, CG, FASG, associate editor of *The New England Historical and Genealogical Register* and a consulting editor for the Newbury Street Press, is the author of several articles on Massachusetts published on *NewEnglandAncestors.org*.

Ruth Quigley Wellner is the NEHGS Research Services Coordinator. She was founder and first president of the Central Massachusetts Genealogical Society and is past treasurer of the Genealogical Speakers Guild. Ruth has over 25 years experience in genealogical research and professional speaking.

A Guide
to the Library of the
New England Historic
Genealogical Society

Using the Library

Researching Your Family Tree

Getting to the New England Historic Genealogical Society (NEHGS) is easy, whether you arrive by plane, train, or automobile, but learning where things are requires orientation. Five floors of material can be intimidating if you don't know where to start. Reviewing basic research techniques will enable you to approach research at NEHGS logically.

A good first step is to plan your trip based on a series of questions — who, what, where, and how. Whom do you want to find? What do you want to know about them? Where did they live? How did they get there? After reviewing first steps, we offer some advanced tips to help you get the most out of your visit. We conclude this introduction with some practical advice on using the library.

Tracing Your Heritage

Initiating Your Project — What do you want to know?

Beginning to research your family history can quickly become a daunting project. To make it easier, focus your attention on one person or family branch at a time. Consult a helpful guide to research, such as Ralph J. Crandall, *Shaking Your Family Tree: A Basic Guide to Tracing Your Family's Genealogy*, 2nd edition (Boston: NEHGS, 2001).

Work from the Known to the Unknown

This is the number one rule of genealogy. Start from what you know about yourself, and work backwards one family event at a time.

Use Home Sources

Interview living relatives about their lives and family history to assist you in your search. Ask them when and where they were born, when they married, what they remember about their parents. It is important to formulate a list of questions before the interview to keep the conversation focused. Record the interview whenever possible.

Other material that you or relatives might have, such as old photos, personal letters, family Bibles, diaries, and material objects might supply names, dates, and other information important to your research.

Use a Record-Keeping System

Once you've sifted through all your home resources, it's time to organize your research before it becomes overwhelming. Whether you record the information on note cards or use computer software, it is important to find a system that is both efficient and easy to use. Make sure that you clearly document each new piece of data and record where it came from.

Develop a Research Strategy

In general, you should start with published materials, such as books and periodicals, searching for printed and abstracted records before moving to original sources and manuscripts. This sequence of events can vary depending on the research problem. You will develop a sense of appropriate research strategies as you become more experienced. You should also create checklists of research tasks.

Verify Your Sources

Transcription errors, editing mistakes, and typographical errors exist in all sorts of documents — handwritten and published — not just those found online. Try to find original sources whenever possible.

Planning Your Research Trip

There are a number of things you can do to make a research trip a success; most of them can be done before you come to the library.

Organize and Review Your Research

The very first item on your checklist should be putting your research notes in order. That means filing all the discoveries from your last research trip and updating your genealogical information for the families you intend to research. It's disappointing to return from doing genealogical research only to discover that you had already found what you were looking for on a previous trip to the library but had forgotten to review your notes beforehand. Make the task manageable by working on it in small pieces. Organizing before you leave home will enable you to leave unnecessary paperwork behind.

Make Lists

Genealogical software allows researchers to make lists to stay focused. Don't make one large list; rather, organize your questions to make research easier.

- Use a spreadsheet to group questions by time period, place, and person. Keep a research log with questions, sources consulted, and the date and place you found the data.

- Highlight missing pieces of information on your family tree or group sheet. This works as a quick reference source.

Go Online

Part of the list-making process is knowing what's available to help you uncover new family information. For instance, it makes sense to explore what libraries have in their collections to make sure you go to the appropriate facility for your question. Most libraries now have online catalogs, so you can start compiling lists of sources before you travel. Use the following to prepare for your research trip.

- *Online catalogs* — Keep track of the latest publications in your area of interest and create a bibliography of new sources to consult.

- *Bookstores* — You may find pertinent items just by browsing bookstore shelves.

- *Websites* — Visit organization, library, and archive websites regularly to stay up-to-date with finding aids and new acquisitions.

- *Connect with Cousins* — Use your family network to share the research load via email.

- *NewEnglandAncestors.org* — Read articles on the website, explore the online catalog, and create an action plan for research in the library.

Call Ahead

Contact the organization you plan to visit beforehand. Libraries, including NEHGS, alter their hours during holiday seasons, bad weather, local holidays, emergencies and special events.

Bring What You Need

Bring pencils, change and small bills, research notes, laptop computer, digital camera — whatever you think you'll need. Consult research policies to see what you're allowed to bring into a facility.

Getting to the Library

NEHGS is in the heart of Boston's Back Bay, near the Public Garden and Boston Common. The address is 99–101 Newbury Street (the nearest cross-street is Clarendon), two blocks west of the Public Garden and two blocks north of the Hancock Tower in Copley Square.

Public transportation is the easiest mode of travel in Boston, but visitors preferring to drive into the city can park in private lots located throughout the Back Bay area for a substantial fee.

Where to Park

The Back Bay Garage

222 Berkeley Street and 500 Boylston Street, one block down and one block over from NEHGS. Call 617-266-7006 for more information.

Entrances on Clarendon Street, between Boylston Street and St. James Avenue, and St. James Avenue between Berkeley and Clarendon streets.

Boston Common Garage

Zero (0) Charles Street, located directly across from the Public Garden and beneath the west end of the Boston Common. Note: the height restriction is 6'3"

For more information please call 617-954-2098. Due to construction on the Central Artery 93 it is best to call for information to verify exit names and numbers.

Fitz Inn Auto Park at Newbury and Dartmouth streets, one block west of NEHGS. For more information, call 617-482-7740 or visit *fitzinn.com*.

John Hancock Garage

Adjacent to the Back Bay Station, four blocks south of NEHGS. Entrance at 100 Clarendon Street. For more information, call 617-572-0151.

Kinney Parking at 10 St. James Avenue, across from the Park Plaza Hotel.

Driving Directions to NEHGS

From West of Boston:

Take the Massachusetts Turnpike (I-90) heading east, going through the Allston/ Brighton tolls, following signs for Boston. Take the "Prudential/Copley Square" exit and bear right in the tunnel following signs for "Copley Square." The tunnel will let you out onto Stuart Street in the Back Bay of Boston. From here there are several parking garages nearby. (See "where to park" for directions to the individual garages from this point).

From each garage head toward Copley Square (a public park across from the Boston Public Library) NEHGS is one block north and one block east, near the corner of Clarendon and Newbury streets.

From North of Boston:

Take Interstate 93 south toward Boston. Take exit 26 "Storrow Drive/ North Station."

From the exit ramp you will be on an access road that will lead you under some bridges to Storrow Drive. Stay towards the left along with the main flow of traffic and you will be emptied out onto Storrow Drive heading west. Follow Storrow Drive westbound along the Charles River and look for the "Copley Square/Back Bay" exit. It should be either the second or third exit once you get onto Storrow Drive

and it will be on the left hand side. The exit will lead you to Beacon Street. After taking the exit, turn left onto Beacon followed by an immediate right onto Arlington Street. From here there are several parking garages nearby (See "where to park" for directions to the individual garages from this point).

From each garage head toward Copley Square (a public park across from the Boston Public Library) NEHGS is one block north and one block east, near the corner of Clarendon and Newbury streets.

From South of Boston:

Take Interstate 93 north toward Boston. Take exit 18 Berkeley Street and follow the exit straight staying in the left lane. At the first light, make a left onto Berkeley Street. Follow Berkeley Street (which bends slightly at the light at Tremont Street, be sure to continue forward on Berkeley) past the old Boston Police headquarters which will be on your left. From here there are several parking garages nearby (See "where to park" for directions to the individual garages from this point).

From each garage head toward Copley Square (a public park across from the Boston Public Library) NEHGS is one block north and one block east, near the corner of Clarendon and Newbury streets.

Street Parking

Newbury and Boylston Streets

There are parking meters for on-street parking, if you can find a spot. On-street parking is monitored so read signs carefully. Cars left in legal parking areas after hours will be towed Rates: Meter parking in 15 minute increments up to a two-hour maximum. Violators are ticketed.

Parking Outside of the City

Alewife Garage, Alewife Brook Parkway, Cambridge, located at the Alewife subway stop on the Red Line. Once you've parked, you may take the Red Line train to Park Street station, change to an Outbound Green Line train and get off at the either the Arlington or Copley station.

Riverside Parking Lot, Grove Street, off Route 128 at Exit 21. Recommended for over-sized vehicles. Once you've parked, you may take the Green D Line train at the Riverside subway stop directly into Boston, getting off at the Arlington or Copley station.

Airports

There are airports in the Boston area — Logan Airport www.massport/logan.com in East Boston; Manchester, New Hampshire, Airport and T. F. Green Airport, in Rhode Island. Logan is the closest to the Library.

Many Boston area hotels offer shuttle service to Logan Airport; ask when you make your reservation or call 1-800-23-Logan. Free buses from the airport connect travelers to Boston's public transportation system, known as the "T" — short for MBTA. Additional information on traveling to and from Logan is available online *massport/logan.com* .

Amtrak

Trains traveling the Northeast Corridor — Boston to Virginia — arrive at South Station in downtown Boston. Many of the trains also stop at the Back Bay Station.

Buses

Greyhound, Bonanza, and Peter Pan bus lines also serve the Boston area. Contact them for additional information.

MBTA (The "T")

Search subway, commuter rail, and intercity bus routes via *mbta.com*. The Library is short walk from public transportation on the Green line (Arlington or Copley Square stops) or from the Orange line (Back Bay Station). Travelers using the Blue or Red lines will need to transfer to either the Orange or Green line to reach the Library. The Green line connects to North Station.

A Tour of the NEHGS Library

Lynn Betlock

When describing the New England Historic Genealogical Society library, it is easy to use superlatives and impressive statistics. NEHGS, founded in 1845, owns the nation's oldest genealogical library. The collection contains more than 200,000 volumes, including comprehensive holdings of published New England genealogies and local histories. The library also contains a growing collection of over 40,000 microfilms of original vital, probate, and land records, city directories, and censuses for New England and eastern Canada. The NEHGS Circulating Library, which allows members to borrow books through the mail, contains over 30,000 volumes. But what do all those impressive statistics mean to the genealogical researcher? What specific resources will help you further your research?

First Floor: Treat Rotunda and Constance Wadley Fuller Reading Room

The Research Library's first floor contains genealogical and historical print publications for the United Kingdom and Ireland, Continental Europe, and beyond. Printed materials relating to all parts of the world outside the Western Hemisphere reside on open shelves on the first floor. (Note that published materials referring to ethnic groups after their arrival in the Americas are not considered international and will be found elsewhere in the Society's collections.) While the collection is very strong on the U.K. and Ireland, there are also considerable holdings relating to Germany, France, and other countries. The first floor has a large assortment of serials and periodicals from all over the world.

Fourth Floor: Dean C. and Roberta J. Smith Technology Room

The Research Library's fourth floor is the technology floor, housing the microtext department, where patrons may access materials on microfilm, microfiche, CD-ROM, and the Internet, regardless of geographical area or record

Reprinted, with updates and revisions from *New England Ancestors* 3:4 (Fall 2002):15–21.

type. The microtext department is particularly strong in primary sources for New England and Eastern Canada.

Five microfiche readers, eighteen microfilm readers (three with high magnification), three microfilm/microfiche reader-printers, and one microfilm/ microfiche CD burner are available for patrons' use. Also available are five computers with Internet access (including free access to most of the databases on *Ancestry.com*) and shortcuts to over 350 CD-ROM titles.

The microtext department contains printed and CD-ROM census indexes for a majority of the pre-1880 United States censuses. There is a complete collection of the federal census for the New England states, 1790 to 1930, some New England state census records, and a nearly complete collection of Canadian censuses prior to 1901. City and town directories for both New England and Canadian communities are on microfiche. The library holds film indexes to the nineteenth- and early-twentieth-century Boston passenger lists (as well as indexes to smaller New England ports) and the St. Albans Canadian border crossings. There are also a large number of vital, church, probate, and land records on microfilm for many locations in New England, the Canadian Maritimes, and Quebec.

Microfilm

Patrons using microfilm machines may use one roll of microfilm at a time. They will be issued a placeholder with their machine number on it. This placeholder should be substituted for the roll of film when it is removed. When they finish, patrons should re-file their film and remove the placeholder.

Microfiche

Patrons using microfiche machines should use the placeholders available in the microfiche area whenever removing microfiche from the cabinet. Microfiche should be returned to the tray above the cabinets. Patrons should *not* re-file microfiche.

Rules for Use of the Smith Technology Room

All patrons must sign up to use microfilm readers, microfiche readers, microtext printers, and computers at the fourth-floor reference desk.

Patrons may use a machine for one hour during busy periods. Patrons may put their name on the waiting list for an additional hour of time *after* they have already used their initial hour. At the end of the hour, patrons must give up their machine to the next patron if there is a waiting list. If there is no waiting list, patrons may continue to use their machine. A Librarian will inform patrons if they must give up their machine.

Patron using a microfilm machine in the Dean C. and Roberta J. Smith Technology Room.

CD-ROMs

CD-ROMs are now located behind the reference desk. Patrons should see a reference librarian to obtain CD-ROMs.

Copies

Printouts made from printers not attached to card readers should be brought to the reference desk for processing.

Fifth Floor: Local History

The Research Library's fifth floor is home to the Society's collection of published book material for all U.S. states, Canadian provinces, the Caribbean, and Latin America. The collection is particularly strong for the New England states and New York, but a wide range of books is available for other areas, particularly Atlantic coastal states and regions to which New Englanders migrated.

The map collection and oversized atlases are located on this floor. Greater Boston is well represented in the map collection, as are many other parts of New England, North America, and Europe.

Interview with David Allen Lambert, Librarian

What are some of the most popular resources in the Smith Technology Room?

- Massachusetts Vital Records 1841–1910
- Computer databases and online resources
- Probates and deeds for New England
- New England and Atlantic Canada resources

In your opinion what is the best day to use the facility?

Wednesdays, because the library is open late.

Are there any overlooked/ underutilized resources at the NEHGS library that patrons should know about?

Yes, many researchers are unaware that the NEHGS library has city directories for Massachusetts on microfiche, the 1855 and 1865 Massachusetts State Census on microfilm, and 1798 Direct Tax list for Massachusetts and Maine which is also now online at *NewEnglandAncestors.org*.

Many people don't realize that the NEHGS Library has the *Columbian Centinel* 1780–1840 (and index); the *Boston Evening Transcript* 1848–1912 (which is a good source for Boston death notices and the query columns are indexed in *American Genealogical Biographical Index*); the *Boston Pilot* 1860–1917; and the *New York Times*, 1852-1899.

Do you have any advice for researchers?

- Keep track of new products and finding aids.
- Create a checklist of what you need to consult or what you'd like to find.
- Focus on answering a question at a time because looking for an entire family in one research trip isn't likely to be productive.
- Don't forget to utilize electronic databases as a shortcut to primary resource documents.

What is a little known fact about the NEHGS library?

You don't have to spend a lot of money on copies. Bring a blank CD or purchase one from the librarian; burn a CD of images from microfiche or film as a Tiff (but you can't copy the whole source due to copyright restrictions).

In addition to the resources mentioned above, the fifth floor houses a vertical file at the librarian's desk, with many college class report books and alumni directories, and published material on the subjects of religious groups, law, business, and art.

A portion of the local history collection — mostly historical (and some genealogical) journals and magazines from states outside New England — is stored in the basement vault. A binder located on the fifth floor provides a listing of these items. Green "vault" call slips can be used to request items found in the catalog with the word "vault" in the call number.

Patrons using the local history collection often make use of the additional seating area on the fifth floor.

Lastly, for patrons who have difficulty reading small print, a electronic book viewer is available to enlarge the image or minimize contrast. Patrons who would like to use the book viewer should ask the reference librarian for assistance.

Floor 5A: R. Stanton Avery Special Collections Department

The R. Stanton Avery Special Collections Department includes over two million manuscript items, dating from the seventeenth century to the present and representing both New England and other regions. The collections includes thousands of unpublished family genealogies; vital records; family Bibles; diaries; account books; ledgers; correspondence; maps; photographs; typescripts; cemetery, church, town, institutional, business, and military records; artwork; and charts. Also in the collection are the papers of family associations and noted genealogists. It is estimated that nearly every New England family prior to 1840 is represented in this collection in some fashion.

Information for Patrons with Special Needs

Visually impaired patrons:

- can use the book viewer, on the fifth floor
- can contact NEHGS volunteer department to arrange for reading assistance,
- can use magnifying glasses on all floors.

Wheelchair users:

- can access all restrooms,
- will be assisted, as requested, by librarians and shelvers in retrieving books or loading microfilm.

Users with arm and hand disabilities:

- can contact the volunteer department for assistance with turning pages or using microfilm readers.

Diaries are an important component of the manuscript collection. Examining the diary collection more closely provides some sense of the scope of both the diaries and the manuscript collection in general. NEHGS houses the work of 272 diarists, who wrote 863 volumes, for a total of 104,222 pages. While most diarists concentrated on family life and daily events, a variety of other themes are represented as well, from military activities to whaling voyages. Most of the diarists were New Englanders — the majority from Massachusetts — but some hailed from New York, Pennsylvania, the Midwest, Canada, and even the Azores and India. Most of the writers (81 percent) were men, and they represent a number of occupations, including minister, soldier, merchant, physician, gold miner and even beekeeper. More information about the NEHGS diary collection can be found online at *New EnglandAncestors.org/libraries/manuscripts*.

Many of the items in the manuscript collection are listed in the online catalog, but patrons should check the card catalogs on floor 5A to ensure a complete search for any unpublished material or original records. The manuscript card catalogs are divided into two classification systems, which contain different items; these catalogs are distinguished by pink or green drawer tabs. The system marked with pink drawer tabs catalogs manuscripts received by NEHGS between 1974 to 1995 and is referred to in-house as the "New Manuscript Collection Card Catalog." The system marked by green drawer tabs catalogs manuscripts received before 1974 and is known as the "Old Manuscript Collection Card Catalog." All manuscripts received after 1995 are in the online catalog. To request a manuscript, submit a completed call slip to the librarian. While everyone is welcome to check the catalogs, use of manuscripts is restricted to NEHGS members. Those examining items from the collection are asked to use pencils or laptop computers — no pens or markers — and make photocopies only with the permission of the librarian on duty.

Sixth Floor: Ruth C. Bishop Reading Room

Patrons will find two kinds of items on the sixth floor: published family genealogies and general reference works. Readers are also encouraged to browse the reference books behind the librarians' desk. The reading room on this floor contains four major sets in almost continual use: the published Massachusetts town vital records to 1850, complete runs of *The New England Historical and Genealogical Register, The American Genealogist (TAG),* and *The New York Genealogical and Biographical Record (NYGBR).*

The rare book collection is also accessed from this floor. NEHGS has been collecting genealogical materials since its founding. Consequently, the Research Library has a large number of rare and limited edition genealogies, local histories, travelogues, heraldic works, and other materials of interest to historians and family history researchers. Currently, all books published prior to 1865 are located in the rare book collection. Some more recent books that are exceptionally valuable or in fragile condition are located in this collection as well. All books in the catalog that have call numbers starting with "RB" are rare books. Access to the rare book collection is a benefit of membership in NEHGS. Members may request rare books from the sixth floor reference desk, and rare books may be used on the sixth floor only. Permission to photocopy certain oversize or fragile items is at the librarian's discretion.

View of the Ruth C. Bishop Reading Room

Interview with David Curtis Dearborn, Librarian

What are some of the most popular resources at the NEHGS Library?

The *Register,* the published Massachusetts vital records, all of the Great Migration materials as well as Torrey's *New England Marriages.*

In your opinion what is the best day of the week to use the facilities?

Wednesday, because the library is open late year round. Researchers can also take advantage of lectures offered on Wednesday.

Is there a good time to visit?

The library is less crowded early in the day. It gets busy after 11 a.m. Spring, summer, and fall are peak research seasons, but the library is less crowded in the winter or whenever the weather is bad.

What are some of the library's overlooked/underutilized resources?

Genealogies in the Library of Congress, compiled by Marion J. Kaminkow, 5 vols. [REF Z5319/U53/2001]

This is useful when someone asks about a book but can't remember the title. This volume is a way to get the full citation.

William Filby's *American and British Genealogy and Heraldry*

Filby's bibliography is a great resource for locating topic specific materials such as "Loyalists in Ohio." It answers a lot of reference questions.

Three books help you find addresses and contact information for libraries, historical societies, and organizations:

American Library Directory (R. R. Bowker, 2 vols. [R.Rm. REF Z731/A53/1997-98]).

Public libraries usually have a more recent edition.

Directory of Historical Organizations in the United States and Canada [R.Rm. REF E172/D5/2002].

Encyclopedia of Associations and Associations Unlimited Reference, 3 vols. [R.Rm. REF AS22/E5/2000].

If you're looking for a society, use this set to find an address, website URL, and a history of the society.

Another overlooked resource is the *World Almanac.* It answers non-genealogical but historically based questions.

What is your advice to researchers?

Even though the library has open stacks, don't use the wandering-the-shelves method to locate what you need, use the card catalog.

First time users shouldn't be afraid of asking the librarian a question or for an orientation.

The library staff is a valuable resource, knowledgeable about materials in the library as well as other materials available at area institutions.

Using the Online and Card Catalogs

The NEHGS library maintains several different catalogs. Searching all the catalogs is the only way to ensure locating all the materials pertaining to a particular subject area, family name, location, title, or author:

- *Online "Sydney" Catalog.* This database contains the majority of the titles in the library. The retrospective cataloging project is entering new records for old library materials on a daily basis. The materials in the online catalog are cataloged in the Library of Congress classification system. There are slight variations in searching capabilities in the computer catalog in the library and the one available online. Instructions provided here are for the in-house version. Use the directions on the *NewEnglandAncestors.org* website when searching the catalog from home.

- *Library of Congress Card Catalog.* Located on the fifth floor, this catalog has white labels with authors, titles, and subjects all listed together alphabetically. These materials are cataloged in the Library of Congress classification system. This was closed in 1994; all books cataloged after that year can be found in Sydney.

- *Old NEHGS Card Catalog.* Located on the sixth floor, this catalog is split into three sections: a yellow-labeled catalog of genealogies listed alphabetically by surname, a blue-labeled catalog of geographic places listed alphabetically, and a white-labeled catalog of subjects listed alphabetically.

- *New Manuscript Collection Card Catalog.* Located on floor 5A, this is a pink-labeled catalog that refers to unpublished material received by NEHGS from 1974 to 1995 (all manuscript collections received after 1995 are referenced in the online catalog).

- *Old Manuscript Collection Card Catalog.* Located on floor 5A, this green-labeled catalog refers to unpublished material received by NEHGS before 1974.

Where Do I Find . . .

The first letters before and after the call number tells you where in the library the item is located. The following key lists where different subjects can be found in the NEHGS library. The abbreviation (LC) refers to call numbers in the Library of Congress classification. For first letters not listed here, show the citation and call number to a librarian.

First Letters of Call # *Last Letters of Call #	Meaning	Location
Atlas... (LC)	Atlas	Fifth Floor
A-AZ (LC)	General Works	Fifth Floor
B-BX [see note below]	Religion and Philosophy (LC)	Fifth Floor
*... Bindery	Unbound small books and pamphlets	Fifth Floor
C-CC, CT (LC)	Archaeology and Biography	Fifth Floor
CD... (LC)	Archives Collections	First Floor (Eastern Hemisphere) and Fifth Floor (Western Hemisphere)
*... CD	Compact Disk	Fourth Floor
CR ... (LC)	Heraldry	Called at the first-floor reference desk
CS 1–71 (LC)	General Genealogy and American Family Genealogies	Sixth Floor
CS 90 (LC)	Canadian Family Genealogies	Sixth Floor
CS 400-438; 440-478; 480-498; 500-2195 (LC)	European, Asian, and Pacific Genealogy	First Floor
CS 439 (LC)	English Family Genealogies	First Floor
CS 479 (LC)	Scottish Family Genealogies	First Floor
CS 499 (LC)	Irish Family Genealogies	First Floor
CS 599, 629, 699, 739, 829, 846, 859, 1169, 1425, 2009 (LC)	Other European, Asian, and Australian Family Genealogies	First Floor
CS 2200-2600 (LC)	American and Ethnic-American surnames	Fifth Floor
CT (LC)	General Biography	Fifth Floor
DA-DU 619 (LC)	European, Asian, and Pacific History	First Floor
DU 620, E-F (LC)	U.S. and North American History	Fifth Floor
G ... (old class)	Old Class Genealogy	Sixth Floor
G ... (LC)	Geography	First Floor (Eastern Hemisphere) and Fifth Floor (Western Hemisphere)

First Letters of Call # *Last Letters of Call #	Meaning	Location
H-LD (LC)	Non-Genealogy Subjects	Fifth Floor
LF (LC)	European Colleges and Schools	First Floor
M-X (LC)	Non-Genealogy Subjects	Fifth Floor
Intl OS . . . or Intl Oversize . . .	International Oversize	First Floor
Intl R.Rm. . . . or Intl REF . . .	International Reference	First Floor
Map . . .	Map	Fifth Floor
*. . .microfiche or *. . .microfilm	Microfiche or Microfilm	Fourth Floor
Mss . . .	Manuscript	Called at floor 5A or sixth floor reference desk (evenings and Saturdays)
MT . . . or Microtext . . .	Microtext Book	Fourth Floor
OS. . .or Oversize. . .	Oversize Book	Sixth floor for sixth-floor call numbers; fifth floor for fifth-floor call numbers
OS RB . . . or Oversize RareBook	Oversize Rare Book	Called at the sixth-floor reference desk
*. . . Pamphlet Box	Small books and pamphlets	Fifth Floor
R. Rm. REF . . . or R.R. REF . . .	Reading Room Reference Book	Sixth Floor
RB . . . or RareBook . . .	In Rare Book collection	Called at the sixth-floor reference desk
REF . . .	Reference Book	Sixth Floor
TP . . .	Tabular Pedigree Chart	Called at the fifth-floor reference desk
Typescript	Typed volume in Manuscript Collection	Called at the fifth-floor reference desk
VF . . .	Vertical File	Fifth Floor
Z . . . (LC)	Library Science and Bibliography	Sixth-floor reference section

Note: Call numbers BX 9450, assigned to publications of the Huguenot Society of London, are located on the first floor in the Treat Rotunda

Searching Techniques

Locating materials in the online catalog requires some knowledge of how to use the software. **Simple Searches** include the Title Search, which searches just the title field of each catalog record; the Author Search, which searches just the author fields; the Subject Search, which searches just the subject fields; and Call Number Search, which searches just the call number field. An **Advanced Search** enables you to search multiple fields (up to six) at once and thereby broaden or narrow your search. It also provides a way to search a field other than title, author, subject, or call number.

To Perform a Simple Search:

1. Select one of the search methods by clicking on the Title, Author, Subject, or Call Number options in the frame on the left side of your Web browser screen. The default search is a title search.

2. Enter your search text in the box given.

3. Specify how you want your list of search results to be sorted by selecting Title, Call Number, Author, Subject, or Year from the pull-down menu. The default is Title.

4. Indicate how many items you want to display on each page of your search results by selecting a choice from the pull-down menu. The default is 10.

5. If you wish to limit your search to just the Circulating Library, Research Library, or Manuscripts, you may do so by clicking in the circle next to the appropriate option. The default is "All Libraries."

6. When you are ready to submit your search, click on the "search" button. Or, if you wish to remove the search information you have entered, click on the "clear" button.

Note: When the word LOAN appears in a call number, it indicates that a copy of the item is held by the Circulating Library.

Tips and Examples for Specific Searches —

Title Search

Enter a word or words that you believe will be found in the title of the item(s) you're looking for. Less is better. You do not need to enter the entire title in the search box. You will most often get better results if you enter only words that are apt to be less common in the catalog.

Author Search

Enter either all or one part of an author's name. When searching by first name and surname together, you may enter the names in any order. No punctuation is required and searches are not case sensitive.

Example: *caroline brown*

Example: *brown caroline*

Example: *filby*

Subject Search

Enter a word or words that might describe the topic that interests you.

Example: *carroll family*

Example: *vermont civil war*

Example: *cemeteries illinois*

Example: *boston registers births* (*Registers of births, etc.* is the term used for all vital records — birth, marriage, death — so remember to always search by births.)

Example: *west indies genealogy* Example: *italian americans*

Call Number Search

The call number indicates the shelving location at NEHGS. A call number is assigned according to the subject of the item. Enter as much or as little of the call number as you wish, followed by an asterisk.

Example: *cs71j88* (to search for material on the Joy family)*

Example: *f127d8* (to search for material on Dutchess County, N.Y.)*

Advanced Search Techniques

An **Advanced Search** allows you to broaden or narrow your search results by querying up to six fields at once. You may search on any combination of the following fields:

Corporation (a.k.a., corporate author) — e.g., New England Historic Genealogical Society

Series — e.g., Canterbury and York Society Series; Images of America

Notes — miscellaneous notes about item

Contents — description of item contents, if available

Publisher — name of publisher

Year — year of publication

Document Type — specifies the format of a title — e.g., compact disc, manuscripts, map, microform, monograph (book), painting, print, serial (journal, periodical, etc.)

Sub-location — e.g., Circulating Library, Research Library, Manuscripts

Uniform Title — an alternate title for a work — e.g., a copy in original language, if library has translation

Added Title — an alternate or related title — e.g., a title on the book's cover, if different from the one on title page

System Key – the unique ID for a catalog record

To Perform an Advanced Search:

1. Select the fields you wish to search from the pull-down menus.

2. Click on the *Search* button. This will bring you to the search screen.

3. Enter your search information in the appropriate boxes.

4. Choose AND, OR, or NOT where necessary. This allows you to broaden or narrow your search. The default is AND.

5. Choose how you want your list of search results to be sorted by selecting Title, Call number, Author, Subject, or Year from the pull-down menu. The default is Title.

6. When you are ready to submit your search, click on the *Search* button.

To move through the online catalog, the general procedure is:

Highlight Your Choice. With the mouse, move the arrow to your choice from the list on your screen. Your choice will be highlighted in blue.

Initiate Action. Press <Enter>, or indicate action desired by clicking on one of the gray action buttons on your screen. (Example: "Search, "View", "Print".)

If the search menu is not on screen, press <Enter> or click on "Search." The menu choice is Title, Author, Subject, or Call Number. Move the blinking cursor to the beginning to the black line beside your choice with the <Tab> key, the directional arrow key or the mouse.

NOTE*:* The computer is set to perform a Keyword Search, which means every word within the field you choose will be searched to find a match for your request. Should you wish to search only the first word in a field, you must make an adjustment before you begin your search. Click on the "Options" button at the top of your screen. From the menu, select "Left justified search." This option is particularly useful when searching for an author's last name, which appears as the first word of the author field. You may also choose "Phrase search" to search for a specific group of words within a title. You must enter the phrase exactly, including punctuation.

Searching with Hyperlinks

When you view a list of search results or a detailed item view, you will notice that some information (Author, Corporation, Subject, and Series) is underlined and highlighted. These are hyperlinks. By clicking on one, you can initiate a search on that term. For example, if you come across a book by George Freeman Sanborn Jr., and you want to find other works he has authored that are in the catalog, click on his name to retrieve a list of those works.

Special Tips for Searching

Searching by Family Name. When searching for items about a family, enter a Subject Search according to this example:

> *williams family*

Do not enter any first names. Remember to search for all the spelling variations that might exist for a name. For example, to find material on the McFarlane family, search also by McFarland family. You may also try searching for a family name by using a Title Search, but in a Title Search you should not include the word "family" — just enter the name.

Searching by Geographic Location

When searching for items about a particular place, enter a Subject Search according to the following examples (along with the *Common Genealogical Subject Terms* given in the next section).

For countries, U.S. States, and Canadian provinces, enter the place name as you normally would.

> Example: *united states*
>
> Example: *massachusetts*
>
> Example: *nova scotia*

For counties, regions, cities, and towns, enter the place name as you normally would.

> Example: *hartford county*
>
> Example: *hudson river valley*
>
> Example: *philadelphia*

However, some of the U.S. state and Canadian province names that accompany these county and city names appear in two ways in the NEHGS library catalog. For example, Registers of births, etc. **— Maine** — Hancock County *OR* Hancock County (**Me.**) — Genealogy. When a county or city name could appear in more than one U.S. state or Canadian province, and you need to specify which one, the best method is to search by both forms of the name or by using a wild card, if possible (*see Wild Cards, below, for example*).

Example: If you're searching for Hancock County, Maine, enter two searches:

hancock county maine

and

hancock county me

Wild Cards (Truncation)

When searching the NEHGS library catalog, you do not need to enter an entire keyword. Instead, you can enter the first few characters of the keyword followed by an asterisk (also called a wild card).

Example: To find all the titles containing the words *California, genealogy, genealogies, genealogist, genealogists,* and *genealogical,* enter the title search "California genealog*"

Example: To find all the records with the subject headings *Salem (Mass.)* and *Massachusetts — Salem,* enter the subject search "salem mass*"

Common Genealogical Subject Terms

The following terms are some of the standard subject terms used in the NEHGS library catalog. Use this list when entering geographic subject searches in order to narrow your search.

bible records	history
biography	maps
census	marriage records*
church history	military pensions
church records and registers	newspapers
court records	probate records
death notices	real property
deeds	registers of births, etc.**
emigration and immigration	taxation
genealogy	wills

* *Used sometimes when an item contains nothing but marriage records.*
** *Used for all vital records — birth, marriage, death. Always search by births.*

NOTE: The asterisk can be entered only at the end of a string of characters — not at the beginning or in the middle. Example: genealog* but not *enealogy or gen*alogy.

Broadening or Narrowing a Search

You may broaden or narrow a search by using the Advanced Search option. When you select more than one field to search, you will be prompted to combine your search terms with AND, OR, or NOT.

Use the AND and NOT options when you want to minimize your list of results. Think of AND as another way of saying narrow. For example, if you know that the item you want is a book on Vermont genealogy written by Bartley, you could enter a Subject Search for *vermont genealogy,* select AND, and enter an Author Search for *bartley*.

Consider the NOT option as another way of saying exclude. For example, if you were interested in genealogy handbooks, but not those that were published in the 1980s, you could enter a Subject Search for *genealogy handbooks,* click on NOT, and enter a Year Search for *198*.*

Use the OR option to maximize your potential list of search results. Think of OR as another way of saying broaden. For example, if you were searching for information on cemeteries in Bangor and Calais Maine, you could enter a Subject Search for *cemeteries maine bangor*, then select OR, and enter a Subject Search for *cemeteries maine calais*.

Viewing a Record

In the list of search results, a number appears to the left of each item. To view more information about a title, click on the number beside it.

Special Resources

The New England Historic Genealogical Society's collection holds a variety of materials necessary for family history research. From the map that helps you locate where your ancestors lived to photographic portraits and newspapers, the NEHGS library helps you write the social history of your family. Local histories, books on material culture and other special publications can be found on the library's shelves.

Atlases, Maps, and Gazetteers

- Extensive collection of maps and city atlases for greater Boston area
- Variety of atlases and maps for United States (country, states, and cities)
- British Isles (mostly for England and Wales, and some of Scotland)
- Many world, national, and local gazetteers

For a detailed list of our atlas, map, and gazetteer holdings, search the online catalog, consult the Website, or ask a librarian.

Newspapers/Newspaper Abstracts

Many researchers are not aware that the NEHGS library has newspaper holdings. While not comprehensive, the Society's newspaper collection contains the New England newspapers that carried genealogical inquiries and a nearly fifty-year run of the *New York Times* during the nineteenth century.

- Boston — *Columbian Centinel* (began as *Massachusetts Centinel*) — microfilm [F73.1/C65 microfilm]
- Boston — *Evening Transcript,* microfilm, 1848–1912 (contains weekly genealogical columns) [F73.1/B67 microfilm]
- Plymouth, N.H. — *Plymouth Record*, 1887–1957 [F44/P7/P73/microfilm]
- Portland, Maine — Index to newspapers, 1785–1835 [F29/P9/J76/1995]
- Hartford, Conn. — *Hartford Times* genealogical columns, 1934–1967 [F104/H3/H33/1978/microfilm]
- New York City — *New York Times*, 1852–1899 [F128/N49]
- New York — Vital records abstracted from the *New York Evening Post*, 1801–

1890 (NYC/15/14 — deaths; NYC/15/20 — marriages) also available to members on *NewEnglandAncestors.org*.

Periodicals

The NEHGS library has an extensive collection of periodicals as well as periodical finding aids. Search the online catalog for periodicals, family newsletters, and magazines, both current and defunct. Ask a librarian for assistance with items in the vault.

Periodical Source Index (PERSI)

- Indexed by place and surname, PERSI cites where a particular surname or locality appears in genealogical literature.

- On CD-ROM, online, and also in book form [REF CS1/P47]

The New England Historical and Genealogical Register, 1847–present

Published by NEHGS, the *Register* is the oldest journal in the field of American genealogy.

- Composite every-name Index in book form
  Vols. 1–50 [R.Rm. REF F1/N56 v.1-50 INDEX] (name and subject)
  Vols. 51–148 [R.Rm. REF F 1/N567/1995] (name only)

- Vols. 1–148 available on CD-ROM with indexes and search capabilities [Microtext CD]

- Available on *NewEnglandAncestors.org*

National Genealogical Society Quarterly, 1912–present
- Vols. 1 to present [CS42/N4]

- Vols. 1–85 also on CD [Microtext CS42/N42/1998 CD]

The American Genealogist (TAG), 1922–Present
- Vols. 1 (1922) to present [R.Rm. REF F104/N6/A6]

- Vols. 1–8 are also referred to as *Families of Ancient New Haven, New Haven Genealogical Magazine;* reprinted in three volumes

- Vols. 9–13 are listed as *The American Genealogist and New Haven Genealogical Magazine*

- *The American Genealogist* is indexed as follows:

  Composite every-name index for vols. 9–41 on CD-ROM [Microtext F104/N6/A6/INDEX/1998 CD]

Subject index for vols. 1–60 (by Jean Worden) in book form [REF F104/N6/A6/INDEX]

Cross-index for vols. 1–8 (by Helen Love Scranton) in book form [F104/N6/A6/INDEX v.1–8]

The New York Genealogical and Biographical Record, 1870–present
- In book form [R.Rm. REF F116/N28] and on microfiche [F116/N281 microfiche]
- Vols. 1 (1869) to present
- Subject index for vols. 1–113 [R.Rm. REF F116/N28/INDEX]
- Composite every-name index for vols. 1–129 on CD

The Pennsylvania Genealogical Magazine, 1935-present
- Vols. 1 to present [F146/G32]

Examples of additional genealogical journals for other states
- *Jacksonville Genealogical Society Quarterly* (Florida) [F319/J1/J32]
- *Louisiana Genealogical Register* [F366/L55/1966]
- *Ancestor Hunt* (Ohio) [F497/A73/A53]
- *Copper State Bulletin* (Arizona) [F810/C64]
- *Kansas Kin* [F687/R5/K33]

Historical Journals

- *New England Quarterly* [VAULT F1/N62]
- *Pennsylvania Magazine of History and Biography* [VAULT F146/P65]
- *Rowan County Register* (North Carolina) [VAULT F262/R8/R88/1986]
- *North Dakota Historical Quarterly* [VAULT F631/N862]

Ethnic Periodicals

- *Toledot* (Jewish Genealogy) [CS31/T64/1977]
- *Irish at Home and Abroad* [CS496/I7/I74/1993]
- *Yorkshire Genealogist* (England) [DA670/Y6/Y497/1888]
- *Journal of the Afro-American Historical and Genealogical Society* [E185.86/A35]

- *Connections* (French-Canadian/Quebec) [CS88/Q4/C64]
- *Swedish American Genealogist* [E184/S23/S88]

Other Periodicals

- *DAR Magazine* [E202/A12]
- *Markers* [NB1855/M37]
- *The Historical Magazine of Protestant Episcopal Church* [VAULT BX5800/H5]

Photographs

Photographs are part of manuscript collections. Search the online catalog by family name or speak to a member of the Special Collections staff on 5A about their holdings.

Reference Collection

A core collection of reference books is kept on the sixth floor — behind the reference desk and in the stacks. This material is commonly consulted and is within reach of the staff on the sixth floor.

At Your Service!
Research Services at the New England Historic Genealogical Society

Ruth Quigley Wellner

Whether our team of determined researchers is puzzling over a particularly difficult query or creating a detailed report, the Research Services department of the New England Historic Genealogical Society is always busy. Our staff, which boasts many years of experience in the field and great familiarity with all our collections, works onsite in our library to glean the best research results for our patrons. And the action does not stop there. In our offices you will also see volunteers and aides answering the telephone, downloading research requests from *NewEnglandAncestors.org*, responding to e-mail, regular mail, and faxes, and recording correspondence on the computer. Everyone is there to help our patrons with their research requests and to enjoy the challenges presented by each new case.

NEHGS Research Services has taken many forms over the last few years. We have broadened our horizons, adding new categories of research services and enhancing the scope of access to this research. With three major options now available, our patrons are sure to find the one best suited to their particular need.

In-Depth Research

This option provides patrons to get help when they have encountered the proverbial "brick wall." Whether you are a seasoned genealogist with a complicated problem, a beginner with questions about where to start, or a curious patron with plenty of interest but little time, the in-depth service may be the choice for you. The client submits a specific question or problem to the department, including all relevant already gathered. The researcher then searches for answers within the library's holdings and networks with other staff to take advantage of the strengths and experience of the entire department. When an answer is located, or when the specified number of hours of research is completed, the client is sent a report detailing all sources searched and the results of these efforts and offering suggestions for further research.

The most expedient way to access this option is to order online from the Research Services page on *NewEnglandAncestors.org.* You may also request an

Reprinted, with updates and revisions, from *New England Ancestors* 3:2 (Spring 2002):32–35.

order form by writing to NEHGS Research Services, 101 Newbury Street, Boston, MA 02116-3007.

Happily, some recent improvements have been initiated to make this service even more valuable to our customers. For example, our in-house staff now completes all research. This procedure ensures more timely results and simplifies communication. Often, the preliminary analysis of a problem by an expert can save research time and effort. If the documents sought cannot be found at NEHGS, our researchers can take a step beyond our library's walls. We are fortunate to be located in the Boston area, close to many wonderful resources. To obtain the appropriate documents or information, we might venture to the Boston Public Library, Massachusetts Registry of Vital Records and Statistics, the Massachusetts State Archives, or the National Archives Branch, as well as other nearby repositories.

Photocopy Service

Our photocopy service has enabled many patrons to review specific articles or pages in books that would otherwise have been unavailable to them. This service provides photocopies from unrestricted sources found in our collection. In order to undertake this photocopying, we require the title of a specific source and page numbers (or an article title). We adhere to applicable copyright laws and are unable to copy entire books, magazines, or manuscripts.

Consultation/Tutorials Service

There are two types of consultations available through the NEHGS Research Services. *Smart Start* provides first-time visitors to the library with a tour tailored to their own research needs. Your first visit to NEHGS can be overwhelming, as the collection is large and there is much to learn in order to use it wisely. On the day of your appointment, a librarian will meet with you, assess the type of research you want to accomplish, then guide you through the facility to familiarize you with the sources you will need to access.

Our second type of consultation provides a personal, in-depth chart review or problem solving assistance in a one-on-one appointment (either in person or by telephone conference) with one of our knowledgeable librarians to give the patron research advice and direction.

As both types of consultation are available only by appointment, please call 617-226-1233 to schedule your consultation.

Using Research Services

The Research Services staff strives to conduct the best possible research on behalf of our patrons. Feedback from customers concerning the work done is always appreciated. One client wrote to us from San Diego, California, having only a partial article found in the *Parkway Transcript* of October 9, 1931. There was no mention of relatives, and the client wished to know more about her ancestor named in the article. In addition to the information in the short article, the client knew only that her grandmother was the daughter of this person. From this little tidbit, our researchers were able to locate this family in census, birth, and death records. We were able to find the birth dates and places of all the children, the wife's name and her death date and place, her father's name and country of birth, and the death data on the subject of the testimonial. She called to tell us how delighted she was with the results.

In another instance, a patron from Allegan, Michigan, wrote asking for a ship's name and manifest connected to her immigrant ancestor. She knew only that the ship had arrived in Boston on February 14, 1916. She also wanted to know where and when her ancestor had married. We were able to ascertain the name of the ship, photocopy the ship's manifest, and provide a transcription of the marriage record. Following is part of her reaction to our search:

I just received the papers about my request. Just wanted you and whoever did the work [to know] that I was very pleased with the results. My brother had written to Boston trying to find out our parents' wedding date with no results, and we now know why.

Research services are available to members and non-members, and information regarding our options can be accessed through the NEHGS website, regular mail, email, fax, and by telephone.

We encourage our patrons to order our services online at *NewEnglandAncestors.org/marketplace/researchservices* (unless otherwise indicated), as doing so allows for faster communication and expedited results. Orders, when placed on NEHGS Research Services order forms, are also accepted via regular mail, email, and fax. Orders are not accepted over the telephone. Due to the high volume of requests, please allow six to eight weeks for delivery.

NEHGS Research Services looks forward to assisting you in your research. While there are no guarantees that your ancestors will be found, NEHGS Research Services does guarantee that a diligent and careful search of sources for the names you provide us will be made.

So, the next time you have a research challenge, you can be confident that NEHGS Research Services is "at your service!"

Genealogies

A Short History of Genealogical Publishing

Christopher Hartman

The publishing of genealogy, for purposes of this study, commenced in earnest about 1850, with the advent of the New England Historic Genealogical Society, and continues to this day, though in various "waves." The founding of NEHGS in 1845 was succeeded, in fifteen years, by the *Genealogical Dictionary of the First Settlers of New England* (4 vols., 1860–62), compiled by James Savage, sometime president of the Massachusetts Historical Society. A quarter-century after its first issue, the NEHGS scholarly periodical, *The New England Historical and Genealogical Register,* instituted what was to become known as *Register* style. This is a standardized presentation of genealogical data, following a generational progression with a paragraph of vital statistics followed by a listing of issue beneath. Variations of this style will be treated later in this article.

Reprinted, with updates and revisions, from *New England Ancestors* 4:2 (Spring 2003):30–32.

The first bibliography issued by a publisher containing a large selection of his published genealogies was *Bibliotheca Munselliana* (1872). Listed with each entry is, among other things, the print run. Among Munsell's most important published genealogies were *The Wetmore Family in America* (1862), *Hyde Genealogy* (1865), and *The Genealogy of the Benedicts in America* (1870). Subsequent to this came *Catalogue of American and English Genealogies in the Library of Congress* (2nd ed. 1919). The next benchmark came in 1935, with the publishing of Emma Toedteberg's *Catalogue of American Genealogies in the Long Island Historical Society*. This work highlighted what was arguably the most comprehensive catalogued collection of American family histories assembled to that date and was directly the product of Toedteberg's effort to secure copies of every genealogy published.

"... Toedteberg was indefatigable in writing to every author of a genealogy or history to seek a copy for the society, and she was extraordinarily successful ... Miss Edna Huntington [Toedteberg's assistant] continued when she became librarian . . . hampered though she was by the sharply reduced resources of the Society during the depression."[1] These many published family and local histories, pamphlets, and charts were distributed through such bookshops as Goodspeed's Book Shop in Boston and Tuttle's Antiquarian Books of Rutland, Vermont.

The eighty-five intervening years (1850–1935) saw a prodigious output of compiled genealogies, sometimes researched by genealogical scholars, who solicited commissions from wealthy and influential Americans desiring to establish their pedigrees. Genealogists such as Andrew Henshaw Ward, John Adams Vinton, Frederick Clifton Pierce, J. Gardner Bartlett, and Charles Henry Pope produced an astounding number of books on behalf of some of New England's earliest families. The descendants of these families often used such work to cement their social identities in a very class-conscious period. Burke's *Armorial Families* and *Peerage, Knightage and Baronetage* (to name just two of their several associated publications) catered largely to Anglophilic Americans who sought to draw a connection between English royalty and the success of their family's succeeding generations in America. Although the research by Vinton, Pope, Bartlett and, to a lesser extent, Pierce, adhered closely to standards of evidence, there were many others who strayed, sometimes to the point of fantasy. One example is the *Universal International Genealogy and of the Ancient Fernald Families*, by Charles Augustus Fernald, published in 1909. The author attempted to fashion a descent from Adam and Eve, the Apostles, and the ancient kings and kingdoms of Phoenicia and Assyria — among others — to the more contemporary Fernald generations. Its documentation is, of course, scanty, but the reading is really quite entertaining. Also, many compilations of the period used coats of arms often not applicable to most persons carrying the family surname. As arms were granted to individuals and not families, it was (and is) often the case that descendants would claim the arms, only to find that they had no right to them. This time-honored misconception was exploited cynically and extensively in this period of genealogical compilation.

The next crucial time period in the development of genealogical writing and publishing follows the end of World War I, and somewhat later, publication of Emma Toedteberg's *Catalogue*. There emerged a new generation of genealogists who employed a rigorously structured brand of genealogical scholarship and, even though they also generally chronicled the histories of colonial American families, were concerned with the integrity and endurance of their work. Perhaps the greatest genealogist of the half-century between 1920 and 1970 who clearly embodied this idea was Donald Lines Jacobus (1887–1970). Jacobus was the founder and editor-in-chief of *The American Genealogist* (*TAG*) and, in addition to numerous compiled family histories, was the author of *Genealogy as Pastime and Profession* (1930) — a timeless and invaluable textbook discussing the principles of genealogical research, the evaluation of evidence, and relationship of genealogy to chronology, eugenics, and the law.

Specializing largely in the genealogy of colonial Connecticut (such as in his work *The Families of Ancient New Haven*), Jacobus compiled such monumental family genealogies as *The Pardee Genealogy* (1927), *The Bulkeley Genealogy* (1933), *A History of the Seymour Family* (1939), *The Waterman Family* (3 vols., 1939–54), *The Granberry Family and Allied Families* (1945) and *The Shepard Families of New England* (3 vols., 1971–73). These works are notable for their numerous citations, with photographs, drawings, and other supporting material.

Another towering figure in the annals of twentieth-century genealogy was John Insley Coddington. In 1940, Coddington was a cofounder, with Arthur Adams and Meredith Colket, of the American Society of Genealogists (ASG). David Curtis Dearborn, in a 1991 article in *The New England Historical and Genealogical Register*, remembered Mr. Coddington in this very tradition:

> The period between the two World Wars witnessed a movement to elevate the standards of American genealogy. The hallmarks of this movement were a dispassionate and exhaustive study and analysis of all the primary sources available at hand. Many of its chief exponents were New Englanders: George Andrews Moriarty, Elizabeth (French) Bartlett, Mary and Winifred Lovering Holman, Arthur Adams, Clarence Almon Torrey, Donald Lines Jacobus and Walter Goodwin Davis. The examples set by the writings and teaching of these pioneers had a powerful influence on the young Mr. Coddington, whose own temperment and critical mind predisposed him towards the scientific approach to the subject. His subsequent prolific outflow of articles quickly earned him a ranking on a level with that of his older colleagues.[2]

Goodspeed's Bookshop of Boston and Tuttle's Antiquarian Books of Rutland, Vermont, each of which commenced around the turn of the twentieth century, were always involved in the buying and selling of books of genealogical interest, but later on and to a lesser extent also published such books. Such a trend well exemplified the resurgence of genealogy's popularity. With publications such as May Folk Webb and Patrick Mann Estes's *Cary-Estes Genealogy* (1939), and Mabel T. Kittredge's *The Kittredge Family in America* (1936), both of which added much narrative content to statistical data, Tuttle established itself as a force in the publication of lasting genealogies. The following passage from *The Kittredge Family* illustrates the concept of making extraordinary the lives of ordinary people:

> Joseph Kittredge, MD II
>
> Today, as friends and neighbors, we feel a common loss — a loss which all confess, and none would even try to measure. A familiar face has passed from our daily paths; one that we all have loved to meet; gentle, cordial, frank and generous impulses shining through its features by pure forces of nature, and that refinement of social tact and feeling which makes so essential a part of true culture. Here was one who brought healing to your bedsides; who touched your flagging pulses with the cheerful and kindly skill that makes the good physician a household benediction . . . [3]

Present-day genealogical publishing follows very much the scholarly tradition of Jacobus, Coddington, and others; such standards are important when one considers the format for your own compiled family genealogy.

The Newbury Street Press, special publications imprint of NEHGS, maintains a standard of excellence supporting this tradition. Newbury Street Press is not a vanity publisher, but rather one that accepts manuscripts conditionally upon acceptance of these standards. It seeks new, groundbreaking, fully documented compilations that will enhance the entire body of genealogical scholarship. In compiling one's work, it is imperative that the original source records be discovered and presented — that the work not be simply a synthesis of numerous already published sources. Such diligence will ensure that your work will be consulted for years to come.

The general format Newbury Street Press follows is that used in *The New England Historical and Genealogical Register*. There are two basic methods of displaying data: the *Telegraphic* data paragraph and the *Narrative* data paragraph. The latter is written in a more conversational style and highlights accomplishments or other relevant information about the individual.[4]

Illustrations are important. How do you wish to present your research? The most interesting and informative work includes contextual material such

Newbury Street Press is the special publications imprint of NEHGS

as photos, paintings, drawings, and charts. These lend an added dimension to the narrative.

You will also need to consider how you will compile your work. Will it be typewritten so that it will require typesetting? Or, will you work with a computer? If the latter, you might wish to use a standardized genealogical program such as the Master Genealogist, Reunion, or Family Tree Maker. These, however, should really be used in conjunction with a word-processing program such as Microsoft Word or Word Perfect. These will give you flexibility in adding narrative content, eventually formatting your work for the printer.

Formatting, essential in preparing the manuscript to become a book, determines how the text will appear on a page, which size and style of print font will be used, and how the illustrations will sit (whether in the text or in their own stand-alone section).

The final stage is printing, which requires you to determine the number of copies to be made, the binding (cloth or paper), and how the book will be marketed or distributed to the public. Costs largely are determined by the quality of the production and can range from several hundred to several thousand dollars or more.

Generally, the process of publishing a family history should be fun, but most importantly, it should bring your ancestors to life. Your research on them should be available to other family members, researchers, and genealogical scholars for generations to come. In other words, their memory should be honored through your chronicle.

Notes

1. Walton H. Rawls, ed., *The Century Book of the Long Island Historical Society.* (Brooklyn, N.Y.: Long Island Historical Society, 1964), 105.
2. David Curtis Dearborn, "John Insley Coddington," excerpted from *The New England Historical and Genealogical Register* 145 (1991):195–200.
3. Mabel T. Kittredge, *The Kittredge Family in America* (Rutland, Vt.: Tuttle, 1936), 112–13.
4. See Thomas Kozachek, *Guidelines for Authors of Compiled Genealogies* (Boston: Newbury Street Press, 1998), for further explanation.

Genealogies:
An Overview

Maureen A. Taylor

The NEHGS library has a wide variety of published and manuscript genealogical works, from oversize genealogical charts and family registers to small tomes that follow a single line. To get the most out of a genealogy, you need to understand how it was written, the numbering system used to organize the material, and even when it was written. These three factors help you determine the veracity of the information presented, especially when there are no source notes enabling you to retrace the researcher's steps.

Genealogy, the study of lineage or direct descent, is a centuries-old hobby. The first American family histories are handwritten notes about immigrant ancestors from oral history traditions. Today scholarly standards call for re-

Genealogies in the collection range from artistic representations to published volumes. *Cowell Tree: Descendants of John Cowell and his son Joseph, Wrentham, Massachusetts.* Lithograph (Mss. TP/ COW/1161).

search and resource notes. Each generation of researchers created different genres of genealogical expression so that a nineteenth-century genealogy may not resemble one written today.

These genres of genealogical writing also include a variety of focal points: "traditional genealogies" that trace only male descendants bearing the surname (ascending to or descending from the immigrant ancestor), those that trace *all* descendants, and those that trace only female descendants. Genetics research and genealogy merge in the study of female lines, since many genetic disorders are passed on through mothers.

Numbering systems determine whether you can follow the pattern of research or not. Over time, compilers have used a wide variety of numbering systems. Some have fallen out of favor, others are used primarily in Europe, and still others are considered standard, like the *Register* style adhered to by the New England Historic Genealogical Society.

This chapter traces the history of genealogical publishing, explains the different styles of genealogical writing, and provides examples of numbering systems. It also explains how onomastics, or the study of names, can provide genealogical clues. Follow the call numbers to locate genealogies of American or foreign families and use the manuscript collection for handwritten tabular pedigrees, oversize charts, and research notes.

Genealogy Classifications

The following Library of Congress classification numbers identify the categories of published genealogies. U.S. and Canadian genealogies are located on the sixth floor of the Research Library; others are found on the first floor. In addition, the Old Class "G" genealogies are also located on the sixth floor. Any genealogy with rare book in the call number can be requested at the sixth floor reference desk.

CS 71	United States genealogies
CS 90	Canadian genealogies
CS 439	English genealogies
CS 479	Scottish genealogies
CS 499	Irish genealogies
CS 599	French genealogies
CS 629	German genealogies
CS 678	Germanic genealogies
CS 699	Holy Roman Empire (Germanic) genealogies
CS 739	Byzantine genealogies
CS 827	Dutch genealogies
CS 846	Russian genealogies
CS 859	Russian genealogies
CS 1169.5	Chinese genealogies

Matrilineal Lines
Julie Helen Otto*

In recent years geneticists, American genealogists, and specialists in the history of forenames have begun to study matrilineal descents and kindreds. A matrilineal descent runs completely through females—your mother's mother's mother, etc. A matrilineal kindred consists of a woman (often an immigrant) her children, her daughters' children, her daughters' daughters' children, etc. Surnames change with each generation and each married daughter, so the titles of such studies may not include surnames. Geographical movement (women following husbands) and social mobility can be quite pronounced, so matrilineal descents contain many surprises (e.g., in NEXUS 7 (1990):155–56, Louisa May Alcott's descent from Anneke Jans).

The largest compendium of matrilineal kindreds to date is a compilation by William Addams Reitwiesner, "Matrilineal Descents of the European Royalty" (rev. ed., 1991), on 16 microfiche.

One-Name Studies

A one-name study concentrates on all instances of a particular surname. You can study a surname in one country, or research all occurrences around the world. The Guild of One-Name Studies (*one-name.org*) registers studies that are comprehensive in nature. Anyone can join the organization and receive a subscription to their publication, *The Journal of One-Name Studies*.

The R. Stanton Avery Special Collections Department has several one-name studies that patrons may find useful, including the following:

Cooke, Rollin Hillyer. *The Cook and Lewis Families:* includes most New England families with these surnames [SG/COO/8].

Curtis, Harold E. *Curtis Family:* all Curtis families of New England; index [Mss 269].

Daffin, Hildegarde S. *Hildegarde Snow Daffin Papers:* relating to the descendants of Nicholas Snow (1599–1676), who settled in Massachusetts, Maine, Connecticut, Nova Scotia, and throughout North America; Mormon descendants of Richard Snow (1608–1677) in Utah; and Snow family members in Arkansas [Mss 231]

---

*Updated and revised from its original version in NEXUS 9:1 (1992):25.

Davis, Edwin Gerry. *Davis Families:* includes most New Englanders with this surname; difficult arrangement, even though it is indexed [SG/DAV/33].

Freeman, Willis. *Freeman Families:* all Freemans of England, New England, and the mid-Atlantic states; 60 volumes, alphabetically arranged by first name, in two parts (male and female) [SG/FRE/55; 111].

Hall, Trella M. *Trella M. Hall Papers:* Sweet family; indexed [Mss 152]

Palmer, Horace Wilbur. *Palmer Families*; descendants of all American Palmers; 13 volumes [Mss 297].

Way, Charles Granville. *Charles Granville Way Papers, 1854–1928:* genealogy, records, notes, and correspondence concerning descendants of Henry Way (d. 1667), of Dorchester, Mass., and allied families, includes the lines of George Way in Connecticut, John Way and Robert Way in Massachusetts, James Way in New York, Nathaniel Way in North Carolina, Robert Way in Pennsylvania, Aaron Way in South Carolina, and Edward Way in Virginia [Mss 50].

Compiled Genealogies

Compiled genealogies are a popular way to present family information, but they can be challenging to use if you are unfamiliar with the format. In his article, Gary Boyd Roberts offers tips on getting the most out of a compiled genealogy and lists his favorites. Finding aids, such as *American Genealogical-Biographical Index* and analytic cards in the card catalog, lead researchers past the single surname title into the multiple families presented in a work.

Using Compiled Genealogies

Gary Boyd Roberts

Several books and articles have appeared in recent years — by Patricia Law Hatcher, Carl Boyer 3rd, Elizabeth Shown Mills, the *National Genealogical Society Quarterly (NGSQ)* and *The Great Migration Newsletter*, plus guides by Joan Ferris Curran, Jane Fletcher Fiske and Margaret F. Costello, Thomas Kozachek, and Henry B. Hoff — on how to research, organize write, edit, and market a compiled family genealogy. This article focuses on how to use the thousands of published compiled genealogies. Published catalogs of such works exist for the Library of Congress, the New York Public Library, the DAR Library in Washington, D.C., and the Circulating Library of NEHGS.

Compiled genealogies fall into two types and two time periods. The two types are agnate and multi-ancestor; the two time periods are roughly 1840–65 through 1920–30, and 1930 to the present. Agnate genealogies cover all male-line descendants — everyone sharing the surname — of an immigrant forebear, usually of the seventeenth or eighteenth centuries. The children of daughters are often covered in these works, sometimes even a daughter's grandchildren (or some of them), but seldom further descendants who do not share the surname. Multi-ancestor genealogies (a term I prefer to "multi-family") treat several, a dozen or more, or even 50 to 100 families, usually of the colonial period and often of one region, that are ancestral to one couple or individual.

Genealogies of the earlier period (from 1840–65 to 1920–30) often use heraldry carelessly, suggest English origins that are often false, and sometimes confuse colonial generations. Works of this era are often strong, however, for roughly the century after the American Revolution, during which migrating pioneers or their children wrote letters to the compilers.

The period since 1920–30 began with the "Jacobus revolution" in standards (generally an examination of record sources, often unorganized in earlier decades). This "revolution" continued via *The American Genealogist*, the *Register*, the *Record*, *NGSQ*, and *The Genealogist* [American], and reached its first major watershed perhaps with the standard of complete will and deed abstraction developed by Mary and Winifred Lovering Holman. In recent decades, as microfilm censuses have become readily available, as some town (meeting) and court minutes have been published, and as much more research is undertaken in English parishes and county record offices, and in American courthouses and state archives, various other records have been used in compiling the standard journal article or "well-documented" genealogy. Finally, as computer preparation of text has become commonplace, footnotes at the bottom of a page have often replaced endnotes or text-embedded source citations.

"Classic" New England Genealogies, 1860–1930: My Favorite 20

1. Henry Adams of Braintree (1898) and Robert Adams of Newbury (1900)

2. Avery of Groton, 2 vols. (1912)

3. George Barbour of Medfield, 11 vols (7 text, 4 index) (1907)

4. William Brewster of the *Mayflower*, 2 vols. (1908)

5. Cleveland/Cleaveland, 3 vols. (1899)

6. Dewey (1898)

7. Dudley, 2 vols. (1886–94)

8. Dwight, 2 vols. (1874)

9. Greenes of R.I., 2 vols. (1903)

10. Hyde, 2 vols. (1864)

11. Humphrey(s), 3 vols. (1883, 1884, n.d.)

12. Loomis (1908) and *Female Branches*, 2 vols. (1880); John Porter, 2 vols. (1893) (Joseph Loomis and John Porter were both sons-in-law of Robert White and Bridget Allgar)

13. Lowell (1899)

14. Pickering, 3 vols. (1897) and 6 vols. Of charts

15. Seven Pierce genealogies, indexed and outlined in *Seven Pierce Families* (1936)

16. Strong, 2 vols. (1871)

17. Wentworth, 3 vols. (1878)

18. Whitman (1889)

19. Henry Whitney, 3 vols. (1878)

20. Winslow, 2 vols. (1877–88)

Note that various of the above are in error about English origins and coats-of-arms; that several confuse colonial generations; and that about half predate 1898.

All-Descendant Genealogies

This group of five- or six-generation all-descendant genealogies was pioneered by Donald Lines Jacobus's *Bulkeley Genealogy* (1933).

1. *Mayflower Families Through Five Generations* (22 volumes to date).

2. *Mayflower Families in Progress* (series title).

3. Rev. F. W. Pyne, *Descendants of the Signers of the Declaration of Independence*, 7 vols. (1997–2002).

4. Ellwood Count Curtis, *The Descendants of John Curtis (1577–1639) & Elizabeth Hutchins (1592–1658)*, 6 vols. covering 7 generations (2000–04).

150 Multi-Ancestor Works

See "My Own Index" by D. L. Jacobus in vol. 3 (1953) of his *Index to Genealogical Periodicals*, since reprinted by Genealogical Publishing Co. (and Carl Boyer, 3rd) (60 works); my list (but not a subject index) of 70 more such works, in the *Register* 135 (1981):196–98, reprinted in Ralph J. Crandall, ed., *Genealogical Research in New England* (1984), pp. 110–12, 114; and my second list, of 20 such works of the 1980s and 1990s (for a total of 150), in the *Register* 150 (1996):467–69. See also *Massachusetts and Maine Families in the Ancestry of Walter Goodwin Davis*, 3 vols. (1996). Other major authors in this genre include Charles Henry Cory, Jr., Mary Walton Ferris, Ernest Flagg, Mary Lovering Holman and Winifred Lovering Holman (Dodge) (mother and daughter), D. L. Jacobus, Herbert Furman Seversmith, Frank Farnsworth Starr, Louis Effingham DeForest, John R. Delafield, Harold Minot Pitman, Edward Elbridge Salisbury, Edith Bartlett Sumner, Alicia Crane Williams, Carl Boyer 3rd, John Anderson Brayton, Paul W. Prindle, Dean Crawford Smith and Melinde Lutz Sanborn, Robert Croll Stevens, and John Brooks Threlfall.

Genealogical Dictionaries

1. James Savage, *A Genealogical Dictionary of the First Settlers of New England* (1860–62, reprinted 1965)

2. J. O. Austin, *The Genealogical Dictionary of Rhode Island* (1887, reprinted with corrections and additions by G.A. Moriarty, 1969)

3. C. H. Pope, *The Pioneers of Massachusetts* (1900, reprinted ca. 1965) (largely superseded — see Torrey, no. 5, below)

4. Sybil Noyes, C. T. Libby and W. G. Davis, *Genealogical Dictionary of Maine and New Hampshire* (1928–39, reprinted 1972)

5. C. A. Torrey, *New England Marriages Prior to 1700* (CD-ROM, 2001)

6. R. C. Anderson, *The Great Migration Begins: Immigrants to New England, 1620–1633*, 3 vols. (1995)

7. R. C. Anderson, G. F. Sanborn and M. L. Sanborn, *The Great Migration: Immigrants to New England 1634–1635* (3 vols.) (in progress)

These genealogies should be examined by any genealogist with a sizable number of New England ancestors. Authors of such works often hired English or American scholars to explore English origins or solve colonial problems; many English origins or resolutions of knotty problems in earlier published genealogies appear nowhere else. Likewise, the periodical literature — notably the *Register,* the *Record, The American Genealogist, The Genealogist,* and *The Virginia Genealogist* — should be examined once or twice in their entirety, and then agnate or multi-ancestor works. Check for an index first, of course, and then check for the spouse of the person you want, or for a child with an unusual first name. Do not check all the men named James, Joseph, Samuel, Thomas, or William of the family surname. Look for several indexes — some even in the book's middle; indexes may exist for first names of the principal surname, for descendants of the immigrant bearing other surnames, for spouses only, for husbands only or wives only, for persons incidentally mentioned, or for "others." Indexes are sometimes divided into those for each section of the book or child of the immigrant, or even for each allied family. The numbers referred to may be page numbers (sometimes a page number in a slightly earlier draft, and therefore consistently a few pages off) or the author-assigned numbers of individuals.

In addition to books, various surnames have experts, often compilers of several genealogies, long-term editors of family newsletters, or compilers of huge databases. Consulting these experts is often the best way to discover what has been found to date on your ancestor. The expert's address is usually in the genealogy, on the copyright page or inside the text, where the current town of residence is generally stated. The newsletter editor can always be contacted at the address for submissions.

Although often corrected by journal articles or English-origins monographs, the original books are mostly right and mostly the work of conscientious scholars or compilers of their period. Compiled genealogies cover a very large percentage of New England families, many New York Dutch and Pennsylvania Quaker settlers, and a large percentage, too, of Tidewater planters. Since the "Roots" phenomenon in the mid-1970s, German and Scotch-Irish genealogies (agnate studies of mostly eighteenth-century settlers) have become popular, and there are now good samples of late-nineteenth and twentieth-century genealogies for most ethnic groups. Since most of our children and grandchildren will be of mixed colonial and ethnic heritage, this large body of work — continually growing — will probably cover a sizable chunk of the ancestry of most future Americans.

Naming Our Ancestors

Julie Helen Otto

Why should the genealogist consider onomastics (names and naming patterns) an important area of study? When choosing names for their children, our ancestors — including many of the illiterate ones — understood and alluded to a rich mix of literary, religious, and popular sources. What choices they made — and why they made them — can be important in tracing their lives, their expectations, and their movements. In the "century of lost ancestors" (1750–1850), we can often estimate or verify the age of someone bearing an unusual name, whose actual birth in some pioneer settlement went unrecorded, by checking the date the name would have gained currency (whether through publication of a popular novel, an important historical event, etc.).

This work began as an intermittent column in the New England Historical Genealogical Society's former newsmagazine *NEXUS* (of which I was then an editor) on personal names as used primarily in the English-speaking world from the sixteenth through the early nineteenth centuries (with some overlap on either side), and with occasional comparisons from other (mainly continental European) naming traditions. In its last decade (1990–2000), *NEXUS* published several onomastic articles: Grace Pittman's classic "O My Son Benoni" (7 [1990]:81–21); "Onomastics: Some Biblical and Literary Examples" and "Stratford-Area Examples of Some Personal Names" by Mary Ann Long Skinner and myself, respectively; "The Name (and Fame) of Elmer Ellsworth" by Margaret F. Costello (11 [1994]:194–98); and "Here I Raise My Ebenezer" by Mrs. Skinner (15 [1998]:71).

Parents' choice of names may indicate something of their religious or political outlook: for example, Quaker families of early Dover, N.H., would probably have thought more than twice about naming a child Hatevil; local patriarch **Hatevil Nutter** (ca. 1603–1675), whose unusual name appears down several generations of his descendants, was a fierce foe of the Friends. Early generations of the Gorton family of Rhode Island were so devoted to radical theology as to believe not only that the sexes were equal, but that the same names could be used for males and females — hence the example of **Mahershallalhashbaz (Gorton) Coles**, wife of Daniel Coles (d. 1692; m. ca. 1662) of Providence, and Oyster Bay, Long Island (J. O. Austin, *Genealogical Dictionary of Rhode Island* [Albany, 1887; repr. Baltimore, 1969], p. 304), whose mouthful of a name was normally inflicted on boys. The early years of the American republic saw much popular sympathy for foreign revolutions and reformers: **Pascalpaoli Spear** (b. Bellingham, Mass. 23 November 1785, son of Benjamin and Elizabeth (Forrestall) Spear, named for the Corsican patriot Gen. Pascal Paoli (1725–1807),

m. Bellingham (int.) 27 February 1811, Betsey Guild and had a namesake son in 1812 (Bellingham VRs, pp. 61, 146). **Paoli Lathrop** (1797–1872) of Wilbraham and South Hadley Falls, Mass., son of Joseph and Rowena (Wells) Lathrop, was named for the same hero (Rev. E. B. Huntington, *A Genealogical Memoir of the Lo-Lathrop Family* [1884], pp. 184–85). When logic failed, fanciful names were chosen from novels, romances, or other popular works because something about a character appealed — or the parents simply liked the sound, a trend that became more evident later in the nineteenth century.

Until the past two hundred years, English and American naming patterns generally involved only one given name per person. The very earliest New England instance I have seen of a middle name is apparently that of **Israel Stoughton Danforth**, b. Dorchester, Mass. 14 October 1687, son of Mr. John Danforth (Dorchester VRs 1 [Boston Rec. Comm. vol. 24]: 33) — and that use seems an obvious commemoration of Mrs. Danforth's grandfather. Middle names do not come into New England common use in until the late eighteenth century. Be aware that multiple given-naming is typical of German and some other European naming traditions, and the occasional appearance of multiple given names in the mid-eighteenth century, especially in such urban centers as Boston, may reflect later immigration to these shores.

The early and mid-eighteenth century also saw the rise of the English novel, with important onomastic consequences. In America, the mid- and late eighteenth century saw a great expansion into new country, in whose wilderness settlements vital records were not kept.

It is never a good idea to infer blood kinships on the basis of naming patterns alone — a rule which goes double or triple for garden-variety first names such as Thomas, Mary, William, Hannah, Sarah, etc., which might well be current in the families of both parents (and those of most of their neighbors). Often, parents chose names to honor family members, to be sure; but — particularly several children along, when the bearable family names were all taken — offspring could be named for in-laws of varying degrees, friends, neighbors, pastors, characters or authors from parental reading matter, and public figures of regional or national importance — not to mention something that just sounded interesting at the time. Even ideas and place names were mined: Bill Powers of Acton, Mass., tells me of **Federal Constitution Vanderburgh** (1788–1868), son of James and Helena (Clark) Vanderburgh of Beekman, N.Y. During the year of his birth, the Constitutional Convention was the great current event, and a family friend suggested the name to the newborn's patriotic parents. (The child's mother balked at the middle name, so in the end "Constitution" was omitted.)

Personal names offer genealogists an opportunity to explore the use of names in their own family. Naming patterns can establish relationships, shed light on a family's politics, religious preferences or literary tastes, uncover a private tragedy or provide clues to new avenues of research. Available in the reference section on the sixth floor are several useful guides to surnames and place names, including Patrick Hanks and Flavia Hodges's *A Dictionary of First*

Names (Oxford and New York: Oxford University Press, 1990 [R.Rm. REF CS2367/H36/1990]), and (in the first-floor International Reference area) the earlier but still extremely useful *The Oxford Dictionary of English Christian Names*, 2nd ed. (Oxford: Clarendon Press, 1950 [Intl REF CS2375/G7/W5/1950]), by E. G. Withycombe. Check the library's online subject catalog under "Names, Personal" for a list of subjects and sub-subjects (this choice will also net you material on surnames as well as given names).

Examples of Naming Patterns

Personal Names as Markers of Family Circumstances

Grace Pittman, in her article in *NEXUS* 7 (1990):17–21 ("O My Son Benoni: A Personal Name as Marker of Family Circumstances"), studied one hundred pre-1780 New England boys named Benoni. Ms. Pittman found evidence to support her theory that the name refers to family circumstances. New Englanders knew their Bibles. The name "Benoni" was taken from Genesis 35:18, which recounts the death in childbirth of Sarah, wife of the patriarch Abraham: "And it came to pass, as her soul was in departing (for she died) that she called his name Benoni: but his father called him Benjamin." She discovered five instances of usage:

- The mother died at or soon after the birth of the child;
- The father died before the child's birth;
- The child was illegitimate or was conceived before his parents married;
- The child died soon after birth; or
- The child was apparently named for his father, a grandfather, or an uncle.

Some Other Name Categories

Flower Names — Although *Rose* has been a reasonably popular English name since medieval times (when that flower was seen not only as a symbol of the Virgin Mary, but also as a poetic metaphor in the courtly love tradition and as a badge denoting political faction), names such as *Daisy, Iris, Hyacinth*, and others did not gain wide currency until the mid-nineteenth century. A rare exception is *Violet*; colonial New England bearers of this name can usually be traced genealogically to Violet (Charnould) Shepard, wife of Edward Shepard of Cambridge, Mass.

Virtue Names — Puritan names honoring desirable feelings, character traits or salvation status (e.g., *Faith, Hope, Charity, Deliverance, Preserved*). Originally unisex, they tended over time (with a few exceptions) to become female names.

Surnames as First and Middle Names

Surname Passes into Common Use

A surname may pass into common use as a first name throughout a town or region. For example, descendants of the early Concord, Mass., settler Simon Willard (1605–1676) bearing other surnames first employed the surname Willard as a given name. After a few generations, however, unrelated families also began to confer the name on their children.

Surnames as Middle Names

A woman marrying and starting a family of her own will often name children for her relatives. She may feel particularly inspired to pass down her maiden surname to perpetuate the memory of parents or siblings if her birth family appears about to "daughter out" because none of her brothers have sur-vived to marry or reproduce. Sometimes parents would honor earlier generations of female ancestors whose families were well known in the community, or of whom they were otherwise proud.

Surnames as First Names

Surnames may also be conferred as given names and can signify descent. Be careful, though, since parents often named their children for famous Americans (e.g., Benjamin Franklin) whom they admired. Much less commonly, surnames may be conferred from novels. If you ever come upon someone with the given name Grandison, you are not descended from a family of this name. The child was undoubtedly named for Sir Charles Grandison, hero of an English novel.

Nicknames

Nicknames, found in documents like census records, diaries, and other less formal paperwork, can mislead researchers who mistakenly look for a person by his or her nickname rather than a formal given name. Often a nickname derives from a later syllable than the first, so will be found elsewhere in the alphabet than the formal name from which it was formed, or will involve a vowel change. A simple chart of nicknames identifies those in common use for specific personal names. There can be variations based on family traditions, ethnic origins, and place of residence.

Nicknames	Given Names
Bess, Beth, Betsy	Elizabeth
Bridey	Bridget
Daisy	Margaret
Datey	Theodate
Delia	Bridget
Dime, Diamah	Phedime/Fatima
Dodie, Dora, Dot	Dorothy
Fannie, Frannie	Frances
Harry	Henry
Hattie	Harriet
Jack	John
Jamie, Jemmy	James
Jenny	Jane, Janet, Jeanette, Virginia
Katy, Kit, Kay	Katherine
Lizzie, Libbie	Elizabeth
Maggie, Midge, Meg, Megan, Peggy	Margaret
Mattie	Martha, Matilda
Milly	Amelia, Pamelia, Millicent, Mildred etc.
Molly	Mary
Mirah	Almira, Elmira, Miranda
Nat	Nathaniel
Nate	Nathan
Ned	Edward, Edmund
Nellie	Eleanor, Ellen, Helen
Noll	Oliver
Nora	Hanorah/Honora, Eleanor
Pat, Patsy, Pattie (female)	Martha, Patience, (later) Patricia
Polly	Mary, Paula
Robin	Robert, Roberta
Sadie, Sally	Sarah
Tad, Ted	Theodore, Edward, Edmund
Tempe	Temperance
Tilly	Matilda, Temperance
Trina	Katherine
Vine	Lavinia
Zeke	Ezekiel
Zina	Melusina

Interpreting Numbering Systems

Maureen A. Taylor

Examine the introduction of each genealogy to see if there is a note regarding the numbering system used. Each one has strengths and weaknesses. Some follow the family generation by generation or branch by branch. Knowing what method the author used will prevent possible confusion. Richard A. Pence's online article, "Numbering Systems in Genealogy," at *saintclair.org/numbers/numahn.html*, and Joan Ferris Curran, Madilyn Coen Crane, and John H. Wray's *Numbering Your Genealogy: Basic Systems, Complex Families, and International Kin* (National Genealogical Society, Special Publication No. 64, Arlington, Va., 1999) are guides to numbering systems in use.

Ahnentafel

Invented by Jerome de Sosa in 1676, the ahnentafel is a list of ancestors rather than a chart. The system begins with you as number 1. Your father is number 2 and your mother is number 3. Continue numbering by doubling each male's number for the next male descendant and adding one to that number for his spouse.

Example of Ahnentafel without citations from "James Coburn: A Genealogical Tribute (1928–2002)" by David Dearborn on NewEnglandAncestors.org.

The actor James Coburn's ancestors are charted by using the ahnentafel, or "Ancestor Table" method of numbering, in which the subject is numbered 1, his father 2, mother 3, paternal grandfather 4, paternal grandmother 5, maternal grandfather 6, maternal grandmother 7, paternal grandfather's father 8, and so forth.

FIRST GENERATION

1   James H[arrison] Coburn, born Laurel, Cedar County, Nebraska, 31 August 1928; died Los Angeles, Calif., 18 November 2002.

SECOND GENERATION

2   James H[arrison] Coburn, born [?Laurel, Cedar Co.?] Neb. 6 October 1902; died Orange County, Calif., 24 December 1975. He appears as head of household at Laurel, Cedar County, Neb. in the 1930 census as James H. Coburn, garage mechanic. He married about 1925,

3   Mylet S. Johnson, born Neb. 15 November 1901; died Orange County, Calif., 20 February 1984. She appears as James' wife in the 1930 census; married 5 years.

THIRD GENERATION

4   Daniel D. Coburn, born Wisconsin 31 May 1868; died Los Angeles County, Calif., 12 November 1946, age 78. He and his wife Altha were living at Laurel, Cedar County, Nebraska in the 1900 census; he was described as a stockman. In 1910 he was at Laurel, described as a merchant — implements, living with wife Altha, 7-year-old son Harrison, and other children. He and his wife are described as married 12 years, and she as the mother of 4 living children, all listed. He was living at Laurel in the 1920 census, a widower, occupation merchant — automobiles. His son is listed in this census as "Harrison," age 17. He married at Lancaster County, Neb. 10 November 1898,

5   Altha Ann Johnson, born Crawford County, Iowa about December 1876; living Laurel, Neb. 1910; died by 1920.

6   ——— Johnson, born Sweden; emigrated to Nebraska.

7   ——— Johnson, born Sweden; emigrated to Nebraska.

Register System

This system's name derives from the fact that it has been used in *The New England Historical and Genealogical Register* since 1870. In this system, the earliest head of family is given the number 1. Each child is represented by a roman numeral, with sequential numbers given to individuals for whom additional research appears in the work. Superscript numbers make it easy to follow the generations.

Example of Register system, with citations removed (from **Register** *157 [2003]:219):*

Children of John² and Elizabeth (James) Hyland:

1. i.   RUTH³ HYLAND, b. 19 Sept. 1695; admitted to the First Church, 16 March 1717/8; evidently d. unm. She witnessed a deed for her father on 6 July 1711. She was called Ruth Hyland in father's will of 8 Dec. 1748. The will of "Ruth Hyland," not recorded, is mentioned in a deed signed by her sister, Anna Cahill (see below).

    ii. ELIZABETH HYLAND, b. 2 Feb. 1697/8; d., presumably unm., prior to 8 Dec. 1748, as she was not mentioned in her father's will of that date.

    iii. MEHITABEL HYLAND, b. say 1700; Mehitabel Hyland, "a daughter of John Hyland," was admitted to the First Church on 8 Sept. 1728. She made her mark, "M," as a witness to a quitclaim made by her niece, Deborah (Jones) Dwelley, 5 May 1747. Her father called her by her maiden name in his will of 8 Dec. 1748, and her namesake niece was called "junior" in 1757. No death record has been found.

2. iv.   JAMES HYLAND, b. 10 March 1701/2; m. MARY TILDEN.

3. v.   JOHN HYLAND, b. 4 July 1704; m. REBECCA WHITE.

4. vi.   SARAH HYLAND, b. 9 Jan. 1706/7; m. ELISHA JONES.

Henry System

This system is named after Reginald Buchanan Henry, who first used it in 1935 in *Genealogies of the Families of the Presidents*. The progenitor is given the number one. Each child of that person is given a number following the progenitor's up to the ninth child and a letter for each child after that. Thus the progenitor's children are 11, 12, 13 . . . up to nine and then lettered X for the tenth, A for the eleventh with additional children the letters of the alphabet. According to Gary Boyd Roberts, the Henry system was popular in genealogies of southern families.

Modified Register System

This system is derived from the Register System, but each person is given a number even if the line is not carried forward. A plus mark next to the number indicates which children are carried forward. The *National Genealogical Society Quarterly* uses this method.

Example of Modified Register System with citations removed from **The Avery Family: The Ancestors and Descendants of Christopher Avery** *(Newbury Street Press, 2003):*

2. JAMES³ AVERY (*Christopher²*, *Christopher¹*) was baptized 22 April 1621 in Wolborough (Newton Abbot) and died 18 April 1700 in Groton, Conn. He married (1) in Gloucester, Mass., on 10 November 1643, JOANNA GREENSLADE. Other forms of her given name, in the fluid spelling of the time, are "Jane" and "Joan." The entry of her marriage to James "Averie" in the published vital records of Gloucester calls her "Joane."

   Joanna (Greenslade) Avery's exact date of death is unknown. On 8 October 1697, Manasseh Minor recorded in his diary that "Capt Avarys wife was bvryed."

Children of James Avery and Joanna Greenslade:

+3. i.   HANNAH AVERY, b. 11 October 1644, Gloucester, Mass.; d. 21 August 1721, Stonington, Conn.

+4. ii. JAMES AVERY, b. 16 December 1646, Gloucester, Mass.; d. 22 August 1728, Groton, Conn.

+5. iii. MARY (MARIE) AVERY, b. 29 February 1647/48, Gloucester, Mass.; d. 2 February 1707/08, Stonington, Conn.

+6. iv. THOMAS AVERY, b. 6 May 1651, New London, Conn.; d. 5 January 1737, Montville, Conn.

7.   v.   JOHN AVERY, b. 10 February 1653/54, New London, Conn.

The only way to understand these systems is to use them. Gary Boyd Roberts suggests that "sometimes an indexing or numbering system is so complex that you will save time simply looking page by page through that part of the book likely to cover the century in which your ancestor lived." This technique is useful when consulting small unindexed publications, publications with a table of contents, or publications with a unique numbering system. Indexes may reference either page number or the number assigned to an individual.

	Key features	*Advantages*	*Disadvantages*
Ahnentafel	You are 1, your father 2, and mother 3.	Presents information in a concise understandable fashion.	Intermarriages are difficult to number; no collateral lines.
Henry System		Works well only with a small family.	Quickly becomes confusing.
Modified Register System	Every individual is numbered; + shows children carried forward.	Works well as long as family doesn't change.	Complex — additional children cause renumbering.
Register System	Only children carried forward are numbered.	Works well as long as family doesn't change.	Complex — additional children to be carried forward cause renumbering.

Rare Books and Manuscripts

Identifying and Using Rare Book Collections

Michael J. Leclerc

One of the many benefits of being a member of NEHGS is access to the contents of the closed stacks in the research library. While most of the NEHGS collection is in open stacks, our rare book and manuscript collections are located in restricted areas. These collections contain a wealth of information just waiting to be tapped. While open stacks help facilitate browsing for materials, it is also important to study card catalogs to ensure that other holdings are not overlooked. Many repositories have put their catalogs online or are in the process of doing so, making access to these collections easier. You can find items from the NEHGS rare book and manuscript collections in the online library catalog, but always remember to ask about separate card catalogs when in a research repository. Many libraries keep different card catalogs for manuscript and rare book collections, or make special notations in their main catalog to

Published online on *NewEnglandAncestors.org,* April 25, 2002.

identify such materials. For example, at NEHGS, all materials in the rare book collection start with "RB" before the Library of Congress call number.

The category of rare books will vary from repository to repository. Each institution decides what it will classify as a rare book. Date of publication, format, and availability of the work are among the factors that are weighed when determining the classification. At NEHGS, any material published in or before 1865 is kept in the rare book collection. Hard to find materials from the late nineteenth and early twentieth centuries also are in this area. We have over 20,000 volumes in our rare book collection, some of which date back to the sixteenth century. Included in our collection are local histories, compiled genealogies, broadsides, journals, diaries, and many volumes on heraldry and the royalty of Europe. NEHGS houses the oldest known published genealogy in America (a broadside from Pennsylvania in 1763) and the oldest known compiled genealogy in New England (1771). Rare books are available to any of our members and can be accessed through the main reference desk in the Ruth C. Bishop Reading Room on the sixth floor of the library. The following is just a small sampling of the gems in the NEHGS rare book collection available to those interested in Canadian research.

Many volumes on the history of the New World as well as many European countries can be found in these collections. Justin Winsor edited a multivolume set entitled *Narrative and Critical History of America*, published by Houghton

Oldest known published genealogy in America is of the Bollinger family, 1763 (Rare Book Y.2).

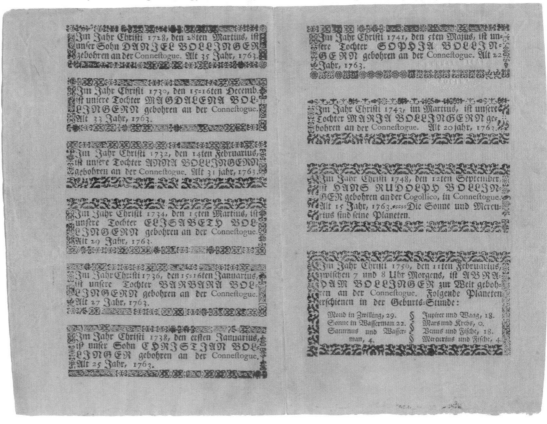

The oldest known genealogy in New England is of the Stebbins Family, 1771 (Rare Book C571/ 581/1771).

Mifflin in 1887. While its title might lead one to believe it is a tome on the United States, this work includes much history of the French colonies in America. Providing a detailed portrait of the settlements in New France and the ultimate loss of Acadia and Québec to the English, these volumes give great insight into the lives of our ancestors. Numerous early maps are included.

Also in our collection is a six-volume English translation of the Rev. P.F.X. de Charlevoix's *History and General Description of New France,* by John Gilmary Shea (1871). These volumes give a detailed history of France's colonies in America with a special focus on Acadia and Québec. There are few illustrations, but the language is quite detailed and colorful and brings vivid images to mind.

It is important to remember when using compiled histories of events that they are told from a specific perspective. As the saying goes, "History is written by the victors." Most versions of world history published in the United States are told from the perspective of the United States and/or England. One gets an entirely different view when reading books from the point of view of the French, who ultimately lost their territories. Which is correct? As in anything, the truth probably lies somewhere in the middle, and a careful balance should be maintained.

For example, Andrew MacFarland Davis's essay on Canada and Louisiana states:

> The scene in which startled villagers were roused from their midnight slumber by the fierce war-whoop, the report of the musket, and the light of burning dwellings, was transferred from the Valley of the St. Lawrence to New England. Upon Vaudreuil must rest the responsibility for the attacks upon Deerfield in 1704 and Haverhill in 1708, and for the horrors of the Abenakis war. The pious Canadians, fortified by a brief preliminary invocation of Divine aid, rushed upon the little settlements and perpetrated cruelties of the same class with those which characterized the brutal attacks of the Iriquois upon the villages in Canada. [1]

Charlevoix describes the attack on Haverhill as follows:

> They then prayed and marched against the fort. Here they met with a vigorous resistance; but at last entered sword and axe in hand, and set it on fire. All the houses were also well defended, and met the same fate.
>
> About a hundred of the English were killed in these attacks; many others, too slow in leaving the fort and houses, were burned in them, and the number of prisoners was large. . . .
>
> During the last combat several of the prisoners taken at the attack on Hewreuil (Haverhill) escaped. All the rest praised highly the kind treatment show them by their captors during the retreat, which was effected without accident. . . . [2]

Each of these narratives focuses on the points that support their version, and, as might be expected, the accounts are very different from each other. No mention is made in the English version of the kind treatment of the prisoners, while the French version says nothing about the reasoning behind the attacks. Reading both versions, however, gives one a better perspective on the events.

Also found in the rare book collection are a number of published sermons. While obviously religious in nature, these served very important political purposes as well. One sermon, given in 1759 by Samuel Cooper, A. M., discusses the recent conquering of Québec by the English:

> The Worth of this Conquest will appear greatly enhanced, if we reflect upon the Character of the Enemy which we have so far subdued — An inveterate and implacable Enemy to our Religion and Liberties; inflamed with *Romish* Bigotry; perfidious, restless, politic, and enterprizing: An Enemy that has ever made War against us in a Manner shocking to Humanity: that has so envied our superior Advantages and Growth, as to deem any Methods just by which we could be distressed; and has accordingly long employed the Barbarity of Savages to drench our Borders with the Blood of the unarmed Villager, and even of Women and Infants.[3]

Thomas Prince of the South Church in Boston gave a sermon on July 18, 1745, which was published and can be found in the collection. In this sermon, he celebrates the taking of Fort Louisbourg and Cape Breton Island by the

English. Prince details many of the reasons for the war with France, and describes one of the most significant concerns in the excerpt below:

> Yea, from the Conseration of such a strong Defence, the Advantage of Wood, Sea-Coal, Fishery, and Free-Gift Lan in this and the neighbouring Islands, the settlement of Thousands of People on them already, and the inuumerable Poor in the Sea-Coast towns of France, ever swarming and coming over to them; — it seems highly probably, that if the Peace continued much longer, there would be in a few Years Time such a Multitude of French Inhabitants, as with the growing Numbers in the bordering Continent of Nova Scotia and Canada, with the addition of the Indian Nations, would exceedingly vex and waste, yea, endanger the Conquest of our English Colonies.[4]

One can also find published church records among these many volumes. One 1859 work contains a list of baptisms and burials made at Fort Duquesne between 1753 and 1756. An important aspect of these records is that they list the home parish of the individuals buried at the fort, making it easier to locate them. For example, on July 29, 1755, a priest buried the body of Jean-Baptiste Dupuis of La Prairie de la Magdeleine, who had been killed in combat against the English.[5] Baptisms and burials can also be found for English soldiers who were perhaps brought to the fort as captives.

Other materials in the collection include old periodicals, such as the *Magazine of American History*. This thirty-volume set was published in New York City from January 1877 to September 1893. It includes hundreds of articles on a wide variety of subjects. The volumes are also generously filled with pictures, drawings, maps, photographs, and reproductions of original documents. In November 1888, Prosper Bender published an essay entitled "A New France in New England." In it he describes the wonder at the masses of French-Canadians moving south into the United States, but especially into the New England area:

> The tide of national feeling on each side of the boundary is turned into different, more honorable and fruitful chanles, each race striving after nobler objects than to vex or destroy the other. The French Canadians pour into the traditional enemy's country, not for war or spoil, but to find homes in their most thirving cities, and to aid in the cultivation of their most fertile fields. The descendants of the old combatants now mingle in peace, to work amicably together in the promotion of American Civilization.[6]

He then goes on to mention the start of mass migration with the Civil War in the United States and discusses the current population and their culture. Bender confidently predicted that French-Canadians and their descendants would outnumber those of English descent in New England by the end of the first quarter of the twentieth century. Other articles about Canada appearing in the same volume included a discussion of Canada's finances and an article on French-Canadian holidays.

Especially fascinating are the published diaries in the collection. For example, Captain William Pote, Jr. of Falmouth, Maine, was a prisoner during the French and Indian War. He was captured May 17, 1745, at Annapolis Basin and released two years later on July 30,1747. In his journal he discusses the daily activities he experienced as a prisoner. He also notes the deaths of other captives such as Captain William Bagley on November 30, 1746, and Geret Vanderverick two days later.[7] The published version is fully indexed, includes several illustrations, and contains a small genealogy of the Pote family as well as a 1749 map by Charles Morris. This hand-colored map details settlements in Acadia, New England, and New York, covering from Newfoundland and Anticosti Island down to East New Jersey and out to Lake Ontario.

Rare book collections can be found in most major repositories. Always contact the repository in advance to find out what the rules are concerning access. For example, access to the rare books and manuscripts at NEHGS is a benefit of membership. In addition, book cradles and white gloves must be used when handling many of the volumes. Most repositories will restrict you to using pencils. Make sure to ask about these additional rules when contacting a repository.

Old compiled genealogies, local histories, diaries and journals, city directories . . . the list goes on and on. Not only can valuable information about individuals and families be found in rare book collections, but a rich amount of material to put your ancestors in historical context is also waiting to be used.

Notes

1. Andrew MacFarland Davis, *Narrative and Critical History of America,* vol. 5, "Canada and Louisiana" (Boston: Houghton Mifflin, 1887), 5.
2. John Gilmary Shea, trans., *History and General Description of New France*, by the Rev. P.F.X. Charlevoix, S.J., in 6 vols. (New York: p.p., 1871) 5:206–7.
3. Samuel Cooper, A.M., *A Sermon Preached Before His Excellency Thomas Pownall, Esq; Captain-General and Governor-in-Chief, The Honourable His Majesty's Council and House of Representatives, of the Province of the Massachusetts-Bay in New-England, October 16th, 1759. Upon Occasion of the Success of His Majesty's Arms in the Reduction of Quebec* (Boston: Green & Russell and Edes & Gill, 1759), 47–48.
4. Thomas Prince, M.A., *Extraordinary Events the Doings of God, and marvellous in pious Eyes. Illustrated in a Sermon At the South Church in Boston, N.E. On the General Thanksgiving, Thursday, July 18, 1745 Occcasion'd by taking the City of Louisbourg on the Isle of Cape Breton, by New-England Soldiers, assisted by a British Squadron* (Boston: D. Henchman, 1745),19.
5. *Registres des Baptesmes et Sepultures Quie se Sont Faits Au Fort Duquesne pendant les années* 1753, 1754, 1755, & 1756 (New York: la Presse Cramoisy de Jean-Marie Shea, 1859), 29–30.
6. Prosper Bender, "A New France in New England," *Magazine of American History* 20:5 (November 1888):387.
7. William Pote, Jr., *The Journal of Captain William Pote, Jr. During His Captivity in the French and Indian War From May, 1745 to August, 1747* (New York: Dodd, Mead, and Company, 1896), 105.

The Wonderful World of Manuscripts

Timothy G. X. Salls

Since our founding in 1845, the New England Historic Genealogical Society has acquired a fantastic collection of resources to help genealogists in their research. Patrons often have many questions about the manuscript collection. What follows is an overview of the primary types of manuscripts we collect, along with some examples of how they can be used to further your research. Patrons can search the library's online catalog to find specific items in our collection. A published guide is also available: *Guide to the Manuscript Collections of the New England Historic Genealogical Society*, edited by Timothy Salls (Boston: NEHGS, 2002).

Account Books

Was your ancestor a subscriber who donated money to fund the construction of the frigate USS *Boston* during 1798 and 1799? Did your ancestor purchase goods from Samuel Townsend, a merchant in Oyster Bay, New York, circa 1739–1775? Account books at NEHGS will provide the answer! Account books are business records that contain the names of customers, dates of transaction, list of goods or services purchased, payment amount, and, in many cases, method of payment (items were often paid for by bartering goods or services). Although some of our account books have no indication of the merchant's name or the location of their business, many others do have this valuable information specifically written in or on the book. Knowing the location is important because these records can be used as evidence that the customer or merchant was living in a particular town during a particular year. An entry in an account book may also be the only record that exists for an individual, especially in areas where the vital statistics were either lost or poorly recorded. Thus, seventeenth- and eighteenth-century account books are particularly valuable since they can provide information where the vital records are lacking.

Every now and then, an account book will include non-business information such as Samuel Sewall's "account of books lent" (Mss 514) or the register of births and deaths for the John and Ruth (Hale) Pearson family of Rowley, Massachusetts included in John Pearson's account book of 1736-1740 (Mss C 4963). An account book of Jason Newell includes a record of tuition for a

Published online on *NewEnglandAncestors.org*.

Jesse Tilson — His Book Anno Domini Stougton May 8th 1759 (Mss A 2006).

Cumberland, Rhode Island, school, circa 1811 (Mss C 4830). NEHGS also collects account books of corporate entities, such as Colonel William Bond's record for the 25th Continental Regiment (Mss C 4883). This account book lists the soldiers in the regiment and notes whether they have firearms, a bayonet, a gun mark, and a gun number. It also contains information concerning the pay of some officers.

Bible Records

Bibles contain birth, marriage, or death information recorded at the same time or shortly after the actual event. As a result, this kind of manuscript can assist researchers by filling in gaps within the published vital records. This is why genealogists seek the title page along with the bible record: the date of publication allows the researcher to determine how close to the events the entries were written (with the assumption that contemporary accounts should be more accurate). Since families often took these heirlooms with them whenever they moved, bible records can sometimes help to locate relatives who "disappear."

A Bible record may also be accompanied by an assortment of items of interest to genealogists including photographs, obituaries, bookmarks, marriage certificates, report cards, handwritten genealogies, wills, etc. NEHGS has published transcriptions of a large portion of Bible records in its collection on a CD-ROM titled *Bible Records from the Manuscript Collections of the New England Historic Genealogical Society;* for more information see Linda Rupnow McGuire's article on this CD-ROM in the Holiday 2001 issue of *New England Ancestors.*

Church and Town Records

Church and town records are often grouped together since they both contain vital statistic information. NEHGS has a very large collection of unpublished transcribed tombstone inscriptions from town cemeteries, family burial grounds, and various churches. These transcriptions were often done for the benefit of the entire community. In addition, our collection includes original and transcribed copies of church registers, which list baptisms (and sometimes the date of birth), marriages, deaths, and, more importantly, admissions. An admission record may reveal the first concrete date for an individual living in a community. Besides the vital records found in transcribed town record books, manuscript town records include items such as handwritten copies of local censuses or tax records, which are also valuable when figuring out who lived in a particular community during a specific year. Information from both town and church records forms a major part of the source material collected by Clarence Bowen for his book *The History of Woodstock, Connecticut* (Plimpton Press, 1926–43), an example of a manuscript collection that focuses on the history of a specific town. Since copying errors and omissions do occur in published vital records, histories, and genealogies, it is important to access the original record or an author's notes to verify whether questionable information was printed correctly. Additionally, a researcher's papers often contain more information than what ends up in their published works.

Correspondence

Correspondence can sometimes provide as much genealogical and historical information as a diary. Many factors influence how much information can be gleaned from any particular collection of correspondence, including general subject matter (personal, business, military, etc.), how often the letters were written, number of authors, and how much detail is provided. Genealogical correspondence may consist of letters written between a genealogist and archivists, curators, town clerks, other genealogists, and/or individuals researching the same surname. The value of genealogical letters should be evident: if someone has already done the work, so much the better, right? At least as long as you credit their work and check their citations. In addition, previous researchers may have had access to sources and repositories that you didn't consider and you may also find additions or corrections to published works.

Personal letters written between family members contain descriptions of their lives in their own words. Family members often discussed the births, marriages, and deaths of family members, friends, and others in their town. Although business letters usually lack vital statistic information often found in genealogical and personal correspondence, they are nevertheless valuable to genealogists since they document a major facet of a person's life. At the very least, the letterheads used by our ancestors on their business letters are often visually interesting and thus can serve not only as an example of the kind of work they did, but also as an interesting image to use in a published genealogy.

Diaries and Journals

Diaries and journals are like time machines that remind us what life was like before such modern conveniences as computers, television, radio, automobiles, electricity, and the like. They are perfect examples of a manuscript's ability to provide insight into the common day-to-day experiences of our ancestors that is so valuable for historians and genealogists. The genealogist's ideal situation would be a firsthand account by an ancestor in which the diary records not only their activities (business, membership in organizations, offices held, leisure, and trips) but their emotions as well. These personal insights, which may include reactions to local and national events, can provide us with a window into the author's life. You will also want to check for diaries written by people living in the same area as your ancestor, as they might contain secondhand accounts concerning the ancestor. For more information and examples on the wealth of information diaries can provide, read Ralph Crandall's article "Diaries and Journals: An Often Neglected Genealogical Resource" (*New England Ancestors,* Summer 2000). Researcher should also peruse our online guide to the diaries in the NEHGS Special Collections Department.

Family Registers

Family registers compile birth, marriage, and death information pertaining to a particular family or families, usually entered by family members themselves. These records may be handwritten notes, hand-drawn and colored registers like frakturs, written additions to preprinted forms (such as those by Currier and Ives), or printed broadsides. Besides the vital statistic information these manuscripts provide, family registers sometimes provide interesting details into the cause of death of a family member, childhood illnesses, and even dowry information. These documents often contain examples of handwriting practice and favorite poems or psalms. Some have an aesthetic quality to them, like

Isaac Ketcham family record, ca. 1817 (Mss C 6).

the colorful Isaac Ketcham family register depicted on the cover of the Winter 2001 edition of *New England Ancestors* vividly demonstrates. Many aspects of these records, including their wonderful folk art qualities, is covered in *The Art of Family: Genealogical Artifacts in New England* (Boston: NEHGS, 2001), edited by D. Brenton Simons and Peter Benes. This book contains numerous illustrations of family registers from the manuscripts holdings of NEHGS as well as examples from the American Antiquarian Society, the Society for the Preservation of New England Antiquities, the Dublin Seminar for New England Folklife, and private collections throughout the United States.

Genealogies

NEHGS has one of the premier collections of genealogical manuscripts in the country, and not surprisingly, they comprise the bulk of our manuscript collection. I have recently cataloged some typescript biographies complete with some tipped-in photographs, which are nice despite the difficult preservation issues they create. What a great legacy for the future to record not just when and where you were born but also to describe your education, places of employment, pets, the cars you've owned, memberships, where you've lived, and other details of your life that only you and your immediate family would know! Thankfully, even when the majority of people go through life as mere players who act their part and then are heard no more, genealogists have continued to make the effort to document members of their families in compiled genealogies. Although early handwritten genealogies, like the Parsons genealogy of 1743, are valuable since the author may have had access to records that might have been lost over time, genealogists must realize that today's standards of documentation and citation weren't established at that time. If you find that a manuscript genealogy contains dates that are questionable, keep in mind that you may also find valuable biographical data not available elsewhere.

You never know what you will find when you ask to view a particular manuscript genealogy in the collection. You may find a modest handwritten record like the forty-page Parsons genealogy, or you might lose yourself in an extensive collection of notes, charts, indexes, and source citations as you face the prospect of 159 boxes of John Insley Coddington Papers before you! How and why manuscript collections are created is no mystery; researchers accumulate a large amount of paperwork in their quest for genealogical information. This includes correspondence, notes taken from published genealogies and histories, extracts, abstracts, transcriptions of government records, and much more. The compilers of the papers in our collection may also have possessed original documents such as letters written by their ancestors, a diary, wills, deeds, photographs, or a family bible. If it was the intention of the genealogist to publish a book, there may be even more records — drafts, annotated copies, and so on. All of these unpublished documents a genealogist compiles as a by-product of their research are manuscripts.

Graphics

The graphics in our collection include photographs, silhouettes, and portraits. Although NEHGS focuses on acquiring photographs such as daguerreotypes, ambrotypes, tintypes, and albumen prints, researchers will also find more modern prints. Photographs are scattered throughout NEHGS's collections. The "scope note" (the brief description of the manuscript provided in the catalog record) and subject headings in a catalog record will indicate when a collection includes photographs or any other graphics. In addition, finding aids (guides to the intellectual and physical arrangement of larger collections) are available. Several collections of family papers at NEHGS include silhouettes, hand painted miniature portraits, or pen and ink sketches. NEHGS also keeps a few collections comprised entirely of photographs, such as the Harriet Merryfield Forbes Collection of New England Gravestones. Patrons can even search in our library catalogs for the large painted portraits in the Society's fine art collection. For more information on other resources for family portraits see D. Brenton Simons' article "Finding Family Portraits: A Bibliography of Selected Sources" (*New England Ancestors*, Holiday 2000) and Maureen A. Taylor's "Photographs in Your Family History" (*New England Ancestors*, Holiday 2001).

Genealogical Papers — Four Cornerstones of the NEHGS Manuscript Collection

Since a member of the Society recently expressed surprise that NEHGS would be interested in their research, it should be noted that our members donate approximately 70 percent to 80 percent of the material in our collection. This material falls into four general types: those that focus on a specific surname, on a specific geographical area, a specific ethnic group, or client research by a professional genealogist. Our collection also includes the records and papers of several family associations. Since many of our patrons are primarily concerned with gathering information on a specific family line, those collections

Mary Potter Clark (born 1867), probably taken ca. 1900 (Mss 395 Brotherton Indian Collection).

What is a Manuscript?

A Glossary for Archivists, Manuscript Curators, and Records Managers, by Lewis and Lynn Bellardo (Chicago, Ill.: Society of American Archivists, 1992) describes a manuscript simply as "a handwritten or typed document; though, a typed document is more precisely called a typescript." This material is unpublished; as a result, manuscripts are usually unique (i.e., only one copy exists).

that focus on an entire family are valuable because they meet the needs of multiple patrons. Sometimes an author will focus on a specific town including the families that lived there, as Fred Crowell did for his articles on New Englanders in Nova Scotia, for which we have the source material. Some genealogists are drawn instead to focus on a specific ethnic group. Rudi Ottery, for instance, compiled a large group of material on the Brotherton Indian tribe. The final type of manuscript collection found at NEHGS are the papers of genealogists hired to do research for clients. The unifying element of such collections is the genealogist, who often specializes in a particular area while their clients' needs vary greatly. Researchers will find more examples of the manuscript collections held by NEHGS by consulting our websites "sample list of holdings." You may also search the manuscript collection by subject, author, or title.

It is difficult to account for every single kind of manuscript that NEHGS has acquired over the past 156 years in such a short article. In addition to the examples outlined above, our collection also includes documents such as military commissions, wills, deeds, estate inventories, sermons, and much more. It is also difficult to account for every possible way manuscripts may be used to further your research. In fact, one of the challenges archivists face is that researchers are constantly using manuscripts in new ways; thus, our cataloging of manuscripts is always evolving to incorporate new research interests and methods. Yet, hopefully, even this short sampling of manuscript types illustrate why they are an important resource for genealogists. Ultimately, because of their contemporary recordings of vital statistic and biographical information, manuscripts are the primary source material that genealogists use to create and enhance the story of their family.

Using Manuscript Collections in Your Research

Michael J. Leclerc

There are many jewels to be found in rare books and manuscript collections. One vastly important difference between the two is that rare books are generally published materials, while manuscript collections usually are unpublished. It is not uncommon, however, to find in a manuscript collection an author's research materials that he or she then used to publish a book. NEHGS has many such collections. The wonderful thing about manuscript collections is that you never know what you will find in them. I have seen everything from notes on families carefully written in *Register* format to scraps of information written on the backs of envelopes. While many collections may have indexes, it is more common to find them not indexed. At most, a finding aid or inventory will be prepared to locate different parts of large collections.

Manuscripts need not be dusty old papers either. Some manuscript collections include carefully prepared charts and family histories printed from computer files in the last decade. Cemetery transcriptions, church records, vital records, and photographs are also in the collections. Captains' logs, broadsides, heraldic drawings, and other materials are also there. The NEHGS collection contains over 3,500 linear feet of manuscripts. Among the more interesting pieces of our collection are an original census book from Norfolk County, Massachusetts, in 1840 and the history of a small central Massachusetts town written in the 1860s that contains graphic opinions of the inhabitants' character from the author's perspective. The following examples from the NEHGS collection will give you some idea of what awaits you in these boxes and envelopes.

While some early diaries have been published, many additional diaries and journals have not, and were donated to institutions and kept in manuscript collections. The diary of Jesse Tilson of Stoughton, Massachusetts, is one such example and offers a fascinating glimpse into the taking of Fort Louisbourg from the French:

> Thursday June ye 28th [1759] in the morning the wind was at East and it Raind at about nine o clock the wid shiftedand Blew at N: W: and upon flood tide the frigget Drouie of from G [?] Island and we landed our cattle upon the

---

Published online on *NewEnglandAncestors.org*, November 9, 2001.

island and I saw a great many acers of wheet, and a great many acers of peas and all the french were gon of the island and carried of all the housestuf and cattle and Left their houses standing their was seven Mass houses upon the island and in sum places ye houses stood verry thick upon ye island & at night they sent down six fire ships. [1]

The papers also include provenance showing how the diary passed from owner to owner and finally ended up at NEHGS.

You will also find books that contain a mixture of handwritten pages, type-written pages, newspaper articles (both loose and pasted in), and other materials. The papers of William P. Brechin, M.D., of Boston contain one such book, which is entitled *The History of Kings County, Nova Scotia* (1910). Among the many notations in the book is the following story:

> I John Lowden of Cornwallis in Kings County do hereby confess That whereas sometime past I have rashly and inadvertently uttered and published a scandalous report of the Rev. James Murdock importing he was disguised with liquor at the dwelling house of Mr. Samuel Starr in Cornwallis which report although I at that time imagined from appearances might be true yet from sufficient evidence I am now fully convinced that my suspicions of Mr. Murdock's being at that time anyways affected or disguised with liquor were false and groundless and that my publishing such a report has greatly injured Mr. Murdock's character and reputation I do therefore hereby further humbly fully and freely acknowledge and confess my fault in publishing such report and heartily beg pardon of the said Mr. James Murdock for the injury I have done him and of all good people who have been offended thereby

> John Lowden
>
> Signed in presence of
William Dickson
D. Sherman Denison

Horton March 24,1768 [2]

This is followed by a similar confession signed by Samuel Starr, dated the same day. While insightful into the characters of the individuals named, there is a problem with this. The first confession starts on the first line of the page. In the top margin was written: "From Nova Scotia Gazetteer of March 24, 1768 Halifax March 31st 1768." Unfortunately these words are then crossed out. Was this a transcription from a newspaper account, or did Mr. Brechin see the original letters? It is impossible to tell from the information contained in the book, which itself appears to be a large number of disparate pages that were once bound together. The surrounding pages are narratives of different stories and shed no light on this entry. Materials such as this are quite common in manuscript collections. While the book's clue may give a researcher reason to find the newspaper mentioned to see if there are more clues contained within, the information itself must be further researched to determine its validity.

Another benefit of manuscript collections is that they may contain references to materials that are no longer extant or whose current whereabouts is unknown. Benjamin G. Gray wrote a seven-page history of the Gray family entitled, "Account of the Early Members of the family of Revd. B. G. Gray late of St. John N.B. deceased especially those in and from Massachusetts." It is dated 9 January 1861, and contains information on individuals from the seventeenth and eighteenth centuries. It is quite likely that the author actually knew many of the individuals born and living in the late 1700s, and thus the information contained about them could be first-hand knowledge. In addition, the account starts out:

> Benjamin Gray of Boston Mass: died in 1741 or 1742: he was the eldest son, and his father the eldest son of his father. About 1738 or 9 this Benjamin Gray received letters from England from a favorite uncle named John Gray of Westminster informing him that he was the next heir to the title and Estate in England. Being however a very great famous bigotted New Light, he wrote back that he would not quit his New Light System to be King of England: and shortly after died, as above mentioned, without male issue.[3]

The above extracted from a letter of Joseph Gray, (a grand nephew of said Benjn Gray) who was born in Massachusetts, but subsequently settled in Halifax, Nova Scotia, as a merchant in the firm of Proctor & Gray.

A side notation shows that the letter was written 8 February 1799. It is quite conceivable that the original letter is now lost to time. If it does exist, it could be difficult or impossible to locate. It may still be in private hands. Sixty-two years after it was written, however, Benjamin Gray allows us to know the contents of that letter and the interesting information contained therein. If he hadn't recorded this correspondence, we may have never known about his namesake.

Transcriptions of original records are often found in manuscript collections. Before the age of microfilm, in the second half of the twentieth century, the only way to examine original records was to travel to the repository where they were held. Transcribing original records was a very popular pastime in the late nineteenth and early twentieth centuries. These transcriptions allowed more people to view the information contained in the original records without having to travel to examine it. In the United States, many typescripts were created by members of the National Society of the Daughters of the American Revolution. Many were also made by the Works Progress Administration (WPA) and deposited at local libraries. Individuals, however, created a huge number of transcriptions that eventually made their way to the author's local libraries. Among the transcriptions in the NEHGS collection is a typescript of the Township Book for Aylesford, Nova Scotia, and land records of the King's Grant in Clements, Annapolis County, Nova Scotia, in 1784. One might also find photocopies of original records, such as those of the Township of Lunenburg, Nova Scotia, which were given to NEHGS.

You may wonder why anyone would want to look at transcriptions or photocopies when microfilm copies of original records are now so easily available. There are several reasons. First, unless you live in Salt Lake City, there is a great likelihood that the films you want to view will have to be rented. It would be nice to view a transcription of the records first to see if the information you are looking for is even in those records. If they contain nothing useful, you could end up saving yourself a considerable amount of money. Even if microfilmed copies of the originals are available, they may be difficult to read. Having a transcription available that was made by viewing the actual documents may make it easier for you to read what you see on the film. Also, parts of the original records may have been lost or destroyed after they were transcribed but before they were microfilmed.

Genealogical notes on families make up the bulk of the information in the NEHGS manuscript collection. They vary in size from small folders to several archive boxes. There are handwritten sheets of paper, index cards, bound notes, and odd scraps of paper, as well as some materials generated by computer. A typical example of family records is a manuscript donated by Dorothea (Whelan) Saavedra on her Newfoundland ancestry. It is a mixture of charts, photocopies of photographs, and narrative. In the opening paragraph, she writes, "This is obviously the first 'rough draft' of a projected four part study of my father's family in Newfoundland. There are many mistakes and empty spaces which will be rectified and filled in time." [4] As is the case with many manuscripts, there is no citation of sources, meaning that all information contained therein would need to be confirmed through primary sources. It is, however, a good place to start. Especially for a place like Newfoundland where few microfilmed records are available outside of the Province.

How can manuscripts be located? One major resource is the National Union Catalog of Manuscript Collections [NUCMC] lcweb.loc.gov/coll/nucmc/nucmc.html. Sponsored by the Library of Congress, NUCMC catalogs manuscript collections at many smaller repositories that may not have the resources to publish their holdings. Larger repositories often have their catalogs on the Internet. Many institutions have also published catalogs of their manuscript collections at different times, such as *The Catalog of Manuscripts of the Massachusetts Historical Society* (Boston: G. K. Hall, 1969).

When checking catalogs also make sure to check for limitations on access. Some collections may have restrictions stipulated by the donor. Repositories may restrict the use of their collections in general. For example, viewing manuscripts at NEHGS is a benefit of membership. Our manuscript collection is not available to non-members. An institution may also enforce special handling rules, such as requiring the use of white gloves, book cradles, or pencils, Additionally, there may be limitations placed on the number of photocopies you can make from any individual collection.

Some of you may be interested in donating your own papers to a local repository. Here are some general guidelines to follow:

* Ask the repository for a copy of their guidelines for donating materials. Once you read them, follow them to the letter. Feel free to ask questions and discuss them with the repository staff, but remember that they have developed these guidelines for a reason.

Manuscript Collections

- Collections donated by genealogists

- Notebooks, index listings, and unpublished genealogies

- Pedigree charts (tabular pedigrees)

- Church records, original town birth registers, diaries

- Account books, letters, personal records, land deeds, wills

- Marriage licenses, intents of marriage, baptismal certificates

- Typescript or manuscript genealogies

- Typescript or manuscript cemetery records

- A wide variety of various unpublished treasures

- Go through your collection and have it neatly organized. Placing it in acid-free folders is a plus, but not absolutely necessary.

- While an index is a wonderful thing, it is not essential. However, a finding aid that shows how the collection is organized is a must. Ask a friend or family member to look at your papers and give you their opinion on how useful your finding aid is. Let them read whatever instructions you have prepared and encourage them to use the materials themselves. Although you may be tempted to try to explain things to them, remember that once the materials are deposited in a library or other institution, you will not always be there to explain things to people using the materials.

- Do not just print out a cascading pedigree chart and ask to submit it. Many repositories would be flooded by such information. Narrative format is best, but even family group sheets will be easier to use and be more valuable than a cascading pedigree.

- Make arrangements to have the materials transported to the repository. Don't expect that repositories will be able to pick materials up from you.

Exploring manuscript collections can be a useful way of finding information that might otherwise be difficult to locate. Do not let the vast amount of original records available detract you from using them. You will often find records that exist nowhere else in the world, and if you happen to find a long-sought answer by researching manuscripts as a last resort, you may regret not having tried it sooner!

Notes

1. Diary and account book of Jesse Tilson and John Spare, 1759, 1764–1766, Mss A 2006.
2. *The History of Kings County, Nova Scotia* - Brechin Collection, Spec. Col. 11/B/3.
3. Benjamin G. Gray, *Account of Early Members of the family of Revd. B.G. Gray late of St. John N.B. deceased especially those in and around Massachusetts,* Mss C 1851.
4. Dorothea M. Saavedra, "My Newfoundland Forebears: A Short Study of the Families Hissock & Manuel of Catalina, Newfoundland & The Families Wells & Whelan of Cupids, Newfoundland," Mss C 1834.

Genealogical Thoughts on NEHGS Manuscripts

Gary Boyd Roberts

I wish to discuss some of the Society's best and most used manuscripts. These fall generally into four categories — those covering towns and regions; treating individual families; containing the papers of major nineteenth- and twentieth-century genealogical scholars; or covering largely English, noble European, or royal families.

Towns and Regions

Proceeding alphabetically by author the first collection is Charlotte Helen Abbott's "Early Records of Families in Andover [Mass]," 14 volumes plus 15 reels of notes, the original of which is at the Andover Historical Society. The quality of this collection is medium leaning to good; much more detail could be obtained from local deeds, wills, and court records. The next two collections are the notes of Charles Edward Banks and Clarence Winthrop Bowen on families of Martha's Vineyard and Woodstock, Connecticut. The former, 25 volumes of "Settlers of Martha's Vineyard," contains the family data used in volume 3 of Banks's history of the island, but also includes an additional unpublished generation. The Bowen collection, 11 cartons, consists of all materials for the eight published volumes of *Genealogies of Woodstock Families,* and was a gift from the American Antiquarian Society. The first six books in this set covered all branches of all families in Woodstock and surrounding towns (especially Pomfret). The last two volumes, covering over half the alphabet, treat only those families in Woodstock proper and only so long as they lived there. The manuscript collection includes much additional data on families Hayward–Z, covered in these last two volumes (ed. by D. L. Jacobus and W. H. Wood after Bowen's death).

The Walter E. (and Lottie A.S.) Corbin and Fred E. Crowell collections — the former 60 linear feet of records and compiled genealogies for central and western Massachusetts, the latter *New Englanders in Nova Scotia* — were both microfilmed, in 1982 and 1979 respectively. I reviewed Corbin in *Register* 139 (1985):150–55 and Crowell in *Register* 135 (1981):67. *The Corbin Collection* is, I believe, the largest regional assemblage of New England source material ever

Gary Boyd Roberts's comments on manuscript collections are part of a series of articles available on *NewEnglandAncestors.org.* They have been updated for this publication.

amassed by professional genealogists. Included are genealogies of all residents of Northampton (outlines only, by Sylvester Judd) and Pittsfield (much more detailed, by Rollin H. Cooke) plus family data also for Belchertown, Southampton, and Wales. This 55-reel collection is now available in many libraries. So too is the Crowell collection, which covers the patrilineal New England ancestry — but not Nova Scotia descendents — of 650 or so immigrants to Nova Scotia in the eighteenth century. Crowell estimated, I might note, that 600 or more additional families could also have been included. Banks, Bowen, and Crowell do not abstract wills or deeds and all have some errors (Crowell more than a few). Each however is immensely useful and by far the best source for its area. The Corbin Collection is also available on CD-ROM — *The Corbin Collection: Vol. 1 Records of Hampshire County, Massachusetts and Vol. 2: Records of Hampden County, Massachusetts* — both edited by Robert J. Dunkle.

The Gilbert Harry Doane collection consists of 38 boxes, 23 of which cover families and records of Fairfield, Vermont (a full 7 the Hungerford family). The Abbie L. and Gustavus A. Hinckley collection, part of which is also a CD published by the Society, consists of 12 volumes of Barnstable town and vital records, 9 volumes of Barnstable County probate records, and assorted other Barnstable materials. The Waldo Chamberlain Sprague collection has been partly microfilmed; the 6100 cards comprising *Genealogies of the Families of Braintree, Massachusetts 1640–1850* is thus widely available (I reviewed it in *Register* 139 [1985]:155–58) and on a CD of the same title through NEHGS. Other parts of the collection, one of our very best in overall quality, include Thayer (8 volumes), Wales, and Curtis genealogies, and Braintree, Quincy, and Randolph vital records through 1850.

The last two collections I wish to mention are middling in quality but still useful. Eugene F. Weedon compiled 86 volumes, over 10 small ledgers, and several notebooks covering families (and including some source records) of Berwick, Maine and Somersworth, New Hampshire. Hamilton Wilson Welch compiled over 250 notebooks on "Early Families of Scituate and Neighboring Towns." This last collection is comprehensive but undocumented, with dates only in years, no will or deed abstraction, and no biographical notes.

Families

Proceeding alphabetically by author, here are the dozen or so greatest collections covering families. The first of these is 53 volumes by Henry Franklin Andrews on his Andrews and Hamlin kinsmen. The Hamlin material was later published; 32 of these volumes, however, cover all descendants (daughters of daughters of daughters, as well as sons of sons of sons) of the author's immigrant patrilineal forebear, John Andrews of Ipswich, died 1708. I believe these volumes are unindexed and have used this enormous collection very rarely.

The second collection is that of Edmund Dana Barbour — 10 bound volumes (now on the open shelves), dated 1907 and indexed, on all descendants, again through female as well as male lines, of Captain George Barbour, a founder of Medfield, Mass. We also have five boxes of the original manuscript and notes. See also *NEXUS* 3 (1987):29. I was especially pleased to find William Marsh Rice of Houston, the founder of Rice University (my family's home when I was born was on Rice Blvd., named after the philanthropist and university) in this set.

The third collection consists of 12 small volumes covering many New England Cook/Cooke families and 31 small volumes covering most Connecticut Lewises. This collection is by Rollin Hillyer Cooke, the great Berkshire Co. genealogist, whose 10 volumes on all early Pittsfield families were copied by W. E. Corbin and are part of that collection (covered above). Mr. Cooke also gave us 9 volumes of Berkshire Co. deed abstracts and two cartons of miscellaneous genealogical notes (see *Register* 139 [1985]:154–55). Another 54 volumes of Berkshire Co. source material collected by Mr. Cooke is at the Berkshire Athenaeum in Pittsfield. I might add that *Mayflower* and Rhode Island Cookes are covered in vol.12 of *Mayflower Families Through Five Generations* and the two-volume 1987 Thomas Cook genealogy by Jane Fletcher Fiske (plus some *TAG* and *Register* contributions).

The fourth collection, by Elwin Gerry Davis and Samuel F. Rockwell, consists of 4 boxes of 14 bound record books that collectively cover most New England Davises. This collection is only partly indexed and should generally be used only after printed sources have been exhausted. The fifth collection to note is 122 volumes of alphabetically arranged lineage papers and membership applications for the Governor Thomas Dudley Association. Gov. Dudley, of royal descent, a major colonial figure, left an extremely large and prominent progeny, including Channings, Danas, Wendells, Holmeses, Elliots, Nortons, Morisons, Lowells, Parkmans, Winthrops, Alsops, Auchinclosses, and various duPonts.

The sixth collection consists of 28 volumes by William Crowninshield Endicott, Jr., on the descendants of Governor John Endicott, 1588–1665/6. Many female lines of this noted Salem family are also included. The Willis Freeman genealogical collection is, in my opinion, one of our major possessions. Its consists of 60 bound folio volumes authoritatively covering almost all Freemans in England, New England, and the mid-Atlantic states, plus numerous southern Freemans. Arranged alphabetically by given names, and then chronologically by birth year, 32 volumes cover male Freemans, 22 volumes treat female Freemans, and 6 volumes cover Freemans of Woodbridge, N.J.

Henry S. Gorham's 28 volumes on the descendants of Captain John Gorham of Barnstable is a massive typescript compiled 1931–44. Captain Gorham was the son-in-law of John Howland of the *Mayflower* and the first four generations of this study (to about 1720) are superseded by Elizabeth P. White's first volume (1990) on the descendants for five generations of that Pilgrim.

The ninth collection consists of 28 volumes on the agnate and some female-line descendants of William Nickerson, first settler of Chatham on Cape Cod. These volumes, by William Emery Nickerson, are a major basis for the ongoing Nickerson genealogy (4 volumes to date) published by the Nickerson Family Association. Also included in the collection are 7 boxes of notes by Anna C. Kingsbury, sponsored by Mr. Nickerson, on over 50 other largely Massachusetts families. Horace Wilbur Palmer's "Palmer Families in America," contains 13 typescript volumes on almost all New England and many mid-Atlantic and southern Palmers. Other copies of the collection are at the New York and Los Angeles Public Libraries. Two parts of this collection, on the descendants of William Palmers of Yarmouth and Duxbury, Mass., respectively, have been published; see *Register* 130 (1976):57–59. This collection was indexed in 1998 by NEHGS volunteer Karen Buss; much of its unpublished section concerns the progeny of Walter Palmer of Stonington.

Wesley Weyman's "Descendants of Captain Myles Standish, Male and Female Lines," 5 cartons, is the largest study to date on the progeny of the military leader of the *Mayflower* company. It is superseded for the first five generations, to about 1720 only, by vol.14 of *Mayflower Families Through Five Generations*. Two other cartons compiled by Mr. Weyman treat Bennetts, Ramsdells, and Wymans.

Many other families are well covered by sizable or large manuscript collections at NEHGS. We also have the original notes for numerous genealogies (those for the John Hayes of Dover, N.H., work are especially voluminous). The above are simply those collections I have much used or noticed and those, with the caveats about indexes, etc., noted above, that I think visitors to the library will most want to use. These collections are open to members but cannot be loaned. I encourage everyone who would like to delve into one or more of them, to visit Boston and NEHGS.

Collections of Major Scholars

I wish to comment on a dozen or more Society collections that are, in effect, the notes and papers of some of the greatest New England genealogists of the last century or more.

Beginning alphabetically, the first of these scholars is Algernon Aiken Aspinwall, whose 55 items, notebooks, or cartons include an undocumented and incomplete, but sixth generation, tracing (through that generation's marriages) of all descendants of the 23 *Mayflower* passengers who became heads of surviving families. This collection may be considered a companion piece to the 41 volumes of *Mayflower* lineages collected in the 1920s and 1930s by Dr. Frank T. Calef (these last at the Rhode Island Historical Society in Providence). I have not used the Calef collection, but until all of the *Mayflower* five-generation "silver books" are published, the Aspinwall notes can be quite useful, especially for the Alden progeny and descendants of younger children of John Howland. Remember, too, that most of the "silver books" go through only the birth of sixth generation descendants, not their marriages.

The second scholar whose work I wish to mention is Claude Willis Barlow, who left us 17 boxes and 4 cartons of alphabetized family notes and correspondence, concerning numerous early residents of Massachusetts and Connecticut. Barlow was a Worcester County specialist and the five-generation *Mayflower* project worker for Richard Warren and John Billington. I knew Mr. Barlow, he used our library often, and died in the late 1970s.

The third set of scholars are Joseph Gardner and Elizabeth (French) Bartlett, whose 17 cartons and other material contain the notes on English origins that both Bartletts collected for the NEHGS Committee on English and Foreign Research. Twenty-two small boxes are a partial, mostly alphabetical, index to English Chancery Proceedings during the reign of Charles I. Two more cartons given by Mrs. Bartlett cover the Mixer-Mixter, Woolson, and Hartshorn families.

A fourth collection of notes is that of Weymouth town genealogist George Walter Chamberlain, who left us 193 items, largely on Massachusetts and New Hampshire families, plus over 80 items separately catalogued by family (we do not have his notes on Weymouth families). I might note, too, that the Rollin Hillyer Cooke and Walter Everett Corbin collections were treated above — the R. H. Cooke collection under Cooke and Lewis families and the Corbin Collection under central and western Massachusetts.

The fifth collection is one of our largest and most valuable — that of Mrs. Mary Campbell Lovering Holman and her daughter Mrs. Winifred Lovering Holman Dodge. Thirty-seven boxes contain authoritative notes on (usually) one line of descent from over 1200 (mostly) Great Migration New England immigrants (their surnames are listed in *NEXUS* 13 [1996]:83–84). Twenty-seven separate volumes contain genealogies prepared for clients, and 5 more volumes consist of various bibliographical aids. These notes include summaries or abstracts, sometimes transcriptions, of all probate and land records for each head of family; this much expanded use of courthouse records became a standard for future New England articles and published genealogies. Mrs. Holman and/or Mrs. Dodge also contributed numerous typescripts to the regular collection and separately catalogued manuscript material on Bentley, Claflin, Fletcher, Lovering, Merrill, and Rice families. The 37 boxes were given to us in 1974, and Mrs. Dodge kept in contact until her death in 1989.

The sixth scholar is Arthur Wentworth Hamilton Eaton, whose 175 items in 18 boxes are largely genealogies of Nova Scotia planters and United Empire Loyalists, notably of Kings and Hants counties; included also are various additions to his published works (see *NEXUS* 3 [1986]:30). The seventh scholar is Merton Taylor Goodrich, whose 45 boxes (22 linear feet) cover most New England Goodriches and over 700 other New England families, especially Austin, Hall, Thyng, and Walker. Henry Winthrop Hardon gave us 54 typescript volumes covering Cole, Horne, Huckins, Huntress, Jackson, Lang, Lord, Peverly, Roberts, and Seward families of New Hampshire and Maine, plus notes, later published, on 18th-century families in Newington, N.H.

The ninth scholar, Royal Ralph Hinman, published *A Catalogue of the Names of the Early Puritan Settlers of the Colony of Connecticut*, covering only A-Danielson and Hinman, in 1853–56. With no Connecticut State Library and no Connecticut Historical Society at that time, we were given the 11 enormous folio volumes of handwritten pasted notes, letters, etc., alphabetically arranged, that were the basis for his *Catalogue*. This collection is probably long superseded on many subjects, but may well contain data found nowhere else.

The tenth scholar, Almon Danforth Hodges Jr., gave us notes collected for his published work, plus items on 70 mostly Massachusetts families. The collection of Samuel Burnham Shackford contains 72 items on largely New Hampshire families. The twelfth scholar was, like the Holmans, one of our greatest. From Clarence Almon Torrey we inherited an early and final version of " New England Marriages Prior to 1700, " microfilmed in 1979, published without references in 1985 (almost 7000 copies of the book have sold to date). A CD-ROM version is now available, prepared in part by David Curtis Dearborn and Marshall Kenneth Kirk, both of whom interpreted Torrey's rather difficult handwriting with great care. Torrey also gave us 14 cartons with much material on the Clark, Fairbanks, Gates, Gawkroger, Gilbert, Gilman, Heald, Roe, Torrey, Whitehead, and Young families, plus the ancestry of presidents John and J.Q. Adams and W. H. Taft. I evaluated Torrey's splendid contribution to seventeenth-century New England genealogy, and to English origins studies, in *Register* 135 (1981):57–61, and in the introduction to the 1985 book.

Marion Charlotte Reed, a protégée of the Holmans, gave us over 14 cartons of notes compiled for clients. This collection covers 1300 families, mostly of New England or New York. I do not really know if this collection is as fine as that of Miss Reed's sponsors. It is underused and may not be fully inventoried.

British and European Collections

There are five manuscript collections with largely British or European content — the collections of John Insley Coddington, John Hutchinson Cook, Joseph Jackson Howard, George Andrews Moriarty Jr., and Gary Boyd Roberts.

In March 1987, the Society was given its largest manuscript gift to date — about 125 cartons of genealogical notes collected over 60 years by John Insley Coddington of Bordentown, N.J., often called the "dean of American genealogists in his generation." Coddington's lifelong interests in this field were royal and noble families, colonial New England (especially Conn. and Fairfield Co.), New Jersey, and Ireland, the last three of which were derived from his own ancestry. An appreciation of his contribution to American genealogy overall and a bibliography of over 200 articles and book chapters appear in *A Tribute to John Insley Coddington, on the Fortieth Anniversary of the American Society of Genealogists* (1980), edited by Neil D. Thompson and Robert Charles Anderson (see also Coddington's obituary in the *Register* 145 [1991]:195–201). Mr. Coddington's large gift also includes the manuscript notes of Mahlon K. A. Schnacke, former librarian of the American Academy of Rome. These latter notes consist in part of a study of the entire known progeny of Maria Brankovic (1466–1495), a Serbian princess who married a marquess of Montferrat, an ancestress of many royal and noble families, and the "gateway" forebear through whom many scholars formerly thought ancestry from the ancient world was most likely to derive. Coddington's notes also cover all families in his own ancestry and all families on which he wrote.

John Hutchinson Cook was Coddington's neighbor in Bordentown and Cook's enormous collection of books, given to the Society in 1987, were the major source for many European articles of both Coddington and Milton Rubincam. John's books, 10,000 or more (probably the largest private genealogical collection ever assembled in this country, on British and European topics at least) have a Latin emphasis; there is greater coverage of France, Spain, Italy, and Belgium than of Germany, the Scandinavian countries, Poland, or Russia. Cook's 23 boxes of manuscripts include 14 of newspaper clippings and photographs — again the largest such collection I know of — covering the marriages and deaths of most kings and British and European noblemen of the twentieth century. Cook was also interested in every intermarriage since about the Civil War of noted Europeans and Americans. His seven boxes of notes, all in pencil but very readable, cover many of these connections and all of the European families that interested him. Cook usually gives sources and obviously used his own books continually. The last two boxes are labeled graphics, and one contains photographs of houses in Burlington Co., N.J. Cook notes also cover all of his own ancestry and were my source for comments on it in his obituary (*NEXUS* 11 [1994]:148). Cook's major American interests were families in New Jersey and South Carolina.

A collection whose history is largely unknown is Joseph Jackson Howard's "Pedigrees of Families of Great Britain," 50 volumes, 1 missing, fully but complexly indexed. Howard was a major British scholar, the editor of many "modern visitation" volumes, and this collection may well have been his lifelong hobby. It carefully, but very partially, and without documentation, traces the royal descents from Alfred the Great and later kings of many British noble and gentry families. This collection is largely unknown in England, but the late Sir Anthony R. Wagner expressed much interest when I told him about it.

George Andrews Moriarty Jr. was the most prolific article writer (over 400) of this century; for almost 50 years he was head of our Committee on English and Foreign Research. For an overall evaluation of his contribution to Anglo-American genealogy see my introduction to the first series of *English Origins of New England Families* (1984), vol. 1, vii–xi. His manuscript holdings here consist of "The Plantagenet Ancestry of Edward III and Queen Philippa," (upon which much of *Royalty for Commoners* and some of the forthcoming Henderson project are based), and 19 ledger volumes and 4 cartons of materials concerning Moriarty's entire known American and medieval ancestry. The bulk of the ledger volumes cover English forebears of Moriarty's five royally descended immigrant ancestors: Edward and Ellen (Newton) Carleton of Rowley, Dr. Richard Palgrave of Charlestown, Rev. William Sargent of Malden, and John Throckmorton of Providence, R.I. This latter ancestry is so extensive that Moriarty treats most of the major families of medieval England.

My own collection is entitled "The Mowbray Connection: An Analysis of the Genealogical Evolution of British, American, and Continental Nobilities, Gentries and Upper Classes Since the End of the Middle Ages," 23 volumes (3 of text, 6 of British charts, 10 of American charts, 2 of continental charts, a bibliography for much of the American section, and an every-name index by Michael J. Wood of the American charts). The charts in this collection outline the royal descents and extent of kinship to Thomas Mowbray, 1st Duke of Norfolk, died 1399, of over 3,500 American, over 1,000 British, and over 500 continental historical figures; see *The Royal Descents of 600 Immigrants* (2004), xvii–xxi. Also at NEHGS are positive microfilm copies of the 140 notebooks on which "The Mowbray Connection" is based, and photocopies of 20 pamphlets covering major notable descendants of various of my New England forebears; 11 comparable pamphlets for the major notable progeny of New England ancestors of the late Princess of Wales and her sons; and various charts beyond what I have published on the genealogical connections of American presidents. I add to these latter volumes frequently.

Most readers will care primarily about our manuscript collections covering New England towns or families, or consisting of the notes of major New England genealogists. I hope, however, that those of you who do find royal, medieval, or gentry ancestry will upon occasion peruse some of the materials in these five collections. I am personally familiar, as well, with the families in Coddington's, Cook's, Moriarty's, and my own ancestry, and will frequently refer readers to the printed or manuscript data compiled by these scholars. New discoveries in these fields — royal descents, American/European connections, or even presidential forebears — are always welcome, and I appreciate knowing about them.

SECTION *4*

New England

New England Overview

Henry B. Hoff

Various regional sources are relevant to most or all of the six New England states. An annotated list is provided here. Some of the sources below are obvious basic sources, while others are particularly valuable in the opinion of the editors. Readers are urged to review all of the following chapters as each was written by a different author, and one author may include a regional source that others did not cite.

Guides and Finding Aids

- Melnyk, Marcia D., *Genealogist's Handbook for New England Research*, 4th ed. (Boston: NEHGS, 1999) REF F3/G466/1999 also LOAN. Lists repositories with details on collections, hours, directions, etc. Includes charts of towns with dates of creation and other relevant data.

- Crandall, Ralph J., ed., *Genealogical Research in New England* (Baltimore: Genealogical Publishing Co., 1984) REF F3/G46/1984 also LOAN. Contains articles on research in each of the six New England states, originally published in *The New England Historical and Genealogical Register.*

- Eichholz, Alice, ed., *Red Book: American State, County, and Town Sources*, 3rd ed. (Provo, Utah: Ancestry, 2004) REF CS49/A55/2004 also LOAN. Contains chapters on research in each state. This edition supersedes the 1992 edition.

- Torrey, Clarence Almon, *New England Marriages Prior to 1700*, contains references to marriages from over 2500 books and a few manuscripts and primary sources, up to 1962. A photocopy of the twelve-volume collection itself is in the sixth-floor reading room. R.Rm. REF F3/T6/1971. However, the cryptic references are often difficult to read. It is best used on CD-ROM (Boston: NEHGS, 2001) or as the bound printout from the CD-ROM (also in the sixth-floor reading room), which contain full citations of all identifiable sources. The marriages without sources were published as *New England Marriages Prior to 1700* (Baltimore: Genealogical Publishing Co., 1992) REF F3/T6/1992 also LOAN.

- Sanborn, Melinde Lutz, *Third Supplement to Torrey's New England Marriages Prior to 1700* (Baltimore: Genealogical Publishing Co., 2003) R.Rm. REF F3/T6/Suppl./2003 also LOAN. Continues Torrey, based on major periodicals, the Great Migration Study Project, and published and unpublished research. Incorporates the contents of two previous supplements.

- *The American Genealogical-Biographical Index* (AGBI), 206 vols. (Middletown, Conn.: Godfrey Library, 1952–2000) REF Z5313/U5/A55. All but the last few volumes are on CD-ROM; the remaining ones are online at *Ancestry.com*. This work indexes over 700 family histories, the genealogical columns of the *Boston Evening Transcript*, and many other sources. See Kory L. Meyerink, "Genealogy's Best-Kept Secret: *The American Genealogical-Biographical Index*," in *Ancestry* 17 (1999):36–40.

- *Periodical Source Index* (PERSI), 16 vols. for 1847–1985, plus subsequent annual volumes (Fort Wayne, Ind.: Allen County Public Library Foundation, 1987–present) REF CS1/P47. Also on CD-ROM and online, the most recent version as part of Heritage Quest Online. Indexes articles in hundreds of genealogical and historical periodicals by surname, location, and topic.

- Colket, Meredith B., Jr., *Founders of Early American Families: Emigrants from Europe 1607–1657*, rev. ed. (Cleveland, Ohio: Order of Founders and Patriots of America, 1985) R.Rm. REF CS61/C64/1985 [A second revised edition, published in 2002, includes minimal revisions]. Lists books and articles on colonists in America by 1657 with living male-line descendants.

- *Donald Lines Jacobus' Index to Genealogical Periodicals*, rev. ed. (Newhall, Calif.: Carl Boyer 3rd, 1983) R.Rm. REF Z5313/U5/J22/1983 also LOAN. Still valuable for finding pre-1953 periodical articles.

- Hoff, Henry B., "New England Articles in Genealogical Journals in 2000," *The New England Historical and Genealogical Register* 156 (July 2002):280–94. Comparable articles published in July 2003 and July 2004 for 2001 and 2002, respectively. Indexes seventeen journals including the following three national journals which have included important compiled accounts of New England families: *National Genealogical Society Quarterly*, 1912–present. CS42/N4 also LOAN; *The Genealogist*, 1980–present. R.Rm. REF CS1/G392; and *The New York Genealogical and Biographical Record*, 1870-present. R.Rm. REF F116/N28.

- Bartley, Scott Andrew, "Seen Elsewhere [Articles on *Mayflower* Genealogical Topics]," *Mayflower Descendant* 51 (2002):71–80; 52 (2003):80, 119–21.

Genealogical and Historical Periodicals

- *The New England Historical and Genealogical Register*, 1847–present. R.Rm. REF F1/N56 also LOAN also fifth floor also Web database. Publishes compiled genealogies (including pre-American origins), problem-solving articles, and source material for the six New England states. Volumes 1–148 (1847–1994) are on CD-ROM and online on *NewEnglandAncestors.org*, with subsequent volumes anticipated to be online. NEHGS published composite every-name indexes for volumes 1–50 (includes subject index) and 51–148. There are two privately-produced subject indexes for volumes after 51, one by Jean D. Worden, the other by Margaret Wellington Parsons. Note also the various compendia of articles from the *Register* (Connecticut Families, English Origins, Mayflower Families, Mayflower Source Records, Rhode Island Families).

- *The Great Migration Newsletter*, 1990–present. REF F7/G73/1990 also LOAN also Intl REF. Vols. 1–10 (1990–99) reprinted as one volume (Boston: NEHGS, 2002). Vol. 11–present is online at *NewEnglandAncestors.org* (by subscription). Contains authoritative articles on seventeenth-century New England, providing insights vital for the genealogist.

- *The American Genealogist*, 1922–present. R.Rm. REF F104/N6/A6 also LOAN. Publishes short compiled genealogies (including pre-American origins) and problem-solving articles for the entire U.S. with emphasis on New England. The first eight volumes were reprinted in three as Donald Lines Jacobus, *Families of Ancient New Haven* (Baltimore: Genealogical Publishing Co., 1974) REF F104/N6/A6/1922 also LOAN. Volumes 9–41 (1932–1965) were reprinted with a subject index (Camden, Maine: Picton Press, 1989), and an every-name index to these volumes was published on CD-ROM by Picton Press in 1998. Jean D. Worden published *The American Genealogist: Index to Subjects in Volumes 1–60* [1922–1984] (Franklin, Ohio: the compiler, 1985) R.Rm. REF F104/N6/A6/Index also LOAN.

- *Mayflower Descendant*, 1899–1937 and 1985–present, published by the Massachusetts Society of Mayflower Descendants. R.Rm. REF F68/M46 also LOAN. Publishes compiled genealogies, problem-solving articles, and source material relevant for families descended from *Mayflower* passengers. Vols. 1–34 (1899-1937) and 1–46 (1899–1996) are on separate CD-ROMs.

Genealogical and Biographical Compendia

- Savage, James, *A Genealogical Dictionary of the First Settlers of New England*, 4 vols. (Boston: Little, Brown & Co., 1860–62; reprinted Baltimore: Genealogical Publishing Co., 1965) R.Rm. REF F3/S2/1860 also LOAN also Rare Book also on CD-ROM. Despite its age, this is still a useful source.

- Anderson, Robert Charles, *The Great Migration Begins: Immigrants to New England 1620–1633,* 3 vols. (Boston: NEHGS, 1995) R.Rm. REF F7/G74/1995 also LOAN also Intl REF. Also on CD-ROM and on *NewEnglandAncestors.org*. This set attempts to identify and provide documented accounts of all Europeans who settled in New England 1620–1633. This set and the following set, plus *The Great Migration Newsletter* (see above), are from the Great Migration Study Project.

- Anderson, Robert Charles, George F. Sanborn Jr., and Melinde Lutz Sanborn, *The Great Migration: Immigrants to New England 1634–1635, Volume I A–B* (Boston: NEHGS, 1999) and *Volume II C–F* (Boston: NEHGS, 2001); Robert Charles Anderson, *The Great Migration: Immigrants to New England 1634–1635, Volume III G–H* (Boston: NEHGS, 2003) R.Rm. REF F7/G742/1999 also LOAN also Intl REF. This set attempts to identify and provide documented accounts of all Europeans who settled in New England in 1634–1635, the peak years of the Great Migration (which ended in 1640).

- *Mayflower Families Through Five Generations*, 22 vols. to date (Plymouth, Mass.: General Society of Mayflower Descendants, 1975–present) REF S63/M39 . . . also LOAN. See also *Mayflower Families in Progress* (Plymouth, Mass.: General Society of Mayflower Descendants, 1986–present) REF F63/M397 . . . also LOAN. The latter volumes ("pink books") are ultimately superseded by the former volumes ("silver books").

Connecticut

Joyce S. Pendery

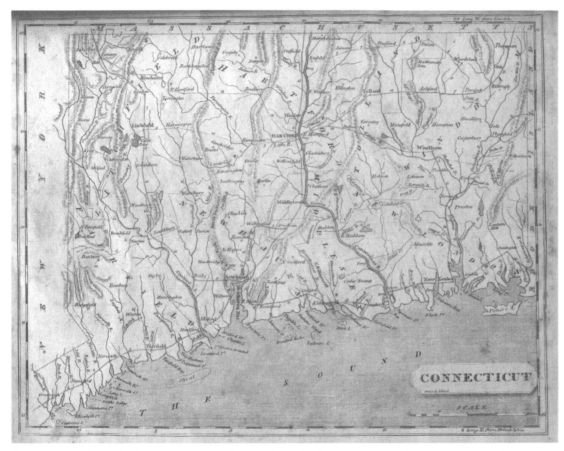

Connecticut from *A New and Elegant General Atlas* by Arrowsmith and Lewis (Boston: Thomas & Andrews, 1805).

Overview

Connecticut records are among the most complete and best preserved in the nation. Most records are kept in towns or in Hartford since county government was abolished in 1960. The NEHGS Library collection of Connecticut records, one of the largest outside the state, is especially rich in resources for eighteenth and nineteenth-century Connecticut. While lacking most land records, the NEHGS Connecticut collection includes many vital, church, cemetery, probate, and census records, as well as an outstanding collection of local histories with genealogies for many Connecticut towns.

Despite good records, Connecticut research can be difficult, particularly for towns that kept few vital records in the first part of the nineteenth century. See, for example, "Identifying the Parents of Eliza DeForest, Wife of Hinman Atwood of Watertown, Connecticut," *The New England Historical and Genealogical Register* 157 (2003):148–54. Eliza and her twelve siblings were born between 1805 and 1830 in Litchfield County but not one had a birth or baptismal record.

Connecticut Colony and New Haven Colony were separate entities until 1662 when they joined together. However, the boundaries of Connecticut were not entirely set until 1827. The boundaries of lower Fairfield County and adjacent Westchester County, New York, were not finalized until 1730. Along the northern border of Connecticut, the towns of Enfield, Somers, Suffield, and Woodstock belonged to Massachusetts until 1749.

Guides and Finding Aids

- Abbe, Elizabeth, "Connecticut Genealogical Research: Sources and Suggestions," *The New England Historical and Genealogical Register* 134 (1980):3–26, reprinted, with additions, in Ralph J. Crandall, ed., *Genealogical Research in New England* (Baltimore: Genealogical Publishing Co., 1984), 77–114. REF F3/G46/1984 also LOAN.

- *The American Genealogical-Biographical Index* [AGBI], 206 vols. (Middletown, Conn.: Godfrey Library, 1952–2000) REF Z5313/U5/A55. See NEW ENGLAND OVERVIEW.

- Collier, Christopher, and Bonnie B. Collier, *The Literature of Connecticut History*, Occasional Papers of the Connecticut Humanities Council, No. 6 (Middletown, Conn.: Connecticut Humanities Council, 1983) R.Rm. REF F94/C65/1983 also LOAN.

- Eichholz, Alice, "Connecticut," in *Red Book: American State, County, and Town Sources*, 3rd ed. (Provo, Utah: Ancestry, 2004), 95–110. REF CS49/A55/2004 also LOAN.

- Kemp, Thomas Jay, *Connecticut Researcher's Handbook* (Detroit: Gale Research Co., 1981) R.Rm. REF F93/K46/1981 also LOAN.

- Melnyk, Marcia D., *Genealogist's Handbook for New England Research*, 4th ed. (Boston: NEHGS, 1999), 22–43. R.Rm. REF F/3/G466/1999 also LOAN.

- Morrison, Betty Jean, *Connecting to Connecticut* (East Hartford, Conn.: Connecticut Society of Genealogists, 1995) R.Rm. REF F93/M67/1995 also LOAN.

- Parks, Roger N., ed., *Connecticut: A Bibliography of its History* (Hanover, N.H.: University Press of New England, 1986) REF F94/C66/1986 also LOAN.

- Pendery, Joyce S., "A Guide to Genealogical Research in Connecticut," *New England Ancestors* 3:3 (Summer 2002):15–23. REF F1/N49 also LOAN. See also the online articles by the same author on *NewEnglandAncestors.org*.

- Roberts, Gary Boyd, "Some Reflections on Modern Connecticut Scholarship," *The Connecticut Nutmegger* 12:3 (December 1979):371–85. F91/C82 also LOAN.

- Sellers, Helen Earle, *Connecticut Town Origins, Their Names, Boundaries, Early Histories and First Families*, 2nd ed. (Chester, Conn.: Pequot Press, 1973) F92/S45/1973.

- Sperry, Kip, *Connecticut Sources for Family Historians and Genealogists* (Logan, Utah: Everton Publishing Co., 1980) F93/S64/1980 also LOAN.

Genealogical and Historical Periodicals

- *Connecticut Ancestry*, 1958–present (Stamford, Conn.: Connecticut Ancestry Society) F93/C8 also LOAN. Vols. 1–14 called *Bulletin of the Stamford Genealogical Society*.

- *Connecticut Historical Society Bulletin*, 1934–94 (Hartford, Conn.: Connecticut Historical Society) F91/C67 also LOAN.

- *Connecticut Historical Society Collections*, 1860–1954, 28 vols. (Hartford, Conn.: Connecticut Historical Society) REF F91/C7 also LOAN.

- *Connecticut History*, 1979–present, a publication of the Association for the Study of Connecticut History (Willimantic, Conn.: Center for Connecticut Studies) F94/C865.

- *Connecticut Maple Leaf*, 1983–present (Tolland, Conn.: French-Canadian Genealogical Society of Connecticut) F91/C81.

- *The Connecticut Nutmegger*, 1968–present (Glastonbury, Conn.: Connecticut Society of Genealogists) F91/C82 also LOAN. See Helen S. Ullmann, *Nutmegger Index: An Index to Non-Alphabetical Articles and a Subject Index to* The Connecticut Nutmegger, *Volumes 1–28, 1968–1996* (Camden, Maine: Picton Press, 1996) F91/C82/Index also LOAN.

- *Connecticut Quarterly Magazine*, 1895–1908, 12 vols. (Hartford, Conn.: Connecticut Quarterly Co.) F91/C8.

- *New Haven Colony Historical Society Journal*, 1952–present (New Haven, Conn.: New Haven Colony Historical Society) F91/N4.

- *The American Genealogist*, 1922–present. R.Rm. REF F104/N6/A6 also LOAN. See NEW ENGLAND OVERVIEW.

- *The New England Historical and Genealogical Register*, 1847–present. R.Rm. REF F1/N56 also LOAN also fifth floor also Web database. See NEW

ENGLAND OVERVIEW. Note *Genealogies of Connecticut Families from* The New England Historical and Genealogical Register, 3 vols. (Baltimore: Genealogical Publishing Co., 1983) F93/G46/1983 also LOAN.

Censuses: Colonial, Federal, and State

Colonial

No censuses of colonial Connecticut were taken. A reconstructed census from various lists is Jay Mack Holbrook, *Connecticut 1670 Census* (Oxford, Mass.: Holbrook Research Institute, 1977) F93/H73/1977.

Federal

Connecticut censuses for the years 1790–1930 are available at NEHGS on microfilm. Some errors in the published 1790 census were listed in Donald Lines Jacobus, "Error in the Census of 1790 (Connecticut)," *The New England Historical and Genealogical Register* 77 (1923):80–81. There are book indexes for the years 1790–1870, book Mortality Schedules for the years 1850, 1860, and 1870, and Soundex indexes on microfilm for the years 1880, 1900, and 1920.

State

Connecticut has never had a state census. Therefore, the Connecticut State Military Preparedness Census of 1917 is unique. While the census itself is not available at NEHGS, the following article provides information about that resource: Thomas Jay Kemp, "The Connecticut State Military Census of 1917," *Connecticut Ancestry* 22:3 (February 1980):117–22. F93/C8 also LOAN.

Vital Records

The Barbour Collection of Connecticut Vital Records is a gem among Connecticut genealogical resources. It is a statewide index to 1850 available in two formats: on microfilm with names arranged alphabetically for the entire state and in books for each town, with names also arranged alphabetically.

- Microfilm: 81 reels. F93/C71 also LOAN.
- Books: 136 vols. (typescript) REF F93/C7, published as 55 vols., Baltimore: Genealogical Publishing Co., 1994–2002. F93/B37/1994 also LOAN.

NEHGS has microfilms of vital records for the following Connecticut towns:

- **Berlin**. Marriages, F104/S8/S785.
- **Greenwich**. Abstracts of births, marriages, and deaths to 1847. F104/G8/M43.

- **New Canaan**. Marriages. F104/S8/S785.

- **Stamford**. Births, marriages, and deaths, 1641–1852. F104/S8/S758.

Vital records published as books include those for the following towns. Early vital records for some towns were published in *The American Genealogist* and other periodicals.

- **Bolton**. *Vital Records of Bolton to 1854 and Vernon to 1852* (Hartford, Conn.: Connecticut Historical Society, 1909) REF F104/B55/1909 also LOAN.

- **Coventry**. *Births, Marriages, and Deaths in Coventry, Connecticut, 1711–1844* (New York: Baker and Taylor, 1897) REF F104/C75/D5/1897 also LOAN.

- **East Granby**. *Sundry Vital Records of East Granby, Connecticut, 1737–1886* (Hartford, Conn.: Albert Carlos Bates, 1947) REF F104/E1/E15/1947 also LOAN.

- **Enfield**. Allen, Francis Talcott, *History of Enfield, Connecticut*, 3 vols. (Lancaster, Pa.: Wickersham Printing Co., 1900) F104/E4/A4/1900 also LOAN.

- **Fairfield**. Welles, Edwin Stanley, *Births, Marriages and Deaths Returned from Hartford, Windsor and Fairfield* (Hartford, Conn.: Case, Lockwood & Brainard, 1898) F104/W7/W4/1898.

- **Hartford**. See Fairfield.

- **Lyme**. Hall, Verne M., and Elizabeth B. Plimpton, trans., *Vital Records of Lyme to 1850* (Lyme, Conn.: American Revolution Bicentennial Commission, 1976) REF F104/L95/V57/1976 also LOAN.

- **Mansfield**. *Births, Baptisms, Marriages, and Deaths from the Records of the Town and Churches in Mansfield, Connecticut, 1703–1850* (New York: Baker and Taylor, 1898) REF F104/M2/D5/1898 also LOAN.

- **New Haven**. *Vital Records of New Haven, 1649–1850*, 2 vols. (Hartford, Conn.: Connecticut Society of the Order of the Founders and Patriots of America, 1917) REF F104/N6/N66/1917 also LOAN.

- **Norwich**. *Vital Records of Norwich, 1659–1848*, 2 vols. (Hartford, Conn.: Society of Colonial Wars in the State of Connecticut, 1913) REF F104/N93/N68/1913 also LOAN.

- **Saybrook**. *Vital Records of Saybrook Colony, 1635–1860, Including Towns of Chester, Deep River, Essex, Old Saybrook, and Westbrook* (Old Saybrook, Conn.: Saybrook Press, 1985) REF F104/S3/V57/1985 also LOAN.

- **Saybrook**. *Vital Records of Saybrook, 1647–1834* (Hartford, Conn.: Connecticut Society of the Order of the Founders and Patriots of America, 1948) REF F104/S3/D42 also LOAN.

- **Seymour**. Sharpe, W. C., *Vital Statistics of Seymour, Connecticut*, 3 vols. (Seymour, Conn.: Record Print, 1883) REF F104/S5/S55/1883 also LOAN.

- **Seymour**. Sharpe, W. C., *Vital Statistics of Seymour, Connecticut, 1901–1910* (Seymour, Conn.: W. C. Sharpe Co., 1911) REF F104/S5/S55/1911 also LOAN.

- **Simsbury**. Bates, Albert C., *Simsbury, Connecticut, Births, Marriages, and Deaths* (Hartford, Conn.: Connecticut Historical Society, 1898) REF F104/S6/S6/1898 also LOAN.

- **Vernon**. See Bolton.

- **Windsor**. See Fairfield.

- **Woodstock**. *Vital Records of Woodstock, 1686-1854* (Hartford, Conn.: Case, Lockwood & Brainard, 1914) REF F104/W9/W9/1914 also LOAN.

Divorce records for five of the eight Connecticut counties have been published:

- Knox, Grace Louise, and Barbara B. Ferris, *Connecticut Divorces: Superior Court Records for the Counties of New London, Tolland, and Windham, 1719–1810* (Bowie, Md.: Heritage Books, 1987) F102/N7/K58/1987 also LOAN.

- Ferris, Barbara B., and Grace Louise Knox, *Connecticut Divorces: Superior Court Records for the Counties of Litchfield, 1752–1922, and Hartford, 1740–1849* (Bowie, Md.: Heritage Books, 1989) IN PROCESS.

See also Thomas Jay Kemp, "Divorces from the Resolves and Private Acts of the State of Connecticut," *Connecticut Ancestry* 31:1 (August 1988):1–24 [1837–1865].

For name changes, see Thomas Jay Kemp, "Changes of Names from the Resolves and Private Acts of the State of Connecticut," *Connecticut Ancestry* 31:1 (August 1988):27–41 [1837–1861].

Note also family records, e.g., Mrs. John L. Buel, *Family Records*, published by the Connecticut Chapter of the National Society, Daughters of the Founders and Patriots of America (New Haven, Conn.: Tuttle, Morehouse & Taylor, 1935) F93/D27/1935 also LOAN.

Church Records

In the 1930s, the Connecticut State Library asked all churches to send their original church records to Hartford for microfilming and safe-keeping. About 600 churches complied, but records of only about 150 churches have been indexed. A useful printed source for marriages is Frederic W. Bailey, ed., *Early Connecticut Marriages as Found on Ancient Church Records Prior to 1800* (1896–

1906; reprinted as 1 vol., Baltimore: Genealogical Publishing Co., 1968) F93/ B16/1968 also LOAN. Also on *Ancestry.com* which serves as a better index.

Microfilms of Connecticut church records at NEHGS includes the following:

- Connecticut Church Records Card Index includes records from nearly 150 Connecticut churches deposited at the Connecticut State Library, 69 reels. F93/C6/1949. Reels 1–33 are an incomplete surname index for many of the churches, and reels 34–69 are films of the slips for the churches not merged into the main index at the time of the filming.

- **Barkhamstead**. Barkhamstead Congregational Church, 1794–1850. Rollin H. Cooke Collection. F72/B5/C66a, reel 49.

- **Darien**. Church records to 1850. F104/S8/S758.

- **East Granby**. Turkey Hills [East Granby] Church, 1776–1860. Rollin H. Cooke Collection. F72/B5/C66a, reel 58.

- **East Hartland**. East and West Hartland Congregational Church, 1762–1880. Rollin H. Cooke Collection. F72/B5/C66a, reel 55.

- **Gilead**. Gilead First Congregational Church, 1752–1900. Walter E. Corbin Collection. F63/C8, reel 43.

- **Greenwich**. Church records. F104/G8/M43.

- **Huntington** (now Shelton). St. Paul's Episcopal Church Records. F104/S54/ S35.

- **Killingly**. Baptist Church Records, 1776–1855. F104/K5/B37.

- **Middle Haddam**. Middle Haddam Congregational Church, 1740–1800. Rollin H. Cooke Collection. F72/B5/C66a, reel 53.

- **North Granby**. North Granby Church, 1794–1843. Rollin H. Cooke Collection. F72/B5/C66a, reel 52.

- **Salisbury**. Salisbury Congregational Church, 1740–1891. Rollin H. Cooke Collection. F72/B5/C66a, reel 56.

- **Shelton**. See Huntington.

- **Stafford**. Stafford First Congregational Church, 1757–1806. Walter E. Corbin Collection. F63/C8, reel 43.

- **Stamford**. Church records to 1850. F104/S8/S758.

- **Turkey Hills**. See East Granby.

- **West Hartland**. See East Hartland.

- **West Stafford**. West Stafford Congregational Church, 1781–1848. Walter E. Corbin Collection. F63/C8, reel 43.

Published Connecticut church records at NEHGS include the following. Those published by the Connecticut State Library are indexes, not full text. There are other church records and indexes at the Connecticut State Library, and various church records have been published in periodicals.

- **Canterbury**. *Records of the Congregational Church in Canterbury, Connecticut, 1711–1844* (Hartford, Conn.: Connecticut Historical Society, 1932) F104/C18/C2/1932 also LOAN.

- **Darien**. Mead, Spencer P., *Abstract of the Church Records of the Town of Darien . . . from the Earliest Records to 1850* (n.p.: the author, 1920) F104/D27/M47/1920 also LOAN.

- **East Granby**. Bates, Albert Carlos, *Records of the Congregational Church in Turkey Hills, now East Granby, Connecticut, 1776–1858* (Hartford, Conn.: the author, 1907) F104/E1/E13/1907 also LOAN.

- **Farmington**. *First Congregational Church Records, 1652–1938* (Hartford, Conn.: Connecticut State Library, 1943) F93/C66/1943 also LOAN.

- **Naugatuck**. Ullmann, Helen S., *Naugatuck Congregational Church Records, 1781–1901* (Bowie, Md.: Heritage Press, 1987) F104/N2/U4/1987 also LOAN.

- **New Preston**. See Washington.

- **Roxbury**. *First Congregational Church Records, 1742–1930* (Hartford, Conn.: Connecticut State Library, 1943) F93/C66/1943 also LOAN.

- **Scotland**. *First Congregational Church Records, 1732–1915* (Hartford, Conn.: Connecticut State Library, 1942) F93/C66/1943 also LOAN.

- **Suffield**. *Records of the Congregational Church, 1710–1836* (Hartford, Conn.: Connecticut Historical Society, 1941) REF F104/S9/S955/1941 also LOAN.

- **Washington**. *First Congregational Church Records in New Preston, 1757–1845* (Hartford, Conn.: Connecticut State Library, 1943) F93/C66/1943 also LOAN.

- **Wethersfield**. *First Congregational Church Records, 1694–1835* (Hartford, Conn.: Connecticut State Library, 1962) F93/C66/1943 also LOAN.

- **Windham**. *Records of the Congregational Church, 1700–1851* (Hartford, Conn.: Connecticut Historical Society, 1943) REF F104/W65/W5/1943 also LOAN.

- **Woodbury**. *First Congregational Church Records, 1670–1908* (Hartford, Conn.: Connecticut State Library, 1943) F93/C66/1943 also LOAN.

Cemetery Records

The Charles R. Hale Collection of Cemetery Inscriptions and Newspaper Notices of Marriages and Deaths, 1932–34 (F93/H35/1949 microfilm), is the principal and most complete source of information on cemetery inscriptions in Connecticut. It is as valuable as the Barbour Collection but not as straightforward, partly because it was filmed before the project was entirely finished. There are five series of films for the Hale Collection:

- Reels 1–157 are a surname index of newspaper death notices and cemetery inscriptions.

- Reels 158–195 are slips abstracting newspaper notices *not* in the indexes at 1–157 or 196–244.

- Reels 196–244 are a surname index of newspaper marriage notices.

- Reels 245–300 are the volumes for each town's cemeteries with an index for each town. The overall index is on reels 1–157 above.

- Reels 301–359 are the abstracted newspaper notices indexed at 1–157 and 196–244.

Other microfilmed cemetery records at NEHGS include the following:

- Eardley's Connecticut Cemeteries, 1673–1911, and Headstone Inscriptions, Stamford, Ct., from the Hale Collection. F93/E2.

- Daniel Hearn Collection, Connecticut Gravestones before 1800, 2 reels. F93/H43.

- **Berlin**. Connecticut Cemeteries, 1673–1911: Stamford, Berlin, Brookfield, New Canaan, and Fairfield. F104/S8/S785.

- **Brookfield**. See Berlin.

- **East Hartford**. Stanley, Anthony D., "Death Book of Known Deaths in East Hartford, 1798–1834." F104/E18/S73.

- **East Windsor**. East Windsor Cemetery Records, 1730–1805. Rollin H. Cooke Collection. F72/B5/C665/1961, reel 59.

- **Fairfield**. See Berlin.

- **Greenwich**. Tombstones: Greenwich, Connecticut, and Middle Patent, New York. F104/G8/M43.

- **New Canaan**. See Berlin.

- **Stafford**. Stafford Leonard District (Stafford Village) Cemetery, 1760–1929. Walter E. Corbin Collection. F63/C8, reel 43.

- **Stamford**. See Eardeley's Connecticut Cemeteries and see Berlin.

- **West Stafford**. West Stafford cemeteries. Walter E. Corbin Collection. F63/C8, reel 43.

- **Willington**. Willington Village Cemetery. Walter E. Corbin Collection. F63/C8, reel 43.

Cemetery records for many Connecticut towns have been published separately, as part of town histories, or in periodicals. Note the following books on the gravestones of soldiers: Joyce Mackenzie Cropsey, comp., *Register of Revolutionary Soldiers and Patriots Buried in Litchfield County* (Canaan, N.H.: Phoenix Publishing Co., 1976) F102/L6/C76/1976 also LOAN, and James S. Hedden, *New Haven County: Register of Graves and Monuments of Patriots, 1775–1783, and Soldiers of Colonial Wars*, 2 vols. (New Haven, Conn.: General David Humphreys Chapter SAR, 1934) F102/N5/H43/1934.

Newspapers

The Hale Collection (see under VITAL RECORDS) is the largest collection of abstracted marriage and death notices for Connecticut. There are abstracted newspaper notices in some of the periodicals listed above. For the colonial period see Kenneth Scott and Rosanne Conway, *Genealogical Data from Colonial New Haven Newspapers* (Baltimore: Genealogical Publishing Co., 1979) F014/N653/A27/1979 also LOAN. Note the genealogical columns in the *Hartford Times*, 1934–1967, on microfilm. F104/H3/H33.

Probate Records

In Connecticut, probate records are kept in probate district courts. From the four probate districts created in Fairfield, New Haven, New London, and Hartford in 1656 (from the original Hartford court and the New Haven Colony), have evolved the current 130 probate districts, not quite one for each of Connecticut's 169 towns. Consult the Connecticut chapter in *Genealogist's Handbook for New England Research*, at 23–29, to determine the probate district for each town, as well as its parent district(s).

Early probate records, sometimes mixed in with other records, may be found in:

- Manwaring, Charles William, comp., *A Digest of the Early Connecticut Probate Records [Hartford District, 1635–1750]*, 3 vols. (1904–06; reprinted Baltimore: Genealogical Publishing Co., 1995) F93/M29/1904 also LOAN.

- Trumbull, J. Hammond, *The Public Records of the Colony of Connecticut, 1636–1776*, vols. 1–3 (Hartford, Conn.: Brown & Parsons, 1850) F97/C7/1850 also LOAN.

- Hoadly, Charles J., *Records of the Colony and Plantation of New Haven, 1638–1649* (Hartford, Conn.: Case, Tiffany & Co., 1857) F98/N8/1857.

- *The Particular Court of the Colony of Connecticut*, Connecticut Historical Society Collections, vol. 22 (Hartford, Conn.: Connecticut Historical Society, 1928) REF F91/C7 v. 22 also LOAN also fifth floor.

- Trumbull, E., ed., *Records of the Particular Court of the Colony of Connecticut, Administration of Sir Edmund Andros, Royal Governor, 1687–88* (Hartford, Conn.: Case, Lockwood & Brainard, 1936) CT/82/20.

- Ullmann, Helen S., "Hartford District Probate Abstracts From 1750, As Abstracted by Lucius Barnes Barbour," *The Connecticut Nutmegger* 34 (September 2001):188–201, (December 2001):363–383, ongoing in 2004. F91/C82 also LOAN.

- Donald Lines Jacobus, "New London (Conn.) Probate Records: Abstracts of Records before 1710," *The American Genealogist* 9 (1932–33):230–33 et seq. to 29 (1953):155–60, with list of exact volumes and pages at 29:160. R.Rm. REF F104/N6/A6 also LOAN.

The Connecticut State Library asked all Connecticut towns to send their probate packages (consisting of wills, bonds, inventories, accounts, and guardianships) to the library for microfilming and safe-keeping. Most, but not all, districts complied. Probate records at Connecticut State Library are available on the following microfilms at NEHGS:

- Connecticut General Index to Probate Records, 1641–1948, 67 reels. F93/C69/1989.

- Connecticut Probate Records to 1880. F93/C69/1989. Records are arranged alphabetically by district. Years included vary by district. Not all districts are included.

- Connecticut Probate Records, 1881–1915. F93/C69/1989. Records are arranged alphabetically by district. Not all districts are included.

- Connecticut Estate Record Card Index, 1915–26. 19 reels. F93/C68/1989.

Fairfield County

Abstracts for all of Fairfield County probate up to 1728 and for Fairfield District to 1757 are available both on microfilm and in book form:

- Microfilm: Mead, Spencer P., Abstract of Fairfield Probate Records 1640–1750 and 1704–1757. F104/F2/M4. Includes all of Fairfield County for period prior to 1728.

- Book: Mead, Spencer P., *Abstract of Probate Records at Fairfield, County of Fairfield and State of Connecticut, 1648–1750* (1929; reprinted Salem, Mass.: Higginson Book Co.) F102/F2/M43/1929 also LOAN.

Abstracts of probate records for Stamford District, including Stamford, Greenwich, Darien (1729–1848), part of New Canaan (1719–1802), and Ridgefield (1729–1746) are also available on microfilm and in book form:

- Microfilm: Abstract of Probate Records for the District of Stamford, County of Fairfield, and State of Connecticut, 1729–1802. F104/S8/S785.

- Book: Mead, Spencer P., *Abstract of Probate Records for the District of Stamford, County of Fairfield, and State of Connecticut, 1729–1802 and 1803–48*, 2 vols. (Greenwich, Conn.: the author, 1924) F104/S8/1924 also LOAN.

Land Records

NEHGS has land records in its microfilm collection for the following Connecticut towns:

- **Farmington**. General Index to Deeds, Grantor Index 1643–1800. F104/F4/F4.

- **Haddam**. Deeds, Grantor-Grantee Index, 1662–1846. F104/H16/H16.

- **Hartford**. General Index of Land Records, Grantor-Grantee Index, 1639–1865, 2 reels. F104/H3/H3.

- **Middletown**. General Index to Deeds, Grantor-Grantee Index, 1654–1746. F104/M6/M6.

- **Simsbury**. Deeds, General Index A-P, Grantor-Grantee Index, 1600–1850. F104/S6/S651.

- **Wethersfield**. Land Records, Grantee and Grantor Indexes, 1640–1916, 2 reels. F104/W4/W4.

- **Windsor**. Deeds, Grantor-Grantee Index, 1640–1820. F104/W7/W7.

Various Connecticut land records have been abstracted in periodicals, especially *The American Genealogist*. The only extensive abstracts of land records for a Connecticut town are Edith M. Wicks, comp., *Genealogical References in Stamford, Ct., Land Records Volumes A through S, 1666-1800+* , Robert W. Spiers, ed. (Stamford, Conn.: Connecticut Ancestry Society, 1999) F104/58/W53/1999 also LOAN.

Town Records

Town records contain an abundance of information about town government, residents, and development. Early records often include vital records and ear mark registrations. While some town record volumes are on microfilm, few have been transcribed, and fewer still published. Some have been abstracted in periodicals, especially *The American Genealogist*. NEHGS has microfilmed town records only for one town: Stamford, Connecticut, Town Meeting Records, 1640–1806, Books 1 and 2. F104/S8/S785.

Published town records include the following towns:

- **Cornwall**. Gannett, Michael R., transc., *Cornwall Documents: Town Meeting Minutes, 1740–1875* (Cornwall, Conn.: Cornwall Historical Society, 1994) F104/C7/C67/1994.

- **Derby**. Phillips, Nancy O., copier, *Town Records of Derby, Connecticut, 1655–1710* (Derby, Conn.: Sarah Riggs Humphrey Chapter DAR, 1901) F104/D4/D4/1901 also LOAN.

- **Enfield**. Allen, Francis Talcott, *History of Enfield, Connecticut*, 3 vols. (Lancaster, Pa.: Wickersham Printing Co., 1900) F104/E4/A4/1900 also LOAN. This three-volume series includes town meeting records as well as land grants and deeds, church records, vital records, probate records, and graveyard inscriptions.

- **Granby**. Williams, Mark, ed., *Granby Town Records*, Vols. I and II (Granby, Conn.: Salmon Brook Historical Society, 1986) F104/G65/G63/1986 also LOAN.

- **Lyme.** Burr, Jean Chandler, ed. and comp., *Lyme Records, 1667–1730* (Stonington, Conn.: Pequot Press, 1968) F104/L95/L89/1968 also LOAN.

- **New Haven**. Dexter, Franklin Bowditch, *New Haven Town Records, 1649–1769*, 3 vols. (New Haven, Conn.: New Haven Colony Historical Society, 1917–1962) F104/N6/N59/1917 also LOAN.

- **Salisbury**. *Salisbury Town Meeting Minutes, 1741–1784* (Salisbury, Conn.: Salisbury Association, 1988) F94/S2/S2/1988 also LOAN.

- **Waterbury**. Pritchard, Katharine A., transc., *Proprietor's Records of the Town of Waterbury, Connecticut, 1677–1761* (New York: Knickerbocker Press, 1911) F104/W3/M38/1911 also LOAN.

Tax Records

Some Connecticut tax records are included within books and microfilms cited elsewhere in this chapter. Some have been published as articles in periodicals, and at least one has been published as a book: Michael R. Gannett, *Cornwall Grand Lists, 1742–1820, and Cornwall Censuses, 1790, 180, 1810, 1820* (Cornwall, Conn.: Cornwall Historical Society, 2003) F104/C7/G27/2003.

Court and Legislative Records

Since Connecticut Colony and New Haven Colony were separate entities until 1662, their records were initially kept separately.

- *Public Records of the Colony of Connecticut, 1636–1776*, 20 vols. (Hartford, Conn.: Brown & Parsons, 1850–80) F97/C7/1850 also LOAN.

- Hoadly, Charles J., *Records of the Colony and Plantation of New Haven, 1638–1649* (Hartford, Conn.: Case, Tiffany & Co., 1857) F98/N8/1857 also LOAN.

- Hoadly, Charles J., *Records of the Colony or Jurisdiction of New Haven* (Hartford, Conn.: Case, Lockwood & Co., 1858) Rare Book F98/N81/1858 also LOAN.

- *Records of the State of Connecticut, 1776–1805*, 12 vols. (Hartford: Case, Lockwood & Brainard, 1894–1986) F99/C7/1894.

See also under PROBATE RECORDS.

Some court records have abstracted in periodicals, especially *The American Genealogist*. Note the following abstracts of court records for Windham County:

- Pasay, Marcella Houle, *Windham County, Connecticut, County Court Records, 1727–1736*, 2 vols. (Bowie, Md., Heritage Books, 2000–02) F102/W7/P38/2000 also LOAN.

- Pasay, Marcella Houle, *Family Secrets: 18th & 19th Century Birth Records Found in the Windham County, CT, County Court Records* (Bowie, Md.: Heritage Books, 2000) 102/W7/P37/2000 also LOAN.

Military Records

Colonial Wars

- Andrews, Frank de Witte. *Connecticut Soldiers in the French and Indian War* (Vineland, N.J.: the author, 1925) F97/A58/1925 also LOAN.

- *Rolls of Connecticut Men in the French and Indian War, 1755–1762*, Connecticut Historical Society Collections, vols. 9–10 (Hartford, Conn.: Connecticut Historical Society, 1903–05) REF F91/C7 v. 9–10 also LOAN.

Revolutionary War, War of 1812, Mexican War

- Johnson, Henry P., *Record of the Service of Connecticut Men in the War of the Revolution, War of 1812, and Mexican War* (Hartford, Conn.: Case, Lockwood & Brainard, 1889) REF E263/C5/C5/1889 also LOAN.

- Jacobus, Donald Lines, *History and Genealogy of the Families of Old Fairfield*, vol. 3: *Revolutionary War Records* (New Haven, Conn.: Tuttle, Morehouse & Taylor, 1932) F104/F2/J17/1932 also LOAN. This last volume of Jacobus's series on Old Fairfield families includes pension documents, muster rolls, and other Revolutionary War records.

- Richards, Josephine Ellis, *Revolutionary Soldiers Honor Roll of Litchfield County* (Litchfield, Conn.: Mary Floyd Tallmadge Chapter DAR, 1912) F102/L6/ D2/1912 also LOAN.

- *Rolls and Lists of Connecticut Men in the Revolution, 1775–1783*, Connecticut Historical Society Collections, vol. 8 (Hartford, Conn.: Connecticut Historical Society, 1901) REF F91/C7/1901 v. 8.

- *Lists and Returns of Connecticut Men in the Revolution, 1775–1783*, Connecticut Historical Society Collections, vol. 12 (Hartford, Conn.: Connecticut Historical Society, 1909) REF F91/C7/1909 v.12 also LOAN.

- Wicks, Edith M., and Virginia H. Olsen, *Stamford's Soldiers: Genealogical Biographies of Revolutionary War Patriots from Stamford, Connecticut* (New Orleans: Polyanthos, 1976) F104/S8/W5/1976 also LOAN.

Loyalists

Many Connecticut residents, particularly members of Anglican churches in southwestern Connecticut, were Loyalists (Tories) during the Revolutionary era. Many Loyalists went to Canada. Studies of Connecticut Loyalists include:

- Tyler, John W., *Connecticut Loyalists: An Analysis of Loyalist Land Confiscations in Greenwich, Stamford, and Norwalk* (New Orleans: Polyanthos, 1977) E277/T9/1977 also LOAN.

- Pond, Edgar LeRoy, *The Tories of Chippeny Hill, Connecticut: A Brief Account of the Loyalists of Bristol, Plymouth and Harwinton, Who Founded St. Matthew's Church in East Plymouth in 1791* (New York: Grafton Press, 1909) F104/B8/ P7/1909 also LOAN.

Civil War

- Connecticut Adjutant General, *Records of Service of Connecticut Men in the Army and Navy of the United States During the War of the Rebellion* (Hartford, Conn.: Case, Lockwood & Brainard, 1889)

- Hewett, Jane B., ed., *Roster of Union Soldiers, 1861–1865*, vol. 4, Connecticut and Rhode Island (Wilmington, N.C.: Broadfoot Publishing Co., 1997) REF E494/H49/1997 also LOAN.

- *Catalogue of Connecticut Volunteer Organizations (Infantry, Cavalry and Artillery) in the Service of the United States, 1861–1865* (Hartford, Conn.: Brown & Gross, 1869) E499.3/C66/1869 also LOAN.

World War I

- Connecticut Adjutant General, *Service Records of Connecticut Men and Women in the Armed Forces of the United States during the World War, 1917–20*, 3 vols. (New Haven, Conn.: U.S. Printing Services, 1941) F93/C663/1941.

NEHGS has a microfilm of Connecticut military records for several wars: Military Veterans: Revolutionary War, War of 1812, War in Mexico, Civil War, Spanish-American War, World War I. F104/S8/S785.

Genealogical and Biographical Compendia (Including Town and County Histories)

Some overall accounts of early Connecticut families include the following:

- Cutter, William Richard, ed., *Genealogy and Family History of Connecticut*, 4 vols. (New York: Lewis Historical Publishing Co., 1911) F93/C99/1911 also LOAN.

- Goodwin, Nathaniel, *Genealogical Notes . . . of the First Settlers of Connecticut and Massachusetts* (1856; reprinted Baltimore: Genealogical Publishing Co., 1969) F93/G65/1969 also LOAN.

- Hinman, Royal Ralph, *A Catalogue of the Names of the First Puritan Settlers of the Colony of Connecticut* (Hartford, Conn.: Case, Tiffany & Co., 1852) Rare Book F93/H65/1852 also LOAN. His manuscript, "Early Connecticut Families," is at SL/CON/12.

Many excellent Connecticut town histories include genealogies of local families. For certain individuals, they may provide the only information available. Use them with caution and try to document information in primary sources. NEHGS has histories for all counties and most towns, including:

- **Bloomfield**. See Windsor.

- **Branford**. See New Haven and Guilford.

- **Bridgeport**. See Stratford.

- **Bridgewater**. See New Milford.

- **Derby**. Orcutt, Samuel, and Ambrose Beardsley, *History of the Old Town of Derby Connecticut, 1642–1880, with Biographies and Genealogies* (Springfield, Mass.: Springfield Printing Co., 1880) F104/D4/O1/1880 also LOAN.

- **Ellington**. See Windsor.

- **Fairfield County**. Jacobus, Donald Lines, *History and Genealogy of the Families of Old Fairfield*, 3 vols. in 4 (1930–32; vols. 1–2 reprinted Baltimore: Genealogical Publishing Co., 1976) F104/F2/J17/1976 also LOAN. One of the best studies. "Old Fairfield" implies the original Town of Fairfield but this work includes some families in nearby towns in Fairfield and New Haven counties.

- **Farmington.** See Hartford.

- **Glastonbury**. See Wethersfield.

- **Greenwich**. Mead, Spencer P., *Ye Historie of Ye Town of Greenwich . . . with Genealogical Notes* (New York: Knickerbocker Press, 1911) F104/G8/M52/1911 also LOAN.

- **Guilford**. Talcott, Alvan, comp., *Families of Early Guilford, Connecticut*, Jacquelyn L. Ricker, ed. (Baltimore: Genealogical Publishing Co., 1984) F104/G9/T35/1984 also LOAN.

- **Haddam**. See Guilford.

- **Hartford**. Barbour, Lucius Barnes, *Families of Early Hartford, Connecticut* (Baltimore: Genealogical Publishing Co., 1977) F104/H3/B37/1977 also LOAN.

- **Killingworth**. See Guilford.

- **Milford**. Abbott, Susan Woodruff, comp., *Families of Early Milford, Connecticut*, Jacquelyn L. Ricker, ed. (Baltimore: Genealogical Publishing Co., 1979) F104/M7/A22/1979 also LOAN.

- **New Canaan**. See Stamford and Norwalk.

- **New Haven County**. Jacobus, Donald Lines, *Families of Ancient New Haven*, 8 vols. (1922–32; reprinted as 3 vols. Baltimore: Genealogical Publishing Co., 1974) R.Rm. REF F104/N6/A6/1922 also LOAN. One of the best. This work covers New Haven and some nearby towns, as explained on the first page of vol. 1.

- **New London**. Parkhurst, Charles, "Early Families of New London and Vicinity," microfilm, 9 reels. F104/N7/P37/1938.

- **New Milford**. Orcutt, Samuel, *History of the Towns of New Milford and Bridgewater, Connecticut, 1703–1882* (Hartford, Conn.: Case, Lockwood & Brainard, 1882) F104/N73/O6/1882 also LOAN.

- **Norwalk**. Hall, Edwin, *The Ancient Historical Records of Norwalk . . . to 1847* (Norwalk, Conn.: J. Mallory & Co., 1847) F104/N9/H2/1847 also LOAN.

- **Norwich.** Caulkins, Frances Manwaring, *History of Norwich, Connecticut, from its Possession by the Indians, to the Year 1866* (Hartford, Conn.: Case, Lockwood & Co., 1866) F104/N93/C4/1874 also LOAN.

- **Stamford**. Huntington, Rev. E. B., *History of Stamford, 1641–1868, Including Darien until 1821* (1868; reprinted Camden, Maine: Picton Press, 1992) F104/S8/H92/1992 also LOAN. The papers of Paul Wesley Prindle, FASG, the bulk of which is his research on Stamford-area families, are at NEHGS (Mss 322).

- **Stonington**. Wheeler, Richard Anson, *History of the Town of Stonington . . . with a Genealogical Register of Stonington Families, 1649–1800* (1900; reprinted Baltimore: Genealogical Publishing Co., 1993) F104/S85/W5/1900 also LOAN.

- **Stratford**. Orcutt, Samuel, *History of the Old Town of Stratford & the City of Bridgeport, Connecticut*, 2 vols. (New Haven, Conn.: Tuttle, Morehouse & Taylor, 1886) F104/S87/06/1886 also LOAN.

- **Waterbury**. Bronson, Henry, M.D., *History of Waterbury, Connecticut . . . with an Appendix of Biography, Genealogy and Statistics* (1858; reprinted Salem, Mass: Higginson Book Co., 1999) F104/W3/B8/1999 also LOAN.

- **Wethersfield**. Stiles, Henry R., *History of Ancient Wethersfield, Connecticut*, 2 vols. (1904; reprint, Somersworth, N.H.: New England History Press, 1987) F104/W4/S74/1987 also LOAN.

- **Windsor**. Stiles, Henry R., *History and Genealogies of Ancient Windsor, South Windsor, Bloomfield, Windsor Locks, and Ellington, 1635–1891*, 2 vols. (1891; reprinted Somersworth, N.H.: New England History Press, 1976) F104/W7/S7/1891 also LOAN.

- **Woodbury**. Cothren, William, *History of Ancient Woodbury, Connecticut*, 3 vols. (1854–79; reprinted Bowie, Md.: Heritage Books, 1992) F104/W88/C6 also LOAN.

- **Woodstock.** Bowen, Clarence Winthrop, *The History of Woodstock Connecticut*, 8 vols. (Norwood, Mass.: Plympton Press, 1926–43) F104/W9/B67/1926 also LOAN. Excellent study; the author's underlying notes are at NEHGS.

Note also the following useful works:

- Knox, Grace Louise, and Barbara B. Ferris, *Some Connecticut Nutmeggers Who Migrated* (Bowie, Md.: Heritage Books, 1988) F93/K56/1988 also LOAN.

- Ritter, Kathy A., *Apprentices of Connecticut, 1637–1900* (Salt Lake City: Ancestry Publishing Co., 1986) F93/R56/1986 also LOAN.

Maps and Atlases

- Hughes, Arthur H., and Morse S. Allen, *Connecticut Place Names* (Hartford, Conn.: Connecticut Historical Society, 1976) R.Rm. REF F92/H83/1976.

- Pease, John C., and John M. Niles, *A Gazetteer of the States of Connecticut and Rhode Island* (1819; reprinted Bowie, Md.: Heritage Books, 1991) R.Rm. REF F92/P36.

- Gannett, Henry, *A Geographic Dictionary of Connecticut and Rhode Island* (Baltimore: Genealogical Publishing Co., 1978) REF F92/G2/1978 also LOAN.

- Long, John H., and Gordon DenBoer, *Connecticut, Maine, Massachusetts, Rhode Island: Atlas of Historical County Boundaries* (New York: Simon & Schuster, 1994) Atlas G1201/F7/A8/1993 also LOAN.

Special Sources for Connecticut

Winthrop's Medical Journal

John Winthrop, Jr. traveled around Connecticut to treat patients from 1656 to 1669, with a break of two years from 1661 to 1663, when he was in England. In his thousand-page journal, Winthrop noted the names of hundreds of patients, dates, locations, brief biographical information, symptoms, and prescriptions. The original journal is at Massachusetts Historical Society in Boston and is available on microfilm elsewhere. Excerpts of journal entries with genealogical information can be found in *The American Genealogist*, vols. 9, 23, and 24; however, these excerpts are not always accurate or complete.

Witchcraft

Many accusations of witchcraft were made against Connecticut residents, primarily in the seventeenth century. The principal published works on the subject are the following:

- Hall, David D., *Witch-Hunting in Seventeenth-Century New England: A Documentary History, 1638–1692* (Boston: Northeastern University Press, 1991) IN CATALOGING.

- Taylor, John Metcalf, *The Witchcraft Delusion in Colonial Connecticut, 1647–1697* (New York: Grafton Press, 1908) BF1576/T25/1908 also LOAN. This work is the classic reference for Connecticut witchcraft.

- Tomlinson, R. G., *Witchcraft Trials of Connecticut* (n.p.: the author, 1978) BF1576/T66/1978.

African Americans and Native Americans

Note articles on African-American families in *The Connecticut Nutmegger*, vols. 34–35.

- Brown, Barbara W., and James M. Rose, ed., *Black Roots in Southeastern Connecticut, 1650–1900* (Detroit: Gale Research Co., 1980) F93/B86/1980.

- Brown, Barbara W., and James M. Rose, ed., *Tapestry: A Living History of the Black Family in Southeastern Connecticut* (New London, Conn.: New London County Historical Society, 1979) F93/R6 also LOAN.

- Pasay, Marcella Houle, *Full Circle, A Directory of Native and African Americans in Windham County, CT, 1650–1900*, 2 vols. (Bowie, Md.: Heritage Books, 2002) IN CATALOGING.

- "Connecticut Blacks and Indians in the American Revolution," in Eric G. Grundset, ed., *African American and American Indian Patriots of the Revolutionary War* (Washington, D.C.: National Society Daughters of the American Revolution, 2001), 65–82. E269/N3/A37/2001.

Yale University

Most Yale students before 1900 were from Connecticut. The principal biographical work is Franklin Bowditch Dexter, *Biographical Sketches of the Graduates of Yale College . . . [1701–1815]*, 6 vols. (New York: Henry Holt, 1885–1912) REF LD6323/D5. For an analysis of the coverage of non-graduates and for the titles of later works, see Francis James Dallett, "Lost Alumni of Yale College: The Non-Graduates of 1771–1805," *The New England Historical and Genealogical Register* 157 (2003):139–43.

Connecticut in Pennsylvania

Connecticut claimed parts of the Wyoming Valley in northern Pennsylvania and many settlers there before the Revolution were from Connecticut. For a full description of this claim and its resulting records, see Donna Bingham Munger, "Following Connecticut Ancestors to Pennsylvania: Susquehanna Company Settlers," *The New England Historical and Genealogical Register* 139 (1985):112–25.

Maine

Joseph C. Anderson II

Overview

On March 15, 1820, Maine became the twenty-third state in the Union, thereby ending more than 150 years in which Maine was under the political and ecclesiastical control of Massachusetts. Because Maine was a part of Massachusetts for so long, Maine developed many of the same strong record-keeping traditions of her neighbor to the south, although circumstances such as war and explosive population growth resulted in the records being less complete than genealogists would desire. Throughout the colonial era, Maine suffered attacks from the French and Indians to the north. On numerous occasions the fledgling settlements along the coast were burned and abandoned, causing a flow of refugees into lower Maine and Massachusetts. When the hostilities ended after the Revolution, settlers from Massachusetts and New Hampshire poured into Maine at the rate of nearly 2,000 per year. In the 25-year period from 1775 to 1800, the Maine population grew nearly eightfold. During this same period, the number of incorporated towns more than tripled from 35 to 126. With such a rapidly expanding population, it was difficult for town clerks and other record keepers to keep track of all of the newcomers.

Maine has a rich assortment of surviving records, with the only major loss being the fire that consumed the Cumberland County probate records in the late nineteenth century. Where town records do not provide the answers to tough genealogical problems, courthouse records such as deeds and probates often come to the rescue. Church, census, and gravestone records offer additional valuable resources for the genealogist. In the last twenty years, Maine has experienced a renaissance in genealogical publishing, led by the Maine Genealogical Society's Special Publications program. Dozens of volumes of vital and church records, probate abstracts, and newspaper notices have been published and most of these are available in the NEHGS library.

Guides and Finding Aids

- Eichholz, Alice, "Maine," in *Red Book: American State, County, and Town Sources*, 3rd ed. (Provo, Utah: Ancestry, 2004), 269–96. REF CS49/A55/2004 also LOAN.

- Frost, John Eldridge, *Maine Genealogy: A Bibliographical Guide*, 2nd ed., rev. (Portland, Maine: Maine Historical Society, 1985) REF F18/F759/1985.

- Frost, John Eldridge, "Maine Genealogy: Some Distinctive Aspects," *The New England Historical and Genealogical Register* 131 (1977):243–66, reprinted, with additions, in Ralph J. Crandall, ed., *Genealogical Research in New England* (Baltimore: Genealogical Publishing Company, 1984), 15–41. REF F3/ G46/1984 also LOAN.

- Haskell, John D., ed., *Maine: A Bibliography of Its History* (Boston: G. K. Hall, 1977) REF F19/M214/1977 also LOAN.

- Melnyk, Marcia D., "Maine," in *Genealogist's Handbook for New England Research*, 4th ed. (Boston: NEHGS, 1999), 45–86. R.Rm. REF F/3/G466/1999 also LOAN.

- *Public Record Repositories in Maine* (Augusta, Maine: Maine State Archives, 1976) CD3274/M4/P8/1976 also Microtext.

- Willis, William, "Bibliography of the State of Maine," typescript (1860) ME/ 57/5.

Genealogical and Historical Periodicals

- *Bangor Historical Magazine*, Joseph W. Porter, ed., 9 vols. (1885–95), reprinted in 4 vols. under new title *The Bangor Historical Magazine Later the Maine Historical Magazine* (Camden, Maine: Picton Press, 1993) F16/M21/1885 also LOAN. Concentration on northern and eastern Maine.

- *Downeast Ancestry*, 16 vols. (1977–93) F18/D6 also LOAN. Statewide in coverage, includes articles on a wide range of genealogical topics. It also has one of the best collections of Maine genealogical queries.

- *The Essex Genealogist*, Journal of the Essex Society of Genealogists (1981–present) F72/E7/E6 also LOAN. Focused on Essex County, Massachusetts, but includes many families that later moved to Maine.

- *Index to the* Maine Seine *and* The Maine Genealogist: *Journals of the Maine Genealogical Society*, Marlene A. Groves, comp. (Rockport, Maine: Picton Press, 1999) F16/M345/Index/ v.1–20.

- *The Maine Genealogist* (formerly *Maine Seine*), quarterly journal of the Maine Genealogical Society, 26 vols. to date (1977–present) F16/M345/v.21 also LOAN. Statewide in coverage, includes problem-solving articles, compiled genealogies, genealogical records, reviews.

- *The Maine Genealogist and Biographer: A Quarterly Journal* (Augusta, Maine: Maine Genealogical and Biographical Society), 3 vols. (1875–78) F16/M155/ 1875–1878 also LOAN. Emphasis on Kennebec County.

- *Maine Historical and Genealogical Recorder*, Stephen Marion Watson, pub., 9 vols. (1884–98), reprinted in 3 vols. (Baltimore: Genealogical Publishing Co., 1973) F16/M18 also LOAN. Contains genealogies, items of historical interest, and sundry church, vital, cemetery, and newspapers records, statewide in coverage but emphasis on Cumberland and York Counties.

- *The New England Historical and Genealogical Register*, quarterly journal of the New England Historic Genealogical Society (1847–present) R.Rm. REF F1/ N56 also LOAN also fifth floor also Web database. See NEW ENGLAND OVERVIEW. The premier genealogical periodical for New England research. Contains many articles on Maine families and many compilations of Maine records.

- *Sprague's Journal of Maine History*, John Francis Sprague, ed., 14 vols. (Dover-Foxcroft, Maine: J. F. Sprague [etc.], 1913–26) F16/S76 also LOAN. Also on CD-ROM (Rockport, Maine, Picton Press, 2000). Emphasis on Piscataquis County.

- *York County Genealogical Society Journal*, quarterly journal of the York County Genealogical Society (1986–present) F27/Y6/Y6. Focused solely on York County genealogy. Many of the early volumes contain material of the late Dr. John Frost. Includes compiled genealogies, early York County court records, cemetery records, and Bible records.

Censuses: Colonial, Federal, and State

Colonial

- Pruitt, Bettye Hobbs, *The Massachusetts Tax Valuation List of 1771* (1978; reprinted Camden, Maine: Picton Press, 1998) REF F63/P838/1998 also LOAN. While not a census, this source serves as a census substitute, although not all of the Maine towns then in existence are included.

Federal

Maine censuses for years 1790–1930 are available at NEHGS on microfilm, with book indexes for years 1790–1870 and the Soundex index on microfilm for the years 1880, 1900, and 1920. In the published 1790 census, the lists for the towns of Nobleborough, Waldoborough, and Bristol were mislabeled (see *The New England Historical and Genealogical Register* 86 [1932]:132). Note John E. Frost, "York County, Maine, Mortality Schedules, U.S. census: 1850, 1860, 1870," typescript (1987) F27/Y6/F76/1987.

A portion of the 1800 federal census for Maine has a feature not found in other states. For parts of Hancock and Kennebec counties, a column was added to the census form giving the place from where the head-of-household had emigrated—particularly important information considering the large migration of settlers into Maine in this period. In the case of Kennebec County the year of emigration was also added. This supplementary data for both of these counties is found on the census microfilm and has been published:

- Davis, Walter Goodwin, "Part of Hancock County, Maine, in 1800," *The New England Historical and Genealogical Register* 105 (1951):204–13, 276–91.

- Anderson, Robert Charles, and Roger D. Joslyn, "Part of Kennebec County, Maine, in 1800," *The New England Historical and Genealogical Register* 145 (1991):346–66.

State

Only a few returns survive from Maine's only state census, conducted in 1837. This census lists the name of the head of household and enumerates the number of persons in the household over 21, between 4 and 21, and under 4. The surviving returns (including those for Bangor, Portland, a number of unorganized localities in what today are Aroostook and Washington counties, and a few other locations) can be accessed at the Maine State Archives in Augusta. Most of these have been transcribed and can be viewed online at *rootsweb.com/ ~meandrhs/history/usdebt/census/maine/1837.html*. In addition, two tax lists—the Massachusetts Tax Valuation List of 1771 and the Massachusetts and Maine Direct Tax Census of 1798—serve as good census substitutes (see above and under TAX RECORDS).

Vital Records

State Vital Records

Maine enacted statewide registration of vital records in 1892. From that year forward, it was required that all records of births, deaths, and marriages occurring in the state be returned to the Bureau of Vital Statistics in Augusta. These vital records were entered on cards and have been microfilmed. The microfilmed records are sorted by year, then by vital event (birth, marriage, death), then alphabetically by name. For most of the years available, these records provide ages, places of birth, and the names and places of birth of the parents when known by the informant. The NEHGS library has a copy of these records through 1955 on microfilm:

- Maine vital records 1892–1955, and brides, grooms, deaths, and divorce indexes 1892–1983, 372 microfilm reels. F18/M344.

In 1927, Maine passed a law requiring town clerks to transcribe and forward to the state all vital records on their town books prior to 1892. When these were received by the state, each record was copied onto an individual card and filed alphabetically by surname. Unfortunately, only about 20 percent of the towns responded to this law. These records are consolidated and arranged alphabetically. Since they are state-wide, these records can be very helpful in tracking people who moved from town to town. The NEHGS library has these records on microfilm:

- Index to Vital Records Prior to 1892 of . . . 80 Towns, 141 microfilm reels. F18/M34 Microfilm.

An index of all Maine marriages 1892–1996 and of Maine deaths 1960–1996, compiled by the Maine State Archives, can be found at the websites shown below. The marriage index includes the name of the bride and groom, their town of residence, and the date of the marriage. The death index includes the name of the decedent, the age of the decedent, and the town where the death occurred:

- thor.dafs.state.me.us/pls/archives/archdev.marriage_archive.search_form
- thor.dafs.state.me.us/pls/archives/archdev.death_archive.search_form

County Marriage Returns

In 1828, the Maine legislature mandated that the town clerks send returns of all marriages to the county clerks. These marriages were then entered into the county commissioners records at the county courthouse. The returns for eight of Maine's counties have been published, as listed below. These volumes include the marriages from 1828, as well as a number of eighteenth-century county marriage returns. These volumes are often helpful to find persons who may have married in towns other than their native towns or to supplement missing or unavailable town records.

Cumberland (1998), **Hancock** (1992), **Lincoln** (2001), **Oxford** (1993), **Penobscot** (1994), **Waldo** (1990), **Washington** (1993), **York** (1993).

Town Vital Records (see TOWN RECORDS below)

Name Changes

See Richard P. Roberts, "Name Changes of Maine Residents 1803–1892," *The Maine Genealogist* 17 (1995):114–18; 18 (1996):35–37, 83–87, 130–34; 19 (1997):31–38, 84–89, 137–39; 20 (1998):33–38, 87–89; 21 (1999):36–42, 91–92; 22 (2000):41–42; 23 (2001):37–44. This series lists all persons whose names were legally changed by the Maine legislature. A good resource for documenting adoptions and divorces not otherwise found in the court records, as well as the nationality of immigrants who Anglicized their names. See also Marquis Fayette King, *Changes in Name by Special Acts of the Legislature of Maine, 1820–1895* (Portland, Maine?: n.p., 1901) F18/K53/1901.

Church Records

Maine has an excellent body of surviving church records. The earliest established churches were Congregational, but by the middle of the eighteenth century churches of other denominations, including Presbyterian, Baptist, and Quaker, began to appear. Finding aids for Congregational and Baptist church records in Maine are shown below:

- Anderson, Joseph C., II, and Lois Ware Thurston, "Early Congregational Church Records in Maine: Location of Original Records and Transcripts," *The Maine Genealogist* 16 (1994):47–49, 72–76.

- Seaman, Dorothy A., "A Search for York County Baptist Church Records," *York County Genealogical Society Journal* 9 (October 1994):1–8; 10 (January 1995):2–7, (July 1995):45–48. F27/Y6/Y6.

The records of a number of Maine's early churches have been published in book form or as serialized articles in periodicals, as follows. In addition, some records were published in the Maine periodicals listed above.

- **Arundel (Kennebunkport):** "A Book of Records of the Church of Christ in Arundel (Kennebunkport), Maine," *The New England Historical and Genealogical Register* 107 (1953):194–201, 269–75; 108 (1954):53–61, 120–24, 188–92. Includes admissions 1771–1815, baptisms 1771–1815, marriages 1771–1815, owners of the covenant 1771–1813.

- **Avon:** Day, Clarence A., "A Record of Marriages Performed by Reverend Nehemiah Hunt (1772–1860) of Wilton and Avon, Maine," *The New England Historical and Genealogical Register* 109 (1955):182–84.

- **Belfast:** Mosher, Elizabeth M., transc., *The Records of Rev. Edward F. Cutter of Maine, 1833–1856* (Camden, Maine: Picton Press, 1989).

- **Berwick:** 1st and 2nd Church: Anderson, Joseph C., II, *Records of the First and Second Churches of Berwick, Maine* (Rockport, Maine: Picton Press, 1999) F29/B6/R43/1999 also LOAN. Incorporates the contents of three articles in *The New England Historical and Genealogical Register*: Rev. Everett S. Stackpole, "Berwick (Maine) Marriages," 55 (1901):309–16, 372–76; Marietta Frances (Stacy) Hilton, "Records of the Second Church of Berwick, Me., 1755–1857," 74 (1920):211–30, 246–67; and John Clark Scates, "Records of the First Church of Berwick (South Berwick), Me.," 82 (1928):71–98, 204–18, 312–33, 500–11; 83 (1929):9–20, 147–56.

  Quaker: "Records of the Society of Friends at Berwick (North Berwick), Me.," *The New England Historical and Genealogical Register* 72 (1918):253–73; 73 (1919):43–51, 124–28; 75 (1921):5–12.

- **Biddeford:** "Records of the First Church of Christ in Biddeford," *Maine Historical and Genealogical Register* 5 (1888):202–06; 6 (1889):293–301, 333–

40, 492–500; 7 (1893):8–14, 82–89, 130–31, 181–85. Contains baptisms 1749–1777, marriages 1742–1773, admissions 1730–1777.

- **Bingham:** Wilson, Frank H., "Baptisms and Funeral Services Conducted by Rev. Obed Wilson of Bingham, Maine," *The New England Historical and Genealogical Register* 103 (1949):296–304. For 1814–1838.

- **Brooklin:** "Maine Marriages of Lucius Bradford," *The New England Historical and Genealogical Register* 140 (1986):264–66. For 1855–1866.

- **Buxton:** *The Records of the Church of Christ in Buxton, Me., During the Pastorate of Rev. Paul Coffin, D.D.* (1868; reprint, Camden, Maine: Picton Press, 1989) F29/B96/C58/1989 also LOAN.

- **China:** Quaker: "Records of the Society of Friends at Harlem (China), Me.," *The New England Historical and Genealogical Register* 70 (1916):268–79, 318–37.

- **Dresden:** "Records of the Dresden, Me., Congregationalist Church," *The New England Historical and Genealogical Register* 66 (1912):2–12.

- **Falmouth:** 1st Church (Portland): King, Marquis F., *Baptisms and Admissions From the Records of First Church in Falmouth, Now Portland, Maine* (Portland, Maine: Maine Genealogical Society, 1898) F29/P9/K5/1898 also LOAN. Contains baptisms 1730–1825, marriages 1750–1753, owners of the covenant, admissions.

  1st Church (Portland): Willis, William, ed., *Journals of the Rev. Thomas Smith and the Rev. Samuel Deane, Pastors of the First Church in Portland* (Portland, Maine: Joseph S. Bailey, 1849) F29/P9/S61/1849 also LOAN.

  2nd Church (Cape Elizabeth): "Marriages in Falmouth (Cape Elizabeth), Solemnized by Rev. Ephraim Clark, Pastor 2d Church," *Maine Historical and Genealogical Register* 3 (1886):101–07, 185–93.

- **Harpswell:** Rev. Elisha Eaton and Rev. Samuel Eaton, Records of Harpswell Congregational Church, 1 microfilm reel. F29/H2/W66. Contains Elisha Eaton's records 1754–1764 of marriages, admissions, baptisms, owners of the covenant; Samuel Eaton's records of marriages 1765–1822; Joseph Eaton's records of marriages 1823–1843.

- **Kennebunkport** (see Arundel).

- **Kittery:** 1st Church: Dunkle, Robert J., and Valerie Ruocco, "Parish Records of the First Church and Society of Kittery, Maine, 1714 to 1791," *The New England Historical and Genealogical Register* 151 (1997):39–58, 217–39, 353–70, 443–62.

  2nd Church: "Kittery, Maine, Second Parish Baptisms 1721–1831: From a Typescript Prepared by Dr. John Eldridge Frost," *The Maine Genealogist* 25 (2003):134–41, 180–90; 26 (2004):43–46, 83–93, to be continued in later issues.

3rd Church: "Kittery, Maine, Third Parish Church Records: From a Manuscript Prepared by Dr. John Eldridge Frost," *The Maine Genealogist* 21 (1999):125–32, 173–76; 22 (2000):25–30, 92–93, 139–40, 180–82; 23 (2001): 13–21.

- **Limington:** "Limington, Maine, Church Records," *The New England Historical and Genealogical Register* 99 (1945):196–203.

- **Livermore:** see Brooklin.

- **Mount Desert:** "Records of the First Church of Mount Desert, Maine, 1792–1867," *The New England Historical and Genealogical Register* 73 (1919):279–91.

- **North Yarmouth:** "Records of Baptisms at the First Church, N. Yarmouth," in Augustus W. Corliss, *Old Times of North Yarmouth, Maine* (Somersworth, N.H.: New Hampshire Publishing Company, 1977), 490–93, 612–18, 662–68, 713–18, 748–53, 801–06, 857–61, 901–06, 939–46, 979–85, 1016–23, 1053–57, 1111–15. Contains baptisms 1730–1849.

- **Portland** (see Falmouth)

- **Saco:** *First Book of Records of the First Church in Pepperellborough (now Saco) Maine* (Saco: York Institute, 1914) F29/S1/S12/1914 also LOAN. Records 1762–98 including admissions, owners of the covenant, baptisms, marriages, deaths.

- **Scarborough:** 1st Church: "Records of the First Congregational Church in Scarborough, Me.," *Maine Historical and Genealogical Register* 1 (1884):51–54, 112–19, 163–71; 2 (1885):29–37, 78–84, 162–69, 230–36; 3 (1886):8–12, 83–90, 144–50, 238–43; 4 (1887):256–62. Contains baptisms 1728–1842, marriages 1729–1852, admissions 1728–1842.

  2nd Church: "Records of the Second Congregational Church in Scarborough, Maine. Marriages," *Maine Genealogical and Historical Register* 4 (1887):29–34, 87–93, 195–97. Contains marriages only 1744–1800.

- **Sidney:** Lang, Sara Drummond, "Marriages by Rev. Asa Wilbur of Sidney, Me., 1793–1840," *The New England Historical and Genealogical Register* 87 (1933):224–42.

- **Vassalborough:** Quaker: "Records of the Society of Friends at Vassalborough, Me.," *The New England Historical and Genealogical Register* 68 (1914):162–69, 242–49, 379–81; 69 (1915):70–82, 171–83, 267–74, 308–19.

- **Waterboro:** Duncan, Margaret, "Maine Marriages Performed by Rev. Henry Leach," *The New England Historical and Genealogical Register* 138 (1984):321–23. For 1815–1850.

- **Wells:** "Records of the First Church of Wells, Me.," *The New England Historical and Genealogical Register* 75 (1921):42–57, 104–23, 310–15; 76 (1922):102–14, 178–97, 247–62. Contains baptisms 1701–1810, members, owners of the covenant.

- **Wilton:** see Avon.

- **Windham (New Marblehead):** "Records of New Marblehead (Windham) 1743–99," *Maine Historical and Genealogical Register* 3 (1886): 287–89. Includes baptisms 1743–1762.

- **York:** 1st Parish: "First Parish, York: Baptisms 1750–1800," transcribed by John E. Frost, *York County Genealogical Society Journal* 4 (January 1989):5–14, (April 1989):9–18, (July 1989):11–20, (October 1989):9–18; 5 (January 1990):11–20, (April 1990):13–20.

   Scotland (Upper) Parish: Bragdon, Lester M., "Births of the Upper Parish in York: Transcribed from the Original Manuscript Book in 1931," *The Maine Genealogist* 23 (2001):119–38, 172–78; 24 (2002):35–42.

Cemetery Records

For many years, the Maine Old Cemetery Association (MOCA) has been locating and recording gravestone inscriptions throughout the state of Maine. To date, three series of MOCA records have been issued comprising hundreds of thousands of inscriptions. The arrangement of the records is first by county, second by town, and third by cemetery or private plot. These records, covering most towns in Maine, are an invaluable resource for Maine researchers. Many of the stones that were transcribed by MOCA have since deteriorated and are no longer legible. A useful index showing which cemeteries and towns are covered in each of the series is found at *rootsweb.com/~memoca/moca.htm*.

- Maine Old Cemetery Association, Cemetery Inscription Project, Series One, 6 microfilm reels. F18/M345/1980 also LOAN microfilm.

- Maine Old Cemetery Association, Cemetery Inscription Project, Series Two, 4 microfilm reels. F18/M345/1982 also LOAN microfilm.

- Maine Old Cemetery Association, Cemetery Inscription Project, Series Three, 6 microfilm reels. F18/M345/1987 also LOAN microfilm.

The MOCA records for two counties have been published with every-name indexes:

- Maine Old Cemetery Association, *Maine Cemetery Inscriptions: York County*, 4 vols. (Camden, Maine: Picton Press, 1995) F27/Y6/M35/1995 also LOAN.

- Maine Old Cemetery Association, *Maine Cemetery Inscriptions: Kennebec County*, CD-ROM (Rockport, Maine: Picton Press, 1999) F27/K3/M35/1999 CD also LOAN.

MOCA has indexed the gravestones of Revolutionary War soldiers:

- Maine Old Cemetery Association, Index of Revolutionary Veterans Buried in Maine. Mss 521.

The NEHGS library contains many published and manuscript compilations of inscriptions of individual cemeteries or of the cemeteries of individual towns, and the library catalog should be checked for these. A few of the more important ones include:

- Jordan, William B., *Burial Records, 1717–1962, of the Eastern Cemetery, Portland, Maine* (Bowie, Md.: Heritage Books, 1987) F29/P9/J762/1987 also LOAN.

- Jordan, William B., *Burial Records, 1811–1980, of the Western Cemetery in Portland, Maine* (Bowie, Md.: Heritage Books, 1987) F29/P9/J764/1987 also LOAN.

- Ketover, Karen Sherman, *Westbrook, Maine, Cemeteries: Plus the Surrounding Towns of Cumberland, Falmouth, Gorham, Portland and Windham* (Bowie, Md.: Heritage Books, 1996) F29/W6/K47/1996 also LOAN. This source covers a large geographical segment of Cumberland County.

- See also the library catalog for the "[Town Name], Maine, Record Book" series of cemetery inscriptions in typescript compiled by John Eldridge Frost for all of the York County towns. Most of these, but not all (notably missing are North Berwick and parts of Waterboro), were incorporated in the *Maine Cemetery Inscriptions: York County*, referenced above.

Newspapers

- Candage, Charles S., and Ruth L. P. Candage, *Vital Records Published in Rockland, Maine, Prior to 1892*, 2 vols. (Camden, Maine: Picton Press, 1989) F29/R6/C36/1989. Contains notices 1846–1891 from the *Rockland Gazette* and the *Lime Rock Gazette*.

- Chipman, Scott Lee, *New England Vital Records from the* Exeter News-Letter, vol. 1, 1831–1840; vol. 2, 1841–1846; vol. 3, 1847–1852; vol. 4, 1853–1858; and vol. 5, 1859–1865 (Camden, Maine: Picton Press, 1993–95) REF F44/E9/C54/1993 also LOAN. Contains many records pertaining to families living in lower Maine.

- Hammond, Otis Grant, *Notices from the New Hampshire Gazette, 1765–1800* (Lambertville, N.J.: Hunterdon House, 1970) F33/H36/1970 also LOAN. Contains 175 marriage and death records for Maine residents before 1800.

- Hammond, Priscilla, "Vital Records Contained in the New Hampshire Gazette, 1756–1800," manuscript, 1937, online database on *NewEnglandAncestors.org*.

- Jordan, William B., *Index to Portland Newspapers, 1785–1835* (Bowie, Md.: Heritage Books, 1995) F29/P9/J76/1995.

- Sullivan, Steven E., *Vital Records from the Thomaston Recorder of Thomaston, Maine, 1837–1846* (Camden, Maine: Picton Press, 1995) REF F29/T4/V58/1995 also LOAN.

- Ward, Mrs. Arthur, "Deaths and Marriages as Published in the *Ellsworth American*, 1866–1891," 3 vols., typescript (1992) F29/E5/W37/1992.

- Wentworth, William Edgar, *Vital Records 1790–1829 from Dover, New Hampshire's First Newspaper* (Camden, Maine: Picton Press, 1995) F44/D7/W46/1994 also LOAN. Includes vital events and notices for many people living in southern Maine.

- Willey, Kenneth L., *Vital Records from the* Eastport Sentinel *of Eastport, Maine, 1818—1900* (Camden, Maine: Picton Press, 1996) REF F29/E2/W56/1996 also LOAN. Includes notices for persons throughout the state of Maine, but largely in Washington County.

- Young, David C., "Index to Death Notices: *Jenks' Portland Gazette*, 1798–1806," typescript (1983) F18/Y67/1983 also LOAN.

- Young, David C., and Elizabeth Keene Young, *Vital Records from Maine Newspapers, 1785–1820*, 2 vols. (Bowie, Md.: Heritage Books, 1993) REF F18/Y68/1993. Statewide in coverage, includes abstracts of genealogical notices from forty Maine newspapers. Contains many records found nowhere else.

- Young, David C., and Benjamin Lewis Keene, *Abstracts of Death Notices (1833–1852) and Miscellaneous News Articles (1833–1924) from the* Maine Farmer (Bowie, Md.: Heritage Books, 1997).

- Young, David C., and Robert L. Taylor, *Death Notices from Freewill Baptist Publications, 1811–1851* (Bowie, Md.: Heritage Books, 1985) F3/Y67/1985 also LOAN.

- Young, David C., and Elizabeth Keene Young, *Marriages and Divorce Records from Freewill Baptist Publications, 1819–1851*, 2 vols. (Bowie, Md.: Heritage Books, 1995) F3/Y672/1994 also LOAN.

- Young, Elizabeth Keene, and Benjamin Lewis Keene, *Marriage Notices from the Maine Farmer, 1833–1852* (Bowie, Md.: Heritage Books, 1995).

Probate Records

Probate records in Maine are kept in the county probate courts. With the exception of Cumberland County, whose probate records were destroyed as a result of several fires in the nineteenth and early twentieth centuries, Maine's probate records provide one of the best sources for genealogical information.

Original Probate Records on Microfilm at NEHGS

- Franklin County, Maine, Records (probate, wills, etc.), 14 reels. F27/F8/ F73.

- Kennebec County, Maine, Records (probate, wills, etc.), 182 reels. F27/K2/ K45.

- Knox County, Maine, Probate Records (1861–1955) and General Index to Probate Records (1860–1928), 34 reels. F27/K7/K59.

- Lincoln County, Maine, Probate Records, 86 reels. F27/L7/L56.

- Piscataquis County, Maine, Records (probate, wills, etc.), 8 reels. F27/P5/ P57.

- Somerset County, Maine, Probate Records, 16 reels. F27/S7/S66.

Probate Records in Transcript or Abstract

The three publications listed below by Frost, Patterson, and Sargent encompass all of the extant probate records recorded in Maine through the year 1800. While extremely valuable, these books were compiled from the probate volumes recorded by the probate clerks and not from the original papers contained in the probate packets at the courthouse. The packets often contain additional information, but they must be searched on site at the county courthouses.

- Anderson, Joseph C., II, ed., *York County, Maine, Will Abstracts, 1801–1858*, 2 vols. (Camden, Maine: Picton Press, 1997) F27/Y6/A53/1997 also LOAN. Includes abstracts of 2,152 wills recorded in York County.

- Frost, John Eldridge, ed., *Maine Probate Abstracts*, 2 vols. (Camden, Maine: Picton Press, 1991) REF F18/F76/1991 also LOAN. Includes abstracts of all previously unpublished records in Maine probate volumes through 1800. An indispensable source for early Maine family research.

- Gray, Ruth, ed., *Abstracts of Penobscot County, Maine, Probate Records 1816– 1866: Including Abstracts of Probate Records from Hancock County 1790–1816 Relating to That Part of Hancock County Set Off as Penobscot County in 1816* (Camden, Maine: Picton Press, 1990) F27/P38/G72/1990 also LOAN.

- Patterson, William Davis, ed., *The Probate Records of Lincoln County, Maine, 1760 to 1800* (1895; reprint, Camden, Maine: Picton Press, 1991) F27/L7/ P2/1895 also LOAN.

- Sargent, William M., *Maine Wills, 1640–1760* (Portland, Maine: Brown, Thurston & Co., 1887) F18/S24/1887 also LOAN.

Land Records

Land records in Maine are surprisingly complete for all counties, and they are one of the best (and most underutilized) sources in the state for solving difficult genealogical problems. These records can be accessed on Family History Library microfilm, NEHGS microfilm, or on site at the county courthouses. The early York County deeds comprise the only published series of land records for Maine:

- York County, Maine, Register of Deeds, *York Deeds*, 18 vols. in 19 (Portland, Maine: Maine Historical Society et al., 1887–1910) F18/Y62 also LOAN. There is a separate index compiled by the Scarborough Historical Society, "York Deeds Index," typescript (1995) FF18/Y62/Index. This indispensable source is a verbatim transcription of the York County deed volumes, 1642–1737. Because York County was the only county in existence in Maine during this time period, the coverage of this work is statewide.

Town Records

Town records in Maine are one of the richest sources of genealogical information available to researchers. Some of the older towns, such as York, Kittery, Wells, Biddeford, and Kennebunkport, began record keeping in the seventeenth century. Most other towns' records date to the eighteenth century. In Maine, town records will list births, deaths, marriages and marriage intentions, as well as town meeting records, appointments of town office holders, cattle marks, real and personal property taxes, records of the poor, and any other business of importance to the town.

Town Records on Microfilm

The original town records of some 400 Maine towns, cities, and plantations have been microfilmed and most, but not all, are available at the NEHGS library. This is possibly the single most important collection for Maine genealogical research: Note, however, that these records generally date from the time the town was incorporated, not from the date of settlement.

Published Town Vital Records

The vital records of some seventy Maine towns have been transcribed and indexed in published volumes, a good portion of these appearing only within the last twenty years. While too numerous to cite individually here, the list below provides the names of the towns whose vital records have been published and the year of the publication. Most of these volumes are available in the NEHGS library and also as a part of the circulating library. Check the catalog for availability and call numbers.

Acton (2003), **Addison** (2003), **Albion** (1998), **Alexander** (1999), **Appleton** (1994), **Augusta** (1933), **Bangor** (births, 2002; deaths, 2003), **Belfast** (1917–19), **Berwick** (1993), **Biddeford** (1998), **Bowdoin** (1944–45), **Bristol** (1947–51), **Brunswick** (2004), **Calais** (2 distinct works, 1998, 2001), **Carmel** (1993), **Clinton** (1909), **Deer Isle** (1997), **Dixmont** (2003), **Etna** (1998), **Fairfield** (1980), **Farmingdale** (1909), **Frankfort** (1999), **Freedom** (1991), **Gardiner** (1914–15), **Georgetown** (1939–43), **Gorham** (1991), **Hallowell** (1924); **Hope** (1990), **Islesboro** (2000), **Jackson** (1989), **Kittery** (1991), **Knox** (1996), **Lebanon** (1922–23), **Lewiston** (2001–2), **Liberty** (1993), **Lincolnville** (1993), **Lisbon** (1995), **Lubec** (1996), **Monroe** (1991), **Montville** (1990), **Mount Desert** (1990), **North Haven** (2002), **Nobleboro** (see Bristol), **North Berwick** (see Berwick), **Northport** (1995), **North Yarmouth** (1993), **Old Town** (1997), **Orrington** (1995), **Otisfield** (1948), **Parsonsfield** (1988), **Penobscot** (1984), **Phippsburg** (1935), **Pittston** (1911), **Prospect** (2000), **Randolph** (1910), **Rockland** (2001), **Saco** (1896), **St. George** (2003), **Searsport** (1993), **Stockton Springs** (1979), **South Berwick** (see Berwick), **South Thomaston** (2001), **Swanville** (1990), **Thomaston** (2002), **Thorndike** (1993), **Topsham** (1929–30), **Troy** (1995), **Unity** (1995), **Vinalhaven** (1994), **Warren** (2004), **West Gardiner** (1997), **Winslow** (1937), **York** (1992).

The following towns' vital records, or a portion of them, have been published in *The New England Historical and Genealogical Register* (volume numbers in parentheses):

Biddeford (71), **Brooksville** (104–110), **Carmel** (83), **Charlotte** (101–103), **Cooper** (85), **Cushing** (90), **Edgecomb** (83), **Georgetown** (80), **Jefferson** (73), **Limington** (85, 87–88), **Lyman** (95–97), **Newcastle** (95), **Newfield** (97–98), **Nobleborough** (84), **Poland** (88), **Sabattus** (148), **Saco** (71), **Tremont** (85), **Waterboro** (90–91), **Webster** (148), **Williamsburg** (94).

Published Town Meeting Records

- **Friendship:** Cook, Melville Bradford, *Records of Meduncook Plantation and Friendship, Maine* (Rockland, Maine: Shore Village Historical Society, 1985) F29/F87/C66/1985 also LOAN.

- **Lewiston:** Hodgkin, Douglas I., *Records of Lewiston, Maine*, vol. 1 (Rockport, Maine: Picton Press, 2001) F29/L63/H63/2001 also LOAN.

Tax Records

Real and personal property taxes in Maine were collected at the town level and recorded by the individual town clerks. The availability of tax records varies from town to town. (See TOWN RECORDS above).

Several statewide Massachusetts tax lists (which included Maine) have been published. Two major tax lists are:

- *Massachusetts and Maine Direct Tax Census of 1798*, 18 reels of microfilm (Boston: NEHGS, 1978) F63/M343/1978 also LOAN also Web database. See also Michael H. Gorn, *An Index and Guide to the Microfilm Edition of the Massachusetts and Maine Direct Tax Census of 1798* (Boston: NEHGS, 1979) REF F63/M343/I53/1979 also LOAN also Microtext.

- Pruitt, Bettye Hobbs, *The Massachusetts Tax Valuation List of 1771* (1978; reprinted Camden, Maine: Picton Press, 1998) REF F63/P838/1998 also LOAN.

Court and Legislative Records

All of Maine's court records for the period 1636–1727 have been published in the *Province and Court Records* series shown below. In that time period, all of Maine was York County.

- *Province and Court Records of Maine*, ed. Charles Thornton Libby (vols. 1–2), Robert Earle Moody (vol. 3), and Neal Woodside Allen (vols. 4–6), 6 vols. (Portland, Maine: Maine Historical Society, 1928–75) F23/M22 also LOAN.

Later court records for Maine are available at the Maine State Archives in the original or on microfilm, and these have not been published. They may also be accessed on Family History Library microfilm. Indexes to the court records of York County (1686–1760), Kennebec County (1799–1854), and Washington County (1839–1845) have been compiled by the Maine State Archives and are available online at *rootsweb.com/~usgenweb/me/mecourt.html*.

Military Records

Most military records for Maine soldiers who fought in wars prior to Maine statehood are located at the Massachusetts Archives in Boston and reference should be made to the Massachusetts chapter in this book for those sources. However, there are a number of good published finding aids and compilations for Maine soldiers and sailors, and these are shown below.

Colonial Wars

- Burrage, Henry Sweetser, *Maine at Louisburg in 1745* (Augusta, Maine: Burleigh & Flynt, 1910) ME/51/45.

- Burrage, Henry Sweetser, *Register of the Officers and Members of the Society of Colonial Wars in the State of Maine: Also History, Roster and Record of Colonel Jedidiah Preble's Regiment, Campaign of 1758; Together with Capt. Samuel Cobb's Journal* (Portland, Maine: Marks Printing House, 1905) E186.3/M22/1905.

- Coleman, Emma Lewis, *New England Captives Carried to Canada Between 1677 and 1760 During the French and Indian Wars*, 2 vols. (Portland, Maine: Southworth Press, 1925; reprinted Bowie, Md.: Heritage Books, 1989) E85/C72/1925 also LOAN. This book, fully cited to primary sources, provides accounts of hundreds of Maine residents killed or captured during the colonial wars.

Revolutionary War

- Fisher, Carleton E., and Sue G. Fisher, comp., *Soldiers, Sailors and Patriots of the Revolutionary War–Maine* (Louisville, Ky.: National Society of the Sons of the American Revolution, 1982) REF E263/M4/F54/1982 also LOAN. Compiled from many sources, this book provides an account of most persons in Maine who fought in the Revolutionary War or performed public service during the war. Make certain to check the references at the back of the book to verify the source of the information. Statewide in scope, this book is also useful as a survey tool for locating the migrations of the soldiers after the war.

- Fisher, Carleton E., *Supplement to Soldiers, Sailors and Patriots of the Revolutionary War–Maine* (Rockport, Maine: Picton Press, 1998) REF E263/M4/F54/1982/Suppl. also LOAN.

- Flagg, Charles Alcott, *An Alphabetical Index of Revolutionary Pensioners Living in Maine* (1920; reprinted Baltimore: Genealogical Publishing Co., 1967) E255/F57/1920 also LOAN.

- House, Charles J., *Names of Soldiers of the American Revolution Who Applied for State Bounty Under Resolves of March 17, 1835, March 24, 1836, and March 20, 1836, as Appears of Record in Land Office* (1893; reprinted Baltimore: Genealogical Publishing Co., 1967) REF E263/M4/H8/1967 also LOAN.

- *Massachusetts Soldiers and Sailors of the Revolutionary War*, 17 vols. (Boston: Wright & Potter, 1896–1908) REF E263/M4/M4/1896 also LOAN. Since Maine was still a part of Massachusetts during the Revolutionary War, the service records of many of Maine's soldiers are found in this series.

- White, Paul R., "Maine Estate Schedules from Revolutionary War Pensions," *The New England Genealogical and Historical Register* 142 (1988):29–38, 197–209, 298–304, 386–91; 145 (1991):44–56, 159–73. This provides abstracts of nearly 400 estate schedules, most of them for Revolutionary War veterans living in the area of Cumberland County and northern York County.

War of 1812

- Massachusetts, Adjutant General, *Records of the Massachusetts Volunteer Militia Called Out by the Governor of Massachusetts to Suppress a Threatened Invasion During the War of 1812–14* . . . (Boston: Wright & Potter, 1913) REF E359.5/M3/1913 also LOAN.

Aroostook War

- *Aroostook War, Historical Sketch and Roster of Commissioned Officers and Enlisted Men Called into Service for the Protection of the Northeastern Frontier of Maine, from February to May 1839 . . .* (Augusta, Maine: Kennebec Journal Print, 1904) ME/58/15.

Civil War

- Jordan, William Barnes, Jr., *Maine in the Civil War: A Bibliographical Guide* (Portland, Maine: Maine Historical Society, 1976).

- *Annual Report of the Adjutant General of the State of Maine [for the Years 1861–1866]*, 5 vols. (Augusta, Maine: Stevens & Sayward, 1862–67) E 492/C58 also Microfiche ME 3, 21, 35, 71, 86.

World War I

- *Roster of Maine in the Military Service of the United States and Allies in the World War, 1917–1919. . .*, 2 vols. (Augusta, Maine: n.p., 1929) F18/M352/1929a also LOAN also Web database.

Genealogical and Biographical Compendia (Including Town and County Histories)

Statewide Compendia

- *Collections of the Maine Historical Society*, Series I, 10 vols. (Portland, Maine: Maine Historical Society, 1831–1906) Rare Book F16/M32 also LOAN.

  Series II, 10 vols. (Portland, Maine: Maine Historical Society, 1890–99) Rare Book F16/M33/2nd ser. also LOAN.

  Series III, 2 vols. (Portland, Maine: Maine Historical Society, 1904–6) Rare Book F16/M33/3rd ser. also LOAN.

- Davis, Walter Goodwin, *Massachusetts and Maine Families in the Ancestry of Walter Goodwin Davis (1885–1966)*, 3 vols. (Baltimore: Genealogical Publishing Co., 1996) CS71/D26/1996 also LOAN. This work, by one of Maine's most respected genealogists, combines sixteen of Davis's "all my ancestors" books with a comprehensive index. Numerous early Maine families are covered here, often with their English ancestry revealed.

- *Documentary History of the State of Maine*, Series II, 24 vols. (Portland, Maine: Maine Historical Society, 1869–1916) Rare Book F16/M38 also LOAN. Includes transcripts of many valuable documents from many sources, including petitions and letters to the General Court of Massachusetts from persons and communities throughout Maine.

- Little, George Thomas, *Genealogical and Family History of the State of Maine*, 4 vols. (New York: Lewis Historical Publishing Co., 1909) F18/L77/1909 also LOAN. While good for clues, use this source with caution.

- *Maine Families in 1790*, ed. Ruth Gray (vols. 1–3), Joseph C. Anderson II and Lois Ware Thurston (vol. 4), Joseph C. Anderson II (vols. 5–8), 8 vols. to date (Camden and Rockport, Maine: Picton Press, 1988–2003) REF F18/M18/1988 also LOAN. This series provides fully-documented three-generation sketches of over 2200 families (to date) living within the state of Maine in the year 1790, more than 13 percent of the entire state population. Considering the sketches include not only the nuclear family under discussion, but also the head-of-household's parents, his spouse's parents, the children's spouses, and the children's spouses' parents, it is evident that a much higher percentage of the population has been covered. This is one of the most important published resources for Maine genealogy.

- Noyes, Sybil, Charles Thornton Libby, and Walter Goodwin Davis, *Genealogical Dictionary of Maine and New Hampshire* (Portland, Maine: Southworth-Anthoensen Press, 1928–39; reprinted Baltimore: Genealogical Publishing Co., 1972) R.Rm. REF F18/N68/1928 also LOAN. One of the best and most reliable sources for persons living in Maine in the seventeenth and early eighteenth centuries, based entirely on original records.

- Pope, Charles H., *The Pioneers of Maine and New Hampshire, 1623 to 1660* (1908; reprinted Baltimore: Genealogical Publishing Co., 1973) R.Rm. REF F18/P82/1908 also LOAN.

- Spencer, Wilbur D., *Pioneers on Maine Rivers, With Lists to 1651* (1930; reprinted Baltimore: Genealogical Publishing Co., 1973) F23/S74/1930 also/LOAN.

County Histories

- **Androscoggin:** Merrill, Georgia Drew, *History of Androscoggin County, Maine* (Boston: W. A. Fergusson & Co., 1891) F27/A5/M5/1891 also LOAN.

- **Aroostook:** Wiggin, Edward, and George H. Collins, *History of Aroostook: Comprising Facts, Names and Dates Relating to the Early Settlement of All the Different Towns and Plantations of the County* (1922; reprinted Salem, Mass.: Higginson Book Co., 2001) F27/A7/W54/1922 also LOAN.

- **Cumberland:** Clayton, W. W., *History of Cumberland Co., Maine, with Illustrations and Biographical Sketches of Its Prominent Men and Pioneers*, 2 vols. (1880; reprinted Bowie, Md.: Heritage Books, 1994) F27/C9/C53/1880 also LOAN.

- **Kennebec:** Kingsbury, Henry D., and Simeon L. Deyo, *Illustrated History of Kennebec County, Maine*, 2 vols. (New York: H. W. Blake & Co., 1892) F27/K2/K5/1892 also LOAN.

- **Penobscot:** *History of Penobscot County, Maine, with Illustrations and Biographical Sketches* (Cleveland: Williams, Chase & Co., 1882) F27/P38/H57/1882.

- **Piscataquis:** Loring, Amasa, *History of Piscataquis County, Maine, from Its Earliest Settlement to 1880* (Portland, Maine: Hoyt, Fogg & Donham, 1880) F27/P5/L8/1880 also LOAN.

- **York:** Clayton, W. W., *History of York County, Maine, with Illustrations and Biographical Sketches of Its Prominent Men and Pioneers* (Philadelphia: Everts & Peck, 1880) F27/Y6/C6/1880 also LOAN.

Town Histories

Histories exist for many towns in Maine and a large number of these compilations include sections providing genealogies of local families, some more reliable than others. While these works are too numerous to cite here in full, the following list provides (1) the name of towns whose histories contain a substantial genealogical section and (2) the year of the book's original publication. Most of these books can be found via a subject search (enter the town name as a subject) in the catalog of the NEHGS library.

Augusta (1870), **Belfast** (1877), **Bethel** (1891), **Blue Hill** (1905), **Boothbay** (1906), **Brewer** (1962), **Brooks** (1935), **Brownfield** (1966), **Brunswick** (1878), **Buckfield** (1915), **Buxton** (1874), **Burlington** (1977), **China** (1975), **Clinton** (1970), **Cornish** (1975), **Deer Isle** (1886), **Dresden** (1931), **Durham** (1899), **Eddington** (see Brewer), **Eliot** (1897–1909) **Ellsworth** (1927), **Embden** (1929), **Farmington** (1885), **Foxcroft** (1935), **Gardiner** (1852), **Gorham** (1903), **Greene** (1938), **Hanover** (1980), **Harpswell** (see Brunswick), **Harrison** (1909), **Hebron** (see Oxford), **Holden** (see Brewer), **Hollis** (1976), **Industry** (1893), **Islesborough** (1893), **Jay** (1995), **Kennebunkport** (1837), **Kittery** (1903), **Lee** (1926), **Leeds** (1901), **Lewiston** (1882), **Lincoln** (1939), **Litchfield** (1897), **Livermore** (1928), **Machias** (1904), **Matinicus Isle** (1926), **Monmouth** (1894), **Morrill** (1957), **New Vineyard** (1976), **Newcastle** (see Sheepscot), **Norway** (1886), **Orrington** (see Brewer), **Otisfield** (1953), **Oxford** (1903), **Paris** (1884), **Parsonsfield** (1888), **Peru** (1911), **Pittston** (see Gardiner), **Portland** (1865), **Rockland** (see Thomaston), **Rumford** (1890), **Saco Valley** (1895), **St. George** (1976), **Sheepscot** (1882), **Skowhegan** (1941), **Sorrento** (see Sullivan), **South Thomaston** (see Thomaston), **Sullivan** (1953), **Sumner** (1899), **Sunday River** (1977), **Thomaston** (1865), **Topsham** (see Brunswick), **Union** (1851), **Wales** (see Monmouth), **Warren** (1877), **Waterford** (1879), **Wayne** (1898), **West Gardiner** (see Gardiner), **Whiting** (1975), **Wilsons Mills** (1975), **Windham** (1916), **Winthrop** (1925), **Woodstock** (1882).

Genealogical Compendia for Maine Towns

A number of works have been published that document the early families in a particular town or location. While these books can be very helpful in sorting out large families in a town, most of them are undocumented and therefore need to be used with caution.

- **Acton:** see Shapleigh.

- **Addison:** see Pleasant River.

- **Beddington:** see Narraguagus River.

- **Bowdoin:** Bickford, Jayne E., and Charlene B. Bartlett, *Early Bowdoin, Maine, Families and Some of Their Descendants* (Bowie, Md.: Heritage Books, 2002) F29/B7918/B53/2002 also LOAN.

- **Calais:** Brooks, Thelma Eye, *Calais, Maine, Families: They Came and They Went* (Bowie, Md.: Heritage Books, 2002) F29/C1/B758/2002 also LOAN.

- **Centerville:** see Pleasant River.

- **Cherryfield:** see Narraguagus River.

- **Columbia and Columbia Falls:** see Pleasant River.

- **Cornish:** Taylor, Robert L., "Early Families of Cornish, Maine," typescript (1985) F29/C74/T3/1985 also LOAN.

- **Deblois:** see Narraguagus River.

- **Gouldsboro:** Johnson, Muriel Sampson, *Early Families of Gouldsboro, Maine* (Camden, Maine: Picton Press, 1990) F29/G7/J64/1990 also LOAN.

- **Harrington:** see Narraguagus River.

- **Lebanon:** Chamberlain, George Walter, "Lebanon, Maine, Genealogies 1750–1892," typescript (Portland, Maine: Maine Historical Society, 1976) F29/L4/C5/1976.

- **Limerick:** Taylor, Robert L., *Early Families of Limerick, Maine* (Camden, Maine: Picton Press, 1993) F29/L64/T39/1993 also LOAN.

- **Limington:** Taylor, Robert L., *Early Families of Limington, Maine* (Bowie, Md.: Heritage Books, 1991) F29/L65/T393/1991.

- **Milbridge:** see Narraguagus River.

- **Narraguagus River:** Lamson, Darryl B., and Leonard F. Tibbetts, *Early Narraguagus River Families of Washington County, Maine* (Rockport, Maine: Picton Press, 2002) F27/W3/L36/2002 also LOAN.

- **Newfield:** Ayers, Ruth Bridges, *Early Families of Newfield, Maine* (Camden, Maine: Penobscot Press, 1995) F29/N62/A94/1995 also LOAN.

- **Pleasant River:** Tibbetts, Leonard F., and Darryl B. Lamson, *Early Pleasant River Families of Washington County, Maine* (Camden, Maine: Picton Press, 1997) F27/W3/T53/1997 also LOAN.

- **Sanford:** Boyle, Frederick R., *Early Families of Sanford–Springvale, Maine* (Portsmouth, N.H.: P. E. Randall, 1988) F29/S2/B69/1988 also LOAN. Boyle, Frederick R., *Later Families of Sanford–Springvale, Maine* (Portsmouth, N.H.: P.E. Randall, 1995) F29/S2/B695/1995 also LOAN.

- **Shapleigh:** Boyle, Frederick R., *Early Families of Shapleigh and Acton, Maine* (Portsmouth, N.H.: P. E. Randall, 2002) F29/S5/B69/2002 also LOAN.

- **Springvale:** See Sanford.

- **Standish:** Sears, Albert J., *Early Families of Standish, Maine* (Bowie, Md.: Heritage Books, 1991) F29/S76/S4/1991.

- **Steuben:** see Narraguagus River.

- **Waldoboro (Germans):** Whitaker, Wilford W., and Gary T. Horlacher, *Early Broad Bay Pioneers: 18th German-Speaking Settlers of Present-Day Waldoboro, Maine* (Rockport, Maine: Picton Press, 1998) F29/W1/W48/1998 also LOAN.

Maps and Atlases

- Attwood, Stanley B., *The Length and Breadth of Maine* (1946; reprinted Orono, Maine: University of Maine, 1973) REF F17/A8 also LOAN. This is the standard work for Maine place names and the history of town creation.

- Long, John H., and Gordon DenBoer, *Connecticut, Maine, Massachusetts, Rhode Island: Atlas of Historical County Boundaries* (New York: Simon & Schuster, 1994) Atlas G1201/F7/A8/1993 also LOAN. Includes beautifully detailed maps outlining all county jurisdictional changes 1606–1917.

- *The Maine Atlas and Gazetteer* (Yarmouth, Maine: David DeLorme and Company, 1978) G1215/D44/1978. An indispensable resource for locating small geographic areas. Sold by all major booksellers.

- The Maine State Bicentennial Commission, *The Maine Bicentennial Atlas: An Historical Survey* (Portland, Maine: Maine Historical Society, 1976) REF F17/M3/1976 also LOAN.

- Varney, George J., *A Gazetteer of the State of Maine, With Numerous Illustrations* (1881; reprinted Bowie, Md.: Heritage Books, 1991) F17/V31/1881 also LOAN. This work provides a brief history of each of the Maine towns and also describes any important geographical features and landmarks.

Special Sources for Maine

- McCausland, Robert R., and Cynthia MacAlmon McCausland, *The Diary of Martha Ballard 1785–1812* (Camden, Maine: Picton Press, 1992) F29/H15/B34/1992 also LOAN. Martha Ballard, a midwife practicing in the Hallowell–Augusta area, recorded in her diary hundreds of deliveries that she performed over a 27-year period. This book is a verbatim transcription of the entire diary. In addition to births and other vital events, the diary records innumerable items of historical and genealogical interest. Martha Ballard's life was the subject of both the Pulitzer Prize-winning study *A Midwife's Tale,* by noted historian Laurel Thatcher Ulrich, and a PBS television special.

- McLane, Charles B., *Islands of the Mid-Maine Coast*. This series contains detailed and scholarly histories of Maine's numerous offshore islands, as well as information on the people who lived there throughout the islands' history.

  Volume I: Penobscot and Blue Hill Bays (Woolwich, Maine: Kennebec River Press, 1982) Oversize F27/P37/M34/1982.

  Volume IA: Blue Hill Bay (Woolwich, Maine: Kennebec River Press, 1985) Oversize F27/B49/M35/1985 also LOAN.

  Volume II: Mt. Desert to Machias Bay (Falmouth, Maine: Kennebec River Press, 1989) Oversize F27/M9/M35/1989.

  Volume III: Muscongus Bay and Monhegan Island (Rockland, Maine: The Island Institute, 1992) F27/M94/M34/1992.

  Volume IV: Pemaquid Point to the Kennebec River (Rockland, Maine: The Island Institute, 1994)

- *Maine State Prisoners 1824–1915* (Rockport, Maine: Picton Press, 2001) F18/R64/2001 also LOAN. One place to look for persons not found in other records.

- "Blacks and American Indians of Maine During the American Revolution," in Eric G. Grundset, ed., *African American and Indian Patriots of the Revolutionary War* (Washington, D.C.: National Society Daughters of the American Revolution, 2001), 1–13. E269/N3/A37/2001.

- Rolde, Neil, *Unsettled Past, Unsettled Future: The Story of Maine Indians* (Gardiner, Maine: Tilbury House, 2004) IN CATALOGING.

Massachusetts

Helen Schatvet Ullmann

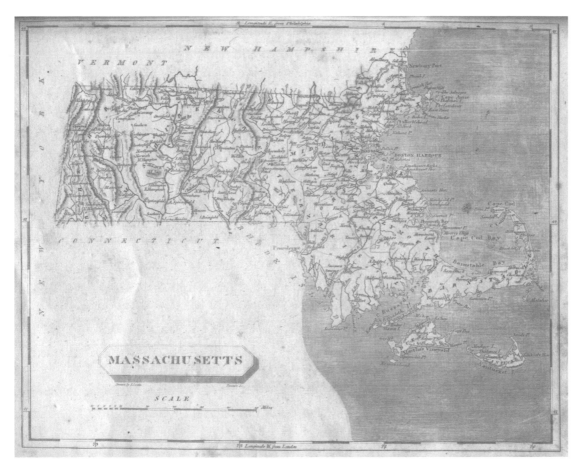

Massachusetts from *A New and Elegant General Atlas* by Arrowsmith and Lewis (Boston: Thomas & Andrews, 1805).

Overview

Massachusetts is incredibly rich in genealogical sources. From town and colony records kept almost from the beginning to special collections in libraries and historical societies to modern electronic databases, there is almost no end to the possibilities for solving sticky research problems. There are perhaps more genealogies published for Massachusetts families than for any other state.

And yet there are gaps. Many towns, especially in the late eighteenth and early nineteenth centuries, did not keep their vital records carefully. Church records, particularly those of non-Congregational churches, can be difficult to locate. Not everyone owned land, or if they did, they may not have traveled to the county courthouse and paid to have deeds recorded.

Nevertheless, most records have survived. An 1827 fire in Barnstable County destroyed early deeds. Fires and floods, particularly in 1955, damaged some local town records. Sometimes records are not in an obvious place. For example, when Hampden County was formed in 1812, the old land records stayed in Springfield, but the old probate records went to Northampton, the new county seat for Hampshire County.

But most problems can be surmounted by thorough research. That probate, land, and court records were kept by the counties is very helpful; the genealogist can check indexes for a wide area all at once. Often it is land records, with the aid of census and other statewide indexes, that help us to follow an individual from town to town and then allows us to zero in on other records, sometimes obscure ones such as diaries or account books, for those towns.

Now that there is so much on microfilm at NEHGS, most Massachusetts families can be well researched on site at 101 Newbury Street.

Guides and Finding Aids

- Melnyk, Marcia D., *Genealogist's Handbook for New England Research*, 4th ed. (Boston: NEHGS, 1999), 87–141. REF F3/G466/1999 also LOAN.

- Crandall, Ralph J., ed., *Genealogical Research in New England* (Baltimore: Genealogical Publishing Co., 1984) 77–114. REF F3/G46/1984 also LOAN. The Massachusetts article has a select bibliography of town histories and compiled genealogies.

- *Research Outline: Massachusetts*, 2nd ed. (Salt Lake City: Family History Library, 1997), ask at fourth-floor desk.

- *Historical Data Relating to Counties, Cities and Towns in Massachusetts*, 5th ed. (Boston: NEHGS, 1997) REF F64/M5/1997 also LOAN. Town by town, this gives complete detail on their formation and border changes. Part 3 of the earlier edition, "Extinct Places," has been incorporated into the main text, and a new index refers the reader to a new category under each town called "Section/Village Names."

- Eichholz, Alice, "Massachusetts," in *Red Book: American State, County, and Town Sources*, 3rd ed. (Provo, Utah: Ancestry, 2004), 310–35. REF CS49/A55/2004 also LOAN.

- Lainhart, Ann S., *A Researcher's Guide to Boston* (Boston: NEHGS, 2003) REF F73.25/L35/2003 also LOAN.

- Holman, Winifred Lovering, "Massachusetts," in *Genealogical Research: Methods and Sources*, Milton Rubincam, ed., 2nd ed., 2 vols. (Washington, D.C.: American Society of Genealogists, 1980–83), 1:139–50. REF CS16/G43/1980 also LOAN. While this does not include post-1980 resources, it is an excellent basic text and more readable than other guides.

- Wright, Norman Edgar, *Genealogy in America: Massachusetts, Connecticut, and Maine* (Salt Lake City, Utah: Deseret Book Company, 1968) REF CS47/W7/1968 also LOAN. This book too is a bit dated, but includes an extensive treatment of Massachusetts sources.

- Gardner-Westcott, Katherine A., ed., *Massachusetts Sources: Part One: Boston, New Bedford, Springfield, Worcester* (Ashland, Mass.: Massachusetts Society of Genealogists, 1988) REF F63/G37/1988.

- *The American Genealogical-Biographical Index* [AGBI], 206 vols. (Middletown, Conn.: Godfrey Library, 1952–2000) REF Z5313/U5/A55. See NEW ENGLAND OVERVIEW.

- Torrey, Clarence Almon, *New England Marriages Prior to 1700*. It is best used on CD-ROM (Boston: NEHGS, 2001) or in the bound printout from the CD-ROM, also in the sixth-floor reading room, which contain full citations of all identifiable sources. See NEW ENGLAND OVERVIEW.

- Sanborn, Melinde Lutz, *Third Supplement to Torrey's New England Marriages Prior to 1700* (Baltimore: Genealogical Publishing Co., 2003) R.Rm. REF F3/T6/Suppl./2003 also LOAN. See NEW ENGLAND OVERVIEW.

- *Periodical Source Index* (PERSI), 16 vols. for 1847–1985, plus subsequent annual volumes (Fort Wayne, Ind.: Allen County Public Library Foundation, 1987–present) REF CS1/P47. Also on CD-ROM and online, the most recent version as part of Heritage Quest Online. See NEW ENGLAND OVERVIEW.

- Ullmann, Helen Schatvet, online articles about Massachusetts on *NewEnglandAncestors.org*.

Genealogical and Historical Periodicals

- *The New England Historical and Genealogical Register*, 1847–present. R.Rm. REF F1/N56 also LOAN also fifth floor also Web database. See NEW ENGLAND OVERVIEW.

- *The Great Migration Newsletter*, 1990–present. REF F7/G73/1990 also LOAN also Intl REF. See NEW ENGLAND OVERVIEW.

- *The American Genealogist*, 1922–present. R.Rm. REF F104/N6/A6 also LOAN. See NEW ENGLAND OVERVIEW.

- *The Berkshire Genealogist*, published by the Berkshire Family History Association, 1978–present. F72/B5/B45. Also an index by Donald L. Lutes to vols. 1–10.

- *Dedham Historical Register*, 14 vols. (1890–1903) F74/D3/D8 also LOAN.

- *Essex Institute Historical Collections*, 129 vols. (1859–1993) F72/E7/E81 also LOAN. Some indexes.

- *The Essex Genealogist*, 1981–present. F72/E7/E6 also LOAN. Subject and every-name index to vols. 1–15 (1981–1996).

- *Essex Antiquarian*, 13 vols. (1897–1909) F72/E7/E4 also LOAN.

- *Historical Collections of the Danvers Historical Society*, 43 vols. (1913–1967) F74/D2D42.

- *Historical Collections of the Topsfield Historical Society*, 31 vols. (1895–1951) F74/T6/T6/1895 also LOAN.

- *Massachusetts Historical Society Collections*, 1792–present. F61/M41.

- *MASSOG: A Genealogical Magazine for the Commonwealth of Massachusetts*, the journal of the Massachusetts Society of Genealogists, 1977–present. F63/M371 also LOAN.

- *Mayflower Descendant*, 34 vols., 1899–1937 and 1985–present. R.Rm. REF F68/M46 also LOAN. See NEW ENGLAND OVERVIEW.

- *Medford Historical Register*, 43 vols. (1898–1940) F74/M5/M35 also LOAN.

- *The Mayflower Quarterly*, 1935–present. REF F68/S64 also LOAN.

- *National Genealogical Society Quarterly*, 1912–present. CS42/N4 also LOAN. Vols. 1-85 on Family Archives CD #210 (Brøderbund, 1998).

Censuses: Colonial, Federal, and State

While there is no true census for the colonial era in Massachusetts, there are many lists of various kinds. A statewide census substitute is Bettye Hobbs Pruitt, *The Massachusetts Tax Valuation List of 1771* (1978; reprinted Camden, Maine: Picton Press, 1998) REF F63/P838/1998 also LOAN.

Microfilms for all federal censuses of Massachusetts, 1790 through 1930 (including an index to the 1890 veterans' census), are in Microtext on the fourth floor, along with Soundex indexes for 1880, 1900, 1910, and 1920. Note Mary Lou Craver Mariner and Patricia Roughan Bellows, *A Research Aid for the Massachusetts 1910 Federal Census* (Sudbury, Mass.: Computerized Assistance, 1988) HA201/1910/T624/1988.

Massachusetts state census for 1855 and 1865 are also in Microtext. Many towns for both censuses have been transcribed and indexed by Ann Smith Lainhart (F74/B2/E4 1986–1992).

Vital Records

When one thinks of vital records in Massachusetts, the first thing that comes to mind is the "official series" collection shelved in the sixth-floor reading room. Other early town volumes, such as Boston, Woburn and Concord, were published before the official series began in the early 1900s. Some town records, such as Sandwich, Charlestown and Townsend, have been published more recently.

There are, however, many towns for which the vital records have not been published. Or they may have been published in a periodical, such as *The New England Historical and Genealogical Register* or the *Mayflower Descendant*. See the list of towns in the *Genealogist's Handbook for New England Research*. This has a key to where such records may be found. Many vital records for central Massachusetts towns were transcribed by Walter E. Corbin and may be searched on microfilm. The Society also has some of the Holbrook Research Institute (now Archives Publishing) microfiches of original records. Other material may be in the manuscript collection. If all else fails, one may order microfilm of original records from the Family History Library.

If multiple transcriptions of a town's records are available, it would be wise to check all of them. For example, Corbin included Hatfield vital records, but there are two other transcriptions, one by Stuart G. Waite (Oversize F74/H45/H33), and the other is part of a collection by R.R. Hinman called "Windham Cullings" (L/WIN/35). While the library does not have the Holbrook fiche for Hatfield, one can order the original town records from the Family History Library.

In the early years of the colony, towns were required to report vital records to the county courts. The marriage records of some counties were published by Frederic W. Bailey in *Early Massachusetts Marriages Prior to 1800* (1897–1914; reprinted as 1 vol., Baltimore: Genealogical Publishing Co., 1968) REF F63/B16/1897 also LOAN. Many, but not all, of these marriages appear in the "official series" volumes.

Another broad collection is that by Nathaniel B. Shurtleff and George Ernest Bowman, *Records of Plymouth Colony: Births, Marriages, Deaths, Burials, and other Records, 1633–1689: Reprinted with "Plymouth Colony Vital Records," a Supplement from the Mayflower Descendant* (Baltimore: Genealogical Publishing Co., 1976) F68/S58/1976.

There are several ways to determine which towns to search:

- The Internet: Many town vital records are on *NewEnglandAncestry.org*. Databases such as the Ancestry World Tree at *Ancestry.com* and the International Genealogical Index, Ancestral File and Pedigree Resource File on *FamilySearch.org* can provide clues as to which town(s) to search.

- *Early Vital Records of the Commonwealth of Massachusetts to about 1850*, CD-ROM (Wheat Ridge, Col.: Search & ReSearch, 1997–2000) provides an efficient way to cover most towns in each county. It includes some materials not otherwise available at NEHGS. However, most town records are indexed only by surname, and it takes time to learn to use these CDs. See a review in *The New England Historical and Genealogical Register* 155 (2001):118–22 for suggestions and warnings. Since these CDs provide images of the original text, they are quite reliable.

- Family Archives CD #220, *Massachusetts Vital Records, 1600s–1800s* (Brøderbund, 2000) is a transcribed index to births and deaths in most of the published books. This may contain errors.

- Family Archives CD #231, *Marriage Index: Massachusetts, 1633–1850* (Brøderbund, 1997), is the same for marriages. This may contain errors.

- Lane, Evelyn C., "Index of Surnames in Early Massachusetts (from printed sources)," 4 vols., typescript (1989) R.Rm. REF F63/I52/1989. This work is a handy reference for uncommon surnames in many of the volumes of published vital records of Massachusetts.

There are volumes on name changes in Massachusetts:

- Pierce, Henry Bailey, *List of Persons whose Names have been Changed in Massachusetts, 1780–1883* (Boston: Wright & Potter, 1885) REF F63/A5/1885.

- *List of Persons whose Names have been Changed in Massachusetts, 1780–1892* (Boston: Wright & Potter, 1893) F63/A5/1893.

- *Index to Names Changed in Massachusetts, 1893–1927, Names Decreed, A-Z* (Boston: Registry of Vital Statistics, 1999) Microtext F63/M364. This is in alphabetical order by the new name.

- Later volumes from the Registry of Vital Statistics through 1944 are indexes to corrections and additions, which include name changes.

Note also family records, e.g., *Bible Records from the Manuscripts Collections of the New England Historic Genealogical Society*, CD-ROM (Boston: NEHGS, 2001).

Church Records

Next to vital records, church records are perhaps the next most sought-after resource in Massachusetts family history research. The Bay Colony having been founded partly for religious reasons, church records begin early. But while many church records are readily available, others can be frustratingly difficult to find and use. Try all of the following:

- The society's online catalog at *NewEnglandAncestors.org*.

- Other catalogs in the NEHGS library.

- The Corbin Collection, which includes many church records, is at NEHGS on microfilm.

- The Rollin H. Cooke Collection, which contains transcriptions of many western Massachusetts church records, can be ordered on microfilm from the Family History Library.

- Although few complete transcriptions of all records for a given church have been published, a journal may have published part of them verbatim or, more frequently, abstracts of baptisms, marriages, etc. *The New England Historical and Genealogical Register* for example, published a new-found volume of Swansea Baptist Church records in January 1985. Articles containing church records can be found using PERSI or other indexes.

Many of the published volumes of town vital records include church records of baptism, marriage and death. However, the "official series" [see the section on vital records] included such records only when there was no corresponding event in town records or when the church record differs in some way. For example, the children of Nicholas Harris appear in the published Wrentham vital records, most of them with birth dates but some with only baptismal dates. However, all of them appear in baptism records of the Original Church of Christ in Wrentham, available only at the church itself.

Although one may not find a transcription at NEHGS, there are some finding aids which will help to locate the records themselves:

- Worthley, Harold Field, ed., *Inventory of the Records of the Particular (Congregational) Churches of Massachusetts, Gathered 1620–1805* in *Harvard Theological Studies, XXV* (Cambridge, Mass.: Harvard University Press, 1970) REF BX7148/M4/W65/1970. This covers, of course, only the Congregational Churches, but is much more detailed and up to date than Wright (see below).

- *A Description of the Manuscript Collections in the Massachusetts Diocesan (Episcopal) Library* (Boston: The Survey, 1939) CD3299/B6/H5/1939.

- Duffy, Mark J., *Guide to the Parochial Archives of the Episcopal Church in Boston* (Boston: Episcopal Diocese of Massachusetts, Diocesan Library and Archives, 1981) REF CD3298/B67/D83/1981.

- Kirkham, E. Kay, *A Survey of American Church Records: for the Period before the Civil War, East of the Mississippi River*, 2 vols. (Salt Lake City: Deseret Book Co., 1959–60) CD3065/K52/1959.

- O'Toole, James M., *Guide to the Archives of the Archdiocese of Boston* (New York: Garland Publishing, 1982) CD3299/B6/O86/1982.

- Wright, Carroll D., Commissioner, *Report on the Custody and Condition of the Public Records of Parishes, Towns and Counties* (Boston: Wright & Potter, 1889) REF CD3290/A2. This is the author's annotated copy. Although this book tells you for what dates records existed in 1889 and their condition, it does not tell you what type of information they contain or where they were located.

Finally, there are some specific published church records which may not appear as such in the NEHGS catalogs. For example, in the *Publications of the Colonial Society of Massachusetts* (F61/C71) are "Records of the First Church in

Boston, 1630–1868," in vols. 39–41. These records also appear on CD-ROM as part of *The Records of the Churches of Boston,* transcribed by Robert J. Dunkle and Ann S. Lainhart (Boston: NEHGS, 2002).

Cemetery Records

While some Massachusetts cemetery records appear in the various books of published vital records, most of which include only records through 1849, many do not. One may find records of specific cemeteries amid records for a particular town or county, in the manuscript collection, and on microfilm, specifically in the Walter E. Corbin Collection.

To locate Massachusetts cemetery records in the library:

- Consult David Allen Lambert's *A Guide to Massachusetts Cemeteries* (Boston: NEHGS, 2002) F63/L36/2002 also LOAN also Microtext. Organized by town, this book specifically identifies transcriptions in the NEHGS library with call numbers.

- Use the various NEHGS catalogs.

- Consult PERSI.

- In the Family History Library Catalog, look under the category "cemeteries" on three levels: town, county and state. Check also under the Daughters of the American Revolution as author.

Newspapers

Some of the principal abstracted newspapers for Massachusetts are listed below. Abstracts of newspapers may be found in the periodicals listed under GENEALOGICAL AND HISTORICAL PERIODICALS. An unusual source with implications for the entire United States is Ruth-Ann Harris and B. Emer O'Keeffe, ed., *The Search for Missing Friends: Irish Immigrant Advertisements Placed in* The Boston Pilot *1831–1920,* 8 vols. (Boston: NEHGS, 1989–1999) REF F73.9/I6/S43/1989 also LOAN also on NEHGS CD-ROM.

- American Antiquarian Society, "Index of Marriages in the *Massachusetts Centinel,* 1784–1840," 7 vols., typescript (1952) REF F73.25/A44.

- American Antiquarian Society, "Index of Deaths in the *Massachusetts Centinel* and *Columbian Centinel,* 1784–1840," 12 vols., typescript (1952) REF F73.25/A45.

- American Antiquarian Society, "Index to Obituary Notices in the *Boston Transcript,* 1875–1899," 2 vols., typescript (Cleveland, Ohio: Bell & Howell, 1968?) F73.25/A40.

- American Antiquarian Society, "Index to Obituary Notices in the *Boston Transcript*, 1900–1930," 3 vols., typescript (Cleveland, Ohio: Bell & Howell, 1968?) F73.25/A40.

- Boston Athenaeum, *Index of Obituaries in Boston Newspapers, 1704–1800*, 3 vols. (Boston: G. K. Hall, 1968) REF F73.25/C6/1968.

- Dunkle, Robert J., and Ann S. Lainhart, *Deaths in Boston, 1700 to 1799*, 2 vols. (Boston: NEHGS 1999) REF F73.25/D86/1999 also LOAN. Includes death notices and estate notices from Boston newspapers.

- Pollock, Andrew, *Index to Advertisements in the Boston News Letter and Massachusetts Gazette*, 2 vols. (Duxbury, Mass.: the author, 1997) F73.1/P64/1997.

- Stevens, Cj, *The Massachusetts Magazine: Marriage and Death Notices, 1789–1796* (New Orleans: Polyanthos, 1978) REF F63/S74/1978.

For newspaper indexes, see New England Library Association, Bibliography Committee, *A Guide to Newspaper Indexes in New England* (Holden, Mass.: the Association, 1978) REF Z6293/N38/1978, and Anita Cheek Milner, *Newspaper Indexes: A Location and Subject Guide for Researchers*, 3 vols. (Metuchen, N.J.: Scarecrow Press, 1977–82) Z6951/M635 also LOAN.

Note the genealogical columns in the *Boston Evening Transcript*, 1848–1912, on microfilm, F73.1/B67.

Probate Records

In Massachusetts probate records are recorded at the county level. The following microfilms of probate records are at NEHGS with some printed indexes:

- Barnstable: General Index 1686–1950; Probate Record Books 1686–1910s (Vols. 1–196). F72/B2/P76.

- Berkshire: General Index 1761–1930; Docket Books 5575–30403 (1835–1917); Probate Record Books 1761–1916 (Vols. 1–224) F72/B5/B76.

- Bristol: General Index 1687–1926; Docket Books 1881–1915 (Vols. 1–31); Probate Record Books 1687–1916 (Vols. 1–379); Probate Files, 1690–1881. F72/B8/B54.

- Dukes: No General Index; Probate Record Books 1690–1885 (Vols. 1–23); other miscellaneous volumes to 1938. F72/M51/P76. Filed alphabetically as if titled Martha's Vineyard.

- Essex: Printed index, 1638–1840. F72/E7/U55/1987. Docket index, 1638–1840 (Vols. 1–16), 1841–1881 (Vols. 17–37); Probate Record Books (old series) 1671–1867 (Vols. 301–424); Probate Record Books (new series) 1638–1691; Probate Record Books (new series) 1816–1867 (Vols. 1–244). F72/E7/P76.

- Franklin: General Index 1812–1965; Docket Books 1–18,800 (1810–1923); Probate Record Books 1812–1894, vols. 1–71. F72/F8/M46.

- Hampden: General Index 1812–1986; Probate Packets 1809–1881 (1–12508); Probate Record Books (Vols. 1–240 [not all volumes included]); Miscellaneous volumes 1858–ca. 1886. F72/H2/H36.

- Hampshire: General Card Index 1660–1971; Probate Records 1660–1916 (Vols. 1–142); other miscellaneous volumes. F72/H3/H35.

- Middlesex: Printed General Indexes 1648–1909. F72/M7/M55; Docket Books, 1–45383; Probate Papers (first series) 1648–1871 (1–45383); Probate Files (second series) 1872–1909 (1–4702); Probate Record Books 1648–1901 (Vols. 1–609). F72/M7/M72.

- Nantucket: No General Index; Probate Record Books 1706–1867. F72/N2/P76.

- Norfolk: Printed Index, 1793–1900. F72/N8/M45/1910; General Index 1793–1929; Docket Books, 1–52476; Probate Record Books 1793–1916 (Vols. 1–275). F72/N8/P76.

- Old Norfolk: see under LAND RECORDS.

- Plymouth: Printed Index, 1686–1881. F72/P7/W6/1988; General Index 1686–1820 (includes dockets); Index with Docket Books, 1685–1881 and 1881–1939; Docket Books 1881–1967 (Vol. 1–76); Probate Record Books 1686–1903 (Vols. 1–214). F72/P7/P72.

- Suffolk: Printed Indexes 1636–1997. F72/S9/M45; Miscellaneous Dockets 1636–1923; Docket Books 1–118,206; Probate Record Books 1628–1916, vols. 1–1102; Docket Books 1900–1916, vols. 95–123; Probate Record Books, new series, 1636–1766, vols. 1–42. F72/S9/S835.

- Worcester: Printed Index, 1648–1871 (Series A); 1871–1920 (Series B) F72/W9/M45; General Index 1731–1881; Docket Books, 1–68399; Probate Record Books (Series A) 1731–1881 (Vols. 1–469). F72/W9/P76.

Probate Records and Abstracts in Print

- Sherman, Ruth Wilder, and Robert S. Wakefield, *Plymouth Colony Probate Guide . . . . 1620–1691* (Warwick, R.I.: Plymouth Colony Research Group, 1983) REF F63/S53/1983 also LOAN.

- Rounds, H. L. Peter, *Abstracts of Bristol County, Massachusetts, Probate Records, 1687–1762,* 2 vols. (Baltimore: Genealogical Publishing Co., 1987–88) F72/B8/R68/1987 also LOAN.

- Dow, George Francis, ed., *The Probate Records of Essex County, Massachusetts, 1635–1681,* 3 vols. (Salem, Mass.: Essex Institute, 1916–20) REF F72/E7/E47/1916 also LOAN.

- Rodgers, Robert H., *Middlesex County in the Colony of the Massachusetts Bay in New England: Records of Probate and Administration, October 1649–December 1660* (Boston: NEHGS, 1999) REF F72/M7/R63/1999 also LOAN; same author and title, . . . *March 1660/61–December 1670* (Boston: NEHGS, 2001) F72/M7/R632/2001 also LOAN.

- McGhan, Judith, *Suffolk County Wills: Abstracts of the Earliest Wills upon Record in the County of Suffolk, Massachusetts, from* The New England Historical and Genealogical Register (Baltimore: Genealogical Publishing Co., 1984) REF F72/S9/S88/1984 also LOAN.

Abstracts of many probate records have appeared in various periodicals, e.g., Worcester County probate in the *Mayflower Descendant*.

Land Records

In Massachusetts land records are recorded at the district level. Counties may have one, two or even three districts for recording deeds. See *Genealogist's Handbook for New England Research*, 104–14, and the *Red Book* (see under GUIDES AND FINDING AIDS) for the towns in each district and the date each district was created. For an explanation of the allocation of probate and land records among Hampshire County and its "daughter" counties, Franklin and Hampden, see the *Red Book*. In addition, town records (especially the proprietors records for a town) often contain land records.

Microfilms of land records are at NEHGS for the following counties:

- Berkshire: General Index 1761–1870; Deeds 1761–1925 (Vols. 1–313) F72/B5/L36. Middle District only.

- Bristol: General Index 1686–1956; Deeds 1686–1900 (Vols. 1–556) F72/B8/D44. Taunton Registry only.

- Dukes: General Index 1649–1895; Deeds 1641–1872 (Vols. 1–42); Proprietor Records 1641–1717. F72/M5/D85. Filed alphabetically as if titled Martha's Vineyard.

- Essex: General Index 1640–1879; Deeds 1640–1866 (Vols. 1–695) F72/E7/E87.

- Franklin: General Index 1787–1899; Deeds 1787–1902 (Vols. 1–485) F72/F8/D44.

- Hampden: General Index 1636–1909; Deeds 1638–1762 (Vols. A–Z); Deeds 1757–1902 (Vols. 1–602) F72/H2/H36.

- Hampshire: General Index 1787–1986; Deeds 1787–1900 (Vols. 1–541) F72/H3/H352.

- Middlesex: General Index 1639–1835; Deeds 1649–1802 (Vols. 1–147) F72/M7/M73.

- Nantucket: General Index 1657–1875; Deeds 1659–1866 (Vols. 1–58) F72/N2/N46.

- Old Norfolk: Deeds, wills, and other records 1647–1714 (Vols. 1–4) F67/N67. Includes index.

- Plymouth: General Index 1685–1859; Deeds (Vols. 1–200) F72/P7/P73.

- Suffolk: General Index 1639–1920; Index to Other Persons 1639–1799; Deeds 1640–1885 (Vols. 1–1706) F72/S9/S845.

- Worcester: General Index 1731–1889; Deeds 1722–1866 (Vols. 1–716) F72/W9/W675.

Land Record Abstracts in Print

- Essex Society of Genealogists, *Essex County Deeds, 1639–1678, Abstracts of Volumes 1–4 Copy Books, Essex County, Massachusetts* (Bowie, Md.: Heritage Books, 2003). IN PROCESS.

- The first fourteen volumes of Suffolk County land records (up to 1697) were published as *Suffolk Deeds*, 14 vols. (Boston: Rockwell & Churchill, 1880–1906) F72/S9/S9 also LOAN.

Town Records

The early official records of some towns have been published in various formats. The best known are probably the forty volumes of Boston records published by the Boston Record Commissioners (R.Rm. REF F73.1/B74 also LOAN). A helpful list of these Boston records is in Ann Smith Lainhart, *A Researcher's Guide to Boston* (Boston: NEHGS, 2003), 20–21, 81–82. REF F73.25/L35/2003 also LOAN.

For using town records, see Ann Smith Lainhart, *Digging for Genealogical Treasure in New England Town Records* (Boston: NEHGS, 1996) F3/L35/1996 also LOAN. Warnings out for some towns have been published, sometimes as a collection for the entire county (e.g., Plymouth and Worcester). Warnings out for Boston, 1745–1773 and 1791–1792, are alphabetically arranged in the Boston Overseers of the Poor Records, 1733–1925, 15 reels of microfilm. F73.25/B67/O6/1988.

Tax Records

Many tax lists appear among town records on microfilm. Others have been reproduced in periodicals or as a book. Two major tax lists are:

- *Massachusetts and Maine Direct Tax Census of 1798*, 18 reels of microfilm (Boston: NEHGS, 1978) F63/M343/1978 also LOAN also Web database. See also Michael H. Gorn, *An Index and Guide to the Microfilm Edition of the Massachusetts and Maine Direct Tax Census of 1798* (Boston: NEHGS, 1979) REF F63/M343/I53/1979 also LOAN also Microtext.

- Pruitt, Bettye Hobbs, *The Massachusetts Tax Valuation List of 1771* (1978; reprinted Camden, Maine: Picton Press, 1998) REF F63/P838/1998 also LOAN.

Some early tax lists are available at the State Library in the State House on Beacon Hill. These include the Massachusetts General Court, Valuation Committee, "Valuations, 1780–1792, 1810–1811," which are also available on microfilm from the Family History Library.

Court and Legislative Records

Most Massachusetts court records are not available in the library itself with the exception of the Supreme Judicial Court for Suffolk County, Records 1689–1799, Minutes 1702–1789. F72/S9/S838 Microfilm. However, some court records have been published, and most pre-twentieth century records may be ordered from the Family History Library.

Published records available in the library include:

- *Acts and Resolves, Public and Private, of the Province of the Massachusetts Bay*, 21 vols. (Boston: Wright & Potter, 1869–1922) Rare Book KFM2425/A2.

- *Journals of the House of Representatives of Massachusetts*, 49 vols. in 55 to date (Boston: Massachusetts Historical Society, 1919–) Vault J87/M4/1919.

- Konig, David Thomas, ed., *Plymouth Court Records, 1686–1859*, 16 vols. (Wilmington, Del.: Michael Glazier, Inc., in association with the Pilgrim Society, 1978–81) F72/P7/P8/1978. Also on CD (Boston: NEHGS, 2002).

- Menand, Catherine S., *A Research Guide to the Massachusetts Courts and their Records* (Boston: Massachusetts Supreme Judicial Court, Archives and Records Preservation, 1987) REF KFM2910/Z9/M4/1987 also LOAN.

- Menand, Catherine S., *A Guide to the Records of the Suffolk County Inferior Court of Common Pleas, in the Custody of the Social Law Library, Boston, Massachusetts* (Boston: Colonial Court Records Project, Social Law Library, 1981) CD3297/S9/1981 also LOAN.

- Noble, John et al., eds., *Records of the Court of Assistants of the Colony of the Massachusetts Bay, 1630–1692*, 3 vols. (Boston: Rockwell & Churchill, 1901–28) F67/M33/1901 also LOAN.

- Dow, George Francis, *Records and Files of the Quarterly Courts of Essex County, 1636-1686*, 9 vols. (Salem, Mass.: Essex Institute, 1911–75) F72/E7/E48/1911 also LOAN.

- Morison, Samuel Eliot, *Records of the Suffolk County Court, 1671–1680*, 2 vols. (Boston: Colonial Society of Massachusetts, 1933) F61/C71/v. 29–30 of *Publications of the Colonial Society of Massachusetts.*

- Shurtleff, Nathaniel B., and David Pulsifer, *Records of the Colony of New Plymouth*, 12 vols. in 10 (Boston: William White, 1855–61) F68/N55 also LOAN.

- Shurtleff, Nathaniel B., *Records of the Governor and Company of the Massachusetts Bay in New England*, 5 vols. in 6 (Boston: William White, 1853–54) Rare Book F67/M32/1853 also LOAN.

- Sanborn, Melinde Lutz, *Ages from Court Records, 1636–1700, Volume I: Essex, Middlesex, and Suffolk Counties, Massachusetts* (Baltimore: Genealogical Publishing Co., 2003) F63/S26/2003.

- Sanborn, Melinde Lutz, *Lost Babes: Fornication Abstracts from Court Records, Essex County, Massachusetts, 1692 to 1745* (Derry, N.H.: the author, 1992) F72/E7/S36/1992 also LOAN.

- Williams, Alicia Crane, "Plaintiff–Defendant Guide" to cases in the Suffolk County Court of Common Pleas from 1701 to 1708 is in the *Mayflower Descendant*, vols. 35–44 (1985–1994) REF F68/M46 also LOAN.

- Smith, Joseph H., ed., *Colonial Justice in Western Massachusetts, 1639–1702* (Cambridge, Mass.: Harvard University Press, 1961) KFM2935/M2.

Military Records

Works that are in databases on *New EnglandAncestors.org* are so indicated as "Web database." A single database, "Massachusetts Soldiers in the Colonial Wars," includes all the references for Colonial Wars except Bodge.

Colonial Wars

- Bodge, George Madison, *Soldiers in King Philip's War*, 3rd ed. (1906; reprinted Baltimore: Genealogical Publishing Co., 1967) REF E83.67/B662/1906 also LOAN.

- Donahue, Mary E., *Massachusetts Officers and Soldiers, 1702–1722: Queen Anne's War to Dummer's War* (Boston: Society of Colonial Wars in the Commonwealth of Massachusetts, 1980) E197/D66/1980 also LOAN also Web database.

- Goss, K. David, and David Zorowin, *Massachusetts Officers and Soldiers in the French and Indian Wars, 1755–56* (Boston: Society of Colonial Wars in the Commonwealth of Massachusetts, 1985) REF/E199/M414 also LOAN also Web database.

- Stachiw, Myron O., *Massachusetts Officers and Soldiers, 1723–1743: Dummer's War to the War of Jenkins' Ear* (Boston: Society of Colonial Wars in the Commonwealth of Massachusetts, 1979) E195/S7/1979 also LOAN also Web database.

- MacKay, Robert E., *Massachusetts Soldiers in the French and Indian Wars, 1744–1755* (Boston: Society of Colonial Wars in the Commonwealth of Massachusetts, 1978) REF/E199/M35/1978 also LOAN also Web database.

- Voye, Nancy S., *Massachusetts Officers in the French and Indian Wars, 1748–1763* (Boston: Society of Colonial Wars in the Commonwealth of Massachusetts, 1975) REF/E199/V84/1975 also LOAN also Web database.

Revolutionary War

- *Massachusetts Soldiers and Sailors of the Revolutionary War*, 17 vols. (Boston: Wright & Potter, 1896–1908) REF E263/M4/M4/1896 also LOAN. A supplement on microfilm is in Microtext. E263/M4/M42.

- Hambrick-Stowe, Charles E., and Donna D. Smerlas, ed., *Massachusetts Militia Companies and Officers in the Lexington Alarm* (Boston: Society of Colonial Wars in the Commonwealth of Massachusetts et al., 1976) REF E/241/L6/H35/1976 also LOAN also Web database.

- Whittemore, Bradford A., *Memorials of the Massachusetts Society of the Cincinnati* (Boston: the Society, 1964) REF E/202.1/M3832/1964. See also the related database on *New EnglandAncestors.org*.

- Maas, David E., *Divided Hearts: Massachusetts Loyalists, 1765–1790* (Boston: Society of Colonial Wars in the Commonwealth of Massachusetts, 1980) REF E/277/M3/1980 also LOAN also Web database.

- Jones, E. Alfred, *The Loyalists of Massachusetts* (London: Saint Catherine Press, 1930) REF E/277/J77 also LOAN.

- Stark, James H., *The Loyalists of Massachusetts* (Boston: the author, 1910) E277/S79/1910 also LOAN.

War of 1812

- Baker, John, *Records of the Massachusetts Volunteer Militia Called Out by the Governor of Massachusetts to Suppress a Threatened Invasion During the War of 1812–1814* (Boston: Wright & Potter, 1913) REF E359.5/M3/1913.

Civil War

- Higginson, Thomas et al., *Massachusetts in the Army and Navy During the War of 1861–1865*, 2 vols. (Boston: Wright & Potter, 1896–1935) E513.3/H63/1895.

- *Massachusetts Soldiers, Sailors and Marines in the Civil War*, 9 vols. (Norwood, Mass.: Norwood Press, 1931–37) REF E513/M32/1931 also LOAN. Also on microfiche and CD-ROM (Novato, Calif.: Brøderbund, 1997).

Genealogical and Biographical Compendia (Including Town and County Histories)

Many town histories include genealogical sections, some more carefully compiled than others. *A Surname Guide to Massachusetts Town Histories* by Phyllis O. Longver and Pauline J. Oesterlin (Bowie, Md.: Heritage Books, 1993) REF F63/L66/1993 also LOAN, helps in locating families, particularly those with unusual surnames.

Besides various county histories, too numerous to include here, other compendia, some every-name searchable on CD and/or the Internet, include:

- Anderson, Robert Charles, *The Great Migration Begins: Immigrants to New England 1620–1633*, 3 vols. (Boston: NEHGS, 1995) REF F7/G74/1995 also LOAN also Intl REF and on *NewEnglandAncestors.org*. See NEW ENGLAND OVERVIEW.

- Anderson, Robert Charles, George F. Sanborn Jr., and Melinde Lutz Sanborn, *The Great Migration: Immigrants to New England 1634–1635, Volume I A–B* (Boston: NEHGS, 1999) and *Volume II C–F* (Boston: NEHGS, 2001); Robert Charles Anderson, *The Great Migration: Immigrants to New England 1634–1635, Volume III G–H* (Boston: NEHGS, 2003) REF F7/G742/1999 also LOAN also Intl REF. See NEW ENGLAND OVERVIEW.

- Brownson, Lydia, et al., "Genealogical Notes of Cape Cod Families," manuscript on microfilm, 8 reels. F72/C3/B88/1972.

- Cutter, William Richard, *Genealogical and Personal Memoirs Relating to the Families of Boston and Eastern Massachusetts* (1908; reprinted Baltimore: Genealogical Publishing Co., 1995) F63/C99/1908 also LOAN.

- *Families of the Pioneer Valley*, CD-ROM (West Springfield, Mass.: Regional Publications, 2000). Includes Thomas B. Warren's manuscript on Springfield families, which is also on microfilm at NEHGS, and various Pynchon vital and court records.

- *Family History: New England Families #1, 1600s–1800s*, CD #117 (Brøderbund, 1996). Includes various family genealogies and town histories.

- *Genealogical Records: Early New England Settlers, 1600s–1800s*, CD #504 (Brøderbund, 1999).

- Goodwin, Nathaniel, *Genealogical Notes . . . of the First Settlers of Connecticut and Massachusetts* (1856; reprinted Baltimore: Genealogical Publishing Co., 1969) F93/G65/1969 also LOAN.

- *Local and Family Histories: Massachusetts, 1620–1930*, CD #207 (Brøderbund, 1998).

- *Mayflower Families Through Five Generations*, 22 vols. to date (Plymouth, Mass.: General Society of Mayflower Descendants, 1975–present) REF F63/

M397 . . . . also LOAN. See also *Mayflower Families in Progress* (Plymouth, Mass.: General Society of Mayflower Descendants, 1986–present) REF F63/ M397 . . . . also LOAN. The latter volumes ("pink books") are ultimately superseded by the former volumes ("silver books").

- Bacon, Edwin M., ed., *Men of Progress: One Thousand Biographical Sketches and Portraits of Leaders in Business and Professional Life in the Commonwealth of Massachusetts* (Boston: New England Magazine, 1896) REF F63/M533/ 1896 also LOAN.

- *Representative Men and Old Families of Southeastern Massachusetts*, 3 vols. (Chicago: J.H. Beers, 1912) F63/R4/1912 also LOAN.

- Savage, James, *A Genealogical Dictionary of the First Settlers of New England*, 4 vols. (Boston: Little, Brown & Co., 1860–62; reprinted Baltimore: Genealogical Publishing Co., 1965) R.Rm. REF F3/S2/1860 also LOAN also Rare Book. Also on CD #113, *Family History Collection: 217 Genealogy Books* (Brøderbund, 1995) and on CD #169 *Genealogical Records: Genealogical Dictionary of New England, 1600s–1700s* (Brøderbund, 1998).

- Thomas, M. Halsey, ed., *The Diary of Samuel Sewall, 1674–1729*, 2 vols. (New York: Farrar, Straus & Giroux, 1973) F67/S48/1973.

- Stratton, Eugene Aubrey, *Plymouth Colony: Its History & Its People, 1620–1691* (Salt Lake City: Ancestry, 1986) F68/S87/1986 also LOAN.

- Lockwood, John Hoyt, *Western Massachusetts, a History, 1636–1925*, 4 vols. (New York: Lewis Historical Publishing Co., 1926), vols. 3–4 contain biographies. F64/L76/1926 also LOAN.

NEHGS has published some collections on CD-ROM, including:

- Bond, Henry, *Genealogies of the Families and Descendants of the Early Settlers of Watertown, Massachusetts*, on CD-ROM together with *Watertown Records* (Boston: NEHGS, 2002).

- Sprague, Waldo Chamberlain, *Genealogies of the Families of Braintree, Massachusetts* (Boston: NEHGS, 2001). Also on microfilm. The original manuscript is at NEHGS, SG/SPR/17.

- Thwing, Annie Haven, *Inhabitants and Estates of the Town of Boston, 1630–1800 and The Crooked and Narrow Streets of Boston, 1630–1822* (Boston: NEHGS and the Massachusetts Historical Society, 2001).

- Corbin, Walter E., *The Corbin Collection, Volume 1, Records of Hampshire County, Massachusetts* and *Volume 2, Records of Hampden County, Massachusetts*, Robert J. Dunkle, ed., CD-ROM (Boston: NEHGS, 2003–04). This collection on microfilm contains records of other towns and compiled genealogies. F63/ C8 Microfilm also LOAN.

Maps and Atlases

Statewide

- *Historical Data Relating to Counties, Cities and Towns in Massachusetts*, 5th ed. (Boston: NEHGS, 1997) REF F64/M5/1997 also LOAN. See under GUIDES AND FINDING AIDS above.

- Davis, Charlotte Pease, *Directory of Massachusetts Place Names, Current and Obsolete, Counties, Cities, Towns, Sections or Villages, Early Names* (n.p.: Massachusetts Daughters of the American Revolution, 1987) REF F62/D39/1987.

- Gannett, Henry, *A Geographic Dictionary of Massachusetts*, originally published as U.S. Geological Survey, Bulletin no. 116 (Washington, D.C.: U.S. Government Printing Office, 1894; reprinted Baltimore: Genealogical Publishing Co., 1978) REF F6/G36/1978.

- Hayward, John, *A Gazetteer of Massachusetts*, rev. ed. (Boston: J. P. Jewett, 1849) REF F62/H42/1849.

- Nason, Elias, *A Gazetteer of the State of Massachusetts*, rev. ed. (Boston: B. B. Russell, 1890) REF F62/N27/1890.

- Spofford, Jeremiah, *A Gazetteer of Massachusetts* (Newburyport, Mass.: C. Whipple, 1828) Rare Book F62/S76/1828.

- Wilkie, Richard W., and Jack Tager, *Historical Atlas of Massachusetts* (Amherst, Mass.: University of Massachusetts Press, 1991) G1230/H5/1991.

- Walker, O. W., *Atlas of Massachusetts* (Boston: Geo. H. Walker, 1891) No call number. This shows much detail.

County Atlases

- *Atlas of Barnstable County, Massachusetts* (Boston: G. H. Walker, 1880). Reprinted as *1880 Atlas of Barnstable County, Massachusetts: Cape Cod's Earliest Atlas* (Yarmouthport, Mass.: On Cape Publications, 1998) Atlas G1233/C3/E54/1998.

- Gibson, Marjorie Hubbell, *Historical & Genealogical Atlas & Guide to Barnstable County, Mass. (Cape Cod)* (Falmouth, Mass.: Falmouth Genealogical Society, 1995; reprinted with addendum, Teaticket, Mass.: Falmouth Genealogical Society, 1998) F72/C3/G5/1995 and 1998.

- *Atlas of Bristol Co., Massachusetts, from Actual Surveys* (New York: F. W. Beers, 1871) No call number.

- *Atlas of Essex County, Massachusetts* (Philadelphia: D. G. Beers, 1872) No call number.

- Walker, George H., *The Old Maps of Northeastern Essex County, Massachusetts, in 1884* (Fryeburg, Maine: Saco Valley Printing, 1982) F72/E7/O53/1982.

- Walker, George H., *The Old Maps of Southern Essex County, Massachusetts, in 1884* (Fryeburg, Maine: Saco Valley Printing, 1984) G1233.E7/O4/1984.

- Beers, F. W., *County Atlas of Middlesex, Massachusetts* (New York: J. B. Beers & Co., 1875) No call number.

- *Atlas of Norfolk County, Massachusetts, from Recent and Actual Surveys & Records* (New York: Comstock and Cline, 1876) No call number.

- Hopkins, G. M., *Atlas of the County of Suffolk, Massachusetts*, 5 vols. (Philadelphia: G. Hopkins, 1873–75) No call number.

  See also F. W. Beers atlases on CD-ROM for Berkshire, Bristol, Essex, Franklin, Hampden, Hampshire, Middlesex, and Worcester counties.

Special Sources for Massachusetts

African Americans and Native Americans

- Carvalho, Joseph, *Black Families in Hampden County, Massachusetts, 1650–1855* (Boston: NEHGS, 1984) F72/H2/C37/1984 also LOAN.

- Dorman, Franklin A. *Twenty Families of Color in Massachusetts 1742–1998* (Boston: NEHGS, 1998) E185.93/D67/1998 also LOAN.

- Segel, Jerome D. and R. Andrew Pierce, *The Wampanoag Genealogical History of Martha's Vineyard, Massachusetts . . . Volume 1. . . .* (Baltimore: Genealogical Publishing Co., 2003) E99/W2/S44/2003 also LOAN.

- "Massachusetts Blacks and Indians in the American Revolution," in Eric G. Grundset, ed., *African American and American Indian Patriots of the Revolutionary War* (Washington, D.C.: National Society Daughters of the American Revolution, 2001), 27–52. E269/N3/A37/2001.

Witchcraft

- Hall, David D., *Witch-Hunting in Seventeenth-Century New England: A Documentary History, 1638–1692* (Boston: Northeastern University Press, 1991) IN CATALOGING.

- Roach, Marilynne K., "Records of the Rev. Samuel Parris, Salem Village, Massachusetts, 1688–1696," *The New England Historical and Genealogical Register* 157 (2003): 6–30, and sources cited therein.

Miscellaneous Sources

- Coleman, Emma Lewis, *New England Captives Carried to Canada Between 1677 and 1760 During the French and Indian Wars*, 2 vols. (Portland, Maine: Southworth Press, 1925; reprinted Bowie, Md.: Heritage Books, 1989) E85/C72/1925 also LOAN.

- Hearn, Daniel Allen, *Legal Executions in New England: A Comprehensive Review, 1623–1960* (Jefferson, N.C.: McFarland & Co., 1999) F4/H42/1999 also LOAN.

- Kane, Patricia, et al., *Colonial Massachusetts Silversmiths and Jewelers* (New Haven, Conn.: Yale University Art Gallery, 1998) NK7112/K35/1998.

- Schutz, John A. *Legislators of the Massachusetts General Court 1691–1780: A Biographical Dictionary* (Boston: Northeastern University Press, 1997) REF F67/L4/S38/1997 also Web database

- The Scots' Charitable Society was founded in Boston in 1657. NEHGS has four microfilms titled *Records of the Scots' Charitable Society* (Cambridge, Mass.: General Microfilm Co., 1980) F73.1/S36/R43/1979. These records are indexed in David Dobson, *Scots in New England, 1623–1873* (Baltimore: Genealogical Publishing Co., 2002) F15/S3/D63/2002. See the catalog for related materials.

- *Sibley's Harvard Graduates*. This is actually a series first edited by John Langdon Sibley and continued by Clifford K. Shipton, titled *Biographical Sketches of Graduates of Harvard University*, 18 vols. to date (Boston: Massachusetts Historical Society, 1873–1999) REF LD2139/S5.

New Hampshire

Sherry L. Gould

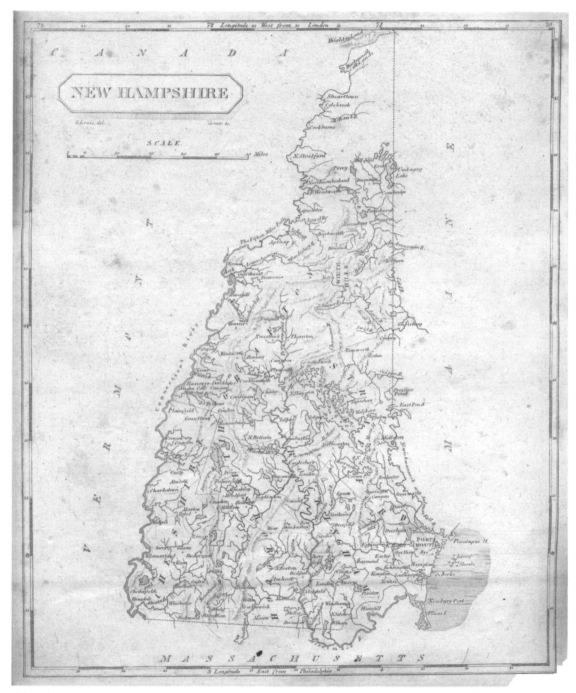

New Hampshire from *A New and Elegant General Atlas* by Arrowsmith and Lewis (Boston: Thomas & Andrews, 1805).

Overview

New Hampshire researchers enjoy an abundance of early records, some of the very earliest being from our seacoast settlements. The New Hampshire collection at NEHGS is one of the most comprehensive areas at the Society, made possible by a generous endowment from Ethel Farrington Smith and gifts from Dean and Roberta Smith. Many probate records, statewide vital records, early town records, and most deeds from across the state may be searched on microfilm right in Boston. The manuscript and printed book collections are equally extensive, allowing researchers really to dig into their ancestry before ever visiting their ancestral homeland for those rare New Hampshire gems found only in the state.

New Hampshire has a large array of town histories, many of which have genealogies and are found at NEHGS. Bill Copeley, librarian at the New Hampshire Historical Society, has compiled an *Index to Genealogies in New Hampshire Town Histories,* listed below. These town histories and the overwhelming collection of family histories can be found by using the library catalogs. Supporting documentation used by authors in compiling family histories may even be found, such as Charles Burleigh's correspondence files used in the compilation of the *Ingalls Genealogy.* Information such as this can assist the researcher in determining the validity of undocumented family histories.

A key source affecting all colonial research is *New Hampshire Provincial and State Papers,* 40 vols. (Concord and Manchester, N.H.: 1867–1943) F34/N54 also LOAN. This set was authorized by the legislature of New Hampshire and is an invaluable aid to researchers. Many of the early state and town records are included within the set. Each volume is individually indexed, and the New Hampshire Division of Records Management and Archives is completing a combined index. See R. Stuart Wallace, "The State Papers: A Descriptive Guide," *Historical New Hampshire* 31 (1976):119–28 (F31/H57), for a full discussion of the contents.

Guides and Finding Aids

- Copeley, William N., *Index to Genealogies in New Hampshire Town Histories* (Concord, N.H.: New Hampshire Historical Society, 2000) R.Rm. REF F33/ C66 also LOAN. This valuable work is arranged by family name and lists every town history that has genealogical information on a given family treated for three or more generations.

- Sanborn, George F., Jr., and Alice Eichholz, ed., "New Hampshire," in *Red Book: American State, County, and Town Sources,* 3rd ed. (Provo, Utah: Ancestry, 2004), 429–45. REF CS49/A55/2004 also LOAN.

- Noyes, Sybil, Charles Thornton Libby, and Walter Goodwin Davis, *Genealogical Dictionary of Maine and New Hampshire* (Portland, Maine: Southworth-

Anthoensen Press, 1928–39; reprinted Baltimore: Genealogical Publishing Co., 1972) R.Rm. REF F18/N68/1928 also LOAN. This is the "Bible" for seventeenth-century New Hampshire families, with excellent documentation.

- Pope, Charles H., *The Pioneers of Maine and New Hampshire, 1623 to 1660* (1908; reprinted Baltimore: Genealogical Publishing Co., 1973) R.Rm. REF F18/P82/1908 also LOAN.

- Lambert, David Allen, "New Hampshire Genealogy Part 2," *New England Ancestors* 1:1 (Premiere Issue, 2000) REF F1/N49 also LOAN.

- Dearborn, David C., "New Hampshire Genealogy: A Perspective," *The New England Historical and Genealogical Register*, 130 (1976):244–58; reprinted in Ralph J. Crandall, ed., *Genealogical Research in New England* (Baltimore: Genealogical Publishing Co., 1984) R.Rm. REF F3/G46/1984 also LOAN.

- Melnyk, Marcia D., *Genealogist's Handbook for New England Research*, 4th ed. (Boston: NEHGS, 1999), 143–69. R.Rm. REF F3/G466/1999 also LOAN.

- Holbrook, Jay Mack, *New Hampshire Residents, 1633–1699* (Oxford, Mass.: Holbrook Research Institute, 1979) F33/H638/1979 also LOAN.

- Towle, Laird C., and Ann N. Brown, *New Hampshire Genealogical Research Guide*, 2nd ed. (Bowie, Md.: Heritage Books, 1983) REF F33/T68/1983 also LOAN.

- Haskell, John D., and T. D. Seymour Bassett, ed., *New Hampshire: A Bibliography of Its History* (Boston: G. K. Hall, 1979) R.Rm. REF F34/N49/1979 also LOAN.

- Hammond, Otis Grant, *Check List of New Hampshire Local History* (Concord, N.H.: New Hampshire Historical Society, 1925) F34/H36/1925 also LOAN. Good source for all New Hampshire town, state, and county histories written by 1925.

- Gould, Sherry L., "A Guide to Genealogical Research in New Hampshire," *New England Ancestors* 4 (Holiday 2003):15–21. REF F1/N49 also Loan. See also the online articles by the same author at *NewEnglandAncestors.org*.

Genealogical and Historical Periodicals

- *The New Hampshire Genealogical Record* (Exeter, N.H.: New Hampshire Society of Genealogists, 1903–present) REF F33/N54 also LOAN. This was published from 1903 through 1910, and then revived in 1990 with vol. 8. It is an excellent source for genealogical information for New Hampshire families.

- *American-Canadian Genealogist* (Manchester, N.H.: American-Canadian Genealogical Society, 1975–present) E184/F85/G46 [called *The Genealogist* until 1994]. This is an important source for French-Canadian ancestry.

- *Historical New Hampshire* (Concord, N.H.: New Hampshire Historical Society, 1944–present) F31/H57. Good historical content for a broad range of historical subjects; subject index for vols. 1–35.

- *The Granite Monthly* (Manchester, N.H.: E. T. McShane, 1877–1930) F31/G75 also LOAN. Many excellent articles can be found in this early journal, some of which are listed in this chapter.

- *New Hampshire Genealogical Digest, 1623–1800*, vol. 1 (Bowie, Md.: Heritage Books, 1986) F33/T66/1986 v. 1 also LOAN. Only one volume published.

- *A Collection of New Hampshire Registers with Note and Comment Thereon by Joseph A. Stickney* [Cover Title: *The New Hampshire Register*] (Great Falls, N.H.: Fred L. Shapleigh, 1887) NH/55/14.

- *The New England Historical and Genealogical Register*, 1847–present. R.Rm. REF F1/N56 also LOAN also fifth floor also Web database. See NEW ENGLAND OVERVIEW.

Censuses: Colonial, Federal, and State

Colonial

New Hampshire had no colonial censuses; however there are some tax and other lists that have served as census substitutes for various years:

- Holbrook, Jay Mack, *New Hampshire 1732 Census* (Oxford, Mass.: Holbrook Research Institute, 1981) REF F33/H63/1981.

- Oesterlin, Pauline Johnson, *New Hampshire 1742 Estate List* (Bowie, Md.: Heritage Books, 1994) F33/O32/1994 also LOAN.

- Wilson, Emily S., *Inhabitants of New Hampshire, 1776* (1983; reprinted Baltimore: Genealogical Publishing Co., 1993) F33/W72/1983 also LOAN. This list should not be construed to contain all male inhabitants; some town are not included. A list of included towns appears on p. 123. Also, some towns did not include those men engaged in the American Revolution.

- Holbrook, Jay Mack, *New Hampshire 1776 Census (Oxford, Mass.: Holbrook Research Institute, 1976) REF F33/H64 also LOAN. See preceding note.*

Federal

New Hampshire censuses for the years 1790–1930 are available at NEHGS on microfilm, with indexes for years 1790–1870 and 1890, and Soundex indexes on microfilm for the years 1880, 1900 and 1920, and a book Mortality Schedule for 1850. Parts of Rockingham and Strafford Counties are missing from the 1800 census films. Grafton County and parts of Rockingham and Strafford Counties are missing from the 1820 census films. The 1800 census has been published as John Brooks Threlfall, transcriber, *Heads of families at the second census of the United States taken in the year 1800, New Hampshire* (Madison, Wis.: the transcriber, 1973) Microtext F33/T47 also LOAN. The 1850 census for Hillsborough County has been published as Ann L. Nichols Brown, *1850 Census, Hillsborough County, New Hampshire: Including Population and Mortality Schedules*, 2 vols. bound in 3 (Bowie, Md.: Heritage Books, 1992) F42/H6/B76/1992 also LOAN.

State

New Hampshire has had no state censuses.

Vital Records

In addition to the statewide sources listed below, vital records for many towns have been published as books or as articles in *The New Hampshire Genealogical Record*. A few of these include church and cemetery records, such as George Freeman Sanborn Jr. and Melinde Lutz Sanborn, *Vital Records of Hampton, New Hampshire, to the End of the Year 1900*, 2 vols. (Boston: NEHGS, 1992–98). The marriages for towns in Strafford County have been published in three volumes.

- *New Hampshire Vital Records*. F33/N454 Microfilm. Statewide vital records are filed in a Soundex system using the first and third letters of the surname, followed by the second and fourth letters. This system has confounded some researchers, especially those using the microfilmed records in sites other than the state office. Uncommon surnames are grouped with others sharing the same beginning.

- *Index to Early Town Records of New Hampshire, 1639–1910*. F33/N457 Microfilm. This index, prepared by the WPA, does not index seven towns. Two of the missing towns are Exeter and Dover, both early settlements. The index is to the town records found in the following entry. It does not indicate what the references mention except that a birth or death is indicated as "F.R." and a marriage indicated as "M.R."

- *State of New Hampshire Town Records*. F33/N458 Microfilm. Prior to 1866 all vital records were kept by the towns; the state became an additional repository by law after that date. It took several years for the towns to comply.

- Oesterlin, Pauline Johnson, *New Hampshire Marriage Licenses and Intentions 1709–1961* (Bowie, Md.: Heritage Books, 1991) F33/O37/1991 also LOAN. This represents an important collection of surviving records now housed at the State Archives, many of which may not be recorded elsewhere.

- Cohen, Sheldon S., "What Man Hath Put Asunder: Divorce in New Hampshire, 1681–1784," *Historical New Hampshire* 41 (1986):118–41. F31/H57.

For name changes, see David Paul Davenport, "Name Changes in New Hampshire, 1679–1883," *Genealogical Journal* 15 (1986):67–103, 213–48. CS1/G382 also LOAN, and Richard P. Roberts, *New Hampshire Name Changes, 1768–1923* (Bowie, Md.: Heritage Books, 1996) F33/R63/1996.

Note also family records, especially William N. Copeley, *New Hampshire Family Records* (Bowie, Md.: Heritage Books, 1994) F33/C67/1994. These are taken from the Bible record collection at the New Hampshire Historical Society.

Church Records

The records of many New Hampshire churches have been published as books or as articles in *The New Hampshire Genealogical Record*, *The New England Historical and Genealogical Register*, or *The Granite Monthly*. NEHGS has manuscripts of some New Hampshire church records. All of these can be found using the NEHGS library catalogs, PERSI (see NEW ENGLAND OVERVIEW), the various subject indexes to *The New England Historical and Genealogical Register*, and this author's online column, "New Hampshire Church Records," posted January 10, 2003 on *NewEnglandAncestors.org*.

Two publications with statewide coverage are William Copeley, "Church Records at the New Hampshire Historical Society," *Historical New Hampshire* 39 (1984):152–59, and

Michael J. Denis, *Inventory of the Roman Catholic Church Records in New Hampshire* (Oakland, Maine: Danbury House Books, 1985) F33/H55/1985 (the original inventory done by the Historical Records Survey in 1938 is also at NEHGS, REF F33/H55/1938).

Because of southern New Hampshire's proximity to Maine and Massachusetts, the church records of those two states often include New Hampshire residents. For example, the marriages of the Hampton–Amesbury Quarterly Friends Meeting were published in *Vital Records of the Amesbury, Massachusetts, to the End of the Year 1849* (Topsfield, Mass.: Topsfield Historical Society, 1913) R.Rm. REF F74/A4/A4/1913.

Cemetery Records

The records of many New Hampshire cemeteries have been published as books or as articles in *The New Hampshire Genealogical Record*, *The New England Historical and Genealogical Register*, or *The Granite Monthly*. NEHGS has manuscripts of some New Hampshire cemeteries. All of these can be found using the NEHGS library catalogs, PERSI (see NEW ENGLAND OVERVIEW), and the various subject indexes to *The New England Historical and Genealogical Register*. The New Hampshire Old Graveyard Association (NHOGA) maintains a website (*rootsweb.com/~nhoga*) with a Master Burial Site Index that may be useful.

The New Hampshire Historical Society has an extensive collection of cemetery records. Two published statewide sources are Winifred Lane Goss, *Colonial Gravestone Inscriptions in the State of New Hampshire* (Dover, N.H.: Historic Activities Committee of the National Society of the Colonial Dames of America, New Hampshire, 1942) F33/G6/1942 also LOAN, and Mrs. Josiah Carpenter, *Gravestone Inscriptions Gathered by the Old Burial Grounds Committee of the National Society of the Colonial Dames of the America in the State of New Hampshire* (Cambridge, Mass.: Riverside Press, 1913) Rare Book F33/C37/1913.

Newspapers

Because of southern New Hampshire's proximity to Maine and Massachusetts, newspapers published in those states often include New Hampshire residents. Besides the following abstracts, briefer ones have been published in *The New Hampshire Genealogical Record*. Note that the abstracts of the *New Hampshire Gazette* may overlap with each other.

- *An Index to the Issues of the Farmer's Cabinet: Published at Amherst, New Hampshire from 1802 through 1820* (Baltimore: F.P. O'Neill, 1991) F44/A6/I53/1991 Microfilm. This newspaper carried details about families that may not be found elsewhere.

- Chipman, Scott Lee, *Genealogical Abstracts from Early New Hampshire Newspapers* (Bowie, Md.: Heritage Books, 2000) F33/C48/2000 also LOAN.

- Chipman, Scott Lee, *New England Vital Records from the* Exeter News-Letter, 5 vols. for 1831–1865 (Camden, Maine: Picton Press, 1993–95) REF F44/C54/1993 also LOAN.

- Hammond, Otis Grant, *Notices from the New Hampshire Gazette, 1765–1800* (Lambertville, N.J.: Hunterdon House, 1970) F33/H36/1970 also LOAN.

- Hammond, Priscilla, "Vital Records Contained in the New Hampshire Gazette, 1756–1800," manuscript, 1937, online database on *NewEnglandAncestors.org*.

- Sanborn, Melinde Lutz, "Vital Records from *The Argus and Spectator* of Newport, New Hampshire," *The New Hampshire Genealogical Record*, vols. 15–present.

- Scobie, Robert, *Genealogical Abstracts From the New Hampshire Mercury, 1784–1788* (Bowie, Md.: Heritage Books, 1997) F44/P8/S35/1997.

- Wentworth, William Edgar, *Vital Records 1790–1829 from Dover, New Hampshire's First Newspaper* (Camden, Maine: Picton Press, 1995) F44/D7/W46/1994 also LOAN.

- Young, David C., and Elizabeth K. Young, "Notices from the New Hampshire Gazette (1765–1795)," *Genealogical Journal* 16:4 (Fall/Winter 1987):206–30; 17:1 & 2 (1988/89):39–62. CS1/G382 also LOAN.

- Young, David Colby, and Robert L. Taylor, *Death Notices from Freewill Baptist Publications, 1811–1851* (Bowie, Md.: Heritage Books, 1985) F3/Y67/1985 also LOAN.

- Young, David C., and Elizabeth Keene Young, *Marriages and Divorce Records from Freewill Baptist Publications, 1819–1851*, 2 vols. (Bowie, Md.: Heritage Books, 1995) F3/Y672/1994 also LOAN.

Probate Records

The earliest available probate data is contained in the Provincial records, published in Volumes 31 to 39 of the *New Hampshire Provincial and State Papers*, covering the years between 1635 through 1771. The preface to each of these volumes describes how the records were located and provides useful information for subsequent research. There is a microfilmed index to the probate data in this series (F42/R7/R75). The library also has microfiche of the original provincial probate records (F33/N45/P7 Microfiche) and a related every-name index on microfilm (F33/N45/P7/Index/1987).

The indexes and docket books for many probate records are available on microfilm at NEHGS listed below.

- **Belknap County**: Probate Index 1841–1898 and Docket Books 1–49. F42/B4/M44.

- **Carroll County**: Probate Index 1840–1990 and Probate Packets 1–8432. F42/C3/C31.

- **Cheshire County**: Probate Docket Books 1771–1869, vols. 1–86. F42/C5/C53.

- **Coos County**: Probate Index 1886–1992 and Probate Packets 1885–1931. F42/C7/C662.

- **Grafton County**: Probate Index 1773–1950 and Docket Books 1773–1924, vols. 1–114. F42/G7/G73.

- **Hillsborough County**: Probate Index 1771–1869 and Docket Books 1771–1957, vols. 1–254. F42/H6/H62. The probate index 1771–1884 has also been published.

- **Merrimack County**: Probate Index 1823–1929 and Probate Records 1823–1923. F42/M5/M54.

- **Rockingham County**: Probate Index 1660–1894 and Docket Books 1771–1856, vols. 21–100. F42/R7/R73.

- **Strafford County**: Probate Index 1773–1989 and Docket Books 1773–1943, vols. 1–170. F42/S8/S87.

- **Sullivan County**: Probate Index 1827–1874 and Probate Packets 1827–1850. F42/S87/S872.

Probate Records in Abstract

- Evans, Helen F., *Abstracts of the Probate Records of Rockingham County, New Hampshire 1771–1799*, 2 vols. (Bowie Md.: Heritage Books, 2000) F42/R7/E93/2000.

- Evans, Helen F., *Abstracts of the Probate Records of Strafford County, New Hampshire 1771–1799* (Bowie Md.: Heritage Books, 1983) F42/S8/P46/1990 also LOAN.

Land Records

Land records for the provincial period (up to 1771) are now labeled as vols. 1–100 of Rockingham County deeds. There is a microfilmed index to these deeds (F42/R7/R75) which is actually a calendar with a summary of the contents of each deed.

Some early deeds for New Hampshire are recorded with Old Norfolk County, Massachusetts, deeds, and others with the so-called "Ipswich Deeds."

- Roberts, E. N., "Understanding New Hampshire Town Land Records," *Heritage Quest* 35 (July-August 1991):50. CS1/H47.

- Dearborn, David Curtis, "The Old Norfolk County Records," *The Essex Genealogist* 3 (1983), 194–96. F72/E7/E6 also LOAN.

- Old Norfolk County: Land Records to 1714. F67/N67 Microfilm. Old Norfolk County included the towns of Salisbury, Hampton, Haverhill, Exeter, Dover, and Strawberry Banke. Salisbury and Haverhill are now in Essex County, Massachusetts. Hampton, Exeter, and Strawberry Banke are now in Rockingham County, New Hampshire; and Dover is now in Strafford County, New Hampshire.

- "Ipswich Deeds." F74/I6/D44 Microfilm. These include various documents starting in 1639 for Essex County, Massachusetts.

The following land records are available on microfilm at NEHGS. In addition, town records often contain land records.

- **Belknap County**: Deed (Grantor/Grantee) Index 1765–1896, Index 1896–1915, and Deeds 1771–1901, vols. 51–105. F42/B4/B44.

- **Carroll County**: Deed (Grantor/Grantee) Index 1841–1909. F42/C3/C31, and Deeds 1841–1901, vols. 1–115. F42/C3/C32.

- **Cheshire County**: Deed (Grantor/Grantee) Index 1771–1869 and Deeds 1771–1860, vols. 1–98. F42/C5C52.

- **Coos County**: Deed (Grantor/Grantee) Index 1772–1898 and Deeds 1772–1902, vols. 1–99. F42/C7/C66.

- **Grafton County**: Deed (Grantor/Grantee) Index 1773–1900 and Deeds 1773–1902. F42/G7/G74.

- **Hillsborough County**: Deed (Grantor/Grantee) Index 1771–1869 and Deed (Grantor/Grantee) Index 1870–1909, and Deeds 1771–1851, vols. 1–266. F42/H6/H64.

- **Merrimack County**: Deed (Grantor/Grantee) Index 1823–1850 and Deeds 1823–1852, vols. 1–114. F42/M5/M53.

- **Rockingham County**: Deed (Grantor/Grantee) Index 1643–1864 and Deeds 1643–1852, vols. 1–350. F42/R7/R74. Vols. 1–100 are the deeds up to 1771 for the entire province of New Hampshire (see above).

- **Strafford County**: Only for the area that became Belknap County.

- **Sullivan County**: Deed (Grantor/Grantee) Index 1827–1850 and Deeds 1827–1850, vols. 2–48. F42/S87/S87.

Town Records

See under VITAL RECORDS above for information about microfilmed New Hampshire town records. See also David Allen Lambert's article "New Hampshire Genealogy Part 2" in *New England Ancestors*, cited under GUIDES AND FINDING AIDS, for a complete listing of the towns found in the microfilmed collection of town records. Many towns started annual town reports in the second half of the nineteenth century, often with vital records included. NEHGS has town reports for many New Hampshire towns, and a search of the NEHGS online catalog will show what years given towns are available.

Some towns have published some of their town records, often as part of a town history. Various town records have been published in *The New Hampshire Genealogical Record*.

Tax Records

One of the few recent published tax records for New Hampshire is John S. Fipphen, *1798 Direct Tax New Hampshire District #13, Consisting of the Towns of Alton, Brookfield, Effingham, Middleton, New Durham, Ossippee, Tuftonboro, Wakefield, and Wolfeboro* (Wolfeboro, N.H.: Wolfeboro Historical Society, 1988) REF F42/S8/F56/1988 also LOAN.

In the NEHGS library there are manuscript tax records and published ones like *Invoice and Taxes of the Town of Rindge, New Hampshire: Taken April 1* (Rindge, N.H.: Town of Peterboro, N.H., 1887) Vault F44/R5/I5.

Court and Legislative Records

The early history of the courts in New Hampshire is treated in Elwin L. Page, *Judicial Beginnings in New Hampshire, 1640–1700* (Concord, N.H.: New Hampshire Historical Society, 1959) KFN1708/P34. Other useful sources include the following:

- *New Hampshire Colonial Court Records.* F33/N459 Microfilm. This is an important collection of early court records.

- Bell, Charles Henry, *The Bench and Bar of New Hampshire.* (Boston: Houghton Mifflin, 1894) F33/B43/1894 also LOAN.

- Hulslander, Laura Penny, *Abstracts of Strafford County, New Hampshire Inferior Court Records, 1773–1783* (Bowie, Md.: Heritage Books, 1987) F42/S8/P46/1990 also LOAN.

- Mevers, Frank, and Harriet S. Lacy, "Early Historical Records (c1620-c1817) at the New Hampshire State Archives," *Historical New Hampshire* 31 (1976):108–18. F31/H57.

- Mevers, Frank, and Melinde Lutz Sanborn, "Minutes of the Court of Quarter Sessions [1683–1688]," *The New Hampshire Genealogical Record* 8 (1991):1–13.

- *Index to the records of the Council of New Hampshire from November 17, 1631, to April 17, 1784; in the office of the Secretary of State* (Concord, N.H.: E. N. Pearson, 1896) J87/N45/1896 also LOAN.

- *New Hampshire Provincial and State Papers* (see OVERVIEW), vol. 40. Court records for Dover–Portsmouth, 1640–1692.

Military Records

The basic work for New Hampshire is Chandler Eastman Potter, *The Military History of the State of New Hampshire, from its Settlement, in 1623, to the Rebellion, in 1861: Comprising an Account of the Stirring Events Connected Therewith; Biographical Notices of many of the Officers Distinguished* (Concord, N.H.: McFarland & Jenks, 1866; reprinted Baltimore: Genealogical Publishing Co., 1972) F34/P86/1866 also LOAN. This work and those by Hammond and Ayling listed below are included on *New Hampshire Military Records 1623–1866*, CD-ROM (Boston: NEHGS, 2004). For the colonial period, see also George Madison Bodge,

Soldiers in King Philip's War, 3rd ed. (1906; reprinted Baltimore: Genealogical Publishing Co., 1967) REF/E83/67/B662/1906.

Revolutionary War

- Hammond, Isaac, *Rolls of the Soldiers in the Revolutionary War. . . .*, 4 vols. (Concord, N.H.: P. B. Cogswell, 1885–89) REF F34/N54 v. 14–17 also LOAN. This is vols. 14–17 of the *New Hampshire Provincial and State Papers*.

- Batchellor, Albert Stillman, *Miscellaneous Revolutionary Documents of New Hampshire, Including the Association Test, the Pension Rolls, and Other Important Papers* (Manchester, N.H.: John B. Clarke, 1910) REF F34/N54 v. 30 also LOAN. This is vol. 30 of the *New Hampshire Provincial and State Papers*.

- *New Hampshire Revolutionary Pensioners Records Index* (Concord, N.H.: New Hampshire Historical Society, 1951) E263/N4/N4 Microfilm. This is a typescript abstract of all Revolutionary applications from New Hampshire bound in many volumes and microfilmed. Important genealogical information about the individuals may be included.

- White, Virgil D., *Genealogical Abstracts of Revolutionary War Pension Files*, 4 vols. (Waynesboro, Tenn.: National Historical Publishing Co., 1990–92) R.Rm. REF E255/W55/1990.

Civil War

- Ayling, Augustus D., *Revised Register of the Soldiers and Sailors of New Hampshire in the War of the Rebellion, 1861–1866* (Concord, N.H.: Ira C. Evans, 1895) REF E520.3/N55/1895 also LOAN.

- *New Hampshire Civil War Enlistments* (Concord, N.H.: New Hampshire Division of Records Management and Archives, 198-) E520.3/N4 Microfiche.

World War I

- Nuckols, Ashley Kay, *Deaths, American Expeditionary Force, W.W.I 1917, 1918 New Hampshire* (Bluefield, Va.: the author, 1995) D609/U6/N834/1995.

Genealogical and Biographical Compendia (Including Town and County Histories)

See Copley's *Index to Genealogies in New Hampshire Town Histories* (under GUIDES AND FINDING AIDS) for compendia at the town level. Listed below are biographical compendia at the county and state level. Note that the first four entries are for specific groups within the state.

- Carter, Nathan Franklin, *The Native Ministry of New Hampshire* (Concord, N.H.: Rumford Printing Co., 1906. BR555/N4/C3/1906. Contains biographies of ministers who were born in New Hampshire; valuable but incomplete.

- Brown, H. B., *Biographical Sketches of the Governor, Councilors, and Members of the Senate and House of Representatives of the New Hampshire Legislature for 1895–96* (Concord, N.H.: the compiler, 1895) NH/46/10.

- Brennan, James F., *Irish Settlers of Southern New Hampshire* (reprinted from *Journal of American Irish Historical Society*, vol. 9, 1910) NH/52/5.

- Foss, Gerald D., and Woodbury S. Adams, *Three Centuries of Freemasonry in New Hampshire* (Concord, N.H.: Grand Lodge of New Hampshire, 1972) HS537/N42/F66. Contains biographies.

- Stearns, Ezra Scollay, William Frederick Witcher, and Edward Everett Parker, *Genealogical and Family History of the State of New Hampshire: A Record of the Achievements of Her People in the Making of a Commonwealth and the Founding of a Nation*, 4 vols. (New York: The Lewis Publishing Company, 1908) F33/S79/1908 also LOAN. Useful but undocumented.

- *Biographical Review . . . Containing Life Sketches of Leading Citizens of Belknap and Strafford Counties, New Hampshire* (Boston: Biographical Review Publishing Company, 1897) F42/B4/B6/1897 also LOAN.

- *Biographical Review . . . Containing Life Sketches of Leading Citizens of Cheshire and Hillsboro Counties, New Hampshire* (1897; reprinted Bowie, Md.: Heritage Books, 1992) F42/C5/B56/1992.

- *Biographical Review . . . Containing Life Sketches of Leading Citizens of Hillsboro and Cheshire Counties, New Hampshire* (Boston: Biographical Review Publishing Company, 1897) F42/C5/B61/1897 also LOAN.

- *Biographical Review . . . Containing Life Sketches of Leading Citizens of Merrimack and Sullivan Counties, New Hampshire* (Boston: Biographical Review Publishing Company, 1897) F42/M5/B6/1897 also LOAN.

- Hurd, D. Hamilton, *History of Rockingham and Strafford Counties, New Hampshire, with Biographical Sketches of Many of its Pioneers and Prominent Men* (Philadelphia, J. W. Lewis & Co. 1882) F42/R7/H9/1882 also LOAN.

- Hazlett, Charles A., *History of Rockingham County, New Hampshire, and Representative Citizens* (1915; reprinted Salem, Mass: Higginson Book Co., 2001) F42/R7/H39/1915 also LOAN.

- *Biographical Review; This Volume Contains Biographical Sketches of Leading Citizens of Rockingham County, New Hampshire* (Boston: Biographical Review Publishing Company, 1896) F42/R7/B6/1896 also LOAN.

- Scales, John, *History of Strafford County, New Hampshire, and Representative Citizens* (1914; reprinted Salem, Mass.: Higginson Book Co., 1997) F42/S8/S28/1914 also LOAN.

- *Book of Biographies: The Volume Contains Biographical Sketches of Leading Citizens of Grafton County, New Hampshire* (Buffalo, N.Y.: Biographical Review Publishing Company, 1897) NH/85/3.

- Ketcham, Cyrus, *Ketcham's New Hampshire Biography* (n.p.: n.d.) Mss/A/K48. Six boxes of files, alphabetically by surname, intended to be used for a dictionary of New Hampshire biography which was never completed or published.

- Herndon, Richard, *Men of Progress Biographical Sketches and Portraits of Leaders in Business and Professional Life in and of the State of New Hampshire* (Boston: New England Magazine, 1898) NH/55/39.

Maps and Atlases

- DenBoer, Gordon, and George E. Goodridge, *New Hampshire, Vermont: Atlas of Historical County Boundaries* (New York: Simon & Schuster, 1993) Atlas G1201/F7/A8/1993/NH,VT also LOAN.

- Lane, Paula L., *The New Hampshire Atlas and Gazetteer* (Freeport, Maine: Delorme & Co., 1986) REF G1220/D44/1977.

- Cobb, David A., *New Hampshire Maps to 1900: An Annotated Checklist* (Hanover, N.H.: New Hampshire Historical Society, 1981) REF Z6027/U5/C64.

- Hayward, John, *A Gazetteer of New Hampshire: Containing Descriptions of all the Counties, Towns, and Districts in the State, also of its Principal Mountains, Rivers, Waterfalls, Harbors, Islands, and Fashionable Resorts* (1839; reprinted Bowie, Md.: Heritage Books, 1993) R.Rm. REF F32/H39/1992.

- Hunt, Elmer M., *New Hampshire Town Names and Whence They Came* (Peterborough, N.H.: Noone House, 1970) REF F32/H85/1971.

- Merrill, Eliphalet, *Gazetteer of the State of New Hampshire* (1817; reprinted Bowie, Md.: Heritage Books, 1987) R.Rm. REF F32/M56/1817 also LOAN.

- Farmer, John, and Jacob Bailey Moore, *A Gazetteer of the State of New Hampshire* (Concord, N.H.: J. B. Moore, 1823) Rare Book F32/F23/1823.

- McFarland, Asa, "Names of Counties and Towns in New Hampshire," *The Granite Monthly* 1 (August 1877):120–22. F31/G75 also LOAN. This is dated but still useful.

Special Sources for New Hampshire

Native Americans and African Americans

- Thatcher, B. B., *Indian Biography* (New York: J. & J. Harper, 1832) Rare Book E89/T36/1832. The Pennacook are covered on pages 340–50.

- Day, Gordon M., Michael K. Foster, and William Cowan, ed., *In Search of New England's Native Past: Selected Essays* (Amherst, Mass.: University of Massachusetts Press, 1998) E99/A13/D39/1998. Understanding the history of the larger Abenaki people is essential in conducting genealogical research of this unique group. Chapter 14 discusses oral tradition, so crucial in Native genealogical research in New Hampshire.

- Calloway, Colin G., *The Western Abenakis of Vermont, 1600–1800: War, Migration, and the Survival of an Indian People* (Norman, Okla.: University of Oklahoma Press, 1990) E99/A13/C35/1990. This is an excellent source for understanding the history and movement of Abenaki family groups throughout Dawnland, including New Hampshire.

- "Blacks and Indians of New Hampshire and Vermont in the American Revolution," in Eric G. Grundset, ed., *African American and American Indian Patriots of the Revolutionary War* (Washington, D.C.: National Society Daughters of the American Revolution, 2001), 15–26. E269/N3/A37/2001.

Miscellaneous Sources

- Wentworth, William Edgar, *Journals of Enoch Hayes Place*, 2 vols. (Boston: NEHGS, 1998) F44/S82/P521/1998 also LOAN. This is a major source of vital records for southeastern New Hampshire in the nineteenth century.

- Coleman, Emma Lewis, *New England Captives Carried to Canada Between 1677 and 1760 During the French and Indian Wars*, 2 vols. (Portland, Maine: Southworth Press, 1925; reprinted Bowie, Md.: Heritage Books, 1989) E85/C72/1925 also LOAN.

- 1993 New Hampshire Motor Vehicle Registration information. F33/N459 Microfiche.

Rhode Island

Cherry Fletcher Bamberg

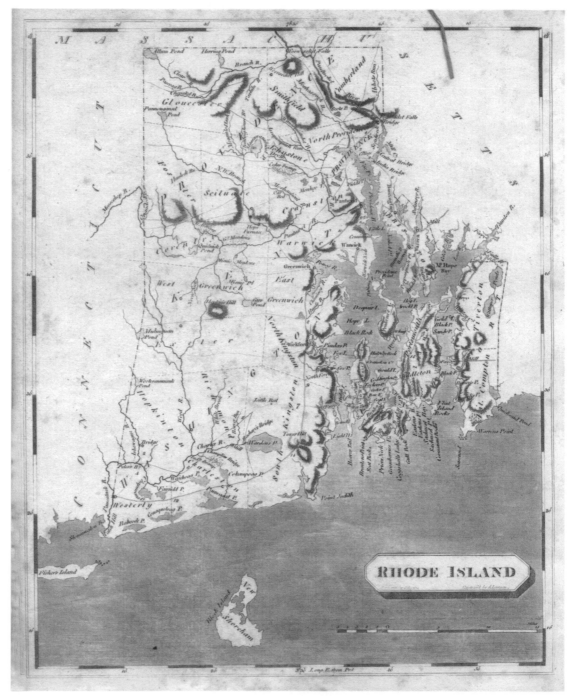

Rhode Island from *A New and Elegant General Atlas* by Arrowsmith and Lewis (Boston: Thomas & Andrews, 1805).

Overview

Rhode Island was founded in the mid-1630s, not as a colony, but as a group of small settlements of men and women rejected by Massachusetts for their failure to conform. In the mid-seventeenth century Rhode Island was a loose federation of towns—Providence, Portsmouth, Newport, and Warwick—that clung precariously to its identity and independence from more powerful neighbors. In 1663 King Charles II granted Rhode Island its famous charter, guaranteeing freedom of religion for the first time in history. The colony became a haven for Baptists, Quakers, Moravians, Seventh Day Baptists, Jews, and even those with no religion at all.

Although early Rhode Islanders rebelled against the religious conformity of Massachusetts, they preserved English traditions of recordkeeping with meticulous care. Just about anything that could have future legal significance— every deed, every piece of probate data, and minutes from town councils and town meetings—were carefully copied, and registered with the town clerks. Where gaps exist, as in Newport or in North Kingstown, it is because later disasters befell the carefully kept documents. No town is completely without its early records, usually kept in the town hall. Published versions of the early records exist for Providence, Portsmouth, and Warwick, and many others are available at NEHGS on microfilm.

The borders of the Rhode Island were not finalized for many years, and minor disputes with Connecticut continue to the present. The most important border changes involved the towns on the east of Narragansett Bay that became part of Rhode Island only in 1747. Previously Bristol, Warren (which included present-day Barrington), Tiverton, and Little Compton were part of Bristol County, Massachusetts, and researchers of early families in those towns need to search in Massachusetts records.

The NEHGS Library in Boston has one of the finest collections of Rhode Island research materials outside that state, allowing the researcher access to original town and census records on microfilm and a wealth of genealogical writings on Rhode Island families. Although the collection includes standard resources for town and state/colony history, its real strength lies in the variety of published and manuscript materials for genealogy.

Guides and Finding Aids

The general finding aids to New England research, such as Torrey's *New England Marriages Prior to 1700*, the Great Migration Study Project series, and PERSI (*Periodical Source Index*) are all useful for Rhode Island research, and library users should consult the NEW ENGLAND OVERVIEW for these and other regional sources.

- Bartlett, John Russell, *Bibliography of Rhode Island: A Catalogue of Books and Other Publications relating to the State of Rhode Island* (Providence, R.I.: A. Anthony, 1864) Rare Book Z1331/B29/1864.

- Eichholz, Alice, "Rhode Island," in *Red Book: American State, County, and Town Sources*, 3rd ed. (Provo, Utah: Ancestry, 2004), 582–92. REF CS49/A55/2004 also LOAN.

- Fiske, Jane Fletcher, "Genealogical Research in Rhode Island," *The New England Historical and Genealogical Register*, 136 (1982):173–219, reprinted, with additions, in Ralph J. Crandall, ed., *Genealogical Research in New England* (Baltimore: Genealogical Publishing Co., 1984), 141–87. REF F3/G46/1984 also LOAN.

- Lamar, Christine, *Genealogical Sources in the Rhode Island State Archives* (Providence, R.I.: Rhode Island State Archives, 1991) R.Rm. REF F78/L35/1991.

- Melnyk, Marcia D., *Genealogist's Handbook for New England Research*, 4th ed. (Boston: NEHGS, 1999), 172–84. R.Rm. REF F3/G466/1999 also LOAN.

- Parks, Roger N., ed., *Rhode Island: A Bibliography of its History* (Hanover, N.H.: University Press of New England, 1993) REF F79/R495/1983 also LOAN.

- Roberts, Gary Boyd, "A Bibliography for 100 Colonial Rhode Island Families," introductory essay in *Genealogies of Rhode Island Families from* The New England Historical and Genealogical Register, 2 vols. (Baltimore: Genealogical Publishing Co., 1989) REF F78/G462/1989 also LOAN.

- Sperry, Kip, *Rhode Island Sources for Family Historians and Genealogists* (Logan, Utah: Everton Publishers, 1986) REF Z1331/S6/1986 also LOAN.

- Taylor, Maureen A., *Research in Rhode Island*, National Genealogical Society Special Publication No. 67, Research in the States Series (Arlington, Va., 2001). Reprinted from *National Genealogical Society Quarterly* 88 (2000):5–31. CS42/N4 also LOAN.

Genealogical and Historical Periodicals

Articles from the six periodicals shown below with an asterisk are included in *Genealogies of Rhode Island Families from Rhode Island Periodicals*, 2 vols. (Baltimore: Genealogical Publishing Co., 1983) F78/G46/1983 also LOAN.

- *The American Genealogist*, 1922–present. R.Rm. REF F104/N6/A6 also LOAN. See NEW ENGLAND OVERVIEW.

- Beaman, Alden G., and Nellie M. C. Beaman, ed., *Rhode Island Genealogical Register*, 21 vols. (East Princeton, Mass., 1978–99) REF F78/R55 also LOAN. This material has been published on an easily searchable, if oddly named

CD: *Vital Records: Rhode Island 1500–1900s,* Family Tree Maker's Family Archives, CD #215. The indexing (in each succeeding volume) makes the printed version somewhat difficult to search. See Helen Schatvet Ullmann, *A Finding Aid for Rhode Island Town Records in Arnold's* Vital Record of Rhode Island, *Beaman's* Rhode Island Vital Records: New Series, *and the* Rhode Island Genealogical Register (Acton, Mass.: the author, 2000) REF F78/U44/2000 also LOAN.

- *The Narragansett Historical Register: A Magazine Devoted to the Antiquities, Genealogy and Historical Matter illustrating the History of the State of Rhode Island and Providence Plantations,* 9 vols. (1882–91) F87/N2/N36/1882 also LOAN. *

- *Bulletin of the Newport Historical Society,* 112 issues (1912–63). F89/N5/N615.

- *Newport History,* 1964–present. F89/N5/N615. Continues *Bulletin of the Newport Historical Society.*

- *The New England Historical and Genealogical Register,* 1847–present. R.Rm. REF F1/N56 also LOAN also fifth floor also Web database. See NEW ENGLAND OVERVIEW.

- *Collections of the Rhode Island Historical Society,* 10 vols. (1827–1902) F76/R47 also LOAN also Rare Book. *

- *The Newport Historical Magazine,* 4 vols. (1880–84) F76/R35 also LOAN. *

- *Publications of the Narragansett Club,* 6 vols. (Providence, R.I., 1866–74) F76/N21.

- *Publications of the Rhode Island Historical Society, New Series,* 8 vols. (1893–1901) F76/R51/1893–1901. *

- *Rhode Island Historical Tracts,* 25 vols. (Providence, R.I.: Sidney S. Rider, 1877–96) F76/R52/1877–1896 also LOAN. *

- *Rhode Island History* (Providence, R.I.: Rhode Island Historical Society, 1942–present) F76/R472 also LOAN. *

- *Rhode Island Roots* (Warwick/Greenville, R.I: Rhode Island Genealogical Society, 1975–present) F78/R2 also LOAN. Quarterly journal of the Rhode Island Genealogical Society.

Censuses: Colonial, Federal, and State

NEHGS holds an extensive collection of Rhode Island material in print and on microfilm. In addition to the sources listed below, see also the tax list of Rochester (Kingstown) taken under Governor Andros in 1687 in *The New England Historical and Genealogical Register* 35 (1881):124, the 1688/9 census of Bristol in *The American Genealogist* 68 (1993):184–85, and a portion of the 1730 census in

Rhode Island Roots 7 (1981):16–17 (Portsmouth), and 10 (1984):8–10 (South Kingstown).

Additional census information on former Rhode Islanders has been distilled from the records of other states as a series called "They Left Rhode Island" in the *Rhode Island Genealogical Register* (see GENEALOGICAL AND HISTORICAL PERIODICALS). NEHGS also has Frank Mortimer Hawes's "New Englanders in the California Census of 1850, Part 5: Persons Born in Rhode Island" (West Hartford, Conn., n.d.) SL/CAL/5.

Colonial

Because of useful introductions, explanations, and more records, the sources cited below are preferable to those compiled by Ronald Vern Jackson.

- MacGunnigle, Bruce, *Rhode Island Freemen, 1747–1755: A Census of Registered Voters* (Baltimore: Genealogical Publishing Co., 1977) REF F78/M32/1977 also LOAN.

- Bartlett, John Russell, *Census of the Inhabitants of Rhode Island and Providence Plantations 1774* (1858; reprinted Baltimore: Genealogical Publishing Co., 1969) Microtext F78/A59/1969 also LOAN. This transcription omits detail on African Americans and Native Americans; see under SPECIAL SOURCES FOR RHODE ISLAND below.

- Chamberlain, Mildred M., *The Rhode Island 1777 Military Census* (Baltimore: Genealogical Publishing Co., 1985) E263/R4/C48/1985 also LOAN.

- Holbrook, Jay Mack, *Rhode Island 1782 Census* (Oxford, Mass.: Holbrook Research Institute, 1979) F78/H47/1979 also LOAN. NEHGS also holds Katherine Minerva Utter Waterman, *Rhode Island Census 1782* (n.p., 1942–45) Rare Book Oversize F78/W38, which was published in vols. 127–129 of *The New England Historical and Genealogical Register*.

Federal

Microfilms for all federal census years, 1790 through 1930, are available in Microtext on the fourth floor, along with Soundex indexes for 1880, 1900, and 1920, and book Mortality Schedule for 1860.

State

Rhode Island has had a state census every ten years from 1865 to 1935 (excluding 1895). NEHGS has the 1865 Rhode Island State Census, F78/R57/1865. Also Microfilm F78/R51/1865/Index, 22 reels.

Vital Records

Before 1850, vital records were kept only in individual Rhode Island towns and then only in a sketchy way. Since one had to pay to register a birth or marriage, many people never bothered. The standard source for the early period is James N. Arnold's twenty-one volumes of transcriptions of Rhode Island vital records for every town as well as church records and newspapers (as described below). The first six volumes contain vital records organized by county and town, with full information for marriages given only under the name of the groom. Arnold's transcriptions are not entirely reliable, and reviewing the original records (see under TOWN RECORDS) is advisable.

From 1850 to 1853 towns kept the information on births, marriages, and deaths; after 1853 the state collected the towns' information into a central repository. NEHGS holds a collection of microfilms of these state records that provide invaluable information. The CD *Rhode Island Vital Records, 1636–1930* (Provo, Utah: MyFamily.com, 2000) attempts to synthesize much of the vital record material from 1636 to 1930, but Arnold and the state records should be consulted.

Because of the changing eastern border of Rhode Island, it is always a good idea to check the vital records of towns now in Bristol County, Massachusetts, for seventeenth and eighteenth-century entries. Important sources include H. L. Peter Rounds, *Vital Records of Swansea, Massachusetts, to 1850* (Boston: NEHGS, 1992) REF F74/S995/R68/1992 also LOAN, and James N. Arnold, *Vital Record of Rehoboth, 1642–1896* (Providence, R.I.: Narragansett Historical Publishing Co., 1897) R.Rm. REF F74/R3/A6/1897 also LOAN.

- Arnold, James N., *Vital Record of Rhode Island: 1636–1850*, 21 vols. (Providence, R. I.: Narragansett Historical Publishing Co., 1891–1912) REF F78/A75 also LOAN. Also on CD as *Vital Record of Rhode Island, 1636–1850* [Arnold Collection], CDventure, Inc., 1998, and also Web database on *NewEnglandAncestors.org*.

- Beaman, Alden Gamaliel, *Rhode Island Vital Records, New Series*, 13 vols. (Princeton, Mass.: the compiler, 1976–87) REF F78/B4 also LOAN. These volumes include vital records deduced from marriage, probate, and gravestones rather than copied from town ledgers. As with Beaman's *Rhode Island Genealogical Register* (see above), this material appears on the easily searchable CD: *Vital Records: Rhode Island 1500s–1900s*, Family Tree Maker's Family Archives, CD #215.

- Ullmann, Helen Schatvet, *A Finding Aid for Rhode Island Town Records in Arnold's* Vital Record of Rhode Island, *Beaman's* Rhode Island Vital Records: New Series, *and the* Rhode Island Genealogical Register (Acton, Mass.: the author, 2000) REF F78/U44/2000 also LOAN.

- Rhode Island Vital Records, 1853–1900 (births, 18 reels; marriages, 21 reels; deaths, 21 reels) F/78/R55/1992 Microfilm.

- Rhode Island Vital Records, Deaths 1901–1945 (183 reels) F/78/R552 Microfilm.

  For name changes, see Maureen Taylor, "Name Changes in Rhode Island, 1800–1880," *The New England Historical and Genealogical Register* 149 (1995):265–94.

Church Records

Rhode Island faith communities, having no such responsibilities to the government as those in Massachusetts did, kept intermittent records at best. A great deal has been written about Rhode Island churches, meetings, and its one colonial synagogue (much of it to be found on the library shelves), but actual records prove much less useful to the genealogist here than in other locations in New England. The most comprehensive single source of early Rhode Island church records is volumes 6–8 and 10–11 of James N. Arnold's *Vital Record of Rhode Island: 1636–1850*. The library also holds an excellent collection of the publications of the American-French Genealogical Society. These volumes—too numerous to list—include transcriptions of baptisms, marriages, and burials from Catholic church records, largely in northern Rhode Island after 1850. As with other aspects of Rhode Island research, records churches and meetings now in Bristol County, Massachusetts, frequently include Rhode Islanders.

Published church records at NEHGS include the following:

- Arnold, James N., *Vital Record of Rhode Island: 1636–1850*, 21 vols. (Providence, R. I.: Narragansett Historical Publishing Co., 1891–1912) REF F78/A75 also LOAN. Also on CD as *Vital Record of Rhode Island, 1636–1850* [Arnold Collection], CDventure, Inc., 1998, also Web database on *NewEnglandAncestors.org*.

- Eddy, Michael, "List of persons married by Rev. Michael Eddy at the First Baptist Church, Newport, R.I., 1790–1835," Mss C 7.

- Hazard, Caroline, *The Narragansett Friends' Meeting in the XVIII Century with a Chapter on Quaker Beginnings in Rhode Island* (Boston: Houghton, Mifflin and Co., 1900) RI/50/0 .

- King, Henry Melville, and Charles Field Wilcox, *Historical catalogue of the members of the First Baptist Church in Providence, Rhode Island* (Providence, R.I.: F. H. Townsend, 1908) F89/P9/P93/1908 also LOAN.

- Mason, George C., *Annals of Trinity Church, Newport, Rhode Island, 1698–1821* (Newport, R.I.: the author, 1890) F89/N5/M372/1890 also LOAN.

- Mason, George C., and George Jehoshaphat Magill, *Annals of Trinity Church, Newport, Rhode Island, 1821–1894, Second Series* (Newport, R.I.: V. M. Francis, 1894) F89/N5/M373/1894.

- Matthews, Margery I., Virginia I. Benson, and Arthur Edward Wilson, *Churches of Foster: A History of Religious Life in Rural Rhode Island* (Foster, R.I.: North Foster Baptist Church, 1978) F89/F74/M37/1978.

- Updike, Wilkins, and James MacSparran, *A History of the Episcopal Church in Narragansett, Rhode Island, including a History of other Episcopal Churches in the State. With an appendix containing a reprint of a work now extremely rare, entitled:* America (New York: H. M. Onderdonk, 1847) Rare Book F89/N2/U63/1847 also LOAN.

Cemetery Records

Recording of Rhode Island cemeteries and research into their history has grown enormously since 1990 when the Rhode Island Historic Cemetery Database Project was founded by John E. Sterling. The database of some 425,000 gravestones, still being compiled and checked, contains comprehensive recording of each of the 3,200 historical cemeteries now identified in the state. All known earlier transcriptions of gravestones, which represent only 60 percent of the total, have been added to the database and are being checked against still-existing stones with modern techniques of gravestone study, and recording errors are being corrected. Out of this research have come books covering over a thousand cemeteries, eight complete towns, and two large cemeteries. An outdated index to the Project is available to NEHGS library users in the microtext department. The best index is to be found on the internet at *rootsweb.com/~rigenweb*.

Two useful sources that do not clearly fit into either the classic or modern transcription category are Alden Gamaliel Beaman's *Births, 1590–1930, from Newport Common Burial Ground Inscriptions* (East Princeton, Mass.: Rhode Island Families Association, 1985) REF F78/B4/v.11 also LOAN, and Vincent F. Luti, *Mallet & Chisel: Gravestone Carvers of Newport, Rhode Island, in the 18th Century* (Boston: NEHGS, 2001) F89/N5/L88/2002 also LOAN.

Older sources

- Arnold, James N., *Inscriptions on the Gravestones in the Old Churchyard of St. Paul's Narragansett, North Kingstown, Rhode Island with a Record of the Inscriptions in the Graveyard of the Old Church at Wickford* (Boston: Merrymount Press, 1909) RI/NOR/25.

- *The Burying Place of Governor Arnold: an Account of the Establishment, Destruction, and Restoration of the Burying Place of Benedict Arnold, First Governor of Rhode Island and Providence Plantations* (Newport, R.I.: Preservation Society of Newport, 1960) F89/N5/B95/1960 also LOAN.

- Carter, Marion Williams Pearce, *The Old Rehoboth Cemetery, "the Ring of the Town": at East Providence, Rhode Island, near Newman's Church* (1932; reprinted Salem, Mass.: Higginson Book Co., 1997) F89/E18/C27/1932 also LOAN.

- Gravestones of the Cemeteries Destroyed in the Construction of the Scituate, Rhode Island Reservoir (n.p., n.d.) SL/RHO/11. A bundle of 244 pages of blueprints.

- Stetson, Oscar Frank, *Copies of Inscriptions taken from Gravestones in the Old East Burial Ground, Juniper Hill Cemetery, Congregational Church Yard, Walker Hill Cemetery, Bristol, Rhode Island: checked with copy made by James Augustus Miller previous to 1900* (193-; reprinted Salem, Mass.: Higginson Book Co., 1997) F89/B8/S74/193– also LOAN.

Modern sources

- Eddleman, Bill, and John E. Sterling, *Coventry, Rhode Island Historical Cemeteries* (Baltimore: Gateway Press, 1998) F89/C7/S73/1998 also LOAN.

- MacGunnigle, Bruce Campbell, *East Greenwich, Rhode Island Historical Cemetery Inscriptions* (East Greenwich, R.I.: East Greenwich Preservation Society and John Peck Rathbun Chapter #4, Society of the Sons of the American Revolution, 1991) F89/E15/M33/1991 also LOAN.

- McAleer, Althea H., *Elm Grove Cemetery Inscriptions, North Kingstown, Rhode Island* (Greenville, R.I: Rhode Island Genealogical Society, 2000) F89/N8/M33/2000.

- McAleer, Althea H., Beatrix Hoffius, and Deby J. Nunes, *Graveyards of North Kingstown, Rhode Island* (North Kingstown, R.I.: the authors, 1992) F89/N8/M34/1992 also LOAN.

- Sterling, John E., and James E. Good, *Exeter, Rhode Island Historical Cemeteries* (Baltimore: Gateway Press, 1994) F89/E9/S73/1994 also LOAN.

- Sterling, John E., *North Burial Ground, Providence, Rhode Island: Old Section, 1700–1848* (Greenville, R.I.: Rhode Island Genealogical Society, 2000) F89/P9/S74/2000.

- Sterling, John E., and James L. Wheaton IV, *South Kingstown, Rhode Island, Historical Cemeteries*, Cherry Fletcher Bamberg, ed. (Greenville, R.I.: Rhode Island Genealogical Society, 2004).

- Sterling, John E., *Warwick, Rhode Island Historical Cemeteries* (Baltimore: Gateway Press, 1997) F89/W2/S74/1997 also LOAN.

- Trim, Robert S., *Rumford Rhode Island Gravestone Records, Carpenter & Hunt Cemeteries*, monograph, 1991. F89/R85/T74.

Newspapers

The most comprehensive single source for genealogical information in newspapers is Arnold's *Vital Record of Rhode Island*, vols. 13–21 (see under VITAL

RECORDS). These volumes contain an alphabetical index of marriages and deaths in many different newspapers. In addition, there are the following books:

- Hammett, Charles Edward, *A Contribution to the Bibliography and Literature of Newport, R. I.; comprising a list of books published or printed, in Newport, with notes and additions* (Newport, R. I.: C. E. Hammett, Jun., 1887) F87/N5/H36/1887 also LOAN.

- *Rhode Island Imprints: A List of Books, Pamphlets, Newspapers and Broadsides printed at Newport, Providence, Warren, Rhode Island between 1727 and 1800* (Providence, R.I.: Rhode Island Historical Society, 1915) Z1331/R55/1915 also LOAN.

- Taylor, Maureen Alice, *Runaways, Deserters, and Notorious Villains from Rhode Island Newspapers, Volume 1:* The Providence Gazette, *1762–1800* (Camden, Maine: Picton Press, 1994) F78/T37/1994 also LOAN.

- Taylor, Maureen A., and John Wood Sweet, *Runaways, Deserters, and Notorious Villains, From Rhode Island Newspapers, Volume 2: Additional Notices from* The Providence Gazette, *1762–1800 as well as advertisements from all other Rhode Island Newspapers from 1732–1800* (Rockport, Maine: Picton Press, 2001) F78/T37/1994 also LOAN.

- Tilley, Edith May, *Items of Newport Interest in Early Boston Newspapers . . .* (Newport, R.I.: Newport Historical Society, 1929) F89/N5/N615/no.69.

Probate Records

Most Rhode Island probate records are kept at the town level. Those at NEHGS on microfilm are listed under TOWN RECORDS for each town. It is a good idea to check the *Genealogist's Handbook for New England Research* (see GUIDES AND FINDING AIDS) for information on location of records in the case of towns that were set off from others. An excellent finding aid to Rhode Island wills is Volume 16 of the *Rhode Island Genealogical Register* which indexes the wills abstracted in the first 15 volumes (see under GENEALOGICAL AND HISTORICAL PERIODICALS).

The exception to the general rule about probate at the town level is that portion of Bristol County, Rhode Island, carved out of Bristol County, Massachusetts in 1747. Before that date, one can search in the more centralized Massachusetts records. A useful printed source is H. L. Peter Rounds, *Abstracts of Bristol County Probate Records 1687–1762*, 2 vols. (Baltimore: Genealogical Publishing Co., 1987–88) REF F72/B8/R68/1987 also LOAN. Swansea town records and Bristol County, Massachusetts, probate records are on microfilm in the Microtext area.

Land Records

Most Rhode Island land records are kept at the town level. Those at NEHGS on microfilm are listed under TOWN RECORDS for each town. It is a good idea to check Marcia D. Melnyk's *Genealogist's Handbook for New England Research* (see GUIDES AND FINDING AIDS) for information on location of records in the case of towns that were set off from others. A useful compendium of seventeenth-century land records is Dorothy Worthington, *Rhode Island Land Evidences, Vol. I, 1648–1696, Abstracts* (Providence, R.I.: Rhode Island Historical Society, 1921) F82/R5/1921 also LOAN.

Town Records

Since most Rhode Island records are kept on the town level, these materials are vital for research in the state. There are published volumes of early records for only a few towns, but scattered transcriptions in periodicals have appeared. The library holds an excellent but still incomplete set of microfilmed town records. Users should be aware that the labels, printed from the suppliers' slips, do not perfectly describe the contents in every case.

Printed Sources

- *Alphabetical Index of the Births, Marriages and Deaths Recorded in Providence*, 32 vols. (Providence, R.I.: Sidney S. Rider, 1879–1945) F89/P9/P86/1879.

- *The Early Records of the Town of Providence*, 21 vols. (Providence, R.I.: Snow & Farnham, 1892–1915) F89/P9/P9 also LOAN. The poor original index is supplemented by Richard LeBaron Bowen's *Index to the Early Records of the Town of Providence, v. I-XXI* (1949; reprinted Salem, Mass.: Higginson Book Co., 2000) F89/P9/P9/Index also LOAN.

- Field, Edward, *Index to the Probate Records of the Municipal Court of the City of Providence, Rhode Island, from 1646 to and including the Year 1899* (Providence, R.I.: Providence Press, 1902) REF F89/P9/P88/1902 also LOAN.

- Chapin, Howard M., *The Early Records of the Town of Warwick* (Providence, R. I.: E. A. Johnson Co., 1926) F89/W2/W18/1926 also LOAN.

- Morgan, Marshall, transcriber, *More Early Records of the Town of Warwick, Rhode Island: "The Book with Clasps" and "General Records,"* Cherry Fletcher Bamberg and Jane Fletcher Fiske, ed. (Boston: NEHGS, 2001) F89/W2/W19/2001 also LOAN.

- Perry, Amos, and Clarence Saunders Brigham, ed., *The Early Records of the Town of Portsmouth* (Providence, R.I.: E. L. Freeman & Sons, 1901) F89/P7/P76/1901 also LOAN.

- Stutz, Jean C., *South Kingstown, Rhode Island Town Council Records, 1771–1795* (Kingston, R.I.: Pettaquamscutt Historical Society, 1988) F89/S7/S87/1988.

Microfilm Sources

- Barrington records (land, vital records, probate) F89/B2/B37, 12 reels.

- Bristol records (deeds, wills and inventories, probate, administrator's accounts, grantors, grantees, land, vital records) F89/B8/B75, 35 reels.

- Burrillville records (probate, land, council books) F89/B9/B87, 18 reels.

- Central Falls records (vital records, land, probate, etc.) F89/C33/C46, 28 reels.

- Charlestown miscellaneous town records; Narragansett Tribe Indian Council Records (1850–1863) F89/C4/C49, 13 reels.

- Cumberland records (vital records, land, probate) F89/C9/C86, 37 reels.

- Exeter probate, probate bonds, probate index and council records. F89/E9/E94, 6 reels.

- Foster records (town meetings, land, probate) F89/F74/F67, 20 reels.

- Glocester records (probate, land, town meeting, town council) F89/G5/G56, 24 reels.

- Hopkinton records (probate, vital records, land, etc.) F89/H7/H66, 29 reels.

- Jamestown miscellaneous town records. F89/J3/J36, 9 reels.

- Johnston miscellaneous town records. F89/J6/J64, 29 reels

- Little Compton records (land, probate) F89/L8/L58, 12 reels.

- Pawtucket records (births, marriages, deaths, land, probate, wills, town records) F89/P3/P39, 81 reels.

- Providence Birth, Marriage, Death, Land, Probate, and Town Records. F89/P9/P7, 536 reels plus 4 reels of out-of-town deaths. F90/P9/P76.

- Warwick records (vital records, probate, land, council, etc.) F89/W2/W37.

- Westerly records, lottery book, town meetings, records. Grantee and grantor indexes; enrolled military records; probate docket and mortgagor and mortgagee indexes. F89/W5/W48.

- Woonsocket records (births, marriages, deaths, deeds, probate) F89/W9/W66, 21 reels.

Tax Records

Such scattered tax records as exist are to be found in transcriptions in periodicals (particularly *Rhode Island Roots*) of town records. Some tax records are on microfilms of town records.

Court and Legislative Records

- Bartlett, John Russell, *Records of the Colony of Rhode Island and Providence Plantations, in New England*, 10 vols. (Providence, R.I.: A. C. Greene and Brothers, 1856–65) F76/R29/1856–1865 also LOAN also on NEHGS CD-ROM. A portion of the original records can be viewed on microfilm: Rhode Island Colony Records, 1646–1715, indexed (2 reels). F/82/R46/1974.

- Fiske, Jane Fletcher, *Gleanings from Newport Court Files 1659–1783* (Boxford, Mass.: the author, 1998) F89/N5/F57/1998 also LOAN.

- Fiske, Jane Fletcher, *Rhode Island General Court of Trials 1671–1704* (Boxford, Mass.: the author, 1998) F78/F57/1998 also LOAN.

- Grimes, J. Stephen, *Record Books of the Rhode Island Courts in the Rhode Island Judicial Archives* (n.p.: the author, 199-) V.F. F79/G75/199-.

- Kimball, Gertrude Selwyn, ed., *The Correspondence of the Colonial Governors of Rhode Island, 1723–1775* (Boston: Houghton, Mifflin, 1902–03) F82/R44/1902 also LOAN.

- *The Public Laws of the State of Rhode Island and Providence Plantations . . . 1798: to which are prefixed, the Charter, Declaration of Independence, Articles of Confederation, Constitution of the United States, and President Washington's address of September 1796* (Providence, R.I.: Carter and Wilkinson, 1798) Rare Book KFR30/A2/1798.

- *Rhode Island Court Records: Records of the Court of Trials of the Colony of Providence Plantations, 1647–1670*, 2 vols. (Providence, R.I.: Rhode Island Historical Society, 1920–22) F82/R4/1920 also LOAN.

- Stetson, Oscar Frank, "Bristol County, Rhode Island Court Records, 1749–1903," Mss 601.

- Smith, Joseph Jencks, *Civil and Military List of Rhode Island, 1647–1800: A list of all officers elected by the General Assembly from the organization of the legislative government of the colony to 1800* (1900; reprinted Salem, Mass.: Higginson Book Co., 1999) F78/S65/1900 also LOAN. Useful for lists of justices and deputies to the General Assembly.

Military Records

The standard source for military data on officers in Rhode Island is Joseph Jencks Smith's *Civil and Military List of Rhode Island, 1647–1850.*

- Smith, Joseph Jencks, *Civil and Military List of Rhode Island, 1647–1800: A list of all officers elected by the General Assembly from the organization of the legislative government of the colony to 1800* (1900; reprinted Salem, Mass.: Higginson Book Co., 1999) F78/S65/1900 also LOAN.

- Smith, Joseph Jencks, and James N. Arnold, *Civil and Military List of Rhode Island, 1800–1850. A list of all officers elected by the General assembly from 1800 to 1850. Also, all officers in revolutionary war, appointed by Continental congress, and in the regular army and navy from Rhode Island, to 1850, including volunteer officers in war of 1812 and Mexican war, and all officers in privateer service during colonial and revolutionary wars, and the war of 1812* (1901; reprinted Salem, Mass.: Higginson Book Co., 1997) F78/S66/1901 also LOAN.

- Smith, Joseph Jencks, *New Index to the* Civil and Military Lists of Rhode Island: *Two volumes in one, giving Christian and Family Names, arranged alphabetically; also, additional indexes of both volumes* (Providence, R.I.: J. J. Smith, 1907) REF F78/S65/1900/Index also LOAN.

Colonial Wars

- Chapin, Howard M., *Rhode Island in the Colonial Wars: A List of Rhode Island Soldiers & Sailors in King George's War, 1740–1748 and a List of Rhode Island Soldiers & Sailors in the Old French & Indian War, 1755–1762* (1918, 1920; reprinted as 1 vol., Baltimore: Genealogical Publishing Co., 1994) E198/C467/1994 also LOAN.

- Chapin, Howard M., *Rhode Island Privateers in King George's War, 1739–1748* (Providence, R.I.: Rhode Island Historical Society, 1926) F82/C483/1926. also LOAN.

- Peirce, Ebenezer Weaver, *Peirce's Colonial Lists. Civil, Military and Professional Lists of Plymouth and Rhode Island Colonies* (Boston: A. Williams & Co., 1880) F68/P37/1881 also LOAN.

- Towle, Dorothy S., *Records of the Vice-Admiralty Court of Rhode Island 1716–1752* (Washington, D.C.: American Historical Association, 1936) RI/10/30.

  In addition to these records, the Society of Colonial Wars in the State of Rhode Island and Providence Plantations has published a number of useful, though often unindexed, transcriptions of original documents relating to Colonial Wars.

Revolutionary War

- Angell, Israel, *Diary of Colonel Israel Angell, commanding the Second Rhode Island Continental Regiment during the American Revolution, 1778–1781*, Edward Field, ed. (Providence, R.I.: Preston and Rounds Co., 1899) E263/R4/A5/1899.

- Baker, Virginia, *The History of Warren, Rhode Island, in the War of the Revolution, 1776–1783* (1901; reprinted Salem, Mass.: Higginson Book Co., 1998) F89/W19/B35/1901 also LOAN.

- Cowell, Benjamin, *Spirit of '76 in Rhode Island: or, Sketches of the efforts of the government and people in the war of the revolution. Together with the names of those who belonged to Rhode Island regiments in the army. With biographical notices* (Boston: A. J. Wright, 1850) Rare Book E263/R4/C8/1850 also LOAN. Reprinted in James N. Arnold's *Vital Record of Rhode Island: 1636–1850*, vol. 12 (see under VITAL RECORDS).

- Gunning, Kathryn McPherson, *Selected Final Pension Payment Vouchers, 1818–1864: Rhode Island* (Westminster, Md.: Willow Bend Books, 1999) F78/G86/1999.

- Mackenzie, Frederick, *The Diary of Frederick Mackenzie giving a daily narrative of his military service as an officer of the regiment of Royal Welch [sic] Fusiliers during the years 1775–1781 in Massachusetts, Rhode Island and New York* (Cambridge, Mass.: Harvard University Press, 1930) E267/M17/1930 also LOAN.

- Murray, Thomas Hamilton, *Irish Rhode Islanders in the American Revolution : with some Mention of Those Serving in the Regiments of Elliott, Lippitt, Topham, Crary, Angell, Olney, Greene, and other Noted Commanders* (1903; reprinted Salem, Mass.: Higginson Book Co., 1998) F90/I6/M87/1903 also LOAN.

- Shipton, Nathaniel N., and David Swain, ed., *Rhode Islanders Record the Revolution: the Journals of William Humphrey and Zuriel Waterman*, Rhode Island Revolutionary Heritage Series No. 4 (Providence, R.I.: Rhode Island Publications Society, 1984) E263/R4/R565/1984 also LOAN.

- Showman, Richard K., ed., *The Papers of General Nathanael Greene*, 12 vols. (Chapel Hill, N.C.: University of North Carolina Press for the Rhode Island Historical Society, 1976–2002) E302/G73/1976.

- White, Virgil D., *Genealogical Abstracts of Revolutionary War Pension Files*, 4 vols. (Waynesboro, Tenn.: National Historical Publishing Co., 1990–92) R.Rm. REF E255/W55/1990.

Civil War

In addition to the official sources listed below, the library holds a strong collection of personal narratives and unit histories.

- Dyer, Frederick H., *A Compendium of the War of the Rebellion (Rhode Island)* (Des Moines, Iowa: Dyer Publishing Company, 1908) Microfiche E 492 also C58/RI/12.

- *Names of Officers, Soldiers and Seamen in Rhode Island Regiments: or Belonging to the State of Rhode Island and Serving in the Regiments of Other States and in the Regular Army and Navy of the United States, Who Lost Their Lives in the Defence of their Country in the Suppression of the Late Rebellion* (1869; reprinted Salem, Mass.: Higginson Book Co., 1998) E528.3/R46/1869 also LOAN.

- *Official Register of Rhode Island Soldiers and Sailors, Who Served in the United States Army and Navy, From 1861 to 1866* (Providence, R.I.: State Printer, 1866) Microfiche E 492 also C58/RI/19.

- *Rhode Island Soldiers and Sailors; Names of Officers, Soldiers, and Seaman of Rhode Island Regiments or Belonging to the State of Rhode Island, and Serving in the Regiments of Other States and in the Regular Army and Navy of the United States, who lost their lives in the Defence of their country in the Suppression of the Late Rebellion* (Providence, R.I.: Providence Press Co., 1869) Microfiche E 492 also C58/RI/44.

Miscellaneous Military Sources

- *Honor Roll of Rhode Island Masons Who Served in the World War 1914–1918 from Statistics of the Masonic War Board of Rhode Island* (Central Falls, R.I.: E. L. Freeman Co., 1921) RI/60/42.

- Kinnicutt, Frances E., *Rhode Island in the War with Spain* (Providence, R.I.: E. L. Freeman & Sons, 1900) E726/R4/R36/1900.

- Nuckols, Ashley Kay, *Deaths, American Expeditionary Force W.W.I 1917, 1918 Rhode Island* (Bluefield, Va.: the author, 1995) REF D609/U6/N838/1995.

Genealogical and Biographical Compendia (Including Town and County Histories)

For county histories and biographical publications, J. Carlyle Parker's, *Rhode Island: Biographical and Genealogical Sketch Index* (Turlock, Calif.: Marietta Pub., 1991) R.Rm. REF F78/P37/1991, is valuable resource. It provides references to unindexed or poorly indexed sources, and the list of sources is valuable in itself.

- Austin, John Osborne, *Ancestry of Thirty-three Rhode Islanders (Born in the Eighteenth Century): Also Twenty-seven Charts of Roger Williams' Descendants to the Fifth Generation. . . .* (Albany, N. Y.: J. Munsell's Sons, 1889) Oversize F78/A93/1889 also LOAN.

- Austin, John Osborne, *The Genealogical Dictionary of Rhode Island; comprising Three Generations of Settlers who came before 1690, with many families carried to the fourth generation* (1887; reprinted with additional material, Baltimore: Genealogical Publishing Co., 1969) R.Rm. REF F78/A935/1887 also LOAN also fifth 5th floor. Though often corrected by subsequent research, it provides good accounts of many early Rhode Island families.

- Bayles, Richard M., *History of Newport County, Rhode Island* (New York: L. E. Preston & Co., 1888) F87/N5/B3/1888 also LOAN.

- Bayles, Richard M., *History of Providence County, Rhode Island*, 2 vols. (New York: W. W. Preston, 1891) F87/P9/B3/1891 also/LOAN.

- *The Biographical Cyclopedia of Representative Men of Rhode Island* (1881: reprinted Salem, Mass.: Higginson Book Co., 1999) F78/B61/1881 also LOAN.

- Cole, J. R., *History of Washington and Kent Counties, Rhode Island* (1889; reprinted Salem, Mass.: Higginson Book Co., 2000) F87/W3/C6/1889 also LOAN.

- Field, Edward, *State of Rhode Island and Providence Plantations at the End of the Century: A History*, 3 vols. (Boston: Mason Publishing Co., 1902) F79/F45/1902.

- Hall, Joseph D., Jr., *Biographical History of the Manufacturers and Business Men of Rhode Island at the Opening of the Twentieth Century* (Providence: J. D. Hall & Co., 1901) RI/80/42 .

- Munro, Wilfred Harold, *Memorial Encyclopedia of the State of Rhode Island*, 2 vols. (Boston: American Historical Society, 1916) RI/80/34

- *Representative Men and Old Families of Rhode Island; genealogical records and historical sketches of prominent and representative citizens and of many of the old families* (1908; reprinted Salem, Mass.: Higginson Book Co., 1997) F78/R42/1908 also LOAN.

- Wilbour, Benjamin Franklin, *Little Compton Families*, 2nd ed. (Little Compton, R.I.: Little Compton Historical Society, 1974) F89/L8/W5/1974 also LOAN.

Maps and Atlases

The library has a good collection of twentieth-century street maps and USGS topographical maps, including the CD, *TOPO! Interactive Maps on CD-ROM. Greater Boston, Cape Cod and Rhode Island* (San Francisco: Wildflower Productions, 1998). Version 1.2.4. Resources of historical interest include the following items, devoted wholly or in part to Rhode Island:

- Long, John H., and Gordon DenBoer, *Connecticut, Maine, Massachusetts, Rhode Island: Atlas of Historical County Boundaries* (New York: Simon & Schuster, 1994) Atlas G1201/F7/A8/1993 also LOAN.

- Pease, John C. and John M. Niles, *A Gazetteer of the States of Connecticut and Rhode Island* (1819; reprinted Bowie, Md.: Heritage Books, 1991) REF F92/ P36.

- Chace, Henry Richmond, *Owners and Occupants of the Lots, Houses and Shops in the town of Providence, Rhode Island, in 1798, located on maps of the highways of that date; also owners or occupants of houses in the compact part of Providence in 1759, showing the location and in whose names they are to be found on the map of 1798* (1914; reprinted Salem, Mass.: Higginson Book Co., 1998) F89/P9/ C531/1914 also LOAN.

Special Sources for Rhode Island

Maritime Records

Rhode Island's connection to the sea provides yet another source of information to researchers. Ships' registers and enrollments contain names of captains and owners, and seamen's protection certificate records offer valuable information on more humble crewmen who had to carry proof of their nationality during the late eighteenth and nineteenth centuries.

- Dixon, Ruth, *Index to Seamen's Protection Certificate Applications and Proof of Citizenship: ports of New Orleans, Louisiana, 1808–1821, 1851–1857, New Haven, Connecticut, 1801–1843, Bath, Maine, 1833–1868, additional ports of Mobile, Alabama, 1819–1859 . . . Newport, Rhode Island, 1813–1817* (Baltimore: Genealogical Publishing Co., 1998) F379/N5/D59/1998.

- *Register of Seamen's Protection Certificates from the Providence, Rhode Island Custom District, 1796–1870: from the Custom House Papers in the Rhode Island Historical Society* (Baltimore: Clearfield, 1995) F89/P9/R44/1995 also LOAN.

- *Ship Registers and Enrollments, Ship Licenses issued to Vessels under Twenty Tons, Ship Licenses on Enrollments issued out of the Port of Bristol–Warren, Rhode Island, 1773–1939* (Providence, R.I.: National Archives Project, 1941) F89/ B8/S87/1941.

- *Ship Registers and Enrollment of Newport, Rhode Island, 1790–1939*, 2 vols. (Providence, R.I.: National Archives Project, 1938–41) F89/N5/S87/1938.

- *Ship Registers and Enrollments of Providence, Rhode Island, 1773–1939*, 2 vols. (Providence, R.I.: National Archives Project, 1941) F89/P9/S87/1941.

- Taylor, Maureen Alice, *Rhode Island Passenger Lists: Port of Providence, 1798–1808; 1820–1872, Port of Bristol and Warren, 1820–1871: compiled from United States Custom House papers* (Baltimore: Genealogical Publishing Co., 1995) REF F78/T38/1995 also LOAN.

Diaries and Journals

- Bamberg, Cherry Fletcher, ed., *The Diary of Capt. Samuel Tillinghast of Warwick, Rhode Island: 1757–1766* (Greenville, R.I.: Rhode Island Genealogical Society, 2000) CS71/T577/2000 also LOAN.

- Hazard, Caroline, ed., *Nailer Tom's Diary: Otherwise the Journal of Thomas B. Hazard of Kingstown, Rhode Island, 1778 to 1840* (Boston: Merrymount Press, 1930) CS71/H428/1930 also LOAN.

- Hazard, Thomas R., *Recollections of Olden Times: Rowland Robinson of Narragansett and his Unfortunate Daughter, with Genealogies of Robinson, Hazard, and Sweet families of Rhode Island; also Genealogical Sketch of the Hazards of the Middle States by Willis P. Hazard* (Newport, R.I.: J. P. Sanborn, 1879) CS71/R66/1879 also LOAN.

- Oatley, Henry Clay, Jr., *Daniel Stedman's Journal, 1826–1859*, Cherry Fletcher Bamberg, ed. (Greenville, R.I.: Rhode Island Genealogical Society, 2003) F89/S7/S74/2003.

- Sherman, Ruth Ann Wilder, ed., *Peleg Burroughs's Journal, 1778–1798: The Tiverton, R. I. Years of the Humbly Bold Baptist Minister* (Warwick, R.I.: Rhode Island Genealogical Society, 1981) F89/T6/B8 also LOAN.

African Americans and Native Americans

The published version of the 1774 census of Rhode Island by John Russell Bartlett (see under CENSUSES) compresses information on African Americans and Native Americans into simple totals, leaving out age and gender data and, in some towns the names of minority heads of households. This census is presently in the process of re-transcription and publication in *Rhode Island Roots*. Library users are urged to use Bartlett's index to identify the location of the person they are researching and then to consult either *Rhode Island Roots* or the microfilm of the original in Microtext HA611.5/1774.

Some relevant published works are the following:

- Cottrol, Robert J., *The Afro-Yankees: Providence's Black Community in the Antebellum Era* (Westport, Conn.: Greenwood Press, 1982) F89/P99/N425/1982 also LOAN.

- Stewart, Rowena, *A Heritage Discovered: Blacks in Rhode Island* (Providence, R.I.: Rhode Island Black Heritage Society, 1975) F90/N4/S8/1975.

- Youngken, Richard C., *African Americans in Newport: An Introduction to the Heritage of African Americans in Newport, Rhode Island, 1700–1945* (Providence, R.I.: Rhode Island Historical Preservation and Heritage Commission and Rhode Island Black Heritage Society, 1995).

- Henry, Lorraine (Rainwaters), *Native American Directory of Maine, Massachusetts, Rhode Island, Connecticut, New York, Wisconsin* (Bowie, Md.: Heritage Books, 1998) E98/G44/H46/1998 also LOAN.

- Recommendation and summary of evidence for proposed finding for federal acknowledgment of the Narragansett Tribe of Rhode Island pursuant to 25 CFR 83 (Washington, D.C.: Bureau of Indian Affairs, 1982) E99/N16/U55/1982.

- "Rhode Island Minorities in the American Revolution," in Eric G. Grundset, ed., *African American and American Indian Patriots of the Revolutionary War* (Washington, D.C.: National Society Daughters of the American Revolution, 2001), 53–63. E269/N3/A37/2001.

Vermont

Scott Andrew Bartley

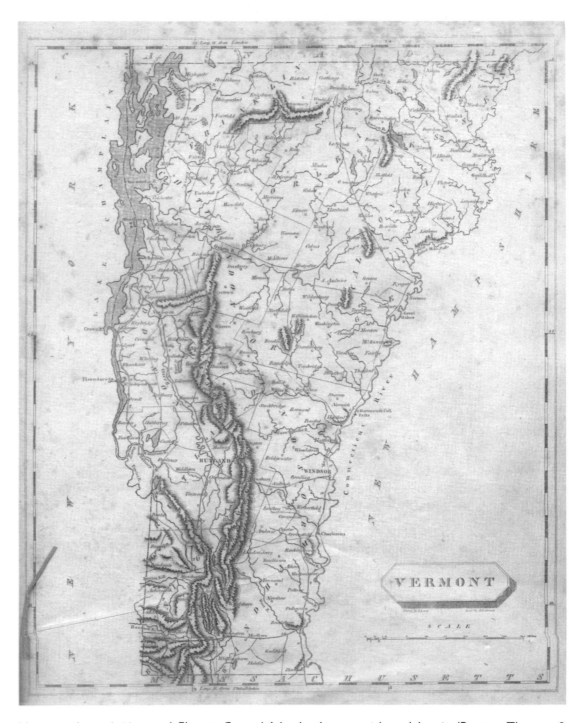

Vermont from *A New and Elegant General Atlas* by Arrowsmith and Lewis (Boston: Thomas & Andrews, 1805).

Overview

The early history of Vermont is a reflection of the political turmoil of the eighteenth century. A researcher needs to be aware that parts of Vermont were claimed at various times by Massachusetts, New Hampshire, and New York. As a result, relevant records for Vermont research may be in the records of jurisdictions adjoining present-day Vermont. In addition, Vermont was independent from 1777 to 1791.

Most original records were created and recorded at the town level. However, courts (including probate) were at the county level or districts that make up a county. Fortunately, most Vermont records of genealogical value have survived and many have been microfilmed. Some cemetery and town records have been abstracted and published as books or articles. The Genealogical Society of Vermont has sponsored or encouraged many of these publications on an ongoing basis, especially through its quarterly journal, *Vermont Genealogy*.

Guides and Finding Aids

- Bartley, Scott Andrew, and Alice Eichholz, "Vermont," in *Red Book: American State, County, and Town Sources*, 3rd ed. (Provo, Utah: Ancestry, 2004), 678–98. REF CS49/A55/2004 also LOAN.

- Melnyk, Marcia D., *Genealogist's Handbook for New England Research*, 4th ed. (Boston: NEHGS, 1999), 185–215. REF F3/G466/1999 also LOAN.

- Leppman, John A., *A Bibliography for Vermont Genealogy* (St. Albans, Vt.: Genealogical Society of Vermont, 2000) F48/L47/2000.

- Eichholz, Alice, *Collecting Vermont Ancestors*, rev. ed. (Montpelier, Vt.: New Trails!, 1993) IN PROCESS. This is the only widely distributed guide devoted exclusively to Vermont.

- *Research Outline: Vermont*, 2nd ed. (Salt Lake City: Family History Library, 1999), ask at fourth-floor desk.

- Crandall, Ralph J., ed., *Genealogical Research in New England* (Baltimore: Genealogical Publishing Company, 1984), 59–75. REF F3/G46/1984 also LOAN.

- Bartley, Scott Andrew, online articles about Vermont at *NewEnglandAncestors.org*.

- Bassett, T. D. Seymour, *Vermont: A Bibliography of Its History* (Boston: G. K. Hall, 1981) REF F49/V37/1981. This work includes books and articles published on Vermont topics in history.

- Carnahan, Paul A., *A Guide to Vermontiana Collections at Academic, Special and Selected Public Libraries* (Burlington, Vt.: Center for Research on Vermont, 1994) F46/C37/1994. This work focuses on manuscript collections of interest to historians and genealogists.

Genealogical and Historical Periodicals

- *Proceedings of the Vermont Historical Society*, 1896–1943, F46/V55/1860-1943. The "Old Series" were published sporadically until 1896, then roughly every two years from 1896 to 1928. The journal started quarterly publication in 1930 as the "New Series"; in 1943 the title changed to:

- *Vermont Quarterly*, 1943–53. F46/V55/1943-1953. The name changed again with vol. 22 (1954) to:

- *Vermont History*, 1954–present. F46/V55. There are four subject and every-name indexes combined in one alphabet for vols. 1–10, 11–20, 21–45, and 46–55.

- *The Vermont Antiquarian*, 3 vols. (1902–05) F46/V42 also LOAN.

- *The Vermonter: The State Magazine*, 51 vols. (1895–1946). There are author and subject indexes for vols. 1–17 and 18–44.

- *Branches & Twigs*, 24 vols. (1972–95), quarterly published by the Genealogical Society of Vermont. F48/B8 also LOAN. A composite every-name index was published by the Society in 2000. *Branches & Twigs* was succeeded by:

- *Vermont Genealogy*, 1996–present. F48/V48/1996 also LOAN. This journal publishes compiled genealogy and abstracted primary sources.

- *Across the Border*, 9 vols. (1988–97) F46/A27. The focus was on the northern counties of Vermont and the Eastern Townships in Quebec.

- *Links*, 1996–present, F46/L56/1996. Semi-annual journal of the Vermont French-Canadian Genealogical Society, focused on the French-Canadian culture and genealogy of Vermont.

- *Rooted in the Green Mountains*, 1997–present. F57/R9/R66. This is a quarterly newsletter-like publication focused on Addison and Rutland counties.

- *The New England Historical and Genealogical Register*, 1847–present. R.Rm. REF F1/N56 also LOAN also fifth floor also Web database. See NEW ENGLAND OVERVIEW.

- *The American Genealogist*, 1922–present. R.Rm. REF F104/N6/A6 also LOAN. See NEW ENGLAND OVERVIEW.

Censuses: Colonial, Federal, and State

Colonial

There is only one census from the colonial period. It was taken by the government of New York in 1771 and covered Cumberland and Gloucester counties. The western half of the state was then part of Albany County and this is no listing for that county. An age distribution was given for both counties and the heads of household for the Gloucester County towns of Newbury, Thetford, Moretown, Stafford, and (as one list) Barnet, Ryegate, Lunenburg, and Guildhall. The majority lived in Cumberland County. This census was published in E. B. O'Callaghan, *The Documentary History of the State of New-York*, 4 vols. (Albany, N.Y.: Weed, Parsons & Co., 1849–51), 4:708–09. Rare Book F122/D63/1849 also LOAN, and was reprinted in *Lists of Inhabitants of Colonial New York* (Baltimore: Genealogical Publishing Co., 1979), 288. F118/D62/1979 also LOAN.

All these names were included at part of Jay Mack Holbrook, *Vermont 1771 Census* (Oxford, Mass.: Holbrook Research Institute, 1982) F48.H7/1982. This work lists people residing in Vermont from 1766 to 1775 from a variety of sources.

Federal

Microfilms for all federal census of Vermont, 1790 through 1930 (including an index to the 1890 veterans' census), are on the fourth floor. The 1790 census for Vermont was actually taken on the first Monday in April 1791 after it was admitted as the first new state. The 1800 census was published as *Heads of Families at the Second Census of the United States Taken in the Year 1800: Vermont* (1938; reprinted Baltimore: Genealogical Publishing Co., 1972) Microtext F48/U55 also LOAN also fifth floor. One special case of the state's copy of a census (and never microfilmed) giving more information is found in Scott A. Bartley, transcriber, *Transcription of the State Copy of the 1850 Federal Census for Springfield and Baltimore, Vermont* (Boston: the transcriber, 1993) F59/S7/B38/1993 also LOAN. This version gives the exact town of birth for almost everyone in the two towns.

State

Vermont has had no state censuses.

Vital Records

The first Vermont law requiring vital records registration was in 1779, as described in the duties of the town clerk, though records date back to 1760. However, this did not seem to compel people to register vital events. In these early years, to about 1820, births and deaths were recorded in family groups and occasionally included the marriage of the parents as well. These records were often recorded after all the children were born. This makes them less valuable if there is a discrepancy with other contemporary sources since they were recorded so long after the date of the event. The benefit, however, is that places of birth were often listed — and the oldest children of the earliest families were often not born in Vermont. The volume of recorded vital records seems to diminish greatly in the 1810s. At this time, there was a great out-migration to New York, Quebec, and points beyond. It should be noted that in Vermont, the laws still required registration, though the language was much more vague.

Vital record registration as we think of it today started for Vermont in 1857. Each town clerk was required to transcribe annually all births, marriages, and deaths occurring during the year proceeding the first day of January. The next major change to affect genealogists was the 1919 law that gave the Secretary of State the authority to require town clerks to make a copy of all births, marriages, and deaths that are found "in the possession of the town, and churches, not already returned, and to transmit the same, properly certified, to the secretary of state." The state provided blank forms (actually color-coded index cards) to each town for this purpose. "If the death records of a town prior to 1870 are incomplete, the secretary of state shall notify the selectmen of said town to that effect. The selectmen of such town shall, before October 1, 1919, cause to be copied at the expense of the town under the direction of the secretary of state, the inscription on all gravestones in their town erected to the memory of any person who died prior to 1870 . . . and the name of the cemetery where buried and shall cause such records to be recorded in the town records."

These card files (except the most current five years) are maintained by the Vital Public Records Division of the General Services Administration presently located at Middlesex, Vermont. The cards themselves were closed in the early 1990s, but a microfilm copy of these files is available on location and at NEHGS (F48/V5). They are broken down into the following time periods: 1760–1870, 1871–1908, 1909–1941, 1942–1954, 1955–1979, then yearly starting in 1980 up to 1990. Each section is in a strict alphabetical order. Rarely are variant surname spellings interfiled. The majority of these records are open to anyone without restriction. The pre-1871 events are known to have records missing from the towns of Holland, Maidstone, Sheffield, and Troy. It has been suggested that some of the Burlington records from the 1860s and 1870s were missed, too. As a last resort, if you cannot find a record (especially before 1820 or after 1856) that other sources suggest is there, go back to the original town records. The town is the ultimate source for vital records in Vermont. Related records that genealogists may want to use are the divorce files. There is a statewide index for 1861–1968, 1968–1979, then yearly starting in 1980 up to 1990 (F48/V5), cross indexed by both husband and wife.

Some of the classic turn-of-the-century Vermont town histories in Vermont may have included a chapter on the earliest vital records for the town. Some vital records have been published in the periodicals listed above. Those published as books include the following:

- *Vermont Marriages: Volume I: Montpelier Burlington Berlin* (Boston: Research Publication Co., 1903; reprinted Baltimore: Genealogical Publishing Co., 1967) F48/V55/1903 also LOAN.

- Mallett, Peter S., *Georgia, Vermont Vital Records* (St. Albans, Vt.: Genealogical Society of Vermont, 1995) F59/G3/M35/1995 also LOAN.

- Warner, Rufus S., *Record of Deaths in the Town of Ludlow, Vermont, from 1790 to 1901 Inclusive* (Ludlow, Vt.: the author, 1902) F59/L9/W2/1902 also LOAN.

- Stevens, Ken, *Vital Records of Putney, Vermont, to the year 1900 with Selected Additional Records* (Pittsford, Vt.: Genealogical Society of Vermont, 1992) F59/P9/V58/1992 also LOAN.

- Peck, Thomas Bellows, *Vital Records of Rockingham, Vermont and Records of the First Church of Rockingham, Vermont* (Pittsford, Vt.: Genealogical Society of Vermont, 1994) F59/R7/P43/1994 also LOAN.

- Wheeler, Mary Anne Z., *Sudbury Vermont Genealogies, Vital Records, and Census Records* (Rockport, Maine: Picton Press, 2000) F59/S89/W54/2000.

  For name changes, see Scott Andrew Bartley, "Names Changes in Vermont, 1778–1900," *Vermont Genealogy* 9:1 (January 2004).

Church Records

Unlike southern New England, one church did not dominate the state. Each town had the right to tax households to support a minister or build a church for the majority of the residents. However, a householder could file a religious certificate to support their own church. These certificates have been published as Alden M. Rollins, *Vermont Religious Certificates* (Rockport, Maine: Picton Press, 2003) F48/R637/2003 also LOAN. For an overview of religious issues in the state, see T. D. Seymour Bassett, "Cabin Religion in Vermont, 1724–1791," *Vermont History* 62:2 (Spring 1994):69–87, and John C. DeBoer and Clara Merritt DeBoer, "The Formation of Town Churches," *Vermont History* 64:2 (Spring 1996):69–88. NEHGS has church records on microfilm for the towns of Bradford (Baptist Society), Cabot (Methodist, Congregational, and United Churches), Enosburgh (Protestant Episcopal), Fairfield (Protestant Episcopal and Trinity Parish), Georgia (Congregational), Jericho (First and Second Congregational), and Sudbury (Congregational). As listed above, the records of the First Church of Rockingham have been published, and other church records have appeared in the periodicals listed above.

Cemetery Records

The state government recognized the problem of insufficient access to early vital records. In 1919 the state made monies available to pay town clerks to transcribe the early vital records. Noting the lack of death records recorded in the town books, the town clerks were also offered funds to support their transcriptions of all gravestone inscriptions within town borders. This was to include all gravestones found with dates before 1871. These transcriptions are interfiled in the official statewide vital records card index (see under VITAL RECORDS).

The Vermont Old Cemetery Association (VOCA), founded in 1958, is a non-profit group whose goal is to "encourage the restoration and preservation of neglected and abandoned cemeteries in the State of Vermont" and to be a clearinghouse for information. The group's hard work culminated in the publication of Arthur L. and Frances P. Hyde, ed., *Burial Grounds in Vermont* (Bradford, Vt.: VOCA, 1991) F48/B87/1991 also LOAN, a town-by-town survey of existing cemeteries. For each town there is a map that locates the cemeteries. An accompanying list provides the current names of the town cemeteries, which sometimes vary from the names as read by the state's town clerks. This list also indicates the estimated number of stones, the span of years that burials took place, directions to the location, and remarks. Nearly 1,900 cemeteries are identified. It should be noted that the towns of Averill, Ferdinand, Glastonbury, and Lewis do not have any cemeteries within their borders.

The largest collection of transcriptions has been by Margaret ("Peggy") Jenks. She started transcribing gravestone inscriptions in 1981 and to date she has produced sixteen books covering twenty-seven towns:

- Benson–Hubbardton–Sudbury. F59/B43/J46/1993 also LOAN.
- Brandon. F59/B74/J46/1994 also LOAN.
- Castleton. F59/C321/J4/1989 also LOAN.
- Chittenden–Mendon–Pittsfield–Sherburne. F59/C52/J46/1992.
- Clarendon–Shrewsbury. F59/C6/J46/1991 also LOAN.
- Danby–Mount Tabor. F59/D2/J4/1993 also LOAN.
- Fair Haven–West Haven. F59/F1/J46/1990 also LOAN.
- Middletown Springs–Ira. F59/M62/J46/1983 also LOAN.
- Pawlet. F59/P3/J46/1985 also LOAN.
- Pittsford–Proctor. F59/P6/J46/1992 also LOAN.
- Poultney. F59/P8/J53/1996.
- Rutland. F57/R9/J45/1995 also LOAN.
- Tinmouth. F59/T5/J4/1985 also LOAN.

- Wallingford–Mount Holly. F59/W18/J46/1992 also LOAN.

- Wells. F59/W4/J4/1981 also LOAN.

- West Rutland. F59/W494/J45/1993 also LOAN.

Joann Nichols created the first survey of published material in 1976 (revised in 1982 and again in 1995). This was the only guide to gravestone records for many years. She culled several manuscript collections and national journals that published this type of material. The current edition is Joann H. Nichols, Patricia L. Haslam, and Robert M. Murphy, *Index to Known Cemetery Listings in Vermont*, 4th ed. (Montpelier, Vt.: Vermont Historical Society, 1999) REF F48/N53/1999. The following are additions (or clarifications) to the 4th edition. Researchers should also look for articles in *Vermont Genealogy*.

- **Irish**: Murphy, Donald Chase, and Janice Church Murphy, comps., *Irish Famine Immigrants in the State of Vermont: Gravestone Inscriptions* (Baltimore: Clearfield, 2000) F60/I6/M87/2000 also LOAN.

- **Addison County**: Farnsworth, Harold P., "Cemetery Records of Addison County, Vermont: Headstones in Addison County Cemeteries of People Born Before 1800," indexed by Richard and Sandra C. King (1992) Mss C 4142.

- **Bennington**: Cassano, Lynne M., *Gravestone Inscriptions from the Village Cemetery, Bennington, Vermont* (Bennington, Vt.: Bennington Museum, 1990) F59/B4/C37/1990.

- **Brattleboro**: Howe, Marjorie Valliere, *A Record of Burials at the Vermont Asylum : later known as the Brattleboro Retreat, 1837–1900* (Williamsville, Vt.: the transcriber, 1999) F59/B8/H695/1999.

- **Brattleboro**: Howe, Marjorie Valliere, *Gravestone Inscriptions of Locust Ridge Cemetery, Brattleboro, Windham Co., Vt.* (Williamsville, Vt.: the transcriber, 1999) F59/B8/H686/1999.

- **Brattleboro**: Howe, Marjorie Valliere, *Gravestone Inscriptions of Prospect Hill Cemetery, Brattleboro, Vt.* (Williamsville, Vt.: the transcriber, 2000) F59/B8/H69/2000.

- **Chelsea**: "Inscriptions in the Old and New Cemeteries in Chelsea, Vermont," Mss C 1066.

- **Dover**: Fiske, Arthur D., "Cemetery Records of Dover, Windham County, Vermont to 1865" (Seattle: the transcriber, 1963) V.F. F59/D75/F57/1963.

- **Duxbury**: Morse, Robert H., *Duxbury & Moretown Cemetery Inscriptions, Washington County, Vermont* (Plainfield, Vt.: Morse, "Version Two," 2000) F59/D89/M67/2000 also LOAN.

- **East Montpelier**: Hill, Ellen C., Bob Webster, and Lois Webster, *The Cemeteries of East Montpelier, Vermont, 1795–1971: An Inventory of Gravestones and Their Poetry* (n.p., 1971) F59/E17/E54/1971 also LOAN.

- **Fairlee**: Neal, Mrs. Philemon C., "South Fairlee (Ely) Cemetery, Fairlee, Vermont: with genealogical notes on Carpenter, Heath, Kibbey" (Massachusetts DAR Genealogical Records Committee, NSDAR Deane Winthrop Chapter, 1955) Mss A 53

- **Fairfield**: Gilbert H. Doane Collection, Mss 16, includes cemeteries in the town of Fairfield.

- **Georgia**: Mallett, Peter S., *Cemeteries of Georgia, Vt.* (Georgia, Vt.: Georgia Historical Society, 1982) F59/G3/C43/1982 also LOAN.

- **Greensboro**: Cutler, Edwin B., "Inscriptions from the Stannard Mountain Cemetery, Greensboro Bend" (1964) Mss A 65.

- **Hartford**: Lubbe, Mrs. George Anthony, "Hartford, Vermont [Cemetery Inscriptions, 1798–1881]" (1881?) Mss A 2316.

- **Middletown Springs**: "Some inscriptions from the Old Cemetery at Middletown Springs, Vt." Mss A 2342.

- **Moretown**: see Duxbury.

- **Strafford**: Bassingthwaighte, George E., "A Record of Gravestones and their Locations in the Kibling Cemetery [Strafford], 1788–1962" (1964) Mss A 51.

- **Westfield**: Soo, Lisa Gilbert, *Gravestone Inscriptions from the Cemeteries of Westfield, Vermont* (Acton, Mass.: the transcriber, 2001) F59/W497/S66/2001.

- **Westminster**: Wright, Charles Byron, *Monuments & Headstones in the "New Cemetery," East Parish, Westminster, Windham County, Vermont, as of November 10, 1999* (Walpole, N.H.: the transcriber, 1999) F59/W5/W75/1999 also LOAN.

- **West Windsor**: Hayden, Arthur B., "Epitaphs and Inscriptions copied from the Old Cemetery at Sheddsville [West Windsor], Vermont," typescript (1954?) Mss A 52.

- **Windsor**: *Old South Burying Ground, Windsor, Vermont* (n.p., 1904) F59/W7/O42/1904 also LOAN.

Newspapers

Abstracts of genealogical data in newspapers can be found in the periodicals listed under GENEALOGICAL AND HISTORICAL PERIODICALS, particularly *Vermont Genealogy*. The only two concerted efforts have been Marsha Hoffman Rising, *Vermont Newspaper Abstracts, 1783–1816* (Boston: NEHGS, 2001) F48/R57/2001, which focuses on Bennington papers, and Dawn H. Hance, transcriber, *Extracts from the Rutland Weekly Herald [1800–1830]*, typed and indexed by Joann H. Nichols, 6 vols. (Rutland, Vt.: the transcriber, 1999–2003) F59/R9/E98.

See also Marlene Simmons, *Index to the Richford, Vt. Gazette and Journal-Gazette 1880–1957: Extracts of Canadian Genealogical Information* (Pointe Claire, P.Q.: Quebec Family History Society, 1994) F59/R56/S56/1994 also LOAN. The WPA created the *Index to the Burlington Free Press in the Billings Library, University of Vermont . . . 1848 [to] 1870*, 10 vols. (Montpelier, Vt.: Historical Records Survey, 1940–42) F59/B9/H57/1940. Anne Kendall Smith and Stuart E. Smith, *Vital Statistics from Saint Johnsbury Caledonian*, 14 vols. (Danville, Vt.: the compilers, 2000–03) F57/C2/S65/2000, covers the period 1870 to 1905.

There are manuscripts at NEHGS by John Eliot Bowman listing Vermont marriages and deaths from Massachusetts and Vermont newspapers between 1790 and 1848. Mss A 38, A 56, and C 3301 through C 3304.

Probate Records

Probate records are filed by district. Each county is one complete district or a county forms two districts. These records were microfilmed up to 1850 and some cases to 1900. They usually have an index in each volume. One thing that you cannot find anywhere else except at the probate court itself is the overall card index to the estate and guardianship records, often up to the 1960s. Some of the indexes are closed as they contain cards for adoption cases. Many Vermont probate records are on microfilm at NEHGS

- Addison County [two courts combined in 1962]: Addison District, 1801–1851. F57/A2/A33, 8 reels, and index for 1852–1959, F57/A2/A33, 2 reels. New Haven District, 1824–1857. F57/A2/N49, 4 reels.

- Bennington County: Bennington District, 1778–1851. FF57/B4/B45, 7 reels. Manchester District, 1779–1850, F57/B4/M36, 5 reels.

- Caledonia County: Caledonia District, 1796–1857. F57/C2/C35, 17 reels, and guardian records, 1839–1881. F57/C2/C35, 2 reels.

- Chittenden County: Chittenden District, 1795–1857. F57/C5/C49, 13 reels, and guardian records, 1838–1856. F57/C5/C49, 1 reel.

- Essex County: Essex District, 1791–1855. F57/E7/E88, 2 reels.

- Franklin County: Franklin District, 1796–1851. F57/F8/F73, 14 reels; includes index volume for 1796–1850.

- Grand Isle County: Grand Isle District, 1796–1859. F57/G7/G73, 4 reels.

- Lamoille County: Lamoille District, 1837–1875. F57/L2/L36, 5 reels.

- Orange County: [two courts combined in 1994]: Bradford District, 1781–1852. F57/O6/B73, 4 reels. Randolph District, 1792–1850. F57/O6/R36, 9 reels.

- Orleans County: Orleans District, 1796–1823. F57/O7/O75, 3 reels.

- Rutland County: Fair Haven District, 1797–1823, 1842–1851. F57/R9/F35, 4 reels. Rutland District, 1784–1850. F57/R9/R88, 9 reels.

- Washington County: Washington District, 1811–1850. F57/W3/W37, 8 reels.

- Windham County: Marlboro District, 1781–1850. F57/W6/M37, 10 reels and estate index 1791–1898, and guardian records, 1821–1849. F57/W6/M37, 1 reel and index 1781–1898. Westminster District, 1781–1851. F57/W6/W47, 7 reels.

- Windsor County: Hartford District, 1783–1851. F57/W7/H37, 10 reels. Windsor District, 1787–1900. F57/W7/W56, 24 reels; both districts indexed in Scott Andrew Bartley and Marjorie-J. Bartley, *Windsor County, Vermont, Probate Index, 1778–1899* (St. Albans, Vt.: Genealogical Society of Vermont, 2000) F57/W7/B37/2000 also LOAN. Also guardian records, 1805–1855. F57/W7/W56, 5 reels.

Land Records

Land records are an underutilized primary source. Land records are created at the town level and so there is no master index on either the county or state level. Each town will have a master grantor and grantee index. They can be an index card system with all cards mixed into a single alphabetical index or ledger book indexes with separate columns for grantors and grantees. Some early land records were recorded at the county level; the only county land records at NEHGS are for Orange County, 1771–1832. F57/O6/O63, 3 reels, with an index for 1771–1952. A list of grantees of Vermont land, 1763–1803, is the basis of Jay Mack Holbrook, *Vermont's First Settlers* (Oxford, Mass.: Holbrook Research Institute, 1976) REF F48/H74 also LOAN. See also land records in volumes 1 and 5–7 of *State Papers of Vermont*, 22 vols. to date (various places and publishers, 1918–91) F46/V35 also LOAN.

Town Records

Town records are the basic source for governmental records in Vermont. The earliest records are those of the proprietors. They normally are meetings (usually not held in the town) and divisions of lands. The next group of records is town meetings. The earliest records of town meetings include everything but land records. Depending on the population of the town, you might see vital records, tax records, school records, poor records, and highway records started as separate series of volumes.

Another important group of records often overlooked but crucial in tracking mobile Vermonters is warnings out. Vermont warnings out cover from 1769 to 1787 and 1801 to 1817. The earlier records are sparse and there was no requirement for them to be recorded in the town books. Most persons warned out during this time were poor and transient. Records for the second period contain more complete information as the town clerk was required by law to record it. The people warned out in the second period were not necessarily poor and most likely did not move out of town. The surviving records for the entire state were abstracted in Alden M. Rollins, *Vermont Warnings Out*, 2 vols. (Camden, Maine: Picton Press, 1995–97) F48/R64/1995 also LOAN.

Abstracted town records have been published for some towns as books or as articles, often in *Vermont Genealogy*. NEHGS has microfilms of original town records for 36 out of 252 towns for Vermont, as follows: Alburgh, Bennington, Bradford, Burke, Cabot, Chelsea, Chester, Corinth, Danby, Danville, Enosburgh, Fairfax, Fairfield, Georgia, Hinesburgh, Huntington, Ira, Jericho, Kirby, Lyndon, Manchester, Marshfield, Milton, Mount Holly, Newbury, Putney, Reading, Royalton, Saint Albans, Sudbury, Vershire, Wallingford, Washington, Weston, Williston, and Woodbury.

Tax Records

Tax lists in Vermont are called Grand Lists. They are first found in the regular town meeting books and, in larger towns, they will form a separate series of books. These lists of ratable polls include adult males over 21 and less than 60 years of age. They excluded ministers and students up to three years after receiving their degree. Improved land and buildings were also subject to tax. If the owner did not live in the town, then the tenant of the land or buildings would be entered on the list. The only dwelling exemption in the 1798 law was a log-house valued at under $1,000.

Court and Legislative Records

Many legislative records were published in *State Papers of Vermont*; an analysis is in Leppman, *Bibliography for Vermont Genealogy* (see GUIDES AND FINDING AIDS).The Vermont Public Records Division has microfilmed copies of some county court records with indexes. The Family History Library has copies of some court records for Bennington, Orange, and Windsor counties.

Military Records

The State Arsenal that housed Vermont's military records was struck by lightning on August 31, 1945, and burned. Fortunately, most of the holdings for the Revolutionary War, War of 1812, Civil War, Spanish American War, and World War I had already been published.

Revolutionary War

- Fisher, Carleton Edward, and Sue Gray Fisher, comp., *Soldiers, Sailors, and Patriots of the Revolutionary War: Vermont* (Camden, Maine: Picton Press, 1992) E263/V5/F58/1992 also LOAN.

- Goodrich, John E., *Rolls of the Soldiers in the Revolutionary War, 1775 to 1783* (Rutland, Vt.: Tuttle, 1904) E263/V5/V5/1904 also LOAN.

- Nye, Mary Greene, *State Papers of Vermont, Volume Six: Sequestration, Confiscation, and Sale of Estates* (Montpelier, Vt.: Office of the Secretary of State, 1941) F46/V35/v.6 also LOAN.

War of 1812

- Clark, Byron N., ed., *A List of Pensioners of the War of 1812* (Burlington, Vt.: Sheldon Press, 1904; reprinted Baltimore: Genealogical Publishing Co., 1996) E359.4/C62/1904 also LOAN. This is from a manuscript by William G. Shaw regarding volunteers from the Burlington area. It contains several appendices including abstracts of payroll records.

- Johnson, Herbert T., *Roster of Soldiers in the War of 1812–14* (St. Albans, Vt.: Messenger Press, 1933) E359.5/V3/R67/1933 also LOAN.

Civil War

- Benedict, G. G., *Vermont in the Civil War. A History of the part taken by the Vermont Soldiers and Sailors in the War for the Union,* 2 vols. (Burlington, Vt.: Free Press Assn., 1886) E533.4/B46/1886 also LOAN.

- *Revised Roster of Vermont Volunteers and lists of Vermonters who served in the Army and Navy of the United States during the War of the Rebellion, 1861–66* (Montpelier, Vt.: Watchman Publishing Co., 1892) Rare Book E533.3/V53/1892.

- Waite, Otis F. R., *Vermont in the Great Rebellion containing historical and biographical sketches, etc.* (Claremont, N.H.: Tracy, Chases and Co., 1869) F53/W34/1869 also LOAN.

Spanish American War

- Johnson, Herbert T., *Vermont in the Spanish-American War* (Montpelier, Vt.: Capital City Press, 1929) VT/50/20.

World War I

- Cushing, John T., and Arthur F. Stone, ed., *Vermont in the World War, 1917–1919* (Burlington, Vt.: Free Press Printing Co., 1928) F54/C8.

- Johnson, Herbert T., *Roster of Vermont Men and Women in the Military and Naval Service of the United States and Allies in the World War, 1917–1919* (Rutland, Vt.: Tuttle, 1927) VT/50/23.

Genealogical and Biographical Compendia (Including Town and County Histories)

For a list of surnames of families with biographical data found in Vermont town histories, see Scott Andrew Bartley's online articles about Vermont at *NewEnglandAncestors.org*. Some published sources are:

- Bartley, Scott Andrew, ed., *Vermont Families in 1791*, 2 vols. (Vol. 1, Camden, Maine: Picton Press, 1992; Vol. 2, St. Albans, Vt.: Genealogical Society of Vermont, 1997) REF F48/V47/1992 also LOAN also fifth floor.

- Carleton, Hiram, ed., *Genealogical and Family History of the State of Vermont* (New York: Lewis Publishing Co., 1903) F48/C28/1903 also LOAN.

- Dodge, Prentiss C., *Encyclopedia Vermont Biography* (Burlington, Vt.: Ullery Publishing Co., 1912) F48/D64/1912 also LOAN.

- Herndon, Richard, *Men of Progress: Biographical Sketches and Portraits of Leaders in Business and Professional Life in and of the Sate of Vermont* (Burlington, Vt.: Free Press Assn., 1898) VT/55/6.

- Hemenway, Abby Maria, ed., *The Vermont Historical Gazetteer*, 5 vols. (various places and publishers, 1867–1923) REF F48/V583 also LOAN also fifth floor also on NEHGS CD-ROM. A compilation of articles written by local historians on all the towns in Vermont starting in the 1850s, though the ones from Windsor County were not published before they burned save Andover. Much information comes from the memories of the elders of the town.

- Jeffrey, William H., *Successful Vermonters: A Modern Gazetteer of Caledonia, Essex, and Orleans Counties* (East Burke, Vt.: Historical Publishing Co., 1904) VT/55/10.

- Jeffrey, William H., *Successful Vermonters: A Modern Gazetteer of Lamoille, Franklin and Grand Isle Counties* (East Burke, Vt.: Historical Publishing Co., 1907) VT/88/15.

- Kent, Dorman B. E., *Vermonters* (Montpelier, Vt.: Vermont Historical Society, 1937) VT/55/8. Originally published as *One Thousand Men* (Montpelier, Vt.: Vermont Historical Society, 1915) VT/55/7.

- Ullery, Jacob G., *Men of Vermont: An Illustrated Biographical History of Vermonters and Sons of Vermont* (Brattleboro, Vt.: Transcript Publishing Co., 1894) F48/U41/1894 also LOAN.

- Williams, Henry Clay, *Biographical Encyclopedia of Vermont of the Nineteenth Century* (Boston: Metropolitan Publishing and Engraving Co., 1885) F48/B61/1885 also LOAN.

Maps and Atlases

For information regarding historical maps, the researcher should consult David Cobb, "Vermont Maps Prior to 1900: An Annotated Cartobibliography" *Vermont History* 39:3–4 (1971). A good current map is *Vermont Atlas & Gazetteer*, 9th ed. (Freeport, Maine: DeLorme, 1996). To understand county border changes, see Gordon DenBoer and George E. Goodridge, *New Hampshire, Vermont: Atlas of Historical County Boundaries* (New York: Simon & Schuster, 1993) Atlas G1201/F7/A8/1993/NH, VT also LOAN. For place names, see Esther Munroe Swift, *Vermont Place Names: Footprints of History* (1977; reprinted Camden, Maine: Picton Press, 1996) R.Rm. REF F47/S84/1977 also LOAN.

Frederick Wilson Beers published a series of atlases for the state. They were all reprinted by the Tuttle Company of Rutland, Vermont, in 1971. The ones NEHGS has in the Atlas section are italicized: *Addison* (1871), Bennington (1869), Caledonia (1875), *Chittenden* (1869), Essex (1878), Franklin and Grand Isle (1871), Lamoille (1878), Orange (1877), *Rutland* (1869), *Washington* (1873), Windham (1869), and *Windsor* (1869). Beers did not publish an atlas for Orleans County.

Special Sources for Vermont

- Duffy, John J., Samuel B. Hand, and Ralph H. Orth, *The Vermont Encyclopedia* (Hanover, N.H.: University Press of New England, 2003) IN CATALOGING. Current coverage of over a thousand Vermont topics.

- Waite, Frederick Clayton, *The Story of a Country Medical College: A History of the Clinical School of Medicine and the Vermont Medical College, Woodstock, Vermont, 1827–1856* (Montpelier, Vt.: Vermont Historical Society, 1945), and *The First Medical College in Vermont: Castleton, 1818–1862* (Montpelier, Vt.: Vermont Historical Society, 1949) F59/C321/W35/1949. These works include biographical sketches of students at two medical colleges that closed by the end of the Civil War.

- "Blacks and Indians of New Hampshire and Vermont in the American Revolution," in Eric G. Grundset, ed., *African American and American Indian Patriots of the Revolutionary War* (Washington, D.C.: National Society Daughters of the American Revolution, 2001), 15–26. E269/N3/A37/2001.

Beyond the Northeast

Ancestors on the Move:
Migrations out of New England

David Curtis Dearborn

When John Dearborn left his home in Wakefield, New Hampshire, in the 1790s for western Pennsylvania, making a small contribution to American history was probably the last thing on his mind. Nevertheless, John's decision to abandon the safe and familiar confines of New England for the frontier put him in the vanguard of what was to become a vast westward movement emblematic of nineteenth-century America. As the Revolution drew to a close, small numbers of people began moving inland, away from the areas already settled, and across the Appalachians. For New Englanders, this movement meant the central and western parts of upstate New York, central and western Pennsylvania, and on to what was then known as the Northwest Territory.

Reprinted from *New England Ancestors* 3:2 (Spring 2002):11–17.

"Emigrants to the West" from S. Augustus Mitchell, *Mitchell's School Geography: A System of Modern Geography...* (Philadelphia: Thomas, Cowperthwait, 1843).

The journey west — whether undertaken by foot, horseback, wagon, or boat — was slow and arduous. It is hard for us to imagine, in this age of coast-to-coast air travel, cell phones, and email, that for some, like John Dearborn, moving west meant cutting off all ties with family. According to a written account, "tradition . . . says, that when he started for the west on foot, one of his [younger] half-brothers, who was much attached to him, went several miles to keep him company, after which none of the family ever received any account of him."[1] How many other similar stories can be told?

Most of you who belong to NEHGS and trace some of your ancestry back to New England do so through lines that migrated west after the Revolution. About two-thirds of NEHGS members live outside New England, with over 2,000 in California alone. One of the most universal genealogical problems faced by many of you is the "brick wall" ancestor, whose trail runs cold in upstate New York in the early nineteenth century. Over the years I have met many of you, either during your visits to the library, or at NEHGS-sponsored events such as Come Home to New England, the New England Summer Conference, or the Salt Lake City Tour. Among your proven New England lines will be some ancestors living in upstate New York or in the Midwest, born in the late eighteenth or early nineteenth century, who are complete dead ends. If you have been involved with genealogy for a decade or more, as many of you have, these "dead end" ancestors are nothing new. Despite your most thorough research through censuses, cemeteries, church records, probates and deeds, they remain frustratingly elusive.

There are several reasons for this quandary:

- The simple fact that your ancestor was migrating creates a disjuncture: he was born in one place but you first find him living in another. Assuming that your ancestor's birth or baptism in New England was recorded, how do you find proof of a connection between the birth/baptism of the person of that name, with your ancestor living elsewhere?

- The period between the Revolution and the Civil War, when most of the migration westward out of New England occurred, is the most difficult period of all in which to trace ancestors. After the Civil War, record-keeping (especially of vital records), the survival of personal documents (letters, family Bibles, etc.), and stories handed down from elderly relatives, make the last 140 years much less fraught with pitfalls. Tracing ancestors before the Revolution, provided that they were in New England, is actually *easier* because 1) there were fewer people the further back you trace, 2) families were more sedentary, and 3) there is a better chance of finding something in print on the family, either in a genealogy, local history, vital records, or the *Register*.

- Not only do the migrations themselves make it difficult to "connect the dots" of your ancestor's life; recordkeeping was usually not up to the task of creating documents of genealogical value. Compared to other regions of the country, New England is a veritable goldmine of records, especially because births, marriages, and deaths were kept by the town clerks. Although these were not always recorded scrupulously for everyone, and some have been lost to fire, floods, and other disasters, they are sufficiently common that, when used with other records, even people of very modest background can usually be traced. Once your ancestors chose to leave New England, they entered the realm of relatively bad recordkeeping.

When searching for your migrating ancestor, always keep in mind the genealogist's Golden Rule: work from the known to the unknown. Just because your ancestor, James Adams, settled in Ohio after the War of 1812, don't assume that he *had* to be a New Englander, even if your great-aunt always claimed that the family was "somehow related to the presidents." If your ancestor had a surname shared by someone famous or by a well-known New England family, such as the Adamses, it is tempting to assume that you are somehow connected. You search Andrew N. Adams's massive 1898 Henry Adams of Braintree genealogy in vain, sadly concluding that somehow, the compiler "missed" your line. Don't rule out the possibility that James or his family had non-New England origins. According to the 1790 census, there were nearly as many Adams households outside New England (592) as there were within (654). A corollary caveat is the notion held by many genealogists with some New England ancestors, that not only must their "dead ends" go back to New England families, they must also descend from "Great Migration" (1620–1640s) immigrants. Even in New England, not all families living at the time of the Revolution trace back to the early 1600s, and the proportion of eighteenth-century immigrant ancestors you will have increases greatly if they lived in New York or points south and west. For example, an ancestor of mine, Rebecca Gillum, who was born near Trenton, New Jersey, in 1800, was a "brick wall" for many years. Just across the Delaware River in Bucks County, Pennsylvania, lived a family named *Gillam*. One Lucas Gillam, who was of an age that he could have been my Rebecca's grandfather, married a member of the locally prominent Dungan family, among whose forebears were Wings and Bachelders of colonial New England. I wanted desperately to tie my Rebecca into this family, but years of searching failed to yield the desired connection. Just a few years ago, I discovered by chance that a distant cousin had in her possession a Gillum family record that showed Rebecca's father to have been an English immigrant who arrived at Trenton with his family about 1798. So much for colonial New England ancestors!

To understand how and why our ancestors left New England, it is necessary to understand New England geography and the history of how it was settled. The first settlements took place along the coast where there was safe anchorage. Those places with the best harbors that had access to drinking water and were easily defensible were the most successful. This is why we see the earliest settlements at Plymouth, Boston, Salem and Gloucester, Portsmouth (New Hampshire), Newport, Providence, Saybrook, and New Haven. By the time of King Philip's War (1675), the area of settlement included much of the coastline of southern New England, all of the coastal plain, as well as the lower Connecticut River valley. By the end of the French and Indian Wars (1763), virtually all of southern New England was settled. Northern New England was a totally different matter. Not only was the possibility of attack by the French and Indians a continuing threat, but geography and climate were against would-be settlers. Aside from the coast, the land is mountainous and ill-suited to farming. The major rivers in the area (the Connecticut, Merrimack, Kennebec, Androscoggin, and Penobscot), along with the parallel mountain ranges, all run from north to south, making east-west travel difficult. Hence, from historical times to the present, the bulk of New England's population has been in the three southern states, with the lion's share in Massachusetts, followed by Connecticut.

Whether our migrating ancestors were from New England or elsewhere, one of the principal motivators for their leaving was the allure of free or cheap land. Thus, as they migrated, they tended to skip over areas that were already settled, because the choicest lands, along rivers and major routes, were claimed by the earlier arrivals. When New Englanders started moving west in large numbers beginning in the 1790s, most passed right through the Hudson and Mohawk valleys, in favor of unclaimed lands further west. As more and more families arrived in an area, the frontier was pushed further west. It was this process of settling and clearing land for farming, building towns and roads, and establishing businesses and commerce, that typifies much of nineteenth-century American history. New Englanders played a major part, both in terms of sheer numbers of settlers, and in terms of contributing New England customs and values to everyday life on the newly settled frontier.

However, because northern New England, especially northern Maine and New Hampshire, was the last area settled, this region maintained its own "frontier" well into the nineteenth century, in a sense acting as a "safety valve," siphoning off families from the more-settled areas, who might otherwise have migrated west. Further, there was an imaginary line, running from about the

White Mountains of New Hampshire, west of the Merrimack, through central Worcester County, and along the Massachusetts–Rhode Island border, that determined in part whether a post-Revolutionary New England family would move east to the unsettled areas of central and northern Maine, or westward to New York and beyond. Typical of this trend was my great-great-great-grandfather Henry Dearborn, a native of Deerfield, New Hampshire, who in 1825 sold his farm in New Durham, New Hampshire (near the southeastern tip of Lake Winnipesaukee), and moved northeastwards with his family about 150 miles to Corinna, Penobscot County, Maine, a town that had been settled only about a dozen years earlier. After the Civil War his son Samuel (my great-great-grandfather) moved even further downeast, to the little town of Lagrange, which even today is at the edge of the vast, unpopulated Maine woods.

Although Maine is probably the least-represented of New England states in terms of westward migration, its sons and daughters are nevertheless to be found scattered all across the northern tier of states. One such migrant was Joseph B. Banton, town clerk of Lagrange and uncle of Samuel Dearborn's wife. A native of Manchester, England, he had settled in Waldo County, Maine, with his parents as a boy. The father of fifteen, he moved in 1845 with his younger children to Clarkson, Monroe County, New York (the three oldest remaining behind and eventually settling in Bangor). By the 1860 census, Joseph was living in Kent County, Michigan, and in 1870 was at Farley, Dubuque County, Iowa, where he died four years later. The children who migrated with him settled in Michigan, Iowa, South Dakota, Washington state, and California.

By the 1870s and 1880s, when settlement in northern New England reached its peak, the region became something of an economic backwater, and its more restless citizens, rather than move west, tended instead to go to the cities of southern New England, especially the Boston area, where economic opportunity was greatest.

Western Massachusetts and Connecticut contributed by far the greatest number of westward migrants. If you have good reason to believe that your "brick wall" ancestor was indeed from New England, this is the area from which he most likely came. The principal destination of many of these settlers was, at least initially, New York.

While the westward flow did not become significant until after the Revolution, the New England–New York connection dates back to the earliest days of colonial settlement. In 1640 Gravesend on Long Island was founded by arrivals from Massachusetts Bay. Southampton was established in 1656 by about forty families from Lynn. The populations of Bedford and Rye were largely composed of families from Connecticut, Rhode Island, and southeastern Massachusetts. A large proportion of the settlers in the Oblong in Dutchess County, New York, were Quakers from Cape Cod. Westchester, Dutchess, and Orange counties in New York saw large waves of migration from Fairfield and Litchfield counties, Connecticut. Many of these settlers or their descendants intermarried with the local population, of Dutch, Huguenot, Scotch-Irish, German, and English backgrounds.

Migrants traveled west by land or water, whatever was most direct or convenient. The earliest overland routes were Indian footpaths widened and improved by the early settlers. The rights of way of many of these, such as the Boston Post Road (to New York City), still survive today. The post road from Boston to Albany, via Worcester and Springfield, was the route by which many headed west. While travel was difficult and the frontier was still dangerous and thinly populated, the rate of in-migration was a relative trickle. Once the frontier was pushed west and the trappings of law, order, and civilization reached the area, the influx increased. Some of the newcomers planned to settle permanently while others, always restless, remained only until some better opportunity presented itself further west. Improved means of transport made the decision whether to stay or move west an easier one. The opening of the Erie Canal in 1825 heralded an unprecedented exodus from New England, though the canal was soon superseded by the coming of the railroad, which made mass movement even easier.

It is important not to overlook the role of Vermont in westward migration. Although serious settlement of Vermont did not begin until after the French and Indian War, it filled up rapidly in the next forty years. Most of the arrivals were from Connecticut and central and western Massachusetts, with a little spillover from New Hampshire. The newcomers found life there hard — heavily forested hilly land, thin stony soil, and poor weather. Beginning with the War of 1812, a combination of hard economic times and bad weather, culminating in 1816, the "Year of No Summer," resulted in a mass exodus. Many Vermonters got no further than the New York counties of Washington, Warren, Essex, Clinton, Franklin, St. Lawrence, and Jefferson, but large numbers also went to Chautauqua County in far western New York, or to points even further west.

A less traveled route but one that should still be noted is the one leading north out of New Hampshire and Vermont to what was called Lower Canada, now Quebec, specifically to the area of Quebec just over the Vermont border, known as the Eastern Townships. The Townships were under British rule but were virgin territory — even the French-speaking native Quebecers had ignored the area. By the 1820s the Eastern Townships were, genealogically speaking, an extension of northern New England. Americans had only to take the oath of allegiance and they were permitted to settle. One such settler was Hananiah Hall, who was born in Wrentham, Massachusetts, in 1758, moved with his parents to Keene, New Hampshire, as a boy, and served as a soldier in the Revolution. The Halls were one of the most prominent families in Keene, though Hananiah's father caused some consternation when he refused to sign the Association Test in 1776. Lured by the promise of a better life, Hananiah moved to Lower Canada with his family, took the Oath in 1799, and spent the next forty years happily farming in the town of Eaton, Quebec.

National events caused some to grapple with their political convictions during the War of 1812. Nathaniel Dearborn, a native of North Hampton, New Hampshire, was living at Northwood, New Hampshire, when he served in the Revolution. By the 1790 census he had moved to Corinth, Vermont, but by 1800 had settled with his family in Barnston, Lower Canada (Quebec). His peaceful life came to an end during the War of 1812, when Nathaniel refused to affirm his loyalty to the crown. Stripped of his lands, he then moved with his sons to Spencer, Tioga County, New York, where he lived to the age of ninety-six. Hananiah Hall and Nathaniel Dearborn both applied for Revolutionary War pensions, and these documents provide the key for tracing their movements.

The majority of westward migrants tended to follow parallel lines of latitude. Thus, the most popular areas of Yankee settlement were upstate New York, the northern tier of Pennsylvania, the northern parts of Ohio, Indiana, and Illinois, plus Michigan, Wisconsin, Minnesota, and Iowa. Few ventured south of the Mason and Dixon Line or the Ohio River. Similarly, Southerners also moved westward roughly in their own latitudes. Most early settlers of Kentucky and Tennessee hailed from Virginia and North Carolina, most early Missourians were from Kentucky, and so many Mississippians were from Alabama, Georgia, and South Carolina.

While we may never be able to untangle the genealogical and migratory strands of all those who left New England, what is certain is that these hardy pioneers influenced their communities and their nation out of all proportion to their numbers. It is estimated that by the Civil War, there were as many people of New England blood living outside New England as there were ones who stayed.

Does this migration mean that New England was depopulated? Not at all. While the populations of Maine, New Hampshire, and Vermont were essentially stagnant from the Civil War until World War II, population grew rapidly in southern New England. This increase was largely due to the huge influx of immigrants, chiefly from Ireland and Italy, but also French-speakers from Canada. Today, a New Englander is as likely to be at least partly of non-western European stock, descending from nineteenth- or even twentieth-century immigrants, as to have ancestors tracing back to the *Mayflower*.

However or whenever your ancestors went west, understanding the migration and settlement patterns peculiar to the areas where they lived will make it easier for you to decide on the best strategies and sources when you begin your quest for their New England origins.

Note

1. Edmund B. Dearborn, "The Dearborn Family," [Mss 374], 95–96.

Suggestions for Further Reading on Migrations out of New England

The following titles, all available at the NEHGS Research Library or from the NEHGS Circulating Library, give valuable, in-depth information on migration out of New England:

Rosenberry, Lois Kimball Mathews, *The Expansion of New England: The Spread of New England Settlements and Institutions to the Mississippi River, 1620–1865* (1909) [F4/ R81/1909].

Holbrook, Stewart H., *The Yankee Exodus: An Account of Migration from New England* (1950) [E179.5/H65/1950].

Davenport, David Paul, "The Yankee Settlement of New York, 1783–1820," *Genealogical Journal* 17 (1988–89):63–88 [CS1/G382].

Geiser, Karl F., "New England and the Western Reserve," *The Massachusetts Magazine* 8 (1915):91–104 [F61/M48].

Hulling, Ray G., "The Rhode Island Emigration to Nova Scotia," *Narragansett Historical Register* 7 (1889):89–135 [F87/N2/N36/1882].

Russell, George Ely, "New Englanders in Maryland," *The Genealogist* 2 (1981):131–49 [CS1/G392].

Thorndale, William, and William Dollarhide, *Map Guide to the U.S. Federal Censuses, 1790–1920* (1987) [G1201/F7T5/1987].

Dept. of Commerce and Labor, Bureau of the Census, *A Century of Population Growth From the First Census of the United States to the Twelfth 1790–1900* (1909; reprinted 1989) [HA195/A5/1989] (contains a very useful table of surnames borne by at least 100 white persons, tabulated by states and territories, in the 1790 census).

Coddington, John Insley, "Migration and Settlement Patterns in Colonial New England," *Mayflower Quarterly* 46 (1980):12–13 [F68/S64]; "Migration Trails," *Detroit Society for Genealogical Research Magazine* 35 (1972):163–72 [F574/ D4/ D547].

The New England Historical and Genealogical Register contains the following helpful articles: Dickoré, Marie, "New England Pioneers in the Cincinnati Area," 111 (1957):288–91; Munger, Donna Bingham, "Following Connecticut Ancestors to Pennsylvania: Susquehanna Company Settlers," 139 (1985):112–25; Tucker, Rufus Stickney, "The Expansion of New England," 76 (1922):301–7 [F1/ N56].

Sources to Aid You in Your Search for Migrating Ancestors

When searching for your migrating ancestor, the most common problem you'll encounter is determining where he/she came from (keep in mind that your ancestor might have moved several times prior to the date of the first record in which you can identify him, and that an earlier place of residence may not be his place of birth). Consider some of the following sources, if they apply to your ancestor:

- Personal family papers. Letters, Bible records, photographs, newspaper clippings, copies of legal documents.

- The U.S. census. Starting in 1850, the census lists state or country of birth.

- County histories and "mug books." Published mainly between the 1860s and 1920s, these reveal the birthplaces of thousands of pioneers.

- Death records. If your migrating ancestor lived into the late nineteenth or early twentieth century, there may be a death record giving place of origin.

- Newspaper obituaries.

- Gravestones. Sometimes give place of birth or other helpful information.

- Land Records (Local and Federal). Sometimes give previous place of residence for newly arrived purchasers of land.

- Powers of attorney. Usually filed in the county courthouse, these nearly always reveal the previous or subsequent residence of the subject.

- Civil or criminal court records.

- Divorce records. May reveal the place and date of marriage.

- Military pension records. Among the most useful sources for tracing nineteenth-century migrants backwards or forwards in time.

New York

Henry B. Hoff

New York from *A New and Elegant General Atlas* by Arrowsmith and Lewis (Boston: Thomas & Andrews, 1805).

Overview

It is hard to generalize about New York genealogical research because its relative difficulty depends on time, place, and group. Researching Dutch-descended New Yorkers in the Hudson Valley in eighteenth century is likely to be easy; researching settlers from New England in the same locale may be difficult.

The survival of civil records for New York is dependent on what records survived the disastrous 1911 fire in Albany that destroyed the state library and what records had previously been transcribed, calendared, abstracted, or indexed. To understand the importance of this event, see "The 1911 State Library Fire and Its Effect on New York Genealogy," *The NYG&B Newsletter* 10 (1999):19–22. F116/N37.

Besides the 1911 fire, the other key aspect of New York genealogy is the settlement of upstate New York by New Englanders. The best article on the subject is David Paul Davenport, "The Yankee Settlement of New York, 1783–1820," *Genealogical Journal* 17 (1988/89):63–88. CS1/G382 also LOAN. Genealogical backtracking from, say, the Midwest into upstate New York and then back into New England is likely to be a difficult project, often because of the family's several moves. Nevertheless, upstate New York problems usually can be solved but often after years of work. A recent NEHGS video publication is *Upstate New York Research*, by Henry B. Hoff, with related syllabus online at *NewEnglandAncestors.org*.

Guides and Finding Aids

- Joslyn, Roger D., "New York," in *Red Book: American State, County, and Town Sources*, 3rd ed. (Provo, Utah: Ancestry, 2004), 472–92. R.Rm. REF CS49/A55/2004 also LOAN.

- *Research Outline: New York*, rev. ed. (Salt Lake City: Family History Library, 1997), ask at fourth-floor desk.

- Austin, John D., Jr., "Genealogical Research in New York State: An Informal Finding List of Published Materials With Supplementary Notes" (Glens Falls, N.Y.: the author, 1983), published for Genealogical Conference of New York (Albany, 1983) REF Z1317/A9/1983.

- Remington, Gordon L., *New York State Towns, Villages, and Cities: A Guide to Genealogical Sources* (Boston: NEHGS, 2002) R.Rm. REF F118/R423/2002 also LOAN.

- *Guide to Historical Resources in _____ County, New York Repositories* (Ithaca, N.Y: Cornell University, 1980–91) [call numbers differ by county]. See website *nysl.nysed.gov*; click on HDI. These are detailed surveys of historical societies and libraries in each county.

- Schweitzer, George K., *New York Genealogical Research* (Knoxville, Tenn.: the author, 1995) REF F118/S29/1988 also LOAN.

- Guzik, Estelle M., *Genealogical Resources in New York* (New York: Jewish Genealogical Society, 2003) R.Rm. REF F128.25/G46/2003 also LOAN.

- Bailey, Rosalie Fellows, *Guide to Genealogical and Biographical Sources for New York City (Manhattan), 1783–1898* (1954; reprinted Baltimore: Clearfield, 1998) REF F128.25/B35/1998 also LOAN.

- Seversmith, Herbert F., and Kenn Stryker-Rodda, *Long Island Genealogical Source Material*, National Genealogical Society Special Publication 24 (Washington, D.C., 1962) F127/L8/S48/1962 also LOAN.

- Epperson, Gwenn F., *New Netherland Roots* (Baltimore: Genealogical Publishing Co., 1994) F118/E66/1994.

- Hoff, Henry B., "Researching New York Dutch Families: A Checklist Approach," *The NYG&B Newsletter* 7 (1996):12–14. F116/N37.

Genealogical and Historical Periodicals

- "New York State Genealogical and Historical Periodicals," *The NYG&B Newsletter* 2 (1991):22–23, 27. F116/N37. See also *Research Outline: New York*, 34–36.

- *Tree Talks* [Central New York Genealogical Society], 1961–present. F118/T7. Subject index 4 vols. 1–28 (1961–1988); see also "Using *Tree Talks*," *The NYG&B Newsletter* 12 (2001):9–12. Every-name indexes for individual county pages have been published by Kinship on CD.

- *Western New York Genealogical Society Journal*, 1974–present. F116/W47/1974 also LOAN.

- *Upstate New York 1685–1910*, CD-ROM (Broderbund, 1995), composite every-name indexes for *The Capital*, *The Columbia*, *The Mohawk* and *The Saratoga*, 1984–1998.

- *The New York Genealogical and Biographical Record*, 1870–present. R.Rm. REF F116/N28 also LOAN. Vols. 1–59 (1870–1928) on CD and more are expected. There is a composite every-name index on CD (NYG&BS, 2002) for vols. 1–129 (1870-1998), and subject indexes in book form for vols. 1–113 (1870–1982) and 114–126 (1983–1995). Note compendia from the *Record* (Long Island Families, Long Island Source Records, English Origins). Website is *NewYorkFamilyHistory.org*.

- *The NYG&B Newsletter*, 1990–2003 [renamed *The New York Researcher* in 2004] F116/N37 also LOAN. Many articles are reproduced at *NewYorkFamilyHistory.org*. There is a composite every-name/place/subject index for vols. 1–6 (1990–1995). New York articles in non-New York journals since 1989 are listed annually; for pre-1989 articles see 5 (1994):11–13; 6 (1995):6–7, 12–13, 28–29; 7 (1996):27.

- *New Netherland Connections*, 1996–present. F122.2/N396/1996. Subject indexes for vols. 1–7 (1996–2002) are in *The NYG&B Newsletter* 10 (1999):5; 13 (2002):30.

- *De Halve Maen: Magazine of the Dutch Colonial Period in America*, 1922–present. F116/H78. There are subject indexes for vols. 1–51 (1923–1977) and vols. 1–64 (1923–1991), and see *The NYG&B Newsletter* 2 (1991):28–29.

- *The New-York Historical Society Quarterly*, 1917–1980. Vault F116/N638. See *The NYG&B Newsletter* 3 (1992):28–29.

- *New York History*, 1919–present. Vault F116/N685.

Censuses: Colonial, Federal, and State

The 1911 fire in Albany destroyed some colonial censuses; others probably had been previously destroyed or lost. Nevertheless, a surprising number of colonial censuses do survive, and these are noted in "Pre-1750 New York Lists: Censuses, Assessment Rolls, Oaths of Allegiance, and Other Lists," *The NYG&B Newsletter* 3 (1992):20–22. Many of the censuses were originally published in E. B. O'Callaghan, *The Documentary History of the State of New-York*, 4 vols. (Albany, N.Y.: Weed, Parsons & Co., 1849–51) Rare Book F122/D63/1849 also LOAN. Most of those were reprinted in *Lists of Inhabitants of Colonial New York* (Baltimore: Genealogical Publishing Co., 1979) F118/D62/1979 also LOAN.

A census for 1771 survives for a few jurisdictions (see *The New York Genealogical and Biographical Record* 107 [1976]:196; 117 [1986]:8), and there was a census in 1776 for Suffolk County, published in *Calendar of Historical Manuscripts Relating to the War of the Revolution*, 2 vols. (Albany, N.Y.: Weed, Parsons & Co., 1868), 1:378–417. NY/5/5. Various lists for New York, Queens, and Suffolk counties (including the 1776 census) were published in a composite volume as *Inhabitants of New York, 1774–1776* (Baltimore: Genealogical Publishing Co., 1993), by Thomas B. Wilson. F128.25/W55/1993.

Between 1825 and 1925, New York State took a census every ten years, with the exception of 1892 instead of 1885. The state copies of those through 1905 were burned in 1911, but many county clerks had retained a copy. These have been microfilmed, and some have been indexed. See "New York State Census Microfilms in the NYG&BS Library," *The NYG&B Newsletter* 5 (1994):7; "Finding Aids at the NYG&BS Library for New York State Censuses," 8 (1997):11–13, 19–21; and "New York State Censuses and Tax Lists," 9 (1998):17–19.

State censuses for 1825, 1835, and 1845 are comparable to federal censuses of the era in that only the head of household is named. However, the 1855 census lists everyone in the household and their relation to the head of household, how long a resident of the town, and county of birth (if born in New York State). As with the federal census, the questions changed slightly with each successive census. See David Paul Davenport, "The State Censuses of New York, 1825–1875," *Genealogical Journal* 14: 4 (Winter 1985–86):172–97. CS1/G382 also LOAN.

New York has all federal census records except for 1890. See "New York Federal Censuses: Indexes and Other Finding Aids," *The NYG&B Newsletter* 8 (1997):5–6. Federal census records are now available online from Heritage Quest, Ancestry, and the Family History Library (1880 only).

Vital Records

Keeping vital records in New York State did not begin until the nineteenth century. There was a brief attempt statewide between 1847 and 1852, and these have been published for many towns in regional and county periodicals or even as a book.

Prior to 1847 there were a few other types of vital records in New York State. The broadest were marriage licenses; these have been collected and published as *New York Marriages Previous to 1784* (Baltimore: Genealogical Publishing Co., 1968) F118/N485/1968 also LOAN. The surviving marriage bonds for the last thirty years of that period have also been published. Some records of civil marriages by mayors or justices of the peace have been published for a few jurisdictions. The town records of some Long Island and Westchester towns include a limited number of vital records, usually births. In 1801 New York City began keeping death records (actually, returns from sextons of cemeteries). New York City and other major cities in the state began keeping vital records between 1847 and 1880. Information on marriages and deaths within the twelve months before the 1855, 1865, and 1875 censuses were given as separate schedules with the censuses; see *The NYG&B Newsletter* 12 (2001):41–42 for the 1855 census.

However, regular statewide vital records do not begin until 1880. Indexes to these records are available in Albany, New York City, Syracuse, and Rochester. A description of these records and the rules governing their availability is in Guzik, *Genealogical Resources in New York*, 294–95.

Divorces were granted by the Chancery Court between 1789 and 1847. For New York City and vicinity these records have been indexed and published in *The New York Genealogical and Biographical Record* 129 (1998):81–88, with an excellent introduction. After 1847 the Supreme Court of each county granted divorces. Note, however, that many New York residents were granted divorces in other states; see, for example, "New Yorkers in Some Connecticut Divorces," *The NYG&B Newsletter* 12 (2001):24–26, 43–46.

For name changes, see John D. Austin, Jr., "Early Changes of Names in New York," *The New York Genealogical and Biographical Record* 127 (1996):137–42, 222–25; 128 (1997):44–48, 997–100.

Church Records

In the relative absence of vital records, church records are particularly important for New York research. Information about guides to church records and where the records of each denomination are deposited may be found in *Research Outline: New York* and Robert Allan Rowe, "Developing a Strategy for Locating Church Records," *Tree Talks* 33 (1993):5–13.

The largest collection of church records for New York is probably the New York DAR Cemetery, Church and Town Records, with a subject index entitled *Revised Master Index to New York State Daughters of the American Revolution Genealogical Records Volumes*, 2 vols. (Zephyrhills, Fla.: Jean D. Worden, 1998) F118/R455/1998. Next is the Vosburgh Collection, a series of typed church records on 101 reels of microfilm (F118/V67/1913), with a subject index in *The NYG&B Newsletter* 9 (1998):53–55. Arthur C. M. Kelly and Jean D. Worden have individually transcribed and published baptisms and marriages of many churches, particularly in the Hudson Valley. Their works are always indexed which Vosburgh's were not; however, Vosburgh also transcribed additional church records such as membership and burials.

Wilson D. Ledley compiled an *Index to Baptismal Surnames in the Reformed Churches of Claverack, Cortlandt. . . .* (New York: Holland Society of New York, 1990) F118/L42/1990, and Arthur Kelly (under the corporate name Kinship) published two CDs: *Marriage Index: New York #1, 1639–1916*, and *New York State Baptism Records: Lower Hudson Valley Church Records.* And many church records have been published in periodicals and in Janet Wethy Foley, *Early Settlers of Upstate New York* (9 vols. 1934–42; reprinted as 2 vols., with every-name index, Baltimore: Genealogical Publishing Co., 1993) F118/E24/1993 also LOAN. Articles have appeared in *The NYG&B Newsletter* on New York City church records. In 1997 and 1998 there were two articles listing New York State Quaker records.

Poor relief was generally administered by churches in the colonial period. For Albany see Janny Venema, *Deacons' Accounts, 1652–1674, First Dutch Reformed Church of Beverwyck/Albany, New York* (Rockport, Maine: Picton Press, 1998) F129/A3/D43/1998 also LOAN. The poor relief accounts of Trinity Church in New York City were published in the *The New York Genealogical and Biographical Record*, vols. 99–102.

Cemetery Records

There are various collections of cemetery records for New York. The largest is probably the New York DAR Cemetery, Church and Town Records, with the *Revised Master Index* as a subject index. Many others are in books, periodicals (particularly the *The New York Genealogical and Biographical Record* and *Tree Talks*), typescripts, manuscripts, and on county websites. "Cemetery records" usually refers to transcriptions of gravestones; nevertheless, the actual records of a few cemeteries have also been published.

Newspapers

Many newspaper abstracts have been published or are available in typescript or on microfilm. The principal guide to these is Fred Q. Bowman and Thomas J. Lynch, *Directory to Collections of New York Vital Records 1726–1989, with Rare Gazetteer* (Bowie, Md.: Heritage Books, 1995) R.Rm. REF F118/B698/1995. Bowman is the author, or coauthor with Thomas J. Lynch, of six other books or extended articles of newspaper abstracts:

• *10,000 Vital Records of Western New York,1809–1850* (Baltimore: Genealogical Publishing Co., 1985) F118/B68/1985 also LOAN.

- *10,000 Vital Records of Central New York, 1813–1850* (Baltimore: Genealogical Publishing Co., 1986) F118/B696/1986 also LOAN.

- *10,000 Vital Records of Eastern New York, 1777–1834* (Baltimore: Genealogical Publishing Co., 1987) F118/B665/1987 also LOAN.

- "1,100 Vital Records of Northeastern New York, 1835–1850," *The New York Genealogical and Biographical Record* 118 (1987):135–42, 203–09; 119 (1988):35–43, 91–98, 166–70.

- *8,000 More Vital Records of Eastern New York, 1804–1850* (Rhinebeck, N.Y.: Kinship, 1991) F118/B666/1991 also LOAN.

- *7,000 Hudson–Mohawk Valley (NY) Vital Records, 1808–1850* (Baltimore: Genealogical Publishing Co., 1997) F118/B697/1997 also LOAN.

There are volumes of newspaper abstracts covering just one newspaper or one county's newspapers. However, coverage frequently extends far beyond county or state boundaries. Many newspaper abstracts have been published in periodicals or in Foley's *Early Settlers of Upstate New York*. Joseph Gavit, *American Deaths and Marriages, 1784–1829*, 2 reels of microfilm (New Orleans: Polyanthos, 1976) F118/G38, is an important source for Albany and upstate.

For the eighteenth century, there are four books by Kenneth Scott: *Genealogical Data from Colonial New York Newspapers [1726–1783]* (Baltimore: Genealogical Publishing Co., 1928) F118/S369/1977 also LOAN; *Genealogical Data from The* New York Post-Boy, *1743–1773*, National Genealogical Society Special Publication No. 35 (Washington, D.C., 1970) F128.25/S329/1980 also LOAN; *Rivington's New York Newspaper: Excerpts from a Loyalist Press, 1773–1783*, Collections of The New-York Historical Society Vol. 84 (New York, 1973) F116/N63 v. 84; and *The New-York Magazine Marriages and Deaths: 1790–1797* (New Orleans: Polyanthos, 1975) CS68/N49/1975.

There are checklists of newspaper abstracts for New York City and Long Island in *The NYG&B Newsletter* 2 (1991):3–5, 20–21. Some of the principal newspaper abstracts for New York City and environs have been available only as typescripts in various libraries. However, two of these are now available online at *NewEnglandAncestors.org*: the *New York Evening Post*, 1801–1890, and the *Christian Intelligencer*, 1830–1870. An unusual set is Rita Susswein Gottesman, *The Arts and Crafts in New York, 1726–1804*, 3 vols., Collections of The New-York Historical Society Vols. 69, 81–82 (New York, 1936–65) F116/N63 v. 69, 81–82, based on detailed information from newspapers.

Probate Records

New York probate is a complex subject, even after the creation of the system of a Surrogate's Court for each county in 1787. Fortunately, there is an excellent book on the subject: Gordon L. Remington, *New York State Probate Records: A Genealogist's Guide to Testate and Intestate Records* (Boston: NEHGS, 2002) R.Rm. REF F118/R42/2002 also LOAN.

Before 1787:

Before 1787 there was probate in county courts and there was centralized probate in New York City for estates worth more than a certain amount. Harry Macy, Jr., "New York Probate Records Before 1787," *The NYG&B Newsletter* 2 (1991):11–15, updated to 2001 online, explains what records have survived for what courts and what records have been transcribed, abstracted, indexed, and/or microfilmed. Besides wills, Macy's article also discusses administrations, inventories, guardianships, probate of New Yorkers who died elsewhere, probate at the county level, and the recording of wills in deed books and town records. Remington expands upon and updates these topics, and lists what is available from the Family History Library.

The key set of abstracts is *Abstracts of Wills on File in the Surrogate's Office, City of New York, 1665–1800* 17 vols., Collections of The New-York Historical Society Vols. 25–41 (New York, 1893–1909), F116/N63 v. 25–41, also on CD from Heritage Books. This set should always be searched, even though the abstracts are not always correct, especially in the earlier volumes. Fortunately, in many cases the original volumes and even the original wills are available on microfilm.

From 1787 On:

The creation of the Surrogate's Court system in 1787 simplified probate in New York, but there were still inconsistencies and overlapping jurisdictions until 1829. In that year a new set of laws and rules improved the system and instituted the requirement of probate petitions naming the heirs at law, regardless of the provisions of the will (if there was one). These probate petitions are a valuable resource for New York research. Remington's book shows that the Family History Library has microfilms of probate packets (that would include the petitions) from only about 40 percent of the counties in the state.

Abstracts of probate records for many of the state's counties are in the NEHGS library as books or periodical articles. In addition, there are typescripts for some counties, including for New York County, 1800–1849. These are all listed Remington's book or Harry Macy, Jr., "Library Resources for Research in New York Probate Records Since 1787," *The NYG&B Newsletter* 3 (1992):3–7.

Probate indexes appear on few, if any, county websites. However, will indexes for several counties are on the website *sampubco.com*.

Land Records

Land records in New York State could be recorded at any of four levels: state, county, town, or "other," the last being a manor, a patent, or a corporate landlord like the Holland Land Company. In addition, some land records were never recorded or were recorded decades after they were made.

At the state level, see "State Patents and Deeds at NYG&BS," *The NYG&B Newsletter* 9 (1998):9 and three other sources: *Calendar of New York Colonial Manuscripts: Indorsed Land Papers, 1643–1803* (1864; reprint Harrison, N.Y.: Harbor Hill Books, 1987) F122/N56/1987; Fred Q. Bowman, *Landholders of Northeastern New York, 1739–1802* (Baltimore: Genealogical Publishing Co., 1987) F118/B65/1983 also LOAN; and *The Balloting Book, and Other Documents Relating to Military Bounty Lands in the State of New York* (Albany, N.Y.: Packard & Van Benthuysen, 1825) NY/5/28.

At the county (or city) level, deeds and deed indexes have been microfilmed for all the counties in the state. There are multi-volume published indexes for New York City and Albany (the latter with descriptions), but abstracts of land records have been published for only a few counties and usually just the first book (with the notable exception of Westchester deeds in *The New York Genealogical and Biographical Record*).

At the town level, land records may be mixed in with other documents, or there may be one or more town deed books (e.g., Huntington, Suffolk County).

For manorial records, see "Manors in New York," *The NYG&B Newsletter* 10 (1999):55–60; 11 (2000):13–17. The land records of some patents, especially in Dutchess County, have been published. Many of the owners of manors and patents leased land to tenants instead of selling it.

An index to some of the records of the Holland Land Company (which owned millions of acres in western New York) has been published as Karen E. Livsey, *Western New York Land Transactions, 1804–1835, Extracted from the Archives of the Holland Land Company*, 2 vols. (Baltimore: Genealogical Publishing Co., 1991–96) F118/L58/1991, 1996 also LOAN.

Town Records

Town records have been published for many of the towns on Long Island (but not those in Kings County) and the Hudson Valley; unfortunately, many are poorly indexed. They usually contain a hodgepodge of town meetings, a few vital records, tax lists, a few wills, land records, and often references to adjacent manors and patents. Rarely have all records of a town been published. Starting in the mid-eighteenth century, the towns on Long Island started keeping records of the Overseers of the Poor. These have been published for the town of Huntington for the period 1752–1861 and include illegitimate births.

For New York City the comparable records are the *Records of New Amsterdam from 1653 to 1674*, 7 vols. (1897; reprinted Baltimore: Genealogical Publishing Co., 1976) F128.4/N53/1976; these included the records of the Mayor's Court 1664–1673. After the brief Dutch reconquest of New York in 1673–74, the records resume as the *Minutes of the Common Council 1675–1776*, 8 vols. (New York: Dodd, Mead, 1905) JS1226/A5/1905.

Tax Records

The survival of tax records for New York is uneven. There is a discussion of known tax lists in "New York State Censuses and Tax Lists," *The NYG&B Newsletter* 9 (1998):17–19, including tax lists published in periodicals for 1767–1908. For prior tax lists, see "Pre-1750 New York Lists: Censuses, Assessment Rolls, Oaths of Allegiance, and Other Lists," *The NYG&B Newsletter* 3 (1992):20–22.

Tax lists begin for many counties in 1779 but continue only sporadically; nevertheless, there are complete tax lists for the entire state for 1799–1804. Dutchess County is unique in having a complete run for most of the eighteenth century, published as Clifford M. Buck, *Dutchess County, NY Tax Lists 1718–1787 with Rombout Precinct. . . .*, Arthur and Nancy Kelly, ed. (Rhinebeck, N.Y.: Kinship, 1991) F127/D8/B82/1991.

Court Records

Research Outline: New York, cited above, has a summary of New York courts at pages 12–13, with notations of what court records have been published as books. In addition, seventeenth-century court records have been published for Albany and environs and for Westchester County. Court records for Ulster County 1693–1782 were published in *National Genealogical Society Quarterly*, vols. 60–61, 68. REF CS42/N4 also LOAN. Despite the existence of a manorial system, there is practically no evidence manorial courts were ever held.

Military Records

Many military records were destroyed in the 1911 fire in Albany, but fortunately, many had already been published. For the colonial period, there are muster rolls, 1664–1775, as published in *Second* and *Third Annual Reports of the State Historian of the State of New York* (Albany, N.Y.: Wynkoop, Hallenbeck & Crawford, 1897–98; reprinted as *New York Colonial Muster Rolls, 1664–1775*, 2 vols., Baltimore: Genealogical Publishing Co., 2000) F118/N492/2000 also LOAN. The rolls for the year 1715 take up more than a hundred pages, providing an effective census of the military age men in those towns and counties. Most of the rolls are for the French and Indian War, 1755–1764, and include age, place of birth, occupation, and physical description. Another version of these rolls was published as *Muster Rolls of New York Provincial Troops, 1755–1764*, Collections of The New-York Historical Society Vol. 24 (New York, 1892) F116/N63 v. 24.

The Revolutionary War caused major upheaval in New York because of the battles fought on New York soil and the British occupation of New York City and environs. Many relevant records were destroyed in the 1911 fire, but some of the key sources had already been transcribed or abstracted: Berthold Fernow,

New York in the Revolution (originally vol. 15 of *Documents Relating to the Colonial History of the State of New York* [F122/D66/v.15]; reprinted New Orleans: Polyanthos, 1972, and Baltimore: Clearfield, 2000); *New York in the Revolution as Colony and State*, 2nd ed. (Albany, N.Y.: Brandow Printing Co., 1898), and *Supplement*, both reprinted Baltimore: Genealogical Publishing Co., 1996. REF E263/N6/N442/1898, 1901; *Calendar of Historical Manuscripts Relating to the War of the Revolution*, 2 vols. (Albany, N.Y.: Weed, Parsons & Co., 1868) NY/5/5; and Edward F. DeLancey, ed., *Muster and Pay Rolls of the War of the Revolution, 1775–1783*, Collections of The New-York Historical Society Vols. 47–48 (New York, 1916; reprinted Bowie, Md.: Heritage Books, 1990) F116/N63 v. 47–48. Some records were copied by the federal government in 1896 and are still available (see *The New York Genealogical and Biographical Record* 120 [1989]:65 for Dutchess County).

Two of the important sources for Loyalists in New York are Harry B. Yoshpe, *The Disposition of Loyalist Estates in the Southern District of the State of New York* (New York: Columbia University Press, 1939) F123/Y68, and Victor Hugo Paltsits, ed., *Minutes of the Commissioners for Detecting and Defeating Conspiracies in the State of New York, Albany County Sessions, 1778–1781*, 3 vols. (Albany, N.Y.: J. B. Lyon, 1909–10) NY/4/5. Because of the proximity of New Jersey (and the lack of a biographical directory for New York Loyalists), it may be useful to consult E. Alfred Jones, *The Loyalists of New Jersey* (1926; reprinted Westminster, Md.: Willow Bend Books, 2002) F131/N62 v.10 also LOAN. The two works by Peter Wilson Coldham on Loyalist claims (see BEYOND THE NORTHEAST) should always be reviewed.

For subsequent wars, see *Research Outline: New York*, 30–31. *Registers of New York Regiments in the War of the Rebellion*, in 43 vols., now has a published index: Richard A. Wilt, *New York Soldiers in the Civil War*, 2 vols. (Bowie, Md.: Heritage Books, 1999).

Genealogical and Biographical Compendia (Including Town and County Histories)

See *Research Outline: New York*, 18–21, for its listing of statewide, regional, and county compendia. Some town histories also include genealogies of local families. Rosalie Bailey's New York City guide has excellent lists of compendia.

For eighteenth-century German immigrants, see Henry Z Jones, Jr., *The Palatine Families of New York*, 2 vols. (Universal City, Calif.: the author, 1985) F130/P2/J66/1985 also LOAN; *More Palatine Families* (Universal City, Calif.: the author, 1991) E184/P3/J66/1991 also LOAN; and [with Lewis Bunker Rohrbach] *Even More Palatine Families*, 3 vols. (Rockport, Maine: Picton Press, 2002) E184/P3/J67/2002 also LOAN.

Frank J. Doherty, *Settlers of the Beekman Patent, Dutchess County, New York*, 7 vols. to date (Pleasant Valley, N.Y.: the author, 1990–2004) F127/D8/D73/1990 also LOAN also on CD; website *beekmansettlers.com*. This is a series on the residents of the southeast corner of Dutchess County, appears to be just a local genealogical dictionary. However, the author has taken it far beyond that — so it has become a major source for New York research. He identifies all the families before they came to Dutchess County (as best he can), he includes records from all over Dutchess County while they were there, and he lists unplaced persons for that surname from all over New York State.

One of the most important new sources for New York is David M. Riker, *Genealogical and Biographical Directory to Persons in New Netherland, From 1613 to 1674*, 4 vols. (Salem, Mass.: Higginson Book Co., 1999) F118/R55/1999, also published as *New Netherland Vital Records, 1600s* on CD-ROM by Family Tree Maker (1999). This is the first genealogical dictionary for seventeenth-century New York. It is generally reliable and extremely useful.

Sometimes the best account of a family is hidden in a book on multiple families. For New York there are lists of these accounts in *The NYG&B Newsletter* 4 (1993):11–13, 21; 7 (1996):24–25; 10 (1999):9–12; and 11 (2000):65–67.

Because many early settlers of Long Island and Westchester County came from New England, it is important to check the Great Migration volumes (see NEW ENGLAND OVERVIEW).

Maps and Atlases

- French, J. H., *Gazetteer of New York State* (1860; reprinted with extra index, Baltimore, Genealogical Publishing Co., 1983) R.Rm. REF F117/F74/1983 also LOAN.

- *County Formations and Minor Civil Divisions of the State of New York* (Salt Lake City: Genealogical Department of The Church of Jesus Christ of Latter-day Saints, 1978).

- Thorne, Kathryn Ford, comp., *New York: Atlas of Historical County Boundaries*, John H. Long, ed. (New York: Simon & Schuster, 1993) Atlas G1201/ F7/A8/1993/New York.

Special Sources for New York

Two excellent genealogical works on upstate Native American ancestry in New York are Barbara J. Sivertsen, *Turtles, Wolves, and Bears: A Mohawk Family History* (Bowie, Md.: Heritage Books, 1996), and David K. Faux, *Understanding Ontario First Nations Genealogical Records: Sources and Case Studies* (Toronto: Ontario Genealogical Society, 2002). For Long Island Native American genealogy, see Gaynell Stone, ed., *The History & Archaeology of the Montauk*, Readings in Long Island Archaeology & Ethnohistory, vol. III, 2nd ed. (Stony Brook, N.Y.: Suffolk County Archaeological Association, 1993).

There are no comparable works for African Americans — but note the following: Vivienne L. Kruger, "Born to Run: The Slave Family in Early New

York," (Ph.D. dissertation, Columbia University, 1985), and the periodical *Afro-Americans in New York Life and History*. For early free African American families, note Henry B. Hoff, "Researching African-American Families in New Netherland and Colonial New York and New Jersey," forthcoming in *The New York Genealogical and Biographical Record*.

For both groups during the American Revolution, note "Minority Revolutionary War Service, New York 1775–1783," in Eric G. Grundset, ed., *African American and American Indian Patriots of the Revolutionary War* (Washington, D.C.: National Society Daughters of the American Revolution, 2001), 83–101. E269/N3/A37/2001.

Beyond the Northeast

Henry B. Hoff

The NEHGS library has quite a good collection for the "other 43 states" (i.e., all but the six New England states and New York). You will be able to begin basic research and plan future non-New England research using the sources in the NEHGS library. Not surprisingly, for advanced research you will need to go to major repositories in the particular state you are researching, to a major "microfilm library" (like the Family History Library), and/or to a major "book library" like the DAR Library in Washington, D.C. The catalogs of all these libraries are available online.

Browsing may be the most enjoyable way to do initial research, but is rarely the most efficient way. The sources you find by browsing may be helpful but not necessarily the best or most current information on the subject or the family.

EXAMPLE: Compare the two published versions of a 1748 baptism in Lancaster County, Pennsylvania:

Elizabeth Kunz, d. Nicholas and Joanna; b. Aug. 25; bap. Sept. 4, 1748 (The Pennsylvania German Society Proceedings and Addresses, *63 vols. Pennsylvania German Society, 1890–1966; material from vols. 3–31 reprinted as* Pennsylvania German Church Records, *3 vols. [Baltimore: Genealogical Publishing Co., 1983], 1:235)*

Elizabeth, daughter of Nicholas Kunz of Waldmoor, Zweibruecken, and Johanna, daughter of John Weyngartman, b. August 25, 1748, bapt. September 4, 1748. Spon: Francis Fortunet and wife (F. Edward Wright, Lancaster County, Pennsylvania, Church Records of the 18th Century, *volume 2 [Westminster, Md.: Family Line Publications, 1994], 12)*

Every state has its nuances. Even if two states have comparable records, there will usually be major differences in what has been indexed and/or published. If you are starting research in a state that is new to you, it is wise to read at least one research guide for that state to determine the highlights and pitfalls. This should help you determine what you can expect, what to look at first — and what you *can* rely on and what you should *not* rely on.

Each state has its own aspects that shape genealogical research, such as missing early federal censuses (New Jersey, Virginia) or states with many "burned counties" whose records are missing (Virginia).

For some states (e.g., Delaware, Maryland, New Jersey, Pennsylvania) there are long sets of published state archives material. These contain useful material, but first you need to find out what has been indexed.

A standard research method is to determine whether there is anything already published on the family or place of interest. A review of library catalogs should determine whether there are relevant books, typescripts, or manuscripts. Articles in periodicals will usually not be catalogued, so to find articles, you will want to consult PERSI (Periodical Source Index, in book form, CD-ROM, or online). In addition, there are finding aids to articles by state (e.g., Earl Gregg Swem, *Virginia Historical Index*), or to books and articles by state (Donald Arleigh Sinclair, *New Jersey Family Index: A Guide to the Genealogical Sketches in New Jersey Collective Sources*).

As you are planning your research, always be aware that there may be useful material that is not neatly categorized by state, county, or town. For example, just as "New England" is usually a category in genealogical libraries, so is "The South." Or maybe you need to review a periodical that covers more than one state or a periodical that covers several counties within a state. If you are lucky, your ancestor may have been part of a planned settlement in which genealogists are interested, like the Huguenot settlers of Manakin Town, Virginia, or the New Jersey settlers of Adams County, Mississippi.

Good genealogical periodicals will be a valuable research tool. For each periodical you will want to determine:

- Can you use it on CD?

- Are there compendia? Are they available on CD or in book form? "Compendia" are collections of articles from a periodical, sometimes on just one subject, usually published by Genealogical Publishing Company, in the 1980s and 1990s. The convenience of having an every-name index for so many articles makes compendia a valuable research tool.

- Are there every-name indexes and/or subject indexes to the periodical? If it is on CD, then it has an every-name index. You can use PERSI as a subject index, but there may also be a subject and/or a place index to it.

You cannot afford to ignore periodicals, and as your research progresses, you may find yourself cycling back through composite every-name indexes [those are indexes to many volumes of a periodical]. You may find the crucial clue in a periodical, like this one:

EXAMPLE: I was looking for Gabriel Mitchell of James City County, Virginia, till 1783, later of North Carolina, whose oldest daughter was named Lucy Jones. The Virginia Genealogist *20 (1976):207, told me that "Bracket Jones and Gabriel Mitchell removed to N. Carolina in the year 1788," according to a list of delinquent taxpayers. This effectively gave me the exact name of Lucy's husband and the year of settlement in North Carolina.*

Abstracted newspaper notices, particularly for marriage and death, are another important source that transcends state boundaries. For example, *Index of Obituaries in Boston Newspapers 1704–1800*; it is in three volumes — of which only one volume is for Boston. The other two are outside Boston — and sometimes in other states and indeed other countries, particularly Canada and the West Indies. Don't confine yourself to the U.S. — abstracted New Brunswick newspapers mention many Americans. People in other states are particularly to be mentioned if they had close relatives living where the newspaper was published.

> *EXAMPLE: At Petersburg [Virginia], on the 30th ult., Mrs. Elizabeth Kidd, in the 66th year of her age. She was sister to the Widow Mitchell of this city. [Issue of 5 May 1801] (Lois Smathers Neal,* Abstracts of Vital Records from Raleigh, North Carolina, Newspapers, *3 vols. [Spartanburg, S.C.: Reprint Co., 1979–80; Raleigh, N.C.: North Carolina Genealogical Society, 1995], 1:283). This death is not reported in Petersburg or Richmond newspapers, and the statement that she was sister to the widow Mitchell is found nowhere else.*

If only marriages and death notices have been abstracted from a newspaper, you may want to look at microfilms of the original newspaper for other genealogical data, especially if your ancestor was involved in an event considered newsworthy. If your family was in a newspaper frequently, you may be able to hypothesize relationships and migration patterns that you later prove by further research.

> *EXAMPLE: In "Almira (Bisbee) Bailey and Her Family in Vermont, Upstate New York, and Wisconsin,"* The New England Historical and Genealogical Register *156 (2002):12–14, author Gloria Bailey Jackson methodically read all "local items" in every issue of a Sun Prairie, Wisconsin, newspaper from 1870 to 1901, and found that other members of Almira's family had settled in Dane County, Wisconsin.*

Of course, watch for misreadings and for missing issues, as best you can. If the newspaper is your only source for a key event, you will want to get a copy of the original.

Probate abstracts and indexes are another key source. For some states there are statewide indexes to wills and administrations (e.g., Virginia to 1800 [1800–1865 in progress], Ohio to 1850, North Carolina to 1900). If you are starting research in a state with an index like this, it probably should be one of the first research tools you use. From there you can determine what will abstracts have been published.

The number of wills and administrations for non-locals in U.S. port cities in the colonial and Federal period is amazing — and you may find reading the abstracts becomes addictive. You may find unexpected clues, making connections you had never thought about.

> *EXAMPLE: While browsing through abstracted Philadelphia wills, I found the will of Robert Tuite, proved in 1760, mentioning relatives in London, Barbados, and Ireland, and a brother James in Maryland. I kept on browsing and later found*

that a copy of the will of James Tuite of Queen Anne's County, Maryland, proved in 1780, had been recorded in Philadelphia. Without further research, this told me in which Maryland county to start my research.

You may find yourself using newspaper and probate abstracts in tandem, a method that may be quicker than using federal and state census records to narrow a search. I was looking for a woman named Mary Codwise, last seen in 1836 in New York City as a widow with grown children. I could have gone through abstracted New York City newspaper death notices from 1836 forward — but instead I saved time by looking at the composite indexes to New York City wills. I found her probate in November 1855, then worked backwards from that date and found her death notice in August 1855.

What makes your family unique for research purposes? There may be aspects to your search that are more important than geography. Some states have works on early colonists and their descendants; two of these are noteworthy: *Adventurers of Purse and Person*, for Virginia, and *The Welcome Claimants*, for Pennsylvania. You may find biographical dictionaries of men who served in a state legislature; those for Pennsylvania and South Carolina are particularly good. Paul Heinegg has produced books treating free African-American families from Delaware to South Carolina.

Here are some other aspects to consider:

Religion: You hope that your family belonged to a church that kept good records, but even if that church didn't, the denomination may have published a newspaper with deaths of members. If you have Quaker ancestry, see *Quaker Genealogies: A Selected List of Books,* by Willard Heiss and Thomas Hamm.

Ethnic background: If you have Scottish ancestry, you may have an ancestor who belonged to the St. Andrew's Society, which published biographies of its members. If your family came from Continental Europe, there is a good chance they will have left records giving the wife's maiden name.

Occupation: There may be books compiled on high-profile occupations — like lawyers, ministers, doctors, silversmiths, artists, and photographers — in that county, area, or state. However, there are also compilations on canal workers, riverboat pilots, carpenters and other woodworkers, cartmen, firemen, accountants, ship builders, booksellers, tavern keepers, butchers, mechanics, and tradesmen. Now, some of these compilations may be little more than names and dates, but that may all you need to open up a new line of research. And if you ancestor worked for someone famous, he or she may be mentioned incidentally in works on that person.

Schools: If there is a chance that anyone in the family attended an organized school, you should look at whatever is available for biographical accounts. For college-level sources, see Francis James Dallett's article in *National Genealogical Society Quarterly* 65 (1977):57–74, "University Archives as a Genealogical Resource," updated by his article in the April 2003 *New England Historical and Genealogical Register*. Note the existence of registers with biographical information for secondary schools like the Moravian schools in Bethlehem, Pennsylvania. And Betty Ring's *Girlhood Embroidery: American Samplers & Pictorial Needlework* contains biographical information about many schoolgirls.

Hereditary societies: If there is any chance someone in the family joined a hereditary society, look for summarized lines of descent, such as those in the *Mayflower Index*, or contact the organization.

Military service: Was anyone in a war? There may be published service or pension records for that war on a national or state level. And there may even be books on veterans of a particular war in a particular county. If you had Loyalist relatives, see *American Loyalist Claims* and *American Migrations 1765–1799*, both by Peter Wilson Coldham.

The role of luck cannot be overlooked, especially for timing and geography. Did your ancestors die after the 1850 census? Did they live in a place with good records — like Madison County, Tennessee? There is a lot in print for that county, and it has a fantastic website with abstracted wills and deeds. But if your family moved away, their next stop may have been a more challenging county. And then you start the research cycle all over again.

Introduction to Canadian Research: Census Records

Michael J. Leclerc

Brief Timeline of Canadian History

To understand the Canadian census records, it is necessary to keep in mind the history of Canadian settlement and government. Samuel de Champlain established the first permanent settlements in Acadia in 1605 and in Québec in 1606. Jean Talon became the intendant in Québec in 1665, at the height of problems between the settlers and the Iroquois. Fighting between France and England spilled over into their colonies in North America. Possession of much of the territory in the Maritimes went back and forth from one country to the other until 1759, when France formally ceded her northern possessions to England. Québec's lands were separated into Upper and Lower Canada in 1791. They

---

Published online on *NewEnglandAncestors.org*, this article has been updated for this publication.

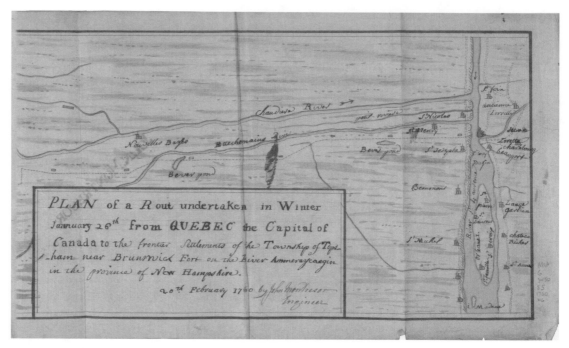

Plan of Route From Quebec to New Hampshire, 1760, by John Montresor (Map G3450/S5/1760/M6)

were reunited in 1841 to become Canada West and Canada East, eventually becoming the provinces Ontario and Québec, respectively.

In 1867 Ontario, Québec, Nova Scotia, and New Brunswick united to become the Dominion of Canada. Manitoba joined the confederation in 1870, British Columbia, in 1873, and Prince Edward Island followed shortly afterward, in 1875. Alberta and Saskatchewan became part of Canada in 1905. The province of Newfoundland and Labrador was added in 1949. Knowing these dates makes it easier to understand why certain censuses were taken when they were.

Census Taking in Canada

The first census in Canada was taken in Québec in 1666 by Intendant Jean Talon. There were 3,215 inhabitants of New France at the time.[1] Censuses were taken at very irregular intervals from then until 1851. The first Dominion census was taken in 1871, and the census has been taken every ten years ever since. The census most recently released to the public is that for 1901. Many of the original pre-1871 census records are housed in repositories in the respective provinces. The National Archives of Canada gathered together and microfilmed as many of these census records as possible. These microfilms are available at NEHGS, the National Archives of Canada in Ottawa, and the Family History Library in Salt Lake City (and available for rental from local Family History Centers). Many other local repositories in the United States and Canada have copies of certain films as well. Microfilms can be ordered from the National Archives of Canada through interlibrary loan at your local public library. All available censuses are listed at the end of this column.

The provinces were divided into census districts and sub-districts. The districts represented electoral districts, which were almost always equivalent to city or county boundaries. Sub-districts were equivalent to towns or townships and wards within cities. In 1871, 1881, and 1891 finding aids were produced that give the exact district and sub-district for localities in each province. Films were made in order by district, and within each district by sub-district. Using these finding aids will also help you locate a particular sub-district on a reel of film.

Information in the Censuses

The information recorded in the records varied from census year to census year. For example, in 1901 the exact date of birth was asked for, not just a person's age or year of birth, as on previous censuses. Pre-1871 census information varies from province to province. For example, the 1861 census for Québec enumerates everyone by name, while a census taken the same year in the province of Nova Scotia names only the heads of household — other members of the household were listed only by age categories.

When using Canadian censuses, it is important to keep in mind the French tradition that women kept their maiden names throughout their lives. This tradition persisted until the early twentieth century. When doing census research on French-Canadians, you will notice that women are usually listed under their maiden name. A typical listing will show the husband under his name, the wife under her maiden name, then the children, who use the surname of the father. The 1881 census starts to show some women under the name of their husband, but it is not until the 1901 census that this becomes the uniform way to record names.

One very valuable piece of information included on the Canadian censuses that does not appear in United States Federal censuses is religion. Taking note of an individual's religion will direct you to church records. It is fairly common, however, to see a husband and wife of different faiths, so be especially attentive to the religion of all members of the household, as records in more than one church may need to be consulted for a particular family. Also, make note of a person's religion in each census, as it was not uncommon for individuals to convert to another faith.

The year for which the most extensive information exists is 1871. The following schedules were microfilmed for this census year:

1. Nominal return of the living
2. Nominal return of deaths within the last twelve months

3. Return of public institutions, real estate, vehicles, and implements

4. Return of cultivated land, field products, and plants and fruits

5. Return of livestock, animal products, homemade fabrics and furs

6. Return of industrial establishment

7. Return of products of the forest

8. Return of shipping and fisheries

9. Return of mineral products

Unlike the United States, where non-population schedules have been microfilmed separately from the population schedules, these schedules were all filmed together by sub-district. Schedules 3–9 can be cross-referenced to schedule one by looking at the page and line references in the first two columns. It is most unfortunate that the 1871 census for Prince Edward Island did not survive.

Census Indexes

Unfortunately, Canadian censuses are not as well indexed as those in the United States. There are many projects underway at local levels to index and/or transcribe census records. For example, the National Archives of Canada and the Ontario Genealogical Society collaborated on a project to index the 1871 census for Ontario.

Remember that indexes to the censuses in Canada are being done by many different groups and usually by volunteers. Criteria for creating indexes, transcriptions, and so on, change from place to place and from census year to census year. If you cannot find an individual that you know should be in a particular location in an index, it is a good idea to look through the actual census for that area. Occasionally specialized indexes are published, such as Glen Eker's Index to Jewish residents in the 1851 and 1861 censuses of Upper Canada and the 1861 census of Lower Canada, which indexes only those in the census who indicated that they were Jewish.

NEHGS has a large collection of Canadian census indexes. The Family History Library in Salt Lake City has copies of these books as well. Unfortunately, they are not available on microfilm at this time. Another place to look for up-to-date indexes is the Internet. Many individuals and organizations are working on various projects to put census indexes online. The Alberta Family History Society has started the Canadian Genealogical Project Registry at *afhs.ab.ca/registry/index.html*. This keeps track of many different genealogical projects, including the compilation of indexes, currently underway on Canadian records.

Post-1901 Census Controversy

No discussion of Canadian census records would be complete without mention of the current work being done in Canada to preserve access to post-1901 census records. There is much debate over whether these records should be transferred from Statistics Canada to the National Archives of Canada. The debate arises from compromises made by Sir Wilfred Laurier's government at the beginning of the century over the release of information. Many individuals feared how the information they provided on the census would be used. The Laurier government promised that census workers would not provide information to tax collectors, the military, and the like. The question now is whether Statistics Canada should turn over the censuses or destroy them.

After much discussion and compromise involving Statistics Canada, the National Archives of Canada, the Privacy Commissioner of Canada, genealogists, historians, and other interested members of the public, Senator Lorna Milne has introduced Bill S-15 to ensure access to all censuses. Under the terms of the bill, censuses older than 30 years would be transferred from Statistics Canada to the National Archives. All censuses would be released to the public 92 years after they were first taken. This last provision is the current schedule of release for censuses.

Availability

Following is a chart of censuses that were microfilmed by the National Archives of Canada:

Province Census Years

Province	Years Available
Alberta	1881, 1891, 1901
British Columbia	1881, 1891, 1901
Manitoba	1831, 1849, 1870, 1881, 1891, 1901
New Brunswick	1851, 1861, 1871, 1881, 1891, 1901
Nova Scotia	1770–71, 1785–87, 1791–95, 1811, 1817–18, 1827, 1838, 1851, 1861, 1871, 1881, 1891, 1901
Ontario	1801, 1803, 1842, 1847, 1848, 1850, 1851, 1861, 1871, 1881, 1891, 1901
Prince Edward Island	1841, 1860–61, 1881, 1891, 1901
Québec	1666, 1667, 1681, 1811, 1813, 1825, 1830, 1831, 1832–35, 1842, 1851, 1861, 1871, 1881, 1891, 1901, 1901
Saskatchewan	1881, 1891, 1901
Territories	1891, 1901

Note

1. Thomas A. Hillman, *Catalogue of Census Returns on Microfilm 1666–1891* (Ottawa, Ont.: Public Archives of Canada, 1987), viii.

Sources for Canadian Research on Microfilm at NEHGS

Michael J. Leclerc

Over the past few years, NEHGS has made a commitment to expanding its microfilm collection. The goal of the New England and Canada Microfilm Acquisitions Project is to acquire all available land, probate, and vital records for each New England state, as well as Québec, Nova Scotia, New Brunswick, and Prince Edward Island. The opportunities to document your research have been greatly enhanced with these records.

Vital Records

New Brunswick

The province of New Brunswick has recently expanded the number of vital records made available to the public. Birth records are available at NEHGS for 1888–1919. There are also late registrations of birth and documentation of those records for the period up to 1887 [CS88/N43/N433]. County marriage books start in 1806 and continue through 1919. Provincial marriage registrations start in 1888 and continue to 1919 [CS88/N43/N432]. Death registrations commenced in 1888 and are available up to 1951 [CS88/N43/N434].

Nova Scotia

Nova Scotia mandated vital records registration starting in 1864, but continued only through 1877 for births and deaths. Marriages continued to be recorded. NEHGS has microfilms of marriage licenses as early as 1849 and as late as 1918. After 1877, mandatory registration for births and deaths was discontinued and not started again until 1906. NEHGS has the records from this brief period of registration [CS88/N64/N64]. There are separate indexes for births, marriages, and deaths. They are filmed in alphabetical order for the entire province, and the indexes are broken down within each letter by county. The records themselves are organized by county.

Published online on *NewEnglandAncestors.org*, March 8, 2002. This version contains additional material.

Prince Edward Island

Pre-1887 birth records in Prince Edward Island are composed of copies of baptismal records from the churches [CS88/P74/P71]. Marriage records from justices of the peace cover the time period 1831–1888 [CS88/P74/P712]. Marriage bonds for the period 1824–1902 are available, with a few dating as early as 1787 [CS88/P74/P717]. Deaths are available up to 1906 [CS88/P74/P713].

Québec

Until the twentieth century, the churches in Québec registered vital records. The Drouin Microfilm Collection [CS88/Q4/I572] contains records of Catholic and Protestant churches and Jewish synagogues located within the province. While many of these records are indexed, there are a large number that are not. The marriages in the Catholic churches have been abstracted and compiled into a separate province-wide index. This index, which covers the period 1760–1930, is available on microfiche [CS88/Q4/I572]. There is also a three-volume set of books located on the fifth floor that covers the period 1608–1760 [CS81/D53/1979].

Land and Probate Records

New Brunswick

In New Brunswick both probate and land records are registered at the county level. The records of Albert County are the only land records held by NEHGS as of December 2001. The index covers 1846–1940, but the records are available only through 1887 [CS88/N431/A41]. All available probate records have been purchased and are available county by county as follows:

Call Number	County	Index Years	Record Years
CS88/N431/A4	Albert	1846-1957	1846-1904
CS88/N431/C3	Carleton	1832-1965	1831-1934
CS88/N431/C5	Charlotte	1785-1965	1785-1942
CS88/N431/G6	Gloucester	1827-1964	1827-1931
	Kent	N/A	N/A
CS88/N431/K5	Kings	1786-1960	1788-1932
CS88/N431/M3	Madawaska	1894-1966	1894-1930
CS88/N431/N77	Northumberland	1860-1966	1860-1930
CS88/N431/Q44	Queens	1785-1976	1785-1941
CS88/N431/R4	Restigouche	1861-1979	1861-1939
CS88/N431/S243	St. John	1785-1904	1785-1932
CS88/N431/S96	Sunbury	1786-1979	1786-1932
CS88/N431/V53	Victoria	1850-1959	1850-1931
CS88/N431/W47	Westmoreland	1787-1953	1787-1905
CS88/N431/Y65	York	1786-1976	1786-1930

The records of Kent County are not available because they were destroyed by fire.

Nova Scotia

In Nova Scotia, the land records are also recorded at the county level. Probate records are registered in probate districts. Some of the counties had two registration districts within the county. NEHGS has recently purchased all of the land records for the province and they are currently available in the microtext department. Following are the records and years available:

Probate Records

Call Number	County	District	Index Years	Record Years
CS88/N643/A16	Annapolis		1763–1979	1763–1970
CS88/N643/A25	Antigonish		N/A	1819–1963
CS88/N643/C2	Cape Breton		1782–1969	1782–1970
CS88/N643/C6	Colchester		1802–1969	1798–1969
CS88/N643/C8	Cumberland		1840–1945	1840–1969
CS88/N643/D5	Digby		1803–1970	1803–1970
CS88/N643/G8	Guysborough	Guysborough	1850–1967	1946–1969
CS88/N643/G8a	Guysborough	St. Mary's	1948–1993	1843–1970
CS88/N643/H3	Halifax		1750–1968	1749–1968
CS88/N643/H4	Hants		1767–1955	1761–1900
CS88/N643/I5	Inverness		1831–1964	1831–1969
CS88/N643/K5	Kings		1785–1925	1783–1968
CS88/N643/L9	Lunenburg			1762–1967
CS88/N643/P6	Pictou		1811–1940	1811–1969
CS88/N643/Q3	Queens		1760–1970	1743–1970
CS88/N643/R5	Richmond		1828–1993	1831–1969
CS88/N643/S5	Shelburne	Barrington		1866–1970
CS88/N643/S5	Shelburne	Shelburne	1784–1956	1784–1970
CS88/N643/S5a	Victoria			1851–1969
CS88/N643/Y3	Yarmouth		1843–1991	1794–1970

Land Records

Call Number	County	District	Index Years	Record Years
CS88/N644/A16	Annapolis		1765–1970	1765–1910
CS88/N644/A25	Antigonish		1784–1969	1785–1907
CS88/N644/C2	Cape Breton		1786–1966	1786–1969
CS88/N644/C6	Colchester		1771–1968	1770–1959
CS88/N644/C8	Cumberland		1764–1968	1764–1967
CS88/N644/D5	Digby		1785–1970	1785–1958
CS88/N644/G8	Guysborough	Guysborough	1785–1969	1785–1967
CS88/N644/G8a	Guysborough	St. Mary's	1815–1911	1815–1969
CS88/N644/H3	Halifax		1749–1967	1749–1967
CS88/N644/H4	Hants		1763–1968	1763–1952
CS88/N644/I5	Inverness		1825–1968	1825–1929
CS88/N644/K5	Kings		1764–1968	1764–1901
CS88/N644/L9	Lunenburg	Chester	1879–1955	1879–1926
CS88/N644/L9c	Lunenburg	Lunenburg	1759–1968	1759–1961
CS88/N644/P6	Pictou		1771–1968	1771–1924
CS88/N644/Q3	Queens		1764–1970	1764–1969
CS88/N644/R5	Richmond		1821–1969	1821–1963
CS88/N644/S5	Shelburne	Barrington	1854–1970	1854–1950
CS88/N644/S5a	Shelburne	Shelburne	1784–1968	1873–1961
CS88/N644/V5	Victoria		1851–1969	1851–1988
CS88/N644/Y3	Yarmouth		1774–1969	1766–1969

Prince Edward Island

Materials in the Land Records Office in Prince Edward Island have been microfilmed for the period 1769–1872 [CS88/P74/L36]. Most of these records deal with land conveyances and mortgages between individuals. Probate records in Prince Edward Island were recorded for the entire island starting in 1771. Records for 1807–1901 are available on microfilm at NEHGS [CS88/P74/W55].

Québec

In Québec, notaries recorded the mortgages and deeds as well as probate records. NEHGS has the notarial records for all areas outside of the cities of Montréal and Québec City. These records are part of the collection held by the Archives Nationales de Québec [CS88/Q4/R44]. The time frame available varies from area to area. There is also a separate set of microfiche with copies of many of the individual notaries' indexes to the records [CS88/Q4/R44]. There is a finding aid available on the fourth-floor to assist you with locating specific notarial records and indexes.

Miscellaneous Records

In addition to the aforementioned records, there are a number of other primary source materials available. For example, there are almost a hundred reels of church records for Prince Edward Island, as well as a few for Nova Scotia and New Brunswick. Another invaluable Prince Edward Island resource is the Master Name Index [CS88/P74/P7]. Compiled from census records, cemetery transcriptions, newspapers, atlases, and many other sources, this index provides a look at all inhabitants on the island.

The microfilm collections of the Archives Nationales de Québec contain a vast number of resources and are also available at NEHGS. In addition to church records and notarial records, one can find surveyor records from the Eastern Townships, court records, family records, and seigneurial records, as well as indexes to adoptions and guardianships in the cities of Montréal and Québec City. A finding aid to the entire collection is available in the microtext department.

For a more complete selection of materials in the NEHGS microtext collection, search the online catalog. If you are interested in donating to the New England and Canada Microtext Acquisitions Project, please contact the Development Office.

The Internet and published print materials are valuable resources for your research, but it is imperative to verify all statements by reviewing original source documents, whenever possible. Besides, it is wonderful to see copies of the actual wills and deeds that your ancestors signed so many years ago.

Summary of Resources

New Brunswick

- *New Brunswick Vital Statistics from Newspapers* (ongoing) 1784–1889, by Daniel F. Johnson [CS88/N43/N48/1982]
- All existing county marriage registers to 1888 [CS88/N43/N432 microfilm]
- Early New Brunswick probate registers, 1785–1835 [CS88/N43/H36/1989]
- Late birth registrations, 1810–1888 [CS88/N43/N432 microfilm]
- Provincial vital records, 1888–1891 [CS88/N43/N433 microfilm]

Newfoundland and Labrador

- 1921 census [HA741/C4/1921 microfilm]
- Vital records from newspapers, 1810–1845 [CS88/N6/H69], 1825–1877 [CS88/N6/C7]

Nova Scotia

- Marriage records, 1864–1918, marriage bonds, 1763–1847, Marriage Licenses, 1849-1918 [CS88/N64/N64/1980 microfilm]

- Nova Scotia vital statistics from newspapers, 1769 onward [CS88/N64/H64]

- Deaths, burials, probates of Nova Scotians, 1749–1799 [CS88/N64/M37 1990]

- Deaths and births, 1864–1877 [CS88/N64/N64/1980 microfilm]

- Land records, various years (see catalog record) [F1039/S5/S5/1975 microfilm]

Prince Edward Island

- Most Roman Catholic Church records to 1900 [CS88/P74/P72/1977 microfilm]

- Many Protestant church records into the twentieth century

- Marriage registers, 1831–1851 [CS88/P74/P714/1979 microfilm]

- All existing marriage bonds for P. E .I., 1849–1902 [CS88/P74/P717 microfilm]

- Deaths recorded at the Division of Vital Statistics, to 1906 [CS88/P74/P712 microfilm]

- Wills recorded at the P. E. I. Supreme Court, 1807–1901 [F1046.8/P74 microfilm]

- Church of Scotland records, 1853–1900 [CS88/P74/ C482-3 microfilm]

- Baptisms to 1886 [CS88/P74/P71 microfilm]

Québec

- Extensive microfilm collection of parish registers (vital records) and notarial records (deeds, *donations entre vifes*, marriage contracts) from the 1600s to the present. [CS88/Q4/R44 microfilm]

- PRDH *Répertoire*
  Books cover vital records 1700–1765 [CS88/Q4/R46]
  CD covers vital records 1766–1799 [CS88/Q4/R46/1998 CD]

- *Dictionnaire National des Canadiens Français* by Drouin
  Books cover 1608-1760 [CS81/D43/1979]
  Microfilm covers 1760-1935 for males [CS88/Q4/I55/1991]; for females [CS88/Q4/I571/1991]

- Various published county marriages

- Family genealogies

- *Dictionnaire Généalogique des Familles du Québec,* by Jetté (families of Québec into the 1720/30s)

- *Dictionnaire Généalogique des Familles Canadiennes,* by Tanguay (families of Québec to the 1780s)

- Non-Catholic records:
  Parish registers, generally after 1759 [CS88/Q4/R44 microfilm]
  Cemetery transcriptions in book form

- Notarial records [CS88/Q4/R44 microfilm]

- Land records: Lower Canada land petitions, 1764–1841 [F1032/P8/L5 microfilm]
  List of lands granted by the Crown in the province of Québec 1763–1890 [CS88/Q4/L5/1891]

Genealogical Research in Nova Scotia

George F. Sanborn, Jr.

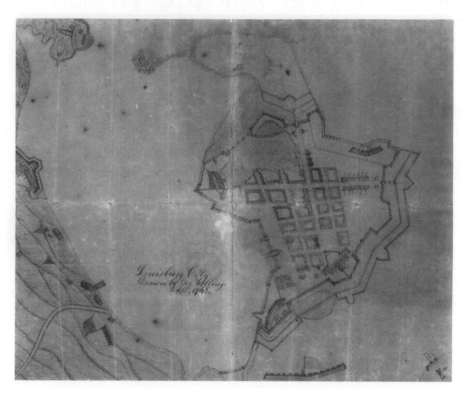

Map of Louisburg City, Nova Scotia, 1745; Drawing by George Follings.

With the history of Nova Scotia and New England so intertwined, it is no wonder that countless Americans have ancestors who resided in or passed through Canada's "Ocean Playground," and no surprise that countless Canadians have ancestors from New England and other parts of the eastern seaboard of the United States. Indeed, we recall with interest that as events heated up prior to the American Revolution, there was considerable sympathy in southern Nova Scotia and along the St. John River Valley, in what became New Brunswick in 1784, for joining Massachusetts and the other twelve colonies to the south in the struggle for independence from England. Had the British Fleet not wisely anchored in Halifax and Saint John harbors, such might have been the case.

Non-Acadian settlement of Nova Scotia by Europeans really did not commence until the arrival of the Cornwallis Fleet at Halifax in 1749. Beginning

Reprinted from *New England Ancestors* 4:2 (Spring 2003):25–29.

about 1758, New England fishermen from Cape Cod and the Islands began to establish themselves along the South Shore of what is now Nova Scotia, followed by the arrival of large numbers of New England Planters (farmers) who settled townships around both sides of southern Nova Scotia, much as townships were settled in New England. The beautiful town of Argyle, Nova Scotia, drew its population largely from the Dover, New Hampshire/Berwick, Maine, area, while the St. John River Valley attracted a large number of planters from Essex County, Massachusetts, especially Rowley, who settled such places as Sheffield, Maugerville [pronounced 'majorville'], and Barker's Point. Not surprising, either, is the Londonderry, New Hampshire, origin of some of the early settlers of Londonderry, Nova Scotia, and neighboring places, while less known to Americans is the significant relocation of large numbers of Rhode Islanders to Hants County communities along the Fundy shore, such as Rawdon, Douglas, Newport, and Falmouth. Similar stories can be told about other communities on both sides of the Bay of Fundy. Interestingly enough, even with daunting obstacles to communication between these new places and their ancestral homes, contact was maintained between the settlers and their former places of residence for many years.

Beginning in 1783, with the arrival of the spring and fall fleets carrying Loyalists and disbanded British troops from collapsing New York, the last stronghold of the Tories in the thirteen colonies, new blood of a more mixed background was introduced into the area. Large numbers of settlers, both black and white, from New York, New Jersey, Pennsylvania, Virginia, and the Carolinas, as well as New England (some having sojourned in Florida, the Bahamas, England, and elsewhere, in an attempt to escape the wrath of the insurrection), moved into such communities as Shelburne, Halifax, Guysborough, Sydney, and Port Hood, along the Nova Scotian shore, and Saint John, Kingston, Fredericton, Kingsclear, and Prince William, among other places, along the St. John River in present-day New Brunswick. In fact, constant complaints by the new Loyalist settlers in New Brunswick to the leaders in Nova Scotia led to the separation and creation of the new colony of New Brunswick in 1784.

Not surprisingly, as the appeal of industrialization increased, accompanied by other social forces of the late nineteenth century, great numbers of descendants of all these groups migrated to the industrial cities of New England and elsewhere in the United States in search of employment. Taking part in this "Second Great Migration" to New England, were descendants of other immigrants to Nova Scotia, too, such as the Yorkshire settlers of the Chignecto Isthmus, the Irish and Newfoundland Irish in various communities on both mainland Nova Scotia and Cape Breton Island, respectively, and the large numbers of Scots and Highland Scots, the latter predominantly from Cape Breton Island and the mainland counties of Antigonish and Pictou. Many other groups and individuals were in the mix as well. Single men came to eastern cities to find employment, while others sought the small towns and familiar employment of work in lumbering regions. Places such as Bangor and Hampden, Millinocket and Milo, and Rumford, in Maine, drew great numbers of

Maritimers, while Gorham, Berlin and Errol in New Hampshire, all had their share of men from "Down East." Some came with families, or returned home only to come again later with families, while others married American women and stayed in their new homes. Single women tended to gravitate to cities, where they could find work as domestics. They often married American husbands. Widows frequently ran boarding houses, largely for other folks from "down home." Some men went directly to the mines in Colorado or Montana, while many settled in California or the Pacific Northwest. Areas of the largest numbers of settlers from Down East in the United States are, in order, the Boston area, followed closely by the San Francisco Bay area; Perth Amboy, New Jersey; and the Seattle area. Important, too, are some other places, such as Pembina County, North Dakota, and parts of Wisconsin and Michigan. But one must always keep in mind that it is not only the British who are ubiquitous (as the magazine ads say) — Canadian Maritimers turn up just about anywhere in the world.

Approaching Our Research

Americans beginning their Nova Scotia research (and even those who have been at it a while) are well advised to exhaust all relevant records in the United States first before blindly plunging into the large quantity of available Nova Scotia data. Review all possible material from family sources (oral history, family scrapbooks, mass or funeral cards, newspaper clippings, old letters, and the like). Obtain copies of vital records from United States sources not only for your ancestors but also their siblings, cousins, and others known to be related. If you do not have obituaries for all of your relatives make a project of trying to find and copy them. Much valuable information and clues to other relationships exist there. Check probate records; the deceased often remembered relatives back home or elsewhere in their wills. The purpose of this research is to give you not only a more complete picture of your family but also to help fix the place or places in Nova Scotia whence they came. Frequently Americans know only "Nova Scotia," and that really is not good enough, especially if the surname is common.

Of less importance for Nova Scotia research are ship manifests, such as those for the Port of Boston, and naturalization records. Usually the place of origin will be stated only as Nova Scotia, or even Canada, and while the records are of interest, they will not, in all probability, dramatically advance your research. An exception could be the so-called St. Albans [Vermont] Border Crossing Records of the Immigration and Naturalization Service, which commence in 1895 and run to 1954. Beginning about 1907, native-born Canadians are also included. While the records are called the St. Albans Border Crossing Records, they cover the entire U.S.-Canada border but were maintained by the St. Albans office of the INS, hence their name. These records, on microfilm at the NEHGS library and at the offices of the National Archives and Records Administration, as well as from the Family History Library in Salt Lake City, provide, among much other useful data, the name, address, and relationship of the nearest kin in Canada, and the name, address, and relationship of the person in the U.S. to whom they were going, as well as dates and places of any prior residence in the United States.

One word of caution when using American vital records referring to native-born Atlantic Canadians: There was and still is a tendency, in northern New England in particular, to refer to anyone from Atlantic Canada as a Nova Scotian, rather than a New Brunswicker, a Prince Edward Islander, or a Newfoundlander. Hence a record will state frequently that someone was born in Nova Scotia when that is not the case. Such confusion is another example of why it is important to view all possible relevant records in the United States, since some of them may say something more specific than Nova Scotia.

United States census records, now open for inspection through and including 1930, are another source of information. Some census forms requested the year of immigration for foreign-born people, and whether or not such people were naturalized citizens. Places of birth, which may be listed just as Nova Scotia or Canada, are also important, especially for the individual's parents. Some odd things do show up, however. In 1870 my relatives, David and Mary E. Adams and their children, appear on the census in Monroe, Waldo County, Maine, with birthplaces given as "Bryant's Island, Nova Scotia." While there is such a place, in the Bay of Fundy, the people in question were actually born in Prince Edward Island! If I had relied on just the 1870 census record and had assumed that it was correct, imagine the time and money I would have wasted trying to locate these people in a place they had probably never heard of. It remains a mystery why the census-taker recorded the birthplace that he did.

Ready to Research

To adapt a well-known phrase from Monday Night Football: "Are you ready to research?" Once your homework has been done, and you have found all the names you can muster, and, one would hope, at least *one* specific place in Nova Scotia where research might begin, let's take a look at what readily available records exist. (If you have been unable to find any records with a Nova Scotia location listed and if you are still at a loss to identify a *place*, you might be aided by Terrence M. Punch's useful book, *In Which County? Nova Scotia Surnames from Birth Registers; 1864 to 1877* (Genealogical Association of Nova Scotia, 1985). You will also want to arm yourself with two other publications: Terrence M. Punch's *Genealogical Research in Nova Scotia*, 4th rev. ed. (Halifax, 1998), and *Genealogist's Handbook for Atlantic Canada Research*, 2nd ed., edited by Terrence M. Punch and George F. Sanborn Jr. (NEHGS, 1997), both available from the NEHGS Book Store and Circulating Library.

Published Sources

There are a number of useful published sources for Nova Scotian research, many available at NEHGS. There are many local community histories and a number of excellent county histories. Did you know that Nova Scotia is the only province in Atlantic Canada that has published county histories such as those common in the United States? Some are of inestimable value, such as that for Inverness County in Cape Breton, which has preserved forever the all-important Gaelic patronymics of most of the early Highland Scots settlers, as well as important oral tradition.

The Genealogical Association of Nova Scotia has published several valuable sources, including newspaper abstracts of vital and other events, as have the now-defunct Cape Breton Genealogical Society and independent researchers such as Wayne Macvicar (*Cape Breton Post*) and James and Shirley McCormick (*The Presbyterian Witness*), among others. Years ago, the Nova Scotia Historical Society and Nova Scotia Archives published some very helpful material. Dr. Allan Everett Marble has compiled two invaluable works, *Deaths, Burials, and Probate of Nova Scotians, 1749–1799, from Primary Sources*, 2 vols. (Halifax, 1990), and *Deaths, Burials, and Probate of Nova Scotians, 1800–1850, from Primary Sources*, 4 vols. (Halifax, 1999). Stephen A. White, at the Centre d'études acadiennes at the Université de Moncton, has prepared a massive and scholarly work, now partly in print, entitled *Dictionnaire généalogique des familles acadiennes, Première Partie 1636 à 1714*, 2 vols. (Moncton, 1999). We must also mention the important and compendious works of the late John Victor Duncanson, *Township of Falmouth, Nova Scotia* (Windsor, 1965); *Newport, Nova Scotia — A Rhode Island Township* (Belleville, Ont., 1985); and *Rawdon and Douglas: Two Loyalist Townships in Nova Scotia* (Belleville, Ont., 1989), as well as Father A. J. MacMillan's *A West Wind to East Bay* (Antigonish, 2001), with genealogies of the pioneer families of East Bay, Cape Breton, and the long-awaited *To The Hill of Boisdale*, rev. ed. (Antigonish, 2001), with genealogies of the pioneer families of the Boisdale area of Cape Breton. And there is the classic by Edwin Crowell, *A History of Barrington Township and Vicinity, Shelburne County, Nova Scotia, 1604–1870* (Yarmouth, 1923). There are many other important and useful works; most are available at NEHGS.

Vital Records

The earliest vital records as such are to be found in the various extant township books for the several Planter townships. Similar to New England town record books, a variety of town business was recorded in them, including vital data. The system of keeping town books fell by the wayside in the second or third decade of the nineteenth century, unfortunately, as descendants of the early settlers seemed to forget the old custom. About half of the township books have been microfilmed and are available at the Nova Scotia Archives, at

NEHGS, and from the Family History Library, while the others must be viewed in their original form at the Nova Scotia Archives in Halifax.

Nova Scotia began keeping birth, marriage, and death records in 1864, but discontinued the practice of registering births and deaths in 1877. Marriages continued to be recorded. Then, in 1908, registration of births and deaths was resumed and has continued to the present day. The 1864–1877 records are conspicuously incomplete, especially in the early years, and it has been observed that many marriages were not recorded even into the twentieth century. One interesting feature of the birth records, at certain periods, was a question asking for the date and place of marriage of the parents, which often preceded 1864. However, I have seen different dates of marriage given for the parents of each child in a family, so a single appearance of a date may or may not be accurate. In the case of death records, the name of the father is occasionally provided which, in the case of a very elderly person, can be a real boon. Even though full recording was resumed in 1908, one should know that the names and birthplaces of parents were not requested on death registrations until approximately 1920. Nova Scotia Archives and Records Management, NEHGS, and the Family History Library, have microfilms of the births and deaths 1864 to 1877, and the marriages from 1864 until the first decade or so of the twentieth century (the final date depends on the county in question). Historical societies, museums, genealogical societies, and/or libraries in the various counties, and other places such as The Beaton Institute in Sydney and the Highland Village in Iona, may have these vital records for their areas.

Deaths less than 50 years old, marriages less than 75 years old, and births less than 100 years old are still retained by the Registrar General. Earlier births, marriages, and deaths have been transferred to Nova Scotia Archives and Records Management. Marriage licenses are more complete, are a much larger collection, and may provide more information. NEHGS has copies of marriage licenses on microfilm as early as 1849 and as late as 1918. Frequently one can find desired information about ancestors and relatives who never left Nova Scotia by searching for the marriage and/or death records, probate records, and obituaries of their siblings in New England, for New England vital records are generally more complete and begin earlier — with fuller information — than those in Nova Scotia. In the case of marriage records, bonds were generally required before a marriage could be performed, normally signed by the groom and a land-owning relative of the bride, attesting that there were no legal impediments to the marriage. Many of the bonds have been lost over the years, but those that survive from 1763 to 1864 have been indexed by the Genealogical Association of Nova Scotia and are now available for sale on CD-ROM.

Before 1864, and even afterwards (especially between 1877 and 1908), one needs to turn to church records, which are often quite full and informative. The Archives in Halifax have endeavored to obtain microfilm copies of all church records, and other repositories, such as The Beaton Institute, will have those for their areas as well. There are restrictions on many of these materials, and permission to view them must first be obtained from the relevant church authority. NEHGS has copies of the Anglican records for Guysborough County, Liverpool, Shelburne, and Annapolis Royal; Presbyterian records for Pictou; and Anglican records (including the old Lutheran records in German script) for Lunenburg, among other scattered holdings, in its collection.

Land and Probate Records

Among the most valuable tools of the genealogist are land and probate records. Those kept in Nova Scotia are similar to those in New England, and are recorded on the county level. The original records are in the various county registries, where one must pay a small fee to search them. However, microfilm copies are available at the Nova Scotia Archives, and at NEHGS, as well as from the Family History Library. With the exception of original Crown grants and various leases, all land records will be found among deeds. The Archives, as well as The Beaton Institute and other places in Nova Scotia, have a fine collection of cadastral maps, showing the boundaries of Crown grants, and the outstanding collection of Ambrose F. Church's maps, dating from the 1860s to the 1880s, depending on the county, and showing nearly every house and the names of householders. All of these maps are available for purchase in Halifax. In addition, the Archives has a set of interesting early maps of the various divisions of colonial Halifax showing the layout of the lots and first grants for each division. Similarly, there are maps of the early lots and land grants to the Loyalists in Shelburne, as well as numerous other such treasures for other places in the province.

Census Records

The story of census records from the early French period, and also the early British period, is complex. Some have been lost; some were statistical; others were head-of-household with numbers of various age and gender groupings in the household. Some census substitutes exist, too, such as the so-called "Victualling Lists" prepared in early Halifax to feed the impoverished settlers brought from England by Cornwallis in 1749. Many of the surviving early census records have been published. A fuller discussion of these will be found in *Genealogist's Handbook for Atlantic Canada Research*, 2nd ed., mentioned above. The earliest census to survive almost in its entirety is that of 1838–1841; however, it does lack most of Cumberland County. The portion for Cape Breton was published by the Cape Breton Genealogical Society. The 1851 census followed, but apparently survives only for Halifax, Kings, and Pictou counties. It is regrettable that the first census of Nova Scotia to list all names in each household is that for 1871, the first federal Canadian census, although earlier ones do provide some useful information (especially the detailed 1861 census). Canadian census records through 1901 are open to the public, and we are hopeful that the 1911 census will be released soon. All available census records are at the Nova Scotia Archives and the Family History Library (from whose branches they may be ordered), and most (including all since 1838) are at NEHGS. An important feature of Canadian census records is the inclusion of each person's religious affiliation (important for deciding which church records to search), as well as the "ethnic origin" of each individual in later records. This last was interpreted as being the nationality of the father's surname line — no matter how many generations removed from the immigration or how diluted by intermarriage with other ethnic groups it might have been.

There are many other sources for research besides those mentioned here, of course. A visit to the Nova Scotia Archives and Records Management in Halifax will reveal numerous manuscript, published, and microfilmed items of interest to all people with Nova Scotian heritage.

Prince Edward Island

George F. Sanborn Jr.

Any genealogical research on Prince Edward Island families will be more meaningful and fruitful if one first has a thorough understanding of the evolution of the Island's institutions. The best overall history is A. B. Warburton's *A History of Prince Edward Island from its Discovery in 1534 until the Departure of Lieutenant-Governor Ready in A.D. 1831* (St. John, N.B., 1923) [CA/22/15], which has the added feature of the little-known 1768 census. Also of distinct importance is Duncan Campbell's *History of Prince Edward Island* (Charlottetown, 1875 [reprinted Bowie, Md., 1990]) [F1048/C35/1875] which has the only surviving record of the province-wide 1798 census. And an indispensable aide, even for the seasoned Island genealogist, is Alan Rayburn's *Geographical Names of Prince Edward Island* (Ottawa, 1973) [REF F1046.4/R38/1973], which has a useful foldout map showing the lots (i.e., townships) and other important features.

Guides and Finding Aids

The most comprehensive guide to research in P.E.I. is Terrence M. Punch and George F. Sanborn Jr., *Genealogist's Handbook for Atlantic Canada Research*, 2nd ed. (Boston, 1997) [REF CS88/A88/G46/1997]. Those wishing to explore the rich world of P.E.I. newspapers will find Heather Boylan's *Checklist and Historical Directory of Prince Edward Island Newspapers 1787–1986* (Charlestown, 1987) [Z6954/C3/B6/1987] of great importance. Newspaper records help fill in the chasm of nonexistent nineteenth-century vital statistics. The Master Name Index, First Series and Second Series (First Series only at NEHGS) [CS88/P74/P7/1985], is an extensive card file of a broad spectrum of records containing cemetery, census, some early newspaper abstracts, some court records, and many other useful things. Other items of broad appeal include the Index to Baptisms to 1886 [CS88/P74/P71] and the Index to Burials to 1906 [CS88/P74/P713], which were prepared by the Department of Health from church records all over the Island.

Genealogical and Historical Periodicals

Foremost among the periodical literature is the valuable P.E.I. Genealogical Society Newsletter [F1046/P75/1977]. Now 25 years old, this quarterly has built up a corpus of important material. Also, *The Island Magazine* (P.E.I. Museum & Heritage Foundation, Charlottetown) [F1046/I8], although not genealogical *per se*, has many important historical articles indispensable to genealogists and for many years included a genealogical article in each issue. Such articles as those listing all the surviving ship passenger lists, the so-called Hill's List of tenants on certain West Prince lots, and the article on the surviving fragment of Bishop MacEachern's baptismal records, come to mind. Similarly, the well-known *Abegweit Review* (Charlottetown, University of Prince Edward Island) [F1046/A23 also LOAN] has interesting articles beneficial to an accurate understanding of Island history and people.

Census: Colonial and Canadian

For the availability of the 1768 and 1798 censuses, see comments above. Censuses were taken thereafter in 1841 [HA741/C4/1841], 1848 [HA741/C4/1848], 1861 [HA741/C4/1861], and 1871 [HA741/C4/1871]. All of these are head-of-household censuses: 1841 is missing 25 of the 67 townships, including many in Prince County; the 1848 census includes only Charlottetown and the royalties round about it as well as Lot 31, while the 1871 census was lost for all but Lots 34 and 36. The first every-name complete census of the Island was taken in 1881 [HA741/C4/1881], followed by those of 1891 (Lots 21 and 22 are lacking) [HA741/C4/1891], and 1901 [HA741/C4/1901] — extracted data from all being found in the Master Name Index. The items of information vary slightly for each one, but all those after 1798 include religious affiliation, which is so important in locating relevant church records.

Vital Records

Official registration of births, deaths, and marriages in Prince Edward Island was not compulsory until 1906. Before that, there are marriage registers, 1831–1888 [CS88/P74/P712] and province-wide marriage licenses, 1787–1805, 1812–1813, and 1824–1851 [CS88/P74/P714]. NEHGS also has Kings County marriage licenses 1879–1970 [CS88/P74/K56], and the province-wide marriage bonds, 1849–December 1902 [CS88/P74/P719]. Baptismal records (including some birth dates) to the end of 1886, and burial records (including some death dates) to 1906, may be found in the Index to Baptisms and the Index to Burials mentioned above.

Church Records

Prior to 1906, and even after that date, church records are the principal source of vital statistics data. NEHGS has scattered church records from various denominations, including nearly all of the pre-1900 Roman Catholic church records and McDonaldite Presbyterian records for the Island.

Cemetery Records

While the P.E.I. Genealogical Society has published transcripts of all the cemetery inscriptions for the Island, the Master Name Index, First Series [CS88/P74/P7/1985], includes the inscriptions arranged alphabetically by the surnames involved.

Newspapers

NEHGS does not actively acquire newspapers, but there are some notable exceptions to this policy. The collection includes the unusual and important newspaper published in Oakland, California, called *The Maple Leaf* (Charlottetown, 1982) [F869/O2/M3/1982]. Published by an expatriate Islander from Summerside, the monthly newspaper's great value comes in the long lists of deaths and other vital statistics from not only the Maritimes but from places such as Massachusetts, where large numbers of Maritimers lived. Often the fastest way to either locate the death of someone who "went away," or to find out where a decedent had come from in Canada, these records accurately report date and place of death, the place of origin in Canada, and often give the name of a parent or other identifying information. Most of the issues missing on the microfilm were later donated to the Public Archives and Records Office in Charlottetown and are available for research there. For newspapers published on the Island, see Heather Boylan's guide to newspapers mentioned see above.

Probate

NEHGS has microfilm copies of P.E.I. wills [copy-book transcripts], 1807–1900, and the Index to Administrations 1897–1901 [CS88/P74/W55]. A private project to abstract and publish all P.E.I. probate records to the mid-nineteenth century is nearly finished, and copies of this much-anticipated book will be promptly added to the collection.

Land Records

Few people bought their own land in P.E.I. during the colonial period; most either squatted or leased their property. Nevertheless, we have microfilm copies of all surviving P.E.I. deeds 1769–1872 [CS88/P74/L36]. For a further discussion of the Island's complicated land-holding history, see the late Ann Coles's article on the subject in *The Island Magazine*, and also the scholarly work of Ian Ross Robertson, *The Prince Edward Island Land Commission of 1860* (Fredericton, 1988) [CS88/P7/P74/1988].

Court Records

While NEHGS does not have any P.E.I. court records as such, some early ones were abstracted in the Master Name Index, First Series (see above), and other significant collections at the Public Archives and Records Office have been described and, in some cases abstracted, in the P.E.I. Genealogical Society Newsletter (see above).

Biographical Compendia

There are no biographical "mug books" or county histories for Prince Edward Island's three counties. However, a large number of community histories have been published, each with some amount of biographical and/or genealogical content. Among the more useful may be cited J. Clinton Morrison, Jr.'s *Along the North Shore: A Social History of Township 11, P.E.I., 1765–1982* (Summerside, P.E.I., 1984) [F1049.5/L5/M6/1984]; the North Tryon Historical Association's *Remember Yesterday: A History of North Tryon, Prince Edward Island 1769–1992*, in two volumes (Summerside, P.E.I., 1993) [CS88/P7/R45/1993]; the Stanley Bridge Community Historical Society's *History of Stanley Bridge, Hub of the Universe* (Sackville, N.B., 1997) [F1049.5/S73/H57/1997]; and the Freetown Historical Society's *Freetown Past and Present* (Summerside, P.E.I., 1985) [F1049.5/F73/F7].

Maps, Atlases, and Toponymic Studies

While numerous maps of individual townships or portions of townships exist from early dates at the Public Archives and Records Office in Charlottetown, the so-called Lake Map of 1863 stands out as being province-wide showing the location of all houses in rural areas with the names of the occupants. NEHGS's copy is on microfilm [G3340/1863/L35], but the best way to view the map clearly is on the most comprehensive and important website for P.E.I. genealogy, at *islandregister.com*.

The ever popular atlas containing similar information for a slightly later time, J. H. Meacham & Co.'s *Illustrated Historical Atlas of The Province of Prince Edward Island* (Philadelphia, 1880 [reprinted Belleville, Ont., 1977]) [G1135/M4/1972] and the Cummins Map Co.'s *Atlas of Province of Prince Edward Island Canada and the World* (Toronto, c1928 [P.E.I. section only reprinted Winnipeg, 1990]) [G1135/A84/1928] round out our collection of these important resources. And useful here, too, is Alan Rayburn's *Geographical Names of Prince Edward Island* (Ottawa, 1973) [REF F1046.4/R38/1973].

Diaries and Account Books

Diaries and account books take on added important in places where few early vital statistics records are found, and the Island has no shortage of such interesting day-to-day journals that traditionally are full of names and dates. Among those in our collection may be cited the "Daybook of Benjamin Chappell" (New London and Charlottetown areas) [CS88/P74/P719]; the "Diaries of the O'Connor and Foley Families" (Kildare Capes area, Lot 3) [CS90/O42/1979]; the "Account Book of Dr. John C. McKeown 1830–1883" (Kings County)

[F1049/K5/M35/1979]; the "Letter Book of John Cambridge 1784–1801"

[F1048/R46]; the "Diaries of George MacDonald 1909–1939" (Queens County)

[F1049/Q6/M33]; the "Diary of Rev. Robert Dyer 1859–1883" (Alberton, Kildare)

[F1049.5/A42/D52/1980]; "William Creed's Account Book 1780-1824"

[F1049.5/C5/C74]; the "Montgomery Store Ledger 1834–1858" (Princetown area)

[F1049.5/P75/M66]; and an Unidentified Store Ledger 1824 (Charlottetown)

[F1049.5/P75/M66].

Miscellaneous Sources

While not heavy in personal names, the U.S. Consular Dispatches 3 June 1857–3 August 1906 (Charlottetown) [CS88/P74/U55] will shed some light on an earlier period of international cooperation between Charlottetown and the eastern United States. Of more genealogical import are the extensive *Soundex Index to Canadian Border Entries through St. Albans, Vt., District 1895–1924, and 1925–1954* [CS68/U61/M1461 and CS68/U61/M1463], and the *Manifests of Passengers in the St. Albans, Vt., District through Canadian Pacific and Atlantic Ports 1895–1954* [Vault CS68/U63/M1464]. From 1907 on, Canadian citizens are included in these records, and the amount of personal detail about each person crossing into the United States, their nearest kin in Canada and the person to whom they were going in the United States, is most interesting and useful, often bringing out earlier travels, relationships, and relatives not previously known.

French-Canadian Research at NEHGS

Michael J. Leclerc

French-Canadians and their Franco-American descendants interested in gene-alogy are very lucky indeed. The records of Québec are among the best in the world. With the exception of minor rebellions, no major war has been fought on Québec soil since the Battle of the Plains of Abraham in the mid-eighteenth century. Because of diligent reporting practices, most parish registers have survived. And major genealogical research has been conducted for over a cen-tury.

Censuses

The first census to be taken in Québec was done by the Intendant Jean Talon in 1666. Other censuses were taken in 1825, 1831, and 1842, but it was not until 1851 that the pattern of decennial censuses was established. The first domin-ion census was taken in 1871 after Confederation in 1867. The census has been taken every ten years since. Records through 1901 are open to the public. They are available at NEHGS or through interlibrary loan from the National Ar-chives of Canada.

While certain individuals and organizations have begun indexing the Ca-nadian censuses, they are for the most part unindexed. Fortunately, most towns outside of the major cities of Québec, Montréal, and Trois-Rivières are not very large, and it does not take long to go through the entire town page by page.

Church Records

Civil registration of church records in the province of Québec did not begin until the 1920s. Prior to that time the churches in the province were required to maintain books of baptisms (births), marriages, and burials (deaths), and send copies of each book to the government. The books were kept as a record of the vital statistics in the province. Fortunately, the records for most Roman Catho-lic parishes survive from their beginnings. Many of the churches in the Protes-tant denominations did not start keeping records immediately, making it more difficult to trace their members.

Published online on *NewEnglandAncestors.org*, February 1, 2002 and June 14, 2002.

Notarial Records

The records of Québec's notaries are perhaps the richest source of material on your French-Canadian ancestors outside of the parish registers. Notaries in Québec are different from notaries in the United States. In Québec, they handle all aspects of contract law, including marriage contracts, which were a requirement for marriage in the province until the 1960s. Employment contracts, land sales, wills, inventories, donations, and sales contracts are among the more valuable records. There were often several notaries in the town so when searching these records, it is important to find out every notary that existed for a town for the years you are looking for.

PRDH

Another important reference is the *Répertoire des Actes de Baptême, Mariage, Sépulture, et des Recensements du Québec Ancien*, published by the Programme de Recherche en Démographie Historique. This forty-seven volume set, commonly referred to as the PRDH, abstracts information from early parish registers (including the names of godparents, witnesses, clergy, and others) as well as early census and hospital records. The PRDH has been produced on CD-ROM for the period 1621–1799. It can be viewed at the NEHGS Library.

Archives Nationales de Québec Publications

In the first half of the twentieth century, archivist Pierre-Georges Roy oversaw the publication of several series of books on historical documents of Québec. The publication, *Inventaire des Contrats de Mariages du Régime Français Conservés aux Archives Judiciaires de Québec*, abstracts many of the early marriage contracts in Québec, providing valuable information on parents' names that may have been left out of the parish registers.

Inventaire des Jugements et Deliberations du Conseil Supérieur de la Nouvelle France de 1717 à 1760 contains records of many who went before the Sovereign Council in the colony. The *Inventaire des Procès-Verbaux des Grands Voyers Conservés aux Archives de la Province de Québec* has records of a number of legal depositions and other testimony. The *Inventaire des Concessions en Fief et Seigneurie Fois et Hommages et Aveux et Denombrements Conservés aux Archives de la Province de Québec* has records of many land transfers.

Vital Records

Civil registration of vital records in the province of Québec did not begin until 1994. Prior to that time, the churches were required to keep duplicate copies of their registers and send them to the civil authorities as the official record of births, marriages, and deaths in the province. The Catholic Church was the first denomination to record these events. After the English took control of Canada, other denominations were added incrementally starting with the Anglican Church. The great majority of French-Canadians, however, were Catholic.

While these records were supposed to be indexed every year, not every parish followed this procedure. Some of the indexes were prepared in order by page number, rather than alphabetically. Thus it is necessary to go through the entire index name by name to find individuals you are looking for. Page numbers in Québec refer to the front and back of a page, rather than facing pages, as they might in the United States. Thus, when scrolling through microfilm images, you will often need to look at two consecutive images to view the entire page.

Québecois naming patterns are important in utilizing these records. Men were often baptized as Joseph, and women as Marie. In addition, French-Canadian women by tradition kept their maiden names throughout their lives. Even on their death records, women were recorded by the name they carried at birth.

The copy of the parish registers that the churches sent to the provincial government is known as the *Registre d'État Civil*. Those registers prior to 1900 are available at the branches of the Archives Nationales de Québec or at the Family History Library in Salt Lake City (and also, of course, through your local Family History Center or NEHGS).

It is important when you are researching in microfilms of parish registers to note whether you are looking at the original parish register or the *Registre d'État Civil*. The original parish records were kept for tracking sacraments in the Catholic Church and nearly all followed the same format. The names of the individuals were written on the left side of the page with the details of the sacrament on the right, which again included the name of the individual. In the margin under the person's name are often notes written by the parish priest. These marginal notes can contain extremely valuable information for your research. For example, a marginal note recorded prior to my grandmother's baptismal record in the Parish of St. Norbert d'Arthabaska stated that the infant's grandmother, my great-great grandmother, was at Sanford, Maine. This was the first indication in the history of my research that placed her at Sanford, and it allowed me to find a marriage record that had eluded me for over seven years! These marginal notes, which are in the original parish registers, are only rarely transferred to the *Registre d'État Civil*.

The Drouin Institute

The Drouin Institute in Montréal began conducting genealogical research in 1899 and continued collecting, transcribing, and selling records and family genealogies for many years. In the 1940s they microfilmed the registers of every Catholic and Protestant parishes in the province, as well as Jewish synagogues. The Drouin Institute ceased to exist in the late 1990s, and their holdings were sold to the American-French Genealogical Society (AFGS) in Woonsocket, Rhode Island. In 1999 AFGS agreed to sell copies of these microfilms to NEHGS, and they remain the only two repositories in the United States where the entire collection is available.

After microfilming of the parish registers was completed, the Drouin Institute abstracted the marriage records from all of the Catholic churches. These records include the names of the individuals who were to be married, as well as the names of their parents. If one of the parties was married previously, the name of the previous spouse appears instead of the names of the parents. Drouin created two master indexes of marriages; one by groom and one by bride. They are indexed by surname, then by first name, then by surname of spouse. The names of the parents and/or previous spouse, and the date and place of marriage are also included in the index. These indexes are in three series and cover the period 1608–1930. The first series covers 1608–1760 and is available in book form. The second series covers 1760–1880, and the third 1881–1930. These are now available on microfilm on the fourth floor.

Compiled Genealogies

Père Cyprien Tanguay and the Dictionnaire Généalogique des Familles Canadiennes depuis la Fondation de la Colonie Jusqu'à nos Jours

Father Tanguay (1819–1902) was a Catholic priest who studied the parish records of early families in Québec. He compiled genealogies of the early families through the mid-eighteenth century. He published the first volume of *Dictionnaire Généalogique des Familles Canadiennes depuis la Fondation de la Colonie Jusqu'à nos Jours* in 1871, and published six additional volumes over the next twenty years.

Father Tanguay's work separates individuals by generation into family groups. The information includes dates and places of marriage as well as names of children, including their dates and places of birth and baptism. The families are in alphabetical order by surname of the husband/father. Because there may be more than one individual with the same name in the same generation, it is often necessary to scrutinize the entries of several families before finding the correct ones.

In addition to these several volumes, Arthur LeBeouf published a volume of additions and corrections to Tanguay in his *Complément au Dictionnaire Généalogique Tanguay* (1957). In addition to re-examining the parish records published by Tanguay, LeBeouf researched additional sources to supplement the original work.

René Jetté and the Programme de Récherche en Demographie Historique

René Jetté is often considered the father of modern French-Canadian genealogy. With a grant from the Québec government, this professor at the University of Montréal started the Programme de Récherche en Demographie Historique (PRDH). The PRDH examined original parish registers, early census records, hospital records, abjuration records, marriage contracts, and other records to create a picture of the early immigrants of New France.

Over the course of time, the PRDH published abstracts of these records in a series of volumes covering the years 1608–1765. These books are separated into different time periods and the records of each place examined are kept together and indexed individually. There is also a master index for each time period. In 1999, the PRDH published a CD-ROM covering the time period 1766–1799, and subsequently released a second CD-ROM containing all of the earlier materials.

In 1983, Jetté published the most important book in French-Canadian genealogical research since Tanguay's work a century earlier. The *Dictionnaire généalogique des familles du Québec dès origines à 1730*, published by the University of Montréal, contains biographies of all families in New France through about 1730. In addition to the primary sources mentioned above, Jetté used over thirty previously published works to add to the biographies. The work is published entirely in French, but most records are very easily translated. Jetté also suggests over a hundred other secondary sources to use for additional research.

Periodicals

The following periodicals contain a great deal of useful genealogical information (all are in English except the second one):

The *French Canadian and Acadian Genealogical Review* was published 1968–1981 by the Centre Canadien des Recherches Généalogiques.

Mémoires de la Société Généalogique Canadienne-Française has been published by the Société Généalogique Canadienne-Française since 1944.

The *American-Canadian Genealogist* is the quarterly journal of the American-Canadian Genealogical Society in Manchester, New Hampshire. The focus of articles is on Acadian, French-Canadian, and Franco-American family history and genealogy. The journal includes articles about Québec and Acadia and the migration of these people from all of French Canada and Acadia into New England, New York, and any other area in North America where descendants of New France settled.

Je Me Souviens is the publication of the American-French Genealogical Society in Woonsocket, Rhode Island. It contains many articles on French-Canadians and their Franco-American descendants, specializing in those who came to New England.

Lost in Canada was published from 1973 to 1994 by Joy Reisinger of Sparta, Wisconsin. It includes many valuable articles on French-Canadians in North America. One of the most interesting is a series of articles on French-Canadians who supported the rebels in the American Revolution. Proof of descent from one of these individuals may allow one to join the Daughters of the American Revolution or Sons of the American Revolution, even though one has no ancestors from the English colonies!

Lifelines is the journal of the Northern New York American-Canadian Genealogical Society in Plattsburgh, New York. Articles include genealogies, queries, and the latest websites for French-Canadian research.

Miscellaneous Published Sources

Nos Ancêtres is a series of volumes published by Gerard Lebel and Thomas La Forest. The series is comprised of thirty volumes, each containing a brief profile of the life of an early colonist, a list of family members, known "dit names" (nicknames that differentiated individuals with the same last name) and other name variations, and (most importantly) end notes with citations to the sources used to produce each profile.

Normand Robert and the Société de Recherche Historique Archiv-Histo are publishing a series of volumes entitled *Nos Origines en France dès débuts à 1825.* Twelve volumes have so far been published in this series, with each book focusing on a particular region of France. Within each regions are brief descriptions of the hometown followed by a list of all immigrants from that particular town.

Marcel Fournier's *Les Europeéns au Canada dès Origines à 1765* (Québec: Editions du Fleuve, 1989) is a fascinating work dealing with immigration from many different countries in Europe. The first part contains historical and statistical information on immigration, while the second part contains brief biographies of these immigrants.

Word Lists

The following basic words appear in many different types of records. Familiarity with these, and a French-English dictionary, will facilitate your research.

Months

French	French Abbreviation	English
janvier	janv	January
février	fév	February
mars	mar	March
avril	avr	April
mai	mai	May
juin	juin	June
juillet	juill	July
aôut	aôut	August
septembre	sept or 7bre	September
octobre	oct or 8bre	October
novembre	nov or 9bre	November
décembre	déc or 10bre	December

Common Terms in French-Canadian Records

French	English	French	English
an(s)	year(s)	mariage	marriage
baptisé	baptised	marrain	godmother
cette	this	mère	mother
cimetière	cemetery	m or mineur	minor
corps	body	moi(s)	month(s)
de	of	né or née	born
décédé	died	ne savoir signer	did not know how to sign their name
déf or défunt	deceased	oncle	uncle
et	and	parrain	godfather
feu	late (deceased)	paroisse	parish
fille	daughter	père	father
fils	son	sauvage	savage (Indian)
hier	yesterday	sauvagesse	savagess (Indian)
illégitime	illegitimate	sépulture	burial
Inconnu	forgotten	sic	as shown in original
indien(ne)	Indian	St or Saint	Saint (male)
inhumé	buried	Ste or Sainte	Saint (female)
jour(s)	day(s)	la veille	the day before
légitime	legitimate	vf or veuf	widower
M or majeur	of age	vve or veuve	widow

Numbers

French	English	French	English	French	English
un	one	onze	eleven	trente	thirty
deux	two	douze	twelve	quarante	forty
trois	three	treize	thirteen	cinquante	fifty
quatre	four	quatorze	fourteen	soixante	sixty
cinq	five	quinze	fifteen	soixante-dix	seventy
six	six	seize	sixteen	quatre-vingt	eighty
sept	seven	dix-sept	seventeen	quatre-vingt-dix	ninety
huit	eight	dix-huit	eighteen	cent	one hundred
neuf	nine	dix-neuf	nineteen	mil	one thousand
dix	ten	vingt	twenty		

Note: Dates are often written out in long form, e.g.: Mil Huit Cent Soixante Dix-Huit = One Thousand Eight Hundred Seventy-Eight = 1878

SECTION 7

British Isles and Ireland

Searching for the "Mill English": The Meadowcrofts of Lancashire

David Curtis Dearborn

Starting in the 1840s, thousands of immigrants from Europe settled in New England, changing forever the ethnic makeup of the region. The mass migration was fueled both by social and political upheavals in Europe and by the Industrial Revolution here, which provided the hope of economic betterment. New England, which until this time had been a rural, agrarian, Yankee society, was transformed over the next eighty years into an industrial giant with a labor force dominated in most areas by the Irish and French-Canadians, but also containing elements of Germans, Scandinavians, Italians, Poles, Portuguese, Greeks, Eastern European Jews, Lebanese, Lithuanians, and other eth-

Reprinted, with updates and revisions, from *NEXUS* 8 (1991):20–23.

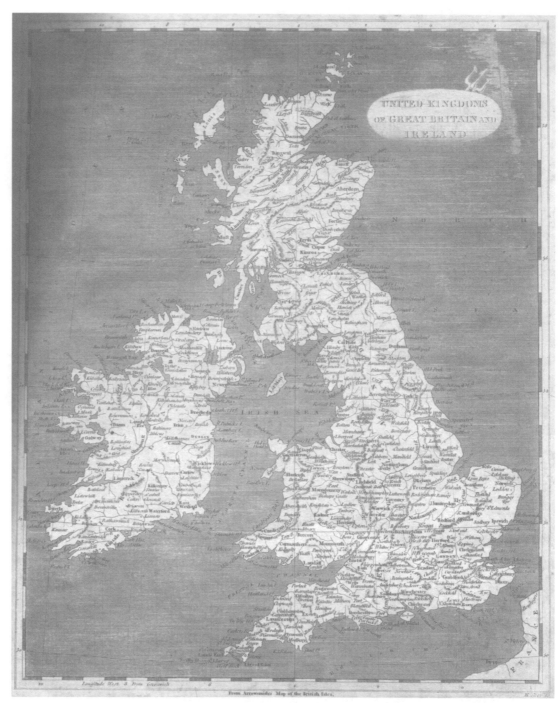

United Kingdoms of Great Britain and Ireland, from *A New and Elegant General Atlas* by Arrowsmith and Lewis (Boston: Thomas & Andrews, 1805).

nic groups. The centers of New England industry were the mill or factory towns that developed mainly along rivers. Some, such as Lynn, Haverhill, and Springfield, Mass., had existed since colonial times, while others, such as Lawrence and Lowell, sprang up almost overnight, with the harnessing of the Merrimack River.

While most of the factory workers were Irish, French-Canadian, or from continental Europe, a small but significant number were English; specifically, from the industrialized portions of southern Lancashire and the West Riding of Yorkshire. Because the so-called "mill English" were mainly Protestant, had English surnames, and spoke English as their native tongue, they often are confused or lumped with the native Yankees (especially when they bore such English surnames as Metcalf or Churchill) and are generally ignored by social historians writing about the immigrant experience in mill towns.

Over time the "mill English" have joined the melting pot, marrying into other immigrant groups and into the indigenous Yankee population. Many marriages crossed religious lines. Thus it is not at all uncommon for a New Englander today (especially of the "baby boom" generation) to have a mixture of Yankee and nineteenth-century immigrant ancestry, in varying proportions. In New England, at least, a person's surname is not necessarily a true indicator of his or her ethnic background.

Tracing nineteenth-century "mill English" ancestry is challenging but by no means impossible. First, learn everything you can about the family in America, keeping alert to those types of records that identify the English town or parish of origin or otherwise extend the pedigree. Such records might be surviving letters and photos among personal items, or public records like certificates of naturalization, ship passenger arrival lists, death certificates, gravestones, or newspaper obituary notices. Second, learn all you can about English genealogical research and the various types of records that exist for the time period when your ancestor emigrated. Some good how-to's include George Pelling, *Beginning Your Family History in Great Britain* (Baltimore: Genealogical Publishing Co. [GPC], 1989), Gerald Hamilton-Edwards, *In Search of British Ancestry*, 4th ed. (GPC, 1983), Angus Baxter, *In Search of Your British and Irish Roots* (GPC, 1989), Anthony J. Camp, *Everyone Has Roots: An Introduction to English Genealogy* (GPC, 1978), David E. Gardner and Frank Smith, *Genealogical Research in England and Wales* (Salt Lake City: Bookcraft, 1956–64), and Paul Milner and Linda Jonas, *A Genealogist's Guide to Discovering Your English Ancestors* (Cincinnati: Betterway Books, 2000).

One of my ancestral families, the Meadowcrofts of Lancashire, may serve to illustrate existing types of records and the level of success possible in nineteenth-century "mill English" genealogy.

According to microfilmed ship passenger arrival lists available through the National Archives and the Family History Library, the widow Hannah Lees arrived in Boston on Christmas Day 1885 from Liverpool aboard the S.S. *Iowa*, accompanied by her two children, Raymond and Mary. [1] The family settled in New Bedford, Mass., and Raymond Lees (my great-grandfather) was naturalized in the Third District Court of Bristol County on 16 October 1894. He stated that he was born in Ashton-under-Lyne, Lancashire, on 20 January 1871.[2] Through interviews with family members, I learned that Hannah Lees had two married sisters who came to Massachusetts from England about the same time, and settled in Lawrence, where the Lees family eventually moved around 1900. All these people worked in the cloth mills, just as they had done in England. From their death records in Massachusetts I found that Hannah Lees and her sisters were born in England in the 1840s and were daughters of John and Elizabeth (Whitehead) Meadowcroft.

For nineteenth-century English research there are four basic classes of records: vital records (beginning 1 July 1837), parish registers (before 1837, with some extending later), censuses (1841, 1851, 1861, 1871, 1881, 1891, 1901), and probates. It is necessary to use all of these types of records to solve a pedigree problem because each provides information not available elsewhere. In some cases, as we shall see, it would be difficult or impossible to find something in one type of record without having searched another. In working from the known to the unknown, each new bit of evidence collected provides a solid base on which to continue the pedigree.

Step one was to confirm the birth of my great-grandfather, Raymond Lees. Most British record sources are vast and poorly indexed, making searching tedious. This deficiency is certainly true of the vital records, for which the nationwide indexes each cover only a quarter year. Thus, if you don't know when a birth or marriage occurred, it may be necessary to search through many rolls of microfilm available through the Family History Library. However, many of the index entries are now on the Free BMD website, *freebmd.rootsweb.com*, which currently contains over 83 million records. Because I already had Raymond's birth date, it was easy in my case to locate his name in the index. At the same time, I searched for the marriage of Raymond's parents, Jonathan and Hannah (Meadowcroft) Lees; Hannah's birth record (about 1844); and the marriage record of her parents, John and Elizabeth (Whitehead) Meadowcroft.

For English vital records the Family History Library has only the indexes on microfilm; actual certificates must be obtained directly by visiting the Family Records Centre in London or by writing to the General Register Office (GRO), PO Box 2, Southport, Merseyside PR8 2JD, England (*statistics.gov.uk*). It is expensive for Americans to request English certificates through the mail.

In my case, the certificates provided valuable information. Raymond Lees, my great-grandfather, happened to have been born at the beginning of the census year 1871; his birth record showed the family residence as 38 Welbeck Street, Ashton-under-Lyne, Lancashire.[3] Thanks to this clue, I could search the 1871 census available on microfilm through the Family History Library. (The 1881 census is available at *familysearch.org* and the 1871, 1891, and 1901 censuses are accessible at *Ancestry.com*). For larger English cities, if you know a street address, you can consult the book street indexes, which provide the enumeration district number (see *familysearch.org*). As each enumeration district is only about twenty pages long, it can be searched rather quickly. The 1871 census showed Raymond, only 13 weeks old, residing with his mother, Hannah Lees, a maternal aunt, Mary E. Lees, and his maternal grandmother, Elizabeth Meadowcroft, age 55. All the women are described as cotton weavers and their birthplace is listed as Ashton. [4] English censuses beginning in 1851 contain a very important feature not found in their American counterpart: exact town or parish of birth (the 1841 census simply indicates whether or not the person was born in the county of residence). This account contains three errors: the aunt, Mary, being unmarried, was a Meadowcroft, not a Lees; Hannah Lees' birthplace is incorrect, and Raymond is called "Maymon"!

The 1866 marriage record in Ashton of Jonathan Lees and Hannah Meadowcroft confirmed that she was the daughter of John Meadowcroft (described as a manager). Jonathan was then 25 and Hannah 22, but the certificate does not ask for place of birth. According to her birth record, Hannah was born at Broadbottom, Cheshire (three miles southeast of Ashton-under-Lyne) on 17 November 1844, daughter of John Meadowcroft, overlooker at weavers, and Elizabeth Meadowcroft, formerly Whitehead. Hannah's parents were married at Oldham, Lancashire, 28 April 1839. John is described as a weaver, son of Thomas Meadowcroft; both parties described their age as "full," while Elizabeth's father's name is simply listed as "dead" (this last bit of information initially frustrated me, but was helpful when I eventually learned that her father, Aaron Whitehead, had died at Ashton in 1824).

Although I now knew that John Meadowcroft's father was Thomas, I had to find John himself in a census in order to learn his age and place of birth. It was relatively easy to locate John and his wife living in Church Court, Ashton-under-Lyne in 1841, with both described as 20, born in the county, he a cotton over-looker and she a weaver, with a year-old son Thomas.[5] Finding them in 1851 proved more difficult. I searched many rolls of microfilm from the Family History Library for Manchester and its suburbs in vain (my research on the Meadowcrofts began over twenty-five years ago). Over the last several years the Manchester & Lancashire Family History Society has produced a series of pamphlet indexes (by surname only) to the 1851 census. Thanks to one of these indexes I located John Meadowcroft and family living at Hollingworth, Cheshire, only a mile and a half northeast of Broadbottom, on the Derbyshire border. The census listed John, then age 33 and born at Middleton, Lancashire (a northern suburb of Manchester),[6] his wife and children, all with ages and places of birth. It seemed sensible to search the 1861 census for Hollingworth also, and indeed I found Elizabeth Meadowcroft still there, now a head of household with marital status described as "wife," and two children under age 10.[7]John and the older children were not to be found. Because Elizabeth was also a head of household ten years later in the 1871 census and is not described as a widow, I suspected that John Meadowcroft was still alive but I had no clue as to where to look for him.

Before proceeding to the search for John Meadowcroft's parents, it is necessary to ask what became of John and his wife Elizabeth. The clue came from their daughter Mary Elizabeth's marriage record. On 9 September 1883, at

Ashton, she married John Howard. Within a few years they had emigrated to America, settling in Lawrence, Massachusetts, where they stayed in close contact with the Lees family. From information from family members I found this marriage record easily. It gives Mary Elizabeth's residence as Glossop, Derbyshire, which, although in a different county, is only about six miles southeast of Ashton-under-Lyne. The 1881 census listed the family in the village of Hadfield, just outside Glossop. We find Elizabeth Meadowcroft, age 66, born Ashton, again called head of household, now "widow," along with daughters Mary E. Meadowcroft, unmarried, 22, and Hannah Gregory, widow, 34, and grandchildren Raymond and Elizabeth Lees, ages 10 and 8.[8]

To my knowledge, Elizabeth Meadowcroft did not come to America with the rest of the family when it emigrated in 1885. It seemed likely that she died before this date, and her death might even have been the catalyst that spurred the others to abandon their native land. Assuming that Elizabeth had died in or near Ashton, I had previously searched the death indexes without success. Now that I had found the family in Derbyshire, I tried again. I quickly discovered that Elizabeth died at Glossop on 13 August 1882, aged 67, of cancer. By American standards, English death certificates are not very helpful, as they list neither birthplace nor parents' names. However, one bit of information was important: the informant on the death record was her son Thomas Meadowcroft, whose address was given as 252 Bury Road, Rochdale. Rochdale is a city about seven miles north of Ashton, and like Ashton, it was a center for cloth weaving. A search of the 1881 census revealed not only the son Thomas living in Rochdale,[9] but his father John, just a few blocks away. As I suspected, John Meadowcroft had indeed remarried and was living with his second wife, Eliza, and son Aaron (Aaron's mother was Elizabeth [Whitehead], and he was named, no doubt, for his maternal grandfather, Aaron Whitehead). The census described John as age 63. born Middleton, Lancashire, overlooker of cotton looms.[10] I still do not know where John was in 1861 or 1871.

Having established that John Meadowcroft was living in middle age at Rochdale, I decided that the next step was to "kill him off," if possible, by searching death indexes, hoping that he did not move again. At the rate of four quarterly indexes per year, this could mean quite a bit of searching, as I had no idea how long he lived. Beginning in 1866, the death indexes give age at death as well as the registration district, so it was possible to eliminate persons of the same name who didn't fit. After much searching, I found a match. The death certificate revealed that John Meadowcroft died at the Union Workhouse at Dearnley Wardle, Rochdale, 4 November 1898, age 81, a cotton loom overlooker. The informant was his son, A[aron] Meadowcroft.

What of John's ancestry? From two censuses I had good confirmation that he was born in the parish of Middleton, Lancashire, about 1818, and from his marriage record I knew that he was the son of Thomas Meadowcroft. The Middleton parish register, recently filmed by the Family History Society, confirmed that John was baptized there on 25 May 1818, eldest child of Thomas and Mary (Cheetham) Meadowcroft.[11]

Thomas Meadowcroft's later children were baptized in the parish church of Ashton-under-Lyne, but the parish register calls him "of Newton or Hyde [Cheshire, overlooker [of weavers]."[12] In the 1840s he became proprietor of an inn, "The Queen's Arms" at 2 Back Lane (now 77 Victoria Street), Newton. The building was still standing when I visited in 1977, and at that time was home to an upholstery business. A local resident told me that The Queen's Arms had been an active pub until at least World War II. The 1851 census shows Thomas at Back Lane, Newton, described as an inn-keeper, age 54, born at Tottington, Lancashire, with wife Hannah (apparently a second wife) and one servant [13] Thomas died there on 23 March 1860, aged 63, of hemiplegia, according to his death certificate.

The Family History Library has microfilmed copies of many English probate records, and has filmed those of the Principal Probate Registry, whose records begin in 1858, down to 1925. From the indexes[14] I learned that Thomas Meadowcroft left a will, which he signed with an "X"; while not rich, he did own a number of cottages in Newton, which he left to his wife Hannah and three children, John, Samuel, and Harriet, the wife of George Gaunt.

Although this account of my progress on my Meadowcroft ancestors is somewhat simplified, it well illustrates what you can hope to find on your own nineteenth-century "mill English" ancestors. As with all genealogists, my research continues. On a visit to the Family History Library several years ago, using microfilmed parish registers of Tottington and Bury, Lancashire, and probates from the Consistory Court of Chester (which had jurisdiction), I successfully extended the family into the early eighteenth century. More recently I have made contact via the Internet with an English Meadowcroft who is a distant cousin, who has traced our common line back to the early 1600s.

The Meadowcrofts were typical working-class people in nineteenth-century industrial southern Lancashire; they were also typical of the "mill English" of southern New England. While they provide less-than-glamorous ancestors, they do present a genealogical challenge. Many Americans share this kind of ancestry, and the Meadowcrofts serve to show how much can be accomplished at the Family History Library. Not all research can be accomplished on one trip, but each visit will provide new bits of information that lead to the next source. Among the things I learned from my research was the high degree of mobility of my family within a small area — they didn't stay in one place very long. I also learned how nearly every record I found provided a clue to finding another record that would reveal more information.

Notes

1. Passenger Lists of Vessels Arriving at Boston, 1820–1891 (National Archives Microfilm M265-381); (Family History Library [FHL] 0419993 [note: "Mary" therein should read "Elizabeth"]).
2. Naturalizations, Third District Court of Bristol Co. [Mass.], 1894, Petition 2622, at National Archives, Waltham, Mass.

3. Copies of all certificates cited are in the author's possession.
4. 1871 Census, R.G. 10/4073, p. 82 (FHL 0846352).
5. 1841 Census, H.O. 107/532, E.D. 3, p. 37 [folio 211] (FHL 0306917).
6. 1851 Census, HO. 107/2239, p. 172 (FHL 0087251).
7. 1861 Census, H.O. R.G. 9/3004, p. 72 (FHL 0543063).
8. 1881 Census, R.G. 11/3460, p. 140 (FHL 1341828).
9. 1881 Census, R.G. 11/4111, p. 45 (FHL 1341983).
10. 1881 Census, R.G. 11/4112, p. 25 (FHL 1341984).
11. Middleton, Lancashire, Parish Register Baptisms, p. 273; Marriages, p. 170 (FHL 1545699).
12. Ashton-under-Lyne, Lancashire [St. Michael's] Parish Register Baptisms, 1814–32 (FHL 0547823).
13. 1851 Census, HO. 107/2236, p. 99 (FHL 0087248).
14. *Calendar of the Grants of Probate and Letters of Administration Made in the Principal Registry and in the Several District Registries of Her Majesty's Court of Probate* [1860] (FHL 0215237).

The "Mill English" —
A Checklist of Sources

David Curtis Dearborn

Background Sources

Thernstrom, Stephan, ed., *Harvard Encyclopedia of American Ethnic Groups* (Cambridge, Mass.: Belknap Press of Harvard University Press, 1980). See especially the chapter on "English," 324–36 [REF E184/A1/H3].

Johnson, Stanley C., *A History of Emigration from the United Kingdom to North America, 1762–1912* (1913; reprinted New York: A. M. Kelley, 1966).

Jones, Maldwyn A., "The Background to Emigration from Great Britain in the Nineteenth Century," *Perspectives in American History* 7 (1973):3–92.

Shepperson, Wilbur S., *British Emigration to North America* (Minneapolis: University of Minnesota Press, 1957).

Berthoff, Rowland T., *British Immigrants in Industrial America, 1790–1950* (Cambridge, Mass.: Harvard University Press, 1953; reprinted New York: Russell & Russell, 1968).

Hardy, Stuart B., "Lancashire in New England: The Textile Migration 1865–1914," *The Manchester Genealogist* 37 (2001):7–12 [CS436/ M2/M24].

Mofford, Juliet Haines, *Greater Lawrence: A Bibliography* (North Andover, Mass.: Merrimack Valley Textile Museum, 1978). Lists sources relating to the history of Lawrence, Massachusetts, the "immigrant city" (and surrounding towns), the focus of this presentation and a major destination of the nineteenth century "mill English" [REF Z1296/L38/M63].

Van Vugt, William E., *Britain to America: Mid-Nineteenth-Century Immigrants to the United States* (Urbana and Chicago: University of Illinois Press, 1999) [E184/B7/V3/1999].

Cole, Donald B., *Immigrant City: Lawrence, Massachusetts, 1845–1921* (Chapel Hill, N.C.: University of North Carolina Press, 1963).

_____. "Lawrence, Massachusetts: Model Town to Immigrant City, 1845–1912," *Essex Institute Historical Collections* 92 (1956): 361–62 [F72/E7/E81].

Dearborn, David Curtis, "Searching for the 'Mill English': The Meadowcrofts of Lancashire," *NEXUS* 8 (1991):20–23. Defines the "mill English" and shows

Adapted from a syllabus of the lecture of the same title.

how a late-nineteenth century immigrant working-class English family can be successfully traced using records available locally and through the Family History Library [REF F3/N522].

_____. "The Mill English," *The Essex Genealogist* 16 (1996):3–13 [F72/ E7/E6].

New England Genealogical Sources

Melnyk, Marcia D., *Genealogist's Handbook for New England Research*. 4th ed. (Boston: NEHGS, 1999) [REF F3/G466/1999]. Describes records and repositories covering both the colonial and the modern period; essential.

Vital Records. NEHGS has birth, marriage, and death records covering the late nineteenth or early twentieth centuries for the following New England states:

Massachusetts: 1841–1910 (Boston 1848–1910), microfilm [F63/M5]; birth index 1901–1950; marriage index 1901–1950; death index 1901–1980 in bound vols.

New Hampshire: 1630s–1900 (births, marriages, deaths), 1901–1937 (marriages, deaths) (microfilm) [F33/N454].

Vermont: early 1700s–1990 (microfilm) [F48/V5].

Maine: 1630s–1891 for 80 selected towns (microfilm) [F18/M34]; Vital records for many other towns individually on microfilm or in print; 1892–1954 (microfilm); later marriage, death, divorce indexes to 1983 [F18/M344].

Rhode Island: births, marriages 1853–1894; deaths 1853–1945 (death index to 1920 only) [F78/R55/R551/R552].

Naturalizations. United States. Immigration and Naturalization Service. "Index to New England Naturalization Petitions, 1791-1906" (Washington, D.C.: National Archives, 1983). 117 reels; 35 mm (National Archives publications. M1299). Index cards are arranged by state (Maine, New Hampshire, Vermont and Massachusetts are together) and then by name of petitioner, arranged according to the Soundex system. Index gives name and location of the court that granted the naturalization, date of naturalization, and volume and page (or certificate) number of the naturalization record. Available at NEHGS [CS68/I53]; original cards (and dexigraph copies of the naturalizations themselves) at the National Archives, Waltham, Mass.

Passenger Arrival Lists. NEHGS has the index to passenger lists of vessels arriving at Boston, 1848–1891 (282 reels; National Archives pub. M265) [CS68/ I532]; 1 January 1902–30 June 1906 (11 reels; T521) [CS68/I533]; and 1 July 1906–31 December 1920 (11 reels; T617) [CS68/I534]. The Boston Public Library (Microtext Dept.) has Boston passenger arrival lists (with gaps) 1820–

1918; arrival lists for miscellaneous ports (16 reels) 1820–1873; and New York 1820–1897 (675 reels) and indexes to same 1820–1846 (103 reels).

City Directories. NEHGS has city directories on microfiche for many cities in which "mill English" settled.

Newspapers. NEHGS has the Boston *Evening Transcript* 1848–March 1912 on microfilm, including a book index to obituaries, 1875–1930. This newspaper, however, was aimed at the Yankee rather than the "mill English" or ethnic population. More popular Boston papers, such as the *Globe, Herald,* and *Post,* can be found in the Microtext Department of the Boston Public Library (BPL), which also has virtually full runs of the daily papers (on microfilm) to the present for all the state's major cities. In addition, BPL has long runs from the late nineteenth century to present of the Hartford (Conn.) *Courant,* Portland (Maine) *Press-Herald,* Manchester (N.H.) *Union Leader,* and Providence (R.I.) *Journal.*

Censuses. NEHGS, the BPL (Microtext Department), and the National Archives in Waltham have complete sets of census films and Soundexes for the New England states, 1790–1930.

English How-To's and Finding Aids

Gardner, David E., and Frank Smith, *Genealogical Research in England and Wales,* 3 vols. (Salt Lake City: Bookcraft, 1956–64). Good discussion and description of the basic classes of records used to research "ordinary" English ancestors of the seventeenth to the nineteenth centuries. Vol. 1 covers newspapers, cemeteries, civil registration, census, parish registers, Bishops' transcripts, non-conformists, and names; vol. 2 covers probate, naval, military and county records; vol. 3 covers paleography [Intl REF CS414/G3].

Cox, Jane, and Stella Colwell, *Never Been Here Before? A Genealogist's Guide to the Family Records Centre* (Kew, Surrey: PRO Publications, 1997). For more on the holdings of the Family Records Centre in London, see below under "English Genealogical Sources" [Intl REF CS415/C69/1997].

Gibbens, Lillian, "Researching English Ancestry. Part I: My Ancestor Left England in the Nineteenth Century," *International Society for British Genealogy and Family History Newsletter* 14 (1992):33, 43–46 [CS410/I5].

International Genealogical Index (IGI), published by the Family History Library of the Church of Jesus Christ of Latter-day Saints (LDS), searchable online at *familysearch.org.* Approximately 40 percent of the total IGI is devoted to England alone. Despite well-known flaws, it is still highly useful (especially when searching for someone with an unusual surname), and should always be checked for pre-1880 individuals. For a discussion, see Elizabeth L. Nichols, "The International Genealogical Index (IGI), 1993 Edition," *Genealogical Journal* 22 (1994):45–58.

Family History Library Catalog (*FHLC*, published by the Family History Library (as above) searchable through the Family History Library's website at *familysearch.org*. Essential, as it lists the film and fiche numbers for the many original sources for English genealogy, including civil records indexes, censuses, probates, and parish registers.

Humphery-Smith, Cecil R., ed., *The Phillimore Atlas and Index of Parish Registers*, 2nd ed., revised (Chichester: Phillimore, 1995) [Intl REF CS415/P54].

Moulton, Joy Wade, *Genealogical Resources in English Repositories* (Columbus, Ohio: Hampton House, 1988) [Z2001/M68/1988].

Tate, W. E., *The Parish Chest: A Study of the Records of Parochial Administration in England* 3rd ed. (Chichester: Phillimore, 1969) [CD1068/A2/T43/1969].

West, John, *Village Records* (London: Macmillan, 1962) [Intl REF DA1/W45/1962].

_____.*Town Records* (Chichester: Phillimore, 1983) [DA690/A1/W47/1983].

Surnames

Reaney, Percy H., *A Dictionary of British Surnames* (1966; reprinted with corrections, London: Routledge & Kegan Paul, 1979). More than 20,000 surnames [CS2505/B4/1967b].

Guppy, Henry B., *Homes of Family Names in Great Britain* (1890; reprinted Baltimore: Genealogical Publishing Co, 1968). Useful for locating family names; gives relative distribution according to counties [CS2502/G85].

McKinley, Richard, *The Surnames of Lancashire*, English Surname Series, vol. 4 (London: Leopard's Head Press, 1981). See especially chapter 8, "Surnames in Salford Hundred, from 1500," the area of southeastern Lancashire (vicinity of Greater Manchester) from which many of the "mill English" came [CS2509/L3/M34/1981].

Redmonds, George, *Yorkshire West Riding*, English Surname Series, vol. 1 (Chichester: Phillimore, 1973). Along with Salford Hundred in Lancashire, the adjoining area of the West Riding of Yorkshire provided the bulk of "mill English" immigrants to New England in the late nineteenth century [CS2509/Y67/R4].

_____. *Surnames and Genealogy: A New Approach* (Boston: NEHGS, 1997). A detailed analysis of the various methods by which surnames developed, particularly in Yorkshire. The author shows how the same surname may have developed independently from different progenitors in different areas; thus, many dictionaries of surnames may mislead when they provide a single origin as the explanation of a surname [CS2505/R42/1997].

English Genealogical Sources

Vital Records. Great Britain. Registrar General, *Index to the Civil Registration of Births, Marriages and Deaths for England and Wales, 1837–1980* (Salt Lake City: filmed by the Genealogical Society of Utah, 1968–86). 1318 reels; also available on microfiche. Films of the quarterly indexes, described fully in Smith and Gardner, *Genealogical Research in England and Wales* (above). The actual certificates must be obtained from the Family Records Centre, 1 Myddelton St., London EC1, either by ordering through the mail or by making a personal visit (you can consult the indexes for free). Many parish registers, covering the period prior to 1837 (and in some cases, beyond), are available in print at NEHGS or on film through the Family History Library; consult the *FHLC* (above) (search under "England/Wales-Civil Registration-Indexes"); consult the IGI, but do so with caution. For up to date information on hours and fees, visit the website of the Office for National Statistics at *statistics.gov.uk/registration*.

Census. The 1841, 1851, 1861, 1871, 1881, and 1891 censuses for England and Wales have been filmed and are available through the Family History Library (search the *FHLC* under "England-Census-[Year]"). All are on 35 mm film, except 1861, which is on 16 mm film, and 1891, which is on microfiche. To determine which film/fiche to order, consult *Index of Place Names Showing the Library Microfilm or Microfiche Numbers for the 1841–1891 Census Records of England, Wales, Channel Islands and the Isle of Man*, available on microfiche at all Family History Centers. The FHL and the Federation of Family History Societies in Great Britain have produced an index to the 1881 census on 19 CD-ROMs that covers England, Wales, and Scotland, available at NEHGS [HA1124/1881]. There is also an index to the 1851 census, on a single CD-ROM, for the counties of Devon, Norfolk, and Warwick only, also available at NEHGS. If your ancestor lived in a large city at or near the time of a census and you know his street address (either from personal knowledge, finding him listed in a trade directory, or from information shown on a civil registration certificate from the Family Records Centre (1 Myddelton St., London EC1 [formerly St. Catherine's House]), you should search the street indexes for larger English cities for the corresponding census year, also available on microfilm through the FHL. These indexes do not list personal names but rather street names and house numbers and give the enumeration district(s) in which they appear, from which the FHL microfilm number can be determined (search the *FHLC* under "England-Census-[Year]-Indexes"). The 1901 census is available online at *pro.gov.uk*.

Probate. Calendar of the Grants of Probate and Letters of Administration Made in the Principal Registry and in the Several District Registries of Her Majesty's Court of Probate (Salt Lake City: 1959, 1986). Covers the years 1858–1987 (search the *FHLC* under "England-Probate Records-Indexes"). The wills themselves from 1858 to 1925 have been filmed as well and may be found in the *FHLC* under "England-Probate Records." The FHL has filmed many of the probate records prior to 1858 (search the *FHLC* under "England-[County]-Probate Records"). For a full description of these records, see Anthony J. Camp, *Wills and Their Whereabouts*, 4th ed. (London, 1974) (NEHGS has the 1963 edition, annotated and brought up to date by this writer) [Intl REF CS434/C3].

List of Surnames

The following is a *selected* list of surnames of persons born in England who are enumerated in the 1910 U.S. census of Lawrence, Massachusetts, generally of "mill English" background, showing the English county where the surname is *principally* found. Quite often, persons of the same surname (or variant spelling) can be found in large numbers in adjacent areas of neighboring counties. Persons bearing common and occupational surnames, such as Smith, Taylor, Baker, etc., have been screened out. Lawrence was chosen because it was an epicenter of "mill English" immigration; similar studies could easily be performed on other southern New England mill cities.

Cheshire: Bancroft, Booth, Buckley, Clayton, Hazlehurst, Royls, Swindell, Trickett.

Derbyshire: Brailsford, Higginbottom, Holling(s)worth, Knott, Morley, Redfern/Redford, Sidebottom, Slater, Thorp, Tomlinson, Wild.

Lancashire (principally Salford Hundred): Ainsworth/Hainsworth, Andrew(s) [note: a common name, but those of Lawrence were principally from Lancashire], Arondale, Ashton, Ashworth, Aspinall, Bardsley, Brierley, Butterworth, Chadwick, Chorley, Crabtree, Cranshaw, Cunliffe, Dewhurst, Duckworth, Edmondson, Entwistle, Fielding, Gar(e)lick, Garside, Greenhalgh, Grimshaw, Hargreaves, Heap, Holt, Hopwood, Howard/Howarth, Isherwood, Kershaw, Lawnsdale/Lonsdale, Lees, Lomax, Longworth, Meadowcroft, Pendlebury, Pickup, Proudlove, Seddon, Stansfield, Stott, Walmesley, Wolstencroft, Wolstenholme.

Staffordshire: Bagnall, Bradbury/Bredbury.

Yorkshire (West Riding): Ackroyd, Barraclough, Broadbent, Cockcroft, Dyson, Firth, Hardesty, Hinchliffe, Illingworth, Ingle(by), Iredale, Jagger, Laycock, Margerison/Marjerison, Murgatroyd, Radcliffe, Rushforth/Rushworth, Saltonstall, Schofield, Shaw, Stead, Sugden, Widdop, Wolfenden, Woodhead.

A Few Other English Resources

Most researchers don't realize that a great deal of English research can be done from U.S. library sources, including Internet resources, publications, and microfiche. Before planning a research trip overseas to access material, use the wide variety of materials available at the NEHGS Library. Here are a few of the underused resources for finding English ancestry.

City Directories

While not comprehensive, a significant number of city directories exist on microfiche for England and Wales. In some cases, there is only a year or two available for a specific locality. Society holdings include directories published in the nineteenth century. Search the online catalog by subject "England directories" for a list of the library's holdings.

County Histories

Look for local history information in the *Victoria History of the Counties of England* series, published by Institute of Historical Research at the University of London. For more than a century, researchers have been compiling comprehensive county histories for England. At present, more than two hundred volumes are in print, with the project not complete. Two general volumes exist for England as well as genealogical volumes for Hertfordshire and Northamptonshire. Some counties are finished while others are still in the beginning stages. These volumes are available on the first floor of the library. [Intl R.Rm DA670 . . .]

In addition to this series of books, the NEHGS library maintains a large collection of county and town histories published by the English Record Societies for counties and by private publishers. Search the online catalog for specific localities to see a list of holdings.

Parish Registers

Consult *The Phillimore Atlas and Index of Parish Registers* [Intl REF CS415/P54/1995] to find out what marriage registers exist and where they can be found. Phillimore also identifies whether the records are indexed. Phillimore can also help you determine the probate jurisdiction(s) for the parish.

Periodicals

Most county record societies published journals. These can be located by searching the county name in the online catalog. Two major genealogical publications are the *Genealogists' Magazine* and *Family Tree* (for post-1700 and colonies).

Pipe Roll Society

In 1883 the Public Record Office in England founded the Pipe Roll Society, which is currently based at the The National Archives in Surrey. That society publishes the annual accounts of Crown revenues sent by sheriffs to the exchequer, arranged by county. These can be useful when searching for families in the period 1155/6 to 1832. Their name derives from the fact that they were wrapped around rods (pipes) for storage. Pipe Rolls until 1222, and related documents from before 1250 have been printed. The Pipe Roll Society began publishing a quarterly journal from 1884 [Vault DA200/P66/1884].

A Few Other English Resources (cont.)

Visitation Pedigrees

Heralds sent by the king granted heraldic rights and validated coats of arms. The records of these visitations are now part of the Harleian Manuscripts at the British Museum. Established in 1869, the Harleian Society began publishing the history and genealogy, including the pedigrees approved at the Heralds Visitations, of various English counties and many of the parish registers of London. Many of these publications are available by searching the online catalog.

Highlights

- Various county parish registers in book form in the Treat Rotunda on the first floor.
- Additional county parish registers in book form in the Rare Book Collection.
- The British Vital Records Index on CD-ROM [CS434/V58/1998 CD also LOAN].
- Various wills and probate indexes for English counties.
- Superb collection of county histories.
- Large selection of both English county history and family history society periodicals.

Scottish Research at NEHGS

George F. Sanborn Jr.

Overview

Among the most popular sections of NEHGS's international collection are our Scottish publications and microform. Numerous early Scots who came to New England, followed later on by the large numbers of Canadians of Scottish descent, as well as immigrants directly from Scotland to New England during the Industrial Revolution and afterward, have all contributed to a large and broad population base with Scottish ties. NEHGS is the leading research facility in the Northeast to study Scottish ancestors.

Guides and Finding Aids

There are two up-to-date and comprehensive guides to Scottish family history research and, used together, they cover virtually all types of records and how to use them. Cecil Sinclair's *Tracing Your Scottish Ancestors: A Guide to Ancestry Research in the Scottish Record Office*, rev. ed. (Edinburgh, 1997) [Intl REF CS463/S56/1997], was prepared by the knowledgeable staff of the Scottish Record Office (now renamed National Archives of Scotland). Kathleen B. Cory's *Tracing Your Scottish Ancestry*, 2nd ed. (Edinburgh, 1996) [Intl REF CS463/C67/1996], with its useful appendices, is highly recommended, as well. A. Rosemary Bigwood's *Scottish Family History: A Handbook* (Edinburgh, 1990) [CS463/B54/1990] is another useful and straightforward resource.

Genealogical and Historical Periodicals

While many of the family history societies around the country publish journals of local interest, there are two major periodicals of general interest to a wide audience of Scottish researchers. First and foremost is *The Scottish Genealogist* [CS460/S35], quarterly journal of The Scottish Genealogy Society. Of interest to researchers of Highland families is the *Highland Family History Society / Comunn Sloinntearachd na Gaidhealtachd Journal* [CS460/H55/1981], the quarterly journal of the Highland Family History Society.

Census

While census records of Scotland, as we commonly think of them, begin only in 1841, numerous useful local census records exist, some of which have been published. NEHGS has *Annan Parish Censuses, 1801–1821*, Scottish Record Society, new series, vol. 4 (Edinburgh, 1975) [CS460/S4/n.s./v. 4], which shows, for that part of Dumfriess-shire in 1801, 1811, and 1821, all families by community, listing the head of the household, whether there was a spouse (not named), and all children by name, and how many in each household were engaged in agriculture of manufacturing. Similarly, *The Urquhart Censuses of Portpatrick, 1832–1853*, Scottish Record Society, new series, vol. 8 (Edinburgh, 1980) [CS460/S4/n.s./v. 8], shows all the families in this busy Galloway parish in two time periods, 1832–1834 and 1844–1853, with wives by their maiden name and all children, their ages, and other details. The fourth floor has microfiche indexes to the 1821 census of Orkney [CS477/O5/O75/1821] and the 1851 census of Orkney [CS477/O5/O75/1851]. We have the four-volume published census of Edinburgh for 1851, compiled by N. R. & S. Carstairs [Intl REF CS477/E2/E35/1993/v. 1–3 (parts 1 and 2)], which is useful for people who had moved to the city because that census requested the parish and county of birth of each person in each household, besides many other useful details. The Family History Library has now released a set of CDs that index the 1881 census of England, Wales, and Scotland and these are found on the fourth floor.

Vital Records

Scotland began civil registration of all births, marriages, and deaths in 1855. Access to indices of post-1854 civil registration through the end of the nineteenth century, and in some cases for several years after 1900, is available through the government website *scotlandspeople.gov.uk*. Researchers will find microfiche indexes to the deaths between 1855 and 1875, inclusive, for the counties of Bute, Lanark, and Sutherland [CS477/A1/M333/1993].

Church Records

The Genealogical Society of Utah indexed the pre-1855 baptismal and marriage records of the Established Church of Scotland [Presbyterian] some years ago, and the records are on microfiche, arranged by county and alphabetically within each county [CS477/A1]. An interesting feature is the possibility of searching by just first name. Many of the same records also appear in the International Genealogical Index (IGI); both the 1992 edition on microfiche, and access to the online edition through *familysearch.org* are available. And it is also possible to search indexes and request certified copies of these same records by visiting *scotlandspeople.gov.uk*.

People searching for records of Covenanters will be glad to know that we have the *Register of Rev. John MacMillan . . .*, edited by Rev. Henry Paton (Edinburgh, 1908) [CS464/M15/1908], which is bound with a typed index to the same. This covers marriages and baptisms in the various Covenanter congregations between 1706 and 1751.

Kirk Session records, while difficult to locate and sometimes difficult to get to see, contain a wealth of information for members of the Church of Scotland [Presbyterian]. It is rare to find any of them in print, but those for South Leith, covering the years 1588–1700, were transcribed and published by D. Robertson, Session Clerk (Edinburgh, 1911) [CS477/L44/R63/1911].

Cemetery Records

The various family history societies in Scotland have been active in transcribing and publishing cemetery inscriptions. NEHGS has a good and growing collection of these, including some for nearly all counties and districts in the country. Keep in mind, however, that it is unusual to find gravestones for ordinary citizens before the nineteenth century in Scotland, and even then they are scarce.

Probate

NEHGS has scattered probate records and indexes, including *Orkney Testaments and Inventories, 1573–1615*, Scottish Record Society, new series, vol. 6 (Edinburgh, 1977) [CS460/S4/n.s./v. 6].

Land Records

For the Outer Isles in the Hebrides, we have the interesting croft history series being published a volume at a time by Bill Lawson, in which a record of the holdings of each croft, as far back as oral tradition and records carry us, reveal, with details about the wives and children, whom they married, and where they went, if known. Each one deals with a separate township or small island, and NEHGS has those that have been published for the islands of Lewis, Harris, Berneray, North Uist, and South Uist.

Rentals and Lists of Inhabitants

Of immense importance in this part of the world are rent rolls and lists prepared locally for various reasons. For example, there is the *West Lothian Hearth Tax, 1691, with County Abstracts for Scotland*, Scottish Record Society, new series, vol. 9 (Edinburgh, 1981) [CS460/S4/n.s./v. 9], and the *Examination Roll of Arbroath, 1752, [and] Town's Duty Roll, 1753*, Scottish Record Society, new series, vol. 13 (Edinburgh, 1987) [CS460/S4/n.s./v.13] which lists residents, their spouses and children, with baptismal dates and other genealogically important information.

An important resource exists in the "Judicial Rental of Sir Donald Macdonald's Estate of North Uist. 1718," in volume 3 of Rev. A. Macdonald and Rev. A. Macdonald, *The Clan Donald*, 3 vols. (Inverness, 1896–1904) [CS479/M2/1896], in which the tenants of North Uist in that year are listed, often with the all-important patronymic or variant surname.

Better than a census is the *List of Inhabitants upon the Duke of Argyle's Property in Kintyre in 1792*, Scottish Record Society, New Series, vol. 17 (Edinburgh, 1991) [CS460/S4/n.s./v. 17], which lists, in typical Scottish fashion, every resident by community with full names (including the maiden name of married women), and the ages of all. From Kintyre came a large number of Highland settlers to North Carolina and Prince Edward Island just a few years before, as well as Highland settlers to Quebec's Eastern Townships somewhat later.

Court Records

NEHGS has the indexed *Records of the Sheriff Court of Aberdeenshire*, prior to 1600, published in three volumes (Aberdeen, 1904–1907), and also *The Gild Court Book of Dunfermline, 1433–1597*, Scottish Record Society, New Series, vol. 12 (Edinburgh, 1986) [CS460/S4/n.s./v. 12].

Maps, Topographical Dictionaries, and Place-Name Books

Serious researchers will want to purchase the relevant Ordnance Survey maps for the areas of their interest; highly recommended is the Landranger series which shows in great detail geographical features, names of streams and hills, parish cemetery locations, roads of all kinds, and so on. Reprints of antique Ordnance Survey maps are also available, but are usually difficult to read. To help you determine the area in which you are interested, a combination of the following will be helpful: Samuel Lewis, *A Topographical Dictionary of Scotland*, 2nd ed., 2 vols. (London, 1851 [reprinted Baltimore, 1989]); Rev. John Wilson, *The Gazetteer of Scotland* (Edinburgh, 1882 [reprinted Milton, Ont., 1999]); and Francis H. Groome, *Ordnance Gazetteer of Scotland*, 3 vols. (London, 1903). As well, diligent researchers will look for, and often find, booklets and pamphlets detailing local place-names, such as one that exists for the Isle of Skye.

Taking the High Road:
Genealogical Research in Scotland — A Checklist of Sources

David Curtis Dearborn

How To's

Irvine, Sherry, *Your Scottish Ancestry: A Guide for North Americans* (Salt Lake City: Ancestry, 1997) [CS463/I78/1997].

Hamilton-Edwards, Gerald, *In Search of Scottish Ancestry*, 2nd ed. (Baltimore: Genealogical Publishing Co. [GPC], 1984) [Intl REF CS463/H35].

James, Alwyn, *Scottish Roots: A Step-by-Step Guide for Ancestor Hunters* (Gretna, Scotland, 1982) [CS464/J255/1982].

Bigwood, A. Rosemary, *Scottish Family History: A Handbook* (Edinburgh, 1990) [CS463/B54/1990].

_____."Sources for Scottish Genealogy: New Register House, Edinburgh," International Society for British Genealogy and Family History [ISBGFH] *Newsletter* 9 (1987):21, 24–25 [CS410/I5].

_____."Sources for Scottish Genealogy: Beyond the Old Parish Registers," ISBGFH *Newsletter* 12 (1990):17, 28–29 [CS410/I5].

_____. "Handbooks for Scottish Family Historians," ISBGFH *Newsletter* 13 (1991):17, 25 [CS410/I5] (critically reviews the "how-to" books by James, Cory, Moody, and Hamilton-Edwards).

_____."Starting Research on Scottish Ancestry," ISBGFH *Newsletter* 14 (1992):33, 42 [CS410/I5].

Cory, Kathleen B., *Tracing Your Scottish Ancestry* (Edinburgh: Polygon, 1990) [Intl REF CS463/C67/1990].

Moody, David, *Scottish Family History* (Baltimore: GPC, 1988; reprinted 1994) [CS463/M66/1994].

Steel, Don J., assisted by Mrs. A.E.F. Steel,, *Sources for Scottish Genealogy and Family History* (London: Society of Genealogists, 1970) (National Index of Parish Registers, vol. 12) [REF CD1068/A2/N3].

Adapted from a lecture of the same title.

Scotland: A Genealogical Research Guide (Salt Lake City: Church of Jesus Christ of Latter-day Saints, 1987) [Intl REF CS463/S4/1987].

Smart, Paul F., "Tracing Scottish Ancestry," *Heritage Quest* 82 [15:4] (July–August 1999):92–94 [CS1/H47].

_____. "Computerized Scottish Research," *Heritage Quest* 65 (September–October 1996):53–57 [CS1/H47].

Eakle, Arlene H., "Finding Ancestors from Scotland: Effective Use of Scottish Church Records, 15 — /1855," *Everton's Genealogical Helper* 55:5 (September/October 1999):12–16 [CS1/G38].

Falley, Margaret Dickson, *Irish and Scotch-Irish Ancestral Research*, 2 vols. (Evanston, Ill., 1962) [Intl REF CS483/F32].

Webster, David W., "Scottish Census Indexes," *Everton's Family History Magazine* 57:5 (September–October 2003):52–57 [CS1/G38].

_____. "Scottish Surnames and Christian Names," *Everton's Family History Magazine* 57:6 (November–December 2003):49–55 [CS1/G38].

North American Sources

Bolton, Charles K., *Scotch-Irish Pioneers in Ulster and America* (1910; reprinted Baltimore: GPC, 1986) [E184/S4B6/1986].

Dickson, R. J., *Ulster Emigration to Colonial America*, 1718–1775 (Belfast: Ulster Historical Foundation, 1988) [E184/S3/D47/1988].

Dobson, David, *Directory of Scottish Settlers in North America, 1625–1825*, 7 vols. (Baltimore: GPC, 1984–93) [E184/S3/D63].

_____. *Scots in New England, 1623–1873* (Baltimore: GPC, 2002) [F15/S3/D63/2002]

_____. *Scottish American Wills, 1650–1900* (Baltimore: GPC, 1991) [E184/S3/D66/1991].

_____. *Scottish-American Court Records, 1733–1783* (Baltimore: GPC, 1991) [E184/S3/D67/1991].

_____. *Directory of Scots in the Carolinas, 1680–1830* (Baltimore: GPC, 1986) [F265/S3/D63].

_____. *Directory of Scots Banished to the American Plantations, 1650–1775* (Baltimore: GPC, 1983) [E184/S3/D6/1983].

_____.*The Original Scots Colonists of Early America, 1612–1783* (Baltimore: GPC, 1989) [Intl REF E184/S3/D64/1989].

_____. *Scottish-American Heirs, 1683–1883* (Baltimore: GPC, 1990) [Intl REF E184/S3/D65/1990].

_____. *Scots in the USA and Canada, 1825–1875* (Baltimore: Clearfield, 1998) [E184/S3/D647/1998].

Hanna, Charles A., *The Scotch-Irish*, 2 vols. (1902; reprinted Baltimore: GPC, 1968) [E184/S2/H21968].

Whyte, Donald A., *A Dictionary of Scottish Emigrants to Canada Before Confederation* (Toronto: Ontario Genealogical Society, 1986) [F1035/S3/W49/1986].

Scottish Sources

Black, George Fraser, *The Surnames of Scotland: Their Origin, Meaning and History* (New York: New York Public Library, 1946; reprinted 1962, 1965) [Intl REF CS24325/B44].

Ferguson, Joan P. S. (comp.), *Scottish Family Histories* (Edinburgh: National Library of Scotland, 1986) [Intl REF Z5313/S4/F4].

Stuart, Margaret, *Scottish Family History: Guide to Works of Reference on the History and Genealogy of Scottish Families* (Edinburgh, 1930; reprinted Baltimore: GPC, 1979) [Intl REF Z5313/S4/S9].

Detailed List of the Old Parochial Registers of Scotland (Edinburgh: HMSO, 1872) [Rare Book CD1098/A2/A2].

Old Parochial Registers Index (Salt Lake City: Church of Jesus Christ of Latter-day Saints, 1990) [CS477/A1 microfiche]; for a description, see A. Rosemary Bigwood, "New Indexes for Scottish OPRs," ISBGFH *Newsletter* 13 (1991):49, 60 [CS410/I5].

Karr, Nole M., "Detailed List of the Old Parochial Registers of Scotland," *National Genealogical Society Quarterly* 44 (1956):134–42; 45 (1957):10–16, 73–76, 144–54 [CS42/N4].

Adam, Frank, and Sir Thomas Innes of Learney, *The Clans, Septs, and Regiments of the Scottish Highlands*, 8th ed. (Edinburgh, 1970) [DA880/ H6/A6].

Scott, Hew, *Fasti Ecclesiae Scoticanae*, 10 vols. (Edinburgh: Oliver & Boyd, 1866–1981) [BX9099/G4].

Lewis, Samuel, *A Topographical Dictionary of Scotland*, 2nd ed., 2 vols. (London, 1851; reprinted Baltimore: GPC, 1989) [Intl REF DA869/ L48/1989].

Stevenson, David, and Wendy B. Stevenson, *Scottish Texts and Calendars: An Analytical Guide to Serial Publications* (London: Royal Historical Society; Edinburgh: Scottish History Society, 1987) (Royal Historical Society Guides and Handbooks, No. 14) [DA20/R92/1938 no. 14].

AA Automaps 3 Mile Road Atlas of Britain, 4th ed. (Basingstoke, Hants: Automobile Assoc., 1987) [Intl REF G1812.2/ P2/A8]. Additionally, you may wish to purchase an Ordnance Survey map for the area(s) of Scotland that interest you. These may be purchased in the U.S. at large bookshops specializing in British local history and travel.

Humphery-Smith, Cecil R., *The Phillimore Atlas and Index of Parish Registers*, 2nd ed. (London: Phillimore, 1995) [Intl REF CS415/P54/1995].

Scottish Genealogy Society volumes of pre-1855 monumental inscriptions, arranged by county or parts of counties [CS477. . .].

Paul, Sir James Balfour, ed., *The Scots Peerage*, 9 vols. (Edinburgh, 1904–14) [CS468/P3].

The Scottish Genealogist, 1954–present [CS460/S35].

Scottish Record Society Publications [CS460/S4] (contains parish registers, commissariot indexes, lists of burgesses and guild brethren, etc.).

Bigwood, A. Rosemary, "Association of Scottish Genealogists and Record Agents," ISBGFH *Newsletter* 9 (1987):29, 36 [CS410/I5].

Some Useful Websites

Family History Library, Salt Lake City, *familysearch.org* (Family History Library Catalog, International Genealogical Index [IGI] which contains, among other things, many (but not all) the births, baptisms and marriages from the Scottish OPRs, and *all* Scottish births and marriages, 1855–1875, from the statutory registers of civil registration).

Cyndi's List of Genealogical Sites on the Web for Scotland, *cyndislist.com/scotland.htm*

General Register Office for Scotland (GROS), *gro-scotland.gov.uk* (information on 1855+ statutory births, marriages and deaths, the census, and links). The website *scotlandspeople.gov.uk* is the official government source of genealogical data for Scotland, including Internet access (for a fee) to indexes of statutory registration, censuses and Old Parochial Registers. For a detailed description, see David W. Webster, "The New Scotlands People Web Site," *Everton's Family History Magazine* 57:2 (March–April 2003):40–48 [CS1/G38].

Scottish Genealogy Society, Edinburgh, *scotsgenealogy.com*

Scots Origins, *scotsorigins.com* (a fee-based research service; formerly provided access to official Scotland governmental records).

Scottish Archive Network, *scan.org.uk* (another online "pay-per-view" site that allows you to search, for free, their index to all Scottish probates, 1500–1900; copies of many of the records themselves can be purchased).

Scot Roots, *scotroots.com* (a fee-based research service for those who want someone else to do the work. The site contains a handy alphabetical parish (OPR) list, giving the parish number, county of location, and date of commencement of OPR).

Scottish town plans online, *nls.uk/maps*, described fully in Sheena Tait, "Scottish Town Plans Online," *Family Tree Magazine* 19:12 (October 2003):40–41 [CS410/F33].

Irish Research Sources at NEHGS

Marie E. Daly

Although most people know about the wonderful collection of early New England records at the Society, the extensive collection of Irish records has been largely a well-kept secret. The types of information available for the Irish-American genealogist range from general guides and how-to's to indexed census and census substitutes, maps and atlases, local histories, church records, tombstone inscriptions, county historical journals, newspaper records, and directories. By performing much of your research here in the United States, you can use your time in Ireland more productively and more enjoyably, i.e., going out to your ancestors' birth places, seeing where they came from, and possibly meeting descendants of the relatives who had been left behind.

In addition, many people have used the heritage centers in Ireland with mixed success and satisfaction. By researching as much as you can on your own, you can increase your chances for a successful search. By furnishing good detailed information to the heritage centers, you can make their searches more focused, and the results more pertinent to your ancestor.

Myth: Not All the Records Were Destroyed

A false rumor has been circulating among genealogists for years — *Finding Irish ancestors is impossible because all the records were burned in 1922*. While there was a fire in 1922 in the Public Record Office (now the National Archives of Ireland) many records were not stored there. For instance, Catholic church records were all locally held, and therefore survive. Although the pre-1901 censuses were destroyed, genealogists can use census substitutes, such as Griffith's Valuation. Irish genealogists have become so adept at maneuvering around the obstacles, that many have successfully traced their ancestors back to the late 1700s. Most of the brick walls actually occur in the seventeenth and eighteenth centuries, when church records, estate records, and deeds peter out. But since many Irish-Americans trace their forebears to mid- to late-nineteenth century immigrants, they would often be satisfied just to find the village or farm from where their ancestor fled the famine.

Reprinted, with updates and revisions, from *New England Ancestors* 1:1 (Premiere Issue 2000):9–15.

Finding the Exact Place of Origin of Your Immigrant Ancestor

Irish surnames and given names are very common, and discerning an ancestor from all the other individuals of the same name in a single county is a daunting task. So Irish-American genealogists must determine the exact origin, i.e., parish or townland, of their ancestor. For the most part, the search for the exact origin is carried out in New World records, not Irish records.

The Society has a large collection of materials to help in the process of identifying immigrants. A good place to begin your research is the 1900, 1910, 1920, or 1930 census, which are indexed and available to search online at the Society. These census records provide the citizenship status, the year of immigration and/or the year of naturalization. In addition to these censuses, NEHGS also has census records from 1790 for the New England states, and online access to all states. Also, NEHGS has a large collection of street directories, passenger arrival lists, newspapers such as *The Boston Pilot*, the *Missing Friends* series, banking records (such as the Emigrant Savings Bank of New York), and civil registrations (births, marriages and deaths) for all of the New England states.

Once you have determined the exact origin of your immigrant ancestor, you will be ready to "make the jump" to the other side of the Atlantic. But before you actually travel to Ireland, you can accomplish a great deal of research with Irish records here at the Society.

General Guides

Several general guides on Irish genealogy can help you begin your search through Irish records. These books will help organize your search, and relate the availability of specific records by county.

- John Grenham, *Tracing Your Irish Ancestors: the Complete Guide*, 2nd ed. (Baltimore: Genealogical Publishing Co., 1999) [Intl REF CS483/G73/1999 also LOAN]. This paperback guide provides a general discussion of the records in the first half of the book, and a listing by county of the available records and their locations, in the second half. The book is particularly useful for its maps of Catholic parish boundaries

- James Ryan, *Irish Records: Sources for Family and Local History* (Orem, Utah: Ancestry, 1997) [Intl REF CS483/R8/1997 also LOAN]. Organized by county, this book provides a good atlas of the parish and barony boundaries. In addition, the book gives a brief history and the available records for each county.

- Dwight A. Radford and Kyle J. Betit, *A Genealogist's Guide to Discovering Your Irish Ancestors* (Cincinnati, Ohio: Betterway Books, 2001) [Intl REF CS483/R33/2001 also LOAN]. This guide not only covers research in Ireland, but also research in the United States, Canada, Great Britain and Australia.

- Margaret Dickson Falley, *Irish and Scotch-Irish Ancestral Research: A Guide to the Genealogical Records, Methods and Sources in Ireland*, 2 vols. (1962; reprinted Baltimore: Genealogical Publishing Co., 1981). [Intl REF CS483/F32 also LOAN]. At one time this comprehensive book was the Bible of Irish genealogy, but it is now out-of-date. Nevertheless, the book presents detailed descriptions of the records and repositories, and may still be profitably consulted by genealogists.

- Robert K. O'Neill, *Irish Libraries, Archives, Museums & Genealogical Centres* (Belfast: Ulster Historical Foundation, 2002]. Written by the Director of the John J. Burns Library at Boston College, this new guide for visitors to Ireland is organized by county, and contains the names, addresses, hours, accessibility and contents of many lesser known repositories.

Locating the Place-Name in Ireland: Maps and Atlases

After consulting the general guides, the next step should be to identify the place-name of your ancestor's origin. The Society has several reference books that will help you identify place-names. Within the thirty-two counties that are familiar to most people, Ireland is divided into *baronies*, which are old administrative divisions arising out of medieval territories; *poor law unions*, which are nineteenth-century administrative divisions; *civil parishes*, which approximate in size an American township; and *townlands*, which are the smallest unit and usually contain only a few hundred acres. Fortunate genealogists will have identified the townland or parish of origin.

A good place to start is the *General Alphabetical Index to the Townlands and Towns, Parishes and Baronies of Ireland: 1851 Census* (Baltimore: Genealogical Publishing Co, 1992) [Intl REF HA1142/1851 also LOAN]. This reference book will identify in what parish, poor law union and barony a townland lays, as well as providing the ordnance survey map number. This information is crucial in using census substitutes such as Griffith's Valuation, explained in more detail below.

Once the townland or parish, barony and poor law union have been identified, the next step is to locate these places on a map. A useful reference is Brian Mitchell's *A New Genealogical Atlas of Ireland*, 2nd ed. (Baltimore: Genealogical Publishing Co., 2002) [Intl REF G1831/F7/M5/2002], which displays the subdivisions by county, and now includes maps of the Roman Catholic parishes. You should make note of the surrounding parishes for later reference. You may discover that there was no church in your ancestor's parish until the later nineteenth century, and that you will have to research the adjacent parishes for earlier dates.

The Society also has townland maps for most counties in Ireland, either on microfiche or in printed form: *Parish Maps of Ireland (depicting all townlands in the four Ulster Counties of Armagh, Donegal, Londonderry and Tyrone)* (Apollo, PA: Closson Press, 1988) [Intl REF G1833/U4/E423/P3/1988]. Also on microfiche are the townland maps for counties in Connaght and Munster provinces. On the fourth floor in the reference area, the research library has an excellent printed source, *Ordnance Survey of Ireland: Indexes to the 1/2500 and 6-inch Scale Maps* [GA803.7/A5]. This represents a complete set of townland maps, with the corresponding ordnance survey maps numbers (discussed below).

The Society has a complete microfiche set of ordnance survey maps with scales of 6-inches-to-1 mile [G5780/T681 microfiche]. Each fiche has only one map on it, so the resolution is finer than that of other sets that have six maps on each fiche or maps on the Internet. With our microfiche printers' ability to enlarge, you can make close-up copies of your ancestor's townland. These maps show the location of details such as houses, trees, streams and narrow country lanes. The ordnance survey map number is provided in the Townland Index mentioned earlier. These are *not* the Valuation maps (available only in Dublin), which correspond with Griffith's Valuation coordinates, and show which house or farm an ancestor occupied. But these ordnance survey maps give you a good perspective of your ancestor's environment and life back in the old country.

The Society also has a number of special Irish atlases that give you excellent descriptions of specific areas. Published by the Clogher Historical Society in conjunction with the Irish Studies Department at Queens University Belfast, *Landscapes of South Ulster*, by Patrick Duffy [Intl Oversize G1833/U4/D84/1993], displays excellent and detailed parish maps for areas in the Catholic Diocese of Clogher. This diocese stretches from Ballyshannon, County Donegal on the west coast, through Counties Fermanagh, Tyrone, and Monaghan to County Louth on the east coast. Not only does the atlas display the maps, but also it assembles a collection of parish descriptions that had been published over the last four hundred years.

These are just a few of the many resources the Society has for identifying the place-name in Ireland. Besides specific county and parish histories, there are numerous books devoted to place-names in Ireland. Among these are *Place-Names of Northern Ireland*, 7 vols., by Nollaig O Muraile and Gerard Stockman (Belfast: QUB, 1992–96) [Intl REF DA990/N46/P53/1992], *The Origin and History of Irish Names of Places*, 3 vols., by P. W. Joyce, (Dublin:1920) [DA979/J7/1920], and *Toponomia Hiberniæ*, 4 vols., by Breandán Ó Cíobháin (Dublin: An Foras Duibhneach, 1978) [DA979/O24/1978].

Local Histories and Descriptions

Once you have located the place-name in Ireland, you should research the history and description of the area as thoroughly as possible. Being knowledgeable about the locale will help you use the genealogical resources, such as census substitutes, more wisely and productively. For instance, townland names and boundaries may have changed over time, ancestors may lease land parcels straddling townland and parish boundaries or the Catholic parish name and boundaries may not correspond with the civil parish. A description listing the major estates and industries within a parish will help you make use of estate records, rental rolls and other local records. Descriptions of ecclesiastical structures and history will help identify church records and cemeteries.

Many researchers use *A Topographical Dictionary of Ireland*, 2 vols., by Samuel Lewis [Intl REF DA979/L48/1984 also LOAN], available in the first-floor reference area, to learn about the history of particular parishes or towns in Ireland. In addition to the Catholic parish maps in *Tracing Your Irish Ancestors* and *A New Genealogical Atlas of Ireland*, Lewis's dictionary gives verbal descriptions of Catholic parishes. Lewis usually starts by providing population statistics from the 1831 census, topographical, archaeological and geological information, a brief history of the parish, a list of the major estates and their owners, and a list and location of the churches of each denomination.

For genealogists with Ulster province roots, the *Ordnance Survey Memoirs* and related documents provide a detailed and fascinating glimpse of individual parishes in the 1830s. Published by The Queens University, the *Ordnance Survey Memoirs*, vols. 1–40 [DA990/46/O85/1990] (located on first floor), give excellent local descriptions of the parishes in the counties of Down, Antrim, Fermanangh, Londonderry, Donegal, and Tyrone. Not only do the books furnish even more detail than Lewis's dictionary, they sometimes delve into highly subjective descriptions of a parish's population.

Another series relating to the Ordnance Survey was published on mimeograph paper in the 1920s by Rev. Michael O'Flanagan. The Society has a three-volume set of *Letters Containing Information Relative to the Antiquities of the County of Galway, Collected During the Progress of the Ordnance Survey* (Bray, 1928) [CS497/G2/O5/1928]. Volumes for other counties may be found in other libraries, such as the Boston Public Library.

Townlands in Ulster: Local History Studies by W. H. Crawford and R. H. Foy (Belfast: Ulster Historical Foundation and Federation for Ulster Local Studies, 1998) [DA990/U6/T69/1998], provides an in-depth examination of particular townlands in Northern Ireland, including Griffith's Valuation and the corresponding Valuation maps. This book is extremely valuable if you are lucky enough to have an ancestor from Forttown, Co. Antrim; Scolbow, Co. Antrim; Ballymagee, Co. Down; Cranfield, Co. Down; Drumskinney and Montiaghroe, Co. Fermanagh; Gallon, Co. Tyrone; Hollyhill, Co. Tyrone; or Owenreagh, Co. Derry.

Irish Townlands: studies in Local History by Brian Ó Dálaigh, Denis A. Cronin, and Paul Connell (Dublin: Four Courts Press, 1998) [DA910/I75/1998 also LOAN], is the companion book for the Irish Republic, and cover the townlands of Drumcavan, Co. Clare; Dysart, Co. Westmeath; Ballynahalsik and Sweet Rockmills, Co. Cork; Kilmacud, Co. Dublin; Cloonfush, Co. Galway; Eskerbaun, Co. Roscommon; Cloncurry, Co. Kildare; Lacken, Co. Wicklow; and Kildoney,

Co. Donegal. Although this book thoroughly examines the localities, the corresponding Valuation maps are not included.

In addition to these sources, the Society has many county and parish histories that give details about specific septs and families within their boundaries, and help to guide your research toward specific records.

Census and Census Substitutes

After determining the location of your ancestor's birthplace, the next step is to research genealogical sources available for that area. Ireland began collecting census data in 1821, and by 1851 had expanded the data collection to include all the members of the family. Unfortunately most of these early records were destroyed. There are census fragments available for certain parishes in certain counties, most notably, for several baronies in several counties for 1821, a large portion of the southern parishes of County Derry in 1831, the parish of Killeshandra in County Cavan in 1841, and four parishes in Kilworth Union, Co. Cork, in 1851. The Society has copies and indexes for these census fragments available in book form, microtext, and on CD. Although the Society does not have the 1901 census of Ireland, you can order the census from the Family History Library in Salt Lake City. In addition, the Society has a number of indexes to the 1901 census, such as *County Longford and its People: An Index to the 1901 Census for County Longford*, by David Leahy (Dublin: Flyleaf Press,1990) [CS497/L68/L42/1990 also LOAN], and the *1901 Census Index, Volume 1, County Fermanagh, and Volume 2, County Tyrone*, by Linda K. Meehan, (Alberta, Canada: Quality Color Press, 1994) [CS484/M43/1994 microfiche].

The record most people use in researching their ancestors is Griffith's Primary Valuation of Ireland (Sir Richard John Griffith, *General Valuation of Rateable Property in Ireland*. Dublin: Irish Microforms Ltd., 1978) [CS484/G46/1978 microfiche], which is a mid-nineteenth-century, head-of-household census of land occupiers. The valuation includes not only landowners, but also people who rented or leased land. The Society has online access to the valuation records through *Otherdays.com*, and also a complete set of the Valuation and the accompanying Householders Index on microfiche, as well as a complete surname index on CD. Since all of the indexes have some problems with omissions in them, you can go directly to the parish valuation record and search through all of the townlands, if you know the parish of origin. You should always keep a wide focus when trolling through records. Even if your ancestor's name is Charles McCarthy, you should make note of other McCarthys within the parish, since they could be relatives. Others with the same surname within the same townland are very likely related. Some people exclude checking Griffith's Valuation because their ancestors emigrated before the Famine. Although the data for Griffith's was collected around 1848, the census takers may have started in some areas years before 1848. In fact, genealogists have come across many cases where their families were listed in Griffith's Valuation, even though they emigrated or died years before.

The next most comprehensive census substitutes available at the Society are the *Tithe Applotment Books*, available on microfilm for the Republic of Ireland and Northern Ireland see Calendar of Tithe Applotment Books (1824–1840) (Belfast: Genealogical Society of Salt Lake City, 1959–78) [CS448/N6/A1 microfilm]. A CD-ROM index, *International Land Records: Tithe Applotment Books 1823–1838* (Novato, Calif.: Broderbund, 1999) [CS497/I55/1999 CD also LOAN], is also available for Northern Ireland. In addition, the Society recently added to its book collections *County Longford Residents Prior to the Famine: A Transcription and Complete Index of the Tithe Applotment Books of County Longford Ireland (1823–1835)*, by Guy Rymsza (South Bend, Ind.: Dome Shadow Press, 2003). In the early decades of the nineteenth century, all land occupiers had to pay tithes to the Church of Ireland, regardless of their religion. The collectors kept records of land acreage and valuation, and the amount they collected from each head-of-household. Dating from about 1824 to 1840, the books document the next generation back from the time of Griffith's Valuation.

For those researchers with Northern Irish roots, the *Ireland Old Age Pension Claims Index*, edited by Janice Beresford Brooks (Dubbo, NSW, Australia: J. B. Brooks, 1994) [CS484/B76/1994 microfiche], may help fill the gap left by the destruction of the 1841 and 1851 census. With the passage of the Old Age Pension Act of 1908, persons age 70 or over had to show proof of age to collect a pension. Since the civil registration in Ireland began for most records after 1864, applicants for pensions had to use the 1841 and 1851 census for proof. The records provide the name and age of the applicant, their parents' names, including in some cases the maiden name of the mother, and their address. In some cases they gave the names of their brothers and sisters, and other records, to prove their age. Located on the fourth-floor, the index consists of 9 microfiche of 39,000 records created between 1908 and 1922 and held in the Public Record Office of Northern Ireland. They cover only the counties of Antrim, Armagh, Derry, Donegal, Down, Fermanagh, and Tyrone.

Another source, *International Land Records: Irish Flax Growers, 1796* (Novato, Calif.: Broderbund, 1999) [CS497/I54/1999 CD], may prove useful to some researchers. As part of a scheme to promote the production of linen, the number of spinning wheels in each household were reported. The lists of head-of-households by parish are more comprehensive for counties most heavily involved in the linen trade, such as Armagh or Mayo. The original lists are located in the Linen Hall Library in Belfast, but the surname indexes are available at the Society on CD-ROM and on microfiche.

Published Church Records

Most Irish church records are accessible only at the local level, at the National Library or Church Representative Body Library in Dublin, or at the National Archives of Ireland or Public Record Office of Northern Ireland. However, NEHGS does have some published Church of Ireland registers for the seventeenth and eighteenth centuries, including from Dublin the churches of St. John the Evangelist, St. Patrick, St. Michan, St. Catherine, the Union of Monkstown, St. Peter and St. Kevin, St. Marie, St. Luke, St. Werburgh, St. Andrew, St. Anne, St. Audran, St. Bride, and St. Nicholas Without; and from Derry, the early records of the Derry Cathedral.

The Society also has a 15-volume set of Albert Eugene Casey's *O'Kief, Coshe Mang, Slieve Lougher, and Upper Blackwater in Ireland* (Birmingham, Ala., 1952–71) [CS497/M8/C3/1952-71 also LOAN]. Casey collected all kinds of records from the area where his ancestors originated, along the Cork–Kerry border. They include indexed copies of Catholic Church records, some of which date back to 1789. The volumes encompass the area between Killarney, Tralee, and Castleisland in Kerry, and over to the baronies of Dunhallow and West Muskerry in Cork. Each printed volume has an index in the back. Many of the baptisms and marriages have been included in the IGI, so researchers can also use the IGI as an index. Of course, you should not just rely on the IGI for information, but consult the original transcription in O'Kief for additional information, such as townland or origin. Furthermore, as the case with any transcriptions, the original records are more accurate and authoritative. You should follow up your research in O'Kief with research in Ireland if at all possible.

About one-third of the Catholic parish registers have been microfilmed by the Family History Library in Salt Lake City, and visitors to the NEHGS library may borrow these films from Salt Lake City.

Other Printed Sources

Since most of the Irish population before the twentieth century lived in rural areas, street directories of cities and towns are not a major source of information. The Society does have some directories on microfiche for all of Ireland 1811–1877, and for Belfast, Cork, Dublin, and Waterford. The people who appear in Irish street directories are most frequently the landed gentry and prominent merchants.

Newspapers are another underused source due to the fact that most of the information in them has not been indexed. Since the ancestors of most Irish-Americans came from the middle and lower classes of Irish society, they are more likely to be found in the reports of county assizes (criminal cases), rather than in biographical notices. But you may find the following periodical and newspaper sources useful: *Irish Marriages, Being an Index to the Marriages in Walker's Hibernian Magazine 1771–1812* by Henry Farrar (Baltimore: Genealogical Publishing Co., 1972) [CS482/F3/1897 also LOAN], *Index to Newspaper Biographical Notices for Limerick, Ennis, Clonmel, and Waterford 1758–1821* (Fethard, Ireland: 1985) [CS497/L5/1985 also LOAN], and *Biographical Notices Relating to Cork and Kerry Collected from Newspapers 1756–1829* (Dublin: Ffolliott, 1969) [CS497/C7/B5/1969], by Rosemary Ffolliott. The Society also has some indices (without the actual newspapers) for some Northern Irish newspapers: *In-*

dex to the Down Recorder by Jack McCoy (Ballynahinch: South Eastern Education and Library Board, 1987) [DA990/D7/I53/1987], and *Index to County Down and Lisburn Items in the Northern Ireland Herald* by Jack McCoy (Ballynahinch: Southeast Education and Library Board, 1992) [DA990/D7/I54/1992].

Genealogical and Historical Magazines

You may find the extensive collection of genealogical and historical magazines more useful than some of the Irish newspapers. The Society holds runs of fifteen Irish genealogical magazines. These periodicals include published genealogies, vital records extracts, tombstone inscriptions, articles on sources and methods, and more. Some notable ones include *Familia: Ulster Genealogical Review* [CS440/F36], *The Irish At Home and Abroad* [CS496/I7/I74/1993], *Irish Family History: the Journal of the Irish Family History Society* [CS480/I715], *The Irish Link (Australia and New Zealand)* [CS2007/I7/1984], *Irish Roots* [Intl Oversize CS480/I74/1992] and *North Irish Roots: the Journal of the North of Ireland Family History Society* [CS449/N67/1984].

NEHGS also has a broad collection of Irish historical magazines, many associated with particular counties. These periodicals include a great deal of information useful to the genealogist: tombstone inscriptions, military records, family and clan histories, local and county histories, and eighteenth and nineteenth century local descriptions and travelogues. The areas covered are Westport, Co. Mayo, the diocese of Clogher (Fermanagh, Tyrone, Monaghan and Louth), Donegal, Dublin, Antrim, Cork, Galway, Kildare, Louth, Upper Ards (Down), Kilkenny, and Ulster.

Estate Records

Many genealogists run into a dead end when they reach the eighteenth century. Most church records, except those in major towns, do not pre-date 1800. Some have estimated that in nineteenth century 95 percent of the land was owned by 5 percent of the population. These major landowners sometimes kept detailed records of their estates, including rental rolls, maps and descriptions of land tenure. Some excellent sources for County Kerry are the Kenmare estate records in *The Kenmare Manuscripts* by V. Kenmare, E. MacLysaght, and K. Cunha (Dublin: Irish University Press, 1970) [CS499/B85/1970]. In this 517-page book, the history of land tenure of various townlands are detailed from the early 1700s. Other estate records have been published in county journals such as *The Clogher Record* and *County Mayo Chronicles*.

Court Records

Most of the probate court records for Ireland were destroyed in the fire at the National Archives in 1922. However, many of the wills and estate administrations had been indexed and/or abstracted in various calendars. Researchers should review the general guide by J. S. W. Gibson, *A Simplified Guide to Probate Jurisdictions: Where to Look for Wills in Great Britain and Ireland* (Baltimore: Genealogical Publishing Co., 1986) [CD1041/G52/1986].

In the nineteenth century, Chief Herald Sir William Betham abstracted some 40,000 wills for the period 1536–1800, and these abstracts are available through the Family History Library (FHL 595939–945, 596139–147). The Society has an index to the wills Betham had abstracted: Sir Arthur Vicars, *Index to the Prerogative Wills of Ireland, 1536–1810,* (Baltimore: Genealogical Publishing Co., 1989) [CS482/V5/1897 also LOAN].

The Society also has indexes to other collections in the National Archives. Readers should consult, *Index of Irish Wills, 1484–1858: Records at the National Archives of Ireland* (Dublin: Eneclann, 1999) [Microtext CS497/A1/163/1999 CD also LOAN]. This CD index contains over 70,000 records and 100,000 names, and does not include the Betham abstracts. About 90 percent of these relate to will transcripts, copies, and abstracts, but 10 percent relate to marriage license grants and bonds.

For the Consistorial Court, Diocese of Dublin (estates valued at over 5 pounds), the Society also has published indexes to act or grant books, and to original wills 1467–1800 in the *Appendix to the 26th Report of the Deputy Keeper of Ireland* (Dublin: Alexander Thom & Co., 1894) [DA905/A2/1894 Appendix] and for 1800–1858 in the *Appendix to the 30th Report of the Deputy Keeper of Ireland* (Dublin: Alexander Thom & Co., 1898) [DA905/A2/1898 Appendix]. The original records included probate records, administrations, wills, will copies and marriage licenses and bonds.

In the late sixteenth century, the lands of the many Irish rebels against the English Crown were confiscated, and then regranted upon their swearing an oath of allegiance to the Crown. Called "Elizabethan Fiants," these regrants and other court documents from the late 1500s were published and indexed in the *Report of the Deputy Keeper of Ireland* in vols. 11, 12, 13, 15, 16, 17, and 18. The index, in vols. 21 and 22, contains about 82,000 names and place-names. The records include not only the major Gaelic and Norman chieftains and leaders, but also waterboys, wood kernes, and horsemen. The records frequently reference not only the parish, but also the townland of residence.

Tombstone Inscriptions

Estate records, deeds, rental rolls, and tombstone inscriptions may be the only sources for pre-nineteenth-century research in Ireland. The Society has in its inventory published tombstone inscriptions (in addition to the ones published in the county historical journals): *Journal of the Association for the Preservation of the Memorials of the Dead in Ireland*, 12 vols., 1892–1931; R. S. J. Clarke, *Gravestone Inscriptions County Down*, 20 vols. (Belfast: Ulster-Scot Historical Foundation, 1966–98) [CS497/D6/G73/1966], R. S. J. Clarke, *Gravestone Inscriptions County Antrim*, 3 vols. (Belfast: Ulster-Scot Historical Foundation, 1966–98) [CS497/A57/G7], and R. S. J. Clarke, *Gravestone Inscriptions Belfast*, 4 vols. (Belfast: Ulster-Scot Historical Foundation, 1966–98) [CS497/B44/1982 also LOAN]. Also on the shelves are a number of individual parish transcriptions of tombstone inscriptions for the Clifton Street Cemetery in Belfast, Old Donagheady Burial Ground (Strabane), and Layde Graveyard (Cushendall, Co. Antrim).

The sources listed here cover some of the larger Irish collections of the Society, but are by no means exhaustive. You should consult the online catalog for a more complete listing. Many of these books, such as O'Kief, can be borrowed through the Circulating Library. Instead of driving from one archives to another, you can save valuable time by coming to the Society to research your ancestors. With many of the major sources collected in one spot, you can access the American census records, vital records, and street directories, and the Irish sources of Griffith's Valuation, the Tithe Applotment Books and the Ordnance Survey maps all in one trip.

Special Research Approaches

How to Analyze Your Research Problems

Henry B. Hoff

A trip to Salt Lake City with NEHGS members reminded me that I might be superfluous there. Every member I had a consultation with knew more about his or her research problems than I ever would, and they usually had done years of research on the problems they presented to me. In thirty minutes or less I was supposed to have fresh thoughts that would be effective, even for research problems I might have seen a few years ago in a previous consultation with the same member.

It sounds like a setup for failure, but oddly enough, it isn't. The members who are devoted enough to come to the NEHGS program in Salt Lake City don't give up. And usually they have been working diligently at research suggestions the NEHGS staff has given them.

Reprinted from *New England Ancestors* 3:2 (Spring 2002):7.

How does the NEHGS staff analyze the research problems of members and try to give useful advice in a short period of time? Here are some of my methods, and I hope you can use them to analyze your own research problems:

Is there a hot new source to recommend?

In November 2001 there was such a source: the online 1880 federal census on banks of computers on each floor of the Family History Library. Not only could it help with ancestors living in 1880; it might even help with ancestors who had children living in 1880 who gave parents' places of birth. For example, one of my great-great-great aunts outlived all her siblings and died in 1881. In the 1880 census she reported that her mother (1769–1807) was born in England, a possibility I had never considered.

Are there sources unique to the place of consultation to recommend?

Since we were at the Family History Library, I tried to think of sources that the member could look at there and nowhere else.

Can I answer questions or fill in blanks, even if they are not the member's principal interest?

Solving secondary problems can be satisfying while working on big "brick wall" problems. And sometimes solving the secondary problems leads to the solution of a bigger problem.

Are there standard sources that should be consulted again in light of new discoveries or new editions of standard works?

A good example is PERSI [*PERiodical Source Index*], which is updated every year or so and should be reviewed for every new surname discovered. Similarly, Torrey's *New England Marriages Prior to 1700* (published on CD by NEHGS) should be reviewed for every seventeenth- and eighteenth-century New England problem.

Can I recommend certain sources in response to certain aspects of this problem?

Could someone be mentioned in a Revolutionary pension? Is there a published genealogy for an allied family? Is the family living in an area where many *Mayflower* descendants lived?

Does some aspect of this problem remind me of a published article?

One of the members had made a breakthrough, resulting in several newly discovered ancestors in Connecticut. Only an early-eighteenth-century wife from Jamaica, Long Island, was unidentified. I suggested the member look at a 1998 *Register* article on a Connecticut family that had been in Jamaica for ideas of sources to search. Instead, the member found the parents of her ancestress in the article!

Solving one research problem will usually lead to . . . a new and earlier research problem! But that's the fun of genealogy. And the NEHGS staff looks forward to helping members with their research problems at 101 Newbury Street and across the country in its programs and seminars.

Research Approaches

Common Sense Research

Throughout your research you'll need to assess the veracity of sources and data. There are two questions you should ask throughout the research process:

Is it correct?

In the case of printed resources, you'll want to know what sources the author consulted. Not all sources are the same. What one states as fact another may disprove. For instance, several sources listed Christopher Avery's birthplace as Salisbury, England, but in fact it is generally thought in more recent sources to be in Devon, England.

Is there something more recent?

Recent doesn't mean correct, but when you are surveying literature it is important to work backwards from the most recent articles and books to older ones. Recent scholarship is usually based on material published in the past. It is also quite possible the author has discovered a new source of information. Manuscripts and documents are "rediscovered" daily in libraries and archives.

Don't Stop with the First Resource — Keep Looking!

A common mistake made by researchers is to stop with the information they find in the book, periodical, or manuscript they consult. If only this were the end of the process! It is generally a good idea to keep looking for information. You might get lucky and select the most up to date and in-depth source as a resource. However in most cases, you'll need to look a little further. The first source may not be complete or error-free.

Indirect Research

Take a new look at an old problem by browsing the library.

- Read the latest genealogical periodicals, examine new books added to the library or consult with a librarian about new strategies.

- Take a break from your direct line pursuit and begin to work on allied families.

- Fill in the background information on a known ancestor by locating biographical material and reading social history.

This may not immediately solve the genealogical mystery you're working on, but the time spent acquiring new skills and resources will help you in the future.

A Piece of Good Advice

Looking at recent scholarship is especially important with colonial families whose ancestry has been re-examined multiple times. In this instance, start with published genealogies then use periodical finding aids, and then go to the original records.

There Must Be Something in Print:
Effective Research in Secondary Sources

Henry B. Hoff

How many times have you wondered whether the answer was on the library shelves — somewhere. If only you knew how to find it! Barring a constant stream good luck or psychic intervention, you and I have to rely on native ingenuity — and asking others for help.

This article will approach the subject of effective research in secondary sources from the point of view of *what are you trying to find* — rather than just describing major sources.

Experienced genealogists sometimes have a sense of what they can expect to find, of what should be there, of what makes sense to look for first. For example, if you know that a brother of your brick-wall dead-end ancestor went to college and became a minister, you might want to be looking for a biography of that brother — rather than a compiled account of the family. If you're descended from a mobile person like a mariner, you may be looking for mere mention of that individual. If you're starting a new project with new family names, probably colonial, you may want to look for what has already been compiled on that family.

A good article on research in secondary sources is Martin Hollick's 1997 article in *The American Genealogist*, "Accessing the Genealogical Literature: Problems Facing Historians and Genealogists." Martin, who was a university reference librarian as well as a genealogist, discusses searching for single-family genealogies, multi-family genealogies [also known as "all my ancestors" works], genealogical dictionaries, genealogical periodicals, biography, and internet resources. He concludes that the field of genealogy needs citation indexes to show what is the best source for a family. To quote Martin, "All too often researchers find secondary sources that cover their ancestry and believe their work is done, not knowing that there is an article or book which shows errors in that source and provides a better and more truthful lineage." So when I called this article "*effective* research in secondary sources," I meant finding *reliable* answers to your genealogical questions — and not stopping at the first discovery.

Adapted from a lecture of the same title.

By reading genealogical periodicals, you can develop a sense of what genealogists are writing about, and so what you are likely to find. For example, my first known Hoff ancestor just appeared in Philadelphia in 1765 and left few descendants — while my mother's male-line ancestor, Richard Smith, appeared on Long Island in 1641 and left a vast descendancy, which has been the subject of more than one compilation. Which family is more likely to have articles and accounts in multi-family genealogies? The Smiths, of course. Yes, common sense should tell you that, but I've picked a rather obvious example. If the Smith male-line descendants had died out in a generation or two, there would probably have been no single family genealogy, even if there was a vast descendancy through daughters, *but* you might still find accounts in multi-family genealogies.

The first source that Martin cites is *The Source: A Guidebook of American Genealogy*, particularly Kory Meyerink's chapter on "Databases, Indexes and Other Finding Aids." More recent is *Printed Sources: A Guide to Published Genealogical Records*, edited by Kory. This is also very useful and it expands some of the ideas in Kory's chapter in *The Source*.

You will notice that I list Family Search and the FHL catalog — as they are essential for basic research — like of like a bed of lettuce upon which more exotic research tidbits are laid. But you can't ignore the bed of lettuce and must keep coming back to it again and again.

Just a word of caution — which you've heard before: Indexes are not infallible. Moreover, subject indexes and even every-name indexes don't always include queries, book reviews, etc. As a result, try to find material by using all possible approaches, and try all indexes, even if you have already found promising material. Variant spellings of surnames are often a big problem. Some every-name indexes are literal (indexed as the name appears), and some group variant spellings together.

Finding Foremothers

Julie Helen Otto

Among any genealogist's greatest frustrations must be the anonymous female ancestor — just as much our forebear as the husband whose name she bears. In vital and church records her children are often listed only as his, even if she died bearing them. When she is finally identified, odd scraps (even "unlikely" places of residence) in her children's later lives make sudden sense — and we may find her ancestry more interesting than her husband's!

Frustrated by it as we may be, we must realize that women's obscurity is not the result of a conspiracy but rather the fruit of cultural factors, often unconscious, and perhaps not so far from our own assumptions as we might find comfortable. Mary (____) certainly knew who she was. Once you find her maiden name, a birth record may well exist; the trick is finding the connection.

A guiding principle of traditional society has been the belief that in marriage, "the two shall become one flesh." Our ancestors took this Biblical text literally; since men were considered heads of household, their wives' identity was subsumed in theirs. Kin of one spouse were assumed to become kin of the other in the same degree. Published genealogies are full of misidentifications from later times, when the "nuclear family" has been the norm.

Example: The 1662 will of John2 Blackman (Rev. Adam1) of Stratford, Conn., calls Moses Wheeler "uncle," but it doesn't necessarily follow that John's mother, Mrs. Jane Blackman, must be a Wheeler. Moses could be related by blood or marriage to John's wife Dorothy Smith, or to any [note emphasis] of John's or Dorothy's parents.

Just because "the two become one flesh," however, it shouldn't be assumed that every relationship between persons not of the same surname must be that of in-laws!

Example: According to the 1901 Tiffany Genealogy, *Elizabeth3 Tiffany (born 1689) married Amos Shepardson. The 1745 will of Elizabeth's much younger half-brother Noah Tiffany (born 1720) mentioned brothers John Tiffany and Amos Shepardson. But Noah Tiffany and Amos Shepardson actually were uterine half-brothers — sons of Elizabeth (Fuller) (Shepardson) Tiffany, whose second marriage to James Tiffany about 1712 was not recorded. Elizabeth Tiffany (born 1689), daughter of James Tiffany by his first wife, remains unidentified.*

Published in *NEXUS* 15:2 (1998):52–53.

In theory, women appear as surrogates for men: as heiresses of their parents or acting in their husbands' interests. In practice, real life intervened. In Massachusetts especially, a married woman usually signed off her dower rights when her husband sold land (even land he had inherited), and widows routinely administered husbands' estates. A wife might leave her husband, or (more commonly) be left by him. The divorce below may be the only record that these two were ever married.

Example: Susannah Nichols of Woodbury, Connecticut, petitioned the Litchfield County Court on 3 August 1767. She had married on 14 November 1752 Richard Nichols of Woodbury; he deserted her on 1 June 1766; in October 1766 she learned he was living in Beekman's Precinct, Dutchess Co., N.Y., and had been married to one Eunice Butler on 29 September 1766 (The American Genealogist 32 [1956]:157).

Married, unmarried, or widowed, women deposed in court; ran farms and businesses; sued and were sued; bequeathed property; or appeared in fornication cases.

Example: The only thing known of one ancestress of the late Princess of Wales was a June 1671 court case: Thomasine (____), wife of Edward Walden of Wenham, witnessed to John Witteredge's being "disguised with drink" (Records and Files of the Quarterly Courts of Essex County, Massachusetts, 4:416).

In the sixth-floor Ruth C. Bishop Reading Room, consult indexes to *The New England Historical and Genealogical Register* (the book form provides more maiden names than the CD-ROM which is now online at *NewEnglandAncestors.org*) and the great journal itself, between the mantel and the window. Also on this wall are full runs (and subject indexes of *The American Genealogist* and *The New York Genealogical and Biographical Record* (hereafter the *Record*). In the sixth-floor reference stacks, over 200 volumes of the *American Genealogical-Biographical Index*, 2nd ed., index many compiled genealogies, the 1790 census ("Heads of Families"), and the *Boston Evening Transcript* genealogical column; even those queries never answered may still be the definitive accounts of many families. Our run of this column is almost complete.

As an auxiliary Family History Center, we also have the International Genealogical Index (IGI), online (at *familysearch.org*) and (in older form) on microfiche on the fourth floor. When using this valuable resource, however, remember that the LDS Church does not pretend to verify information submitted or extracted for this database, nor determine which of several versions is correct. For this reason, it is not sufficient to cite "IGI" as the only source of data when writing a family history. To confirm or deny an IGI clue, check indexes of compiled genealogies (sixth floor); published records of relevant places in the U.S. and Canada (fifth floor) or elsewhere in the world, especially Great Britain (first floor); and — often most important — microfilmed vital, church, census, and other records, as well as computer sources (fourth floor).

Each new town kept vital records (VRs), often quite well given climate, disease, possible Indian attack, and other pioneer realities. Consult published VRs of towns where a foremother lived; she may also appear in VRs of surrounding or parent towns. Published VRs of Massachusetts towns are in the Bishop Reading Room; records for most towns not published are on microfilm, fiche, or manuscript, or at the Boston Public Library. These VRs are also being issued on CD-ROM (fourth floor). Connecticut VRs (Barbour Collection) are in book form (copies of the original typescript on the sixth floor, a mostly complete set of reprints on the fifth), and on microfilm on the fourth floor (by surname, statewide). Remember, however, that the Barbour Collection consists only of records which made it to town clerks to be civically recorded; if your ancestors didn't notify the clerk, you will most likely need to pursue other sources — such as microfilmed probate papers or church record indexes, also on the fourth floor — to find your Connecticut forebear. Other New England holdings include microfilm VRs for Massachusetts (statewide, 1841–1910), Maine (to about 1956), New Hampshire (births to 1900, marriages and deaths to 1937), Vermont (to 1989), and Rhode Island (indexed to 1900); deeds and/or probate for many counties in Massachusetts, New Hampshire, and Maine; much supplemental Connecticut, Maine, New Hampshire, and Rhode Island data; and microfilm vital, church, land, probate, and census records for Atlantic Canada and southern Québec, areas heavily settled from the eighteenth century on by New Englanders. Acquisitions within the last ten years include an index to Connecticut probates to 1948 (and films of probate papers in most districts to 1881, in many to the early years of the twentieth century) and actual probates/indexes for many New Hampshire counties and Vermont districts, with town records for many towns in both states; Québec notarial records; and records of U.S.–Canada border crossings from 1895. A summary of our microform and CD-ROM holdings is at the fourth-floor desk.

Seventeenth Century

Clarence Almon Torrey's manuscript (from which *New England Marriages Prior to 1700* was published in 1985, and the CD-ROM of the same name in 2001) and the 2003 supplement by Melinde Lutz Sanborn (incorporating and adding to the earlier 1991 and 1995 supplements) are indispensable as you determine what has (or hasn't) been published. The late Mr. Torrey wrote a reasonably legible hand, but he did so on onionskin paper, and his blue ink has not always copied well. Consult a librarian if you have questions; we're glad to help decipher. We also have the "Torrey Bibliography" by Alicia Crane Williams, who translated Mr. Torrey's codes (e.g., "Sv" for James Savage's *Genealogical Dictionary of New England* [1860–62]; "AmGen" for *The American Genealogist*). (Or use the CD-ROM version, painstakingly transcribed from the original, which also incorporates Ms. Williams's bibliography.) Never cite Torrey's work as proof in itself. Once you've determined his reference, head for the stacks or the catalog to check the source! If a foremother is not in vital, church, or town data, check records of county, superior, or other courts. Births sooner than about eight months after marriage were seen not as medical miracles but as cases of premarital fornication; details of everyday colonial life and family connections often appear in sharp focus. See, for example, Melinde Lutz Sanborn, *Lost Babes: Fornication Abstracts from Court Records, Essex County, Massachusetts, 1692–1745* (1992).

Keep a "weather eye" on current journals for new seventeenth-century developments. Particularly distinguished in the areas of English origins and colonial maiden-name identifications are *The American Genealogist*, *The Genealogist*, the *Record*, and our own *Register*. To check on journal coverage for specific families or places, use the Periodical Source Index (PERSI). See also "New England Articles in Genealogical Journals" in the July issue of the *Register* starting in 2002.

Eighteenth Century

Mid- and late-eighteenth-century America saw dizzying changes. After the British victory in the French and Indian War, new frontiers (northern New England, upstate New York, Pennsylvania, Ohio, Atlantic Canada, etc.) beckoned growing young families; record-keeping in the new settlements they founded, and often quickly left, was spotty at best. The Appalachians and the Ohio River attracted many settlers from older, more thickly-populated areas from Virginia and the South. As migration increased, the Revolution broke out. Data submitted by soldiers, widows and relatives, and published in Virgil D. White's *Genealogical Abstracts of Revolutionary War Pension Files* in four huge indexed volumes, often include marriage dates, maiden names, and lists (with full birth dates) of children whose vital data more often than not was never recorded.

> *Example: Hannah (Hoyt) (Terrrell) Blackman (1748–post 10 January 1837) of Weston, Conn., widow of two Revolutionary soldiers (Asahel Terrell and Nehemiah Blackman) filed 10 January 1837 on service of her first husband, killed at Saratoga (#W17311). Of the fourteen persons listed (Hannah, her two husbands, and their eleven children) with full birth, marriage and death data given, vital records give only Asahel Terrell's birth (White, 3:448).*

The first federal census of 1790, published early in the 1900s, can often shed light on family groups of several decades earlier. (Our census holdings and indexes are now on the fourth floor.) The later eighteenth century also saw the rise of newspapers, whose reach was not confined to urban areas. Their notices of marriage and deaths often serve as substitutes for actual vital records. At NEHGS we often find that marriage and death abstracts from the *Columbian Centinel* (1784–1840) fill annoying vital record gaps.

Nineteenth Century

The backbone of nineteenth-century American genealogical research has been the U.S. census, taken every ten years since 1790. In 1850 (influenced by Lemuel Shattuck, a founder of NEHGS) the government began every-name enumeration — an improvement over previous numerical listings under heads-of-household. Many women born 1760–1780 make a "last bow" as elderly mothers or in-laws in 1850. Revolutionary War and War of 1812 pension applications (also abstracted or indexed by Virgil D. White) can shed light on nineteenth-century family groups. In urban and suburban areas check city directories; very often you can pinpoint a street, even a building where your ancestor lived — vital clues to nearby relatives and associations. For immigrants, check the 1848–1891 indexes of microfilmed Boston ship passenger lists (at Boston Public Library, 1820–1891), and the index to pre-1906 naturalizations in the six New England states, both on the fourth floor. The fourth floor offers NEHGS patrons online access to searchable census records and images, 1790–1930, via *Ancestry.com* and *heritagequestonline.com*.

Twentieth Century

Only for the century just past do we have living memory — and whole worlds of it disappear each day as people die. Confirm your memories, and your relatives' reminiscences, in census and city directories. For the early part of the century, the census (to 1930) is vital; NEHGS has subscriptions to the online services (*Ancestry.com*, especially for 1850, 1920 and 1930, and *heritagequestonline.com*, especially for 1860, 1870, 1900, 1910, and 1920). NEHGS city directories for many New England areas have been microfiched; Boston and many localities, not confined to Massachusetts, are now available. By the 1920s almost all states had begun systematic vital recordkeeping. For a list of what is available (with sample forms), see Thomas Jay Kemp, *Vital Records Handbook*, 4th ed. (2000), or check online. The Social Security Death Index, on the NEHGS website and at *Ancestry.com*, among other places online, is a huge database of post-1962 decedents giving birth date, zip code of last known mailing address, etc. If your twentieth-century ancestors were born or died, or if they married in Massachusetts, be sure to check the Massachusetts record indexes for births, marriages or deaths. (If using these same index books at the Massachusetts Bureau of Vital Statistics in Boston, you will pay an hourly fee.)

We hope you enjoy finding foremothers at NEHGS. When you do, please tell the librarians (we share your enthusiasm) and publish your findings. Your discoveries are important additions to everyone's knowledge.

Finding Clues to Immigrant Origins

Michael J. Leclerc

One of the most difficult parts of researching your family's origins in Canada is to determine where exactly they came from. In so many frustrating cases, the place of birth is given as just Canada. How can the precise origins be located when the only known information is Canada?

There are two major things to keep in mind before starting your research. The first is the problem of name changes. This is more of a problem for Francophones than any other group. In addition to the usual problems of non-standardized name spellings, English-speaking town clerks had a difficult time understanding many of the French-speaking residents. Names such as Lajoie became Lashua. It is important to sound out names and try different spelling variations when looking for your ancestors.

A common but false assumption is that all French came from Québec and all the Irish and Scots from Nova Scotia. Major migration came into New England from all provinces in the late nineteenth and early twentieth centuries. Francophones inhabited every province in Canada and many Irish families settled in Québec for generations before descendants moved to New England. Always keep an open mind when looking through records and don't make assumptions without the facts to back them up. Even family traditions should be called into question if no substantial evidence exists to prove them. Just because there was a Hebert immigrant to Nova Scotia in the 1600s doesn't mean that your Hebert family came from Lunenburg County instead of Montréal. That being said, let's take a look at some options.

Vital Records

The first step should be to examine all available vital records in the United States for clues. Often these clues are subtle, and unfamiliarity with the terminology contained in these records might lead to erroneous conclusions. For example, a record might give the place of birth as Canada East. On first glance, this might indicate a place of birth as Nova Scotia or New Brunswick. In reality, this record names the exact province of birth — Québec. Unlike the United States, where most states have kept the same name, the names of the provinces of Canada have changed over time. Lower Canada and Canada East are differ-

Published online on *NewEnglandAncestors.org*, July 19, 2002.

ent names for the province of Québec. Familiarize yourself with the various names of each province so that subtle clues like this one can be detected.

In the New England states, vital records are kept on a local level (usually by the town clerk) and a copy is sent to the state. The information on the state copy may not be identical to the information on the local copy. For example, in the state of Massachusetts, early death records on the state level do not include the place of burial but many of the local copies actually give the cemetery name. It is very important to examine both copies or you may miss a crucial piece of information.

It is possible to find three original records relating to the same event, but copied by different persons and kept in different places. For example, doctors or undertakers would usually create death records, especially in large towns and cities. A "Return of Death" form was filled out and filed with the town clerk. The clerk then copied the information into the local death register books. The record would then be copied yet again, this time into the ledger books sent to the state. Information was not always transcribed completely when moving from one version to the next. Examine all copies whenever possible.

Church Records

Once the original vital records have been examined, take the time to look at original church records. Records of baptism, marriage, and burial may contain vital clues. For example, look at the names of the individuals who acted as godparents to children at their baptism. These godparents were often brothers, sisters, aunts, uncles, or cousins. Check the vital records of these individuals for clues to their place of origin as this may help you locate your own ancestors. At the very least the sponsors may have been close family friends that came from the same village in Canada.

Marriage Records

Marriage records, especially in the Catholic Church, can be extremely helpful. In order to be married in the Catholic Church one had to demonstrate proof of baptism. Parish priests often wrote these places of birth in the margins of the parish registers. Many Franco-American Catholic parishes have had their records transcribed and published over the years. These transcriptions can be very helpful, but do not rest there. Make sure to examine the original records, as the marginal notes may not have been copied when the records were transcribed for publication. Also, when writing to a parish for a copy of the original record, ask if it would be possible to have a photocopy of the original. Marginal notes are often left off of the fill-in-the-blank forms that most parishes currently use for providing copies of birth, marriage, and burial certificates. If that is not possible, ask the priest (or church secretary) to make sure that all marginal notes are included when they copy the record for you.

Naturalization Records

Naturalization records can be quite helpful in identifying an immigrant's place of origin. The National Archives Northeast Region in Waltham (380 Trapelo Road, Waltham, MA 02452) has one of the best collections of naturalization records in the United States. They hold the original naturalization records for all federal courts in the New England states from 1790 to 1906. They also have dexigraph copies of naturalization records from most non-federal courts covering the same year span for Maine, Massachusetts, New Hampshire, Rhode Island, and Vermont. Original naturalization records (1790–1906) for the non-federal courts in Connecticut are available as well.

The archives also keep a large collection of post-1906 naturalization records. They have the original records from all federal courts in New England and all courts in Connecticut. The time frame of the holdings varies from state to state.

The dexigraph copies were created as a Works Progress Administration (WPA) project during the Great Depression. The intent was to photostat naturalization records from all courts in New England. Unfortunately, not all of the courts had their records copied. A list of all courts that did have records copied is available at the National Archives in Waltham. In addition to the dexigraph copies, a soundex was created for the pre-1906 records held at the archives.

Naturalization records will often (but not always) give the date and place of birth. The place of birth given may not state the specific town but should at least give the province of origin in Canada as well as the date and place of arrival in the United States. If your ancestor arrived in the United States after 1895, their arrival may be documented in the St. Albans Border Crossing records.

Obituaries

Obituaries can also be a source of information on place of birth. In addition to the place of residence, occupation, and heirs one can often find the place of birth given in the obituaries of individuals who were born in Canada but died in the United States. Daily and weekly newspapers are the most common source of obituaries and death notices. However, organizational and alumni publications will also quite often have necrology columns. Remember that the information in obituaries is usually given by the next of kin and is therefore subject to the limitations of their knowledge.

Voter Registration Records

One little-used source of information is voter registration records. Most of these records start at the late nineteenth or early twentieth centuries. Information recorded usually includes name, residence, occupation, and place of birth. Foreign-born residents had to provide proof of citizenship when they registered to vote. The date and place of their naturalization is usually recorded, sometimes including the actual certificate numbers to make locating the original record easier.

In addition to becoming naturalized in their own right, a person could become naturalized if their father became a citizen while the child was still a minor. A woman could also become a citizen by marrying a citizen of the United States, or if her husband became naturalized. All of the above scenarios are known as derivative citizenship. When a person registered to vote, they were required to provide the date and place of naturalization of their father (or husband). This can be extremely helpful when trying to establish familial relationships between people who have very common names (like Patrick Murphy). Most voter registration records have not yet been microfilmed and are still available in the local town offices.

Military Records

The draft registration cards of World War I provide a fountain of information on male ancestors. There were three registrations of males in the United States for draft lottery purposes. The first registration took place June 5, 1917, for men who were born between 1886 and 1896 (age 21–31 at the time). The registration card included information on the person's name, address, date of birth, place of birth, age, race, citizenship, occupation, employer, marital status, and dependant relatives. The second registration took place June 5, 1918, for men born between 1896 and 97 (age 20–22 at the time). The registration card for these individuals, in addition to the above information, asked for father's place of birth. The third registration occurred September 12, 1918, for men born between 1873 and 1886 and 1897 and 1900 (ages 18–21 and 32–45 at the time). This last card also asked for information on the name and residence of the next of kin.

It is important to note that all males residing in the United States, regardless of their citizenship status, filled out the draft registration cards. If you have an individual who never naturalized, these records may provide an excellent substitute to get you back to the place of origin. The next of kin for recent immigrants may actually list the names and addresses of relatives still living in Canada at the time.

World War I Draft Registration Cards are available on microfilm at the National Archives and through the Family History Library in Salt Lake City. The records are arranged state by state. Each state is organized by draft board. It is necessary to know the address of an individual to locate them in the records. In large cities, it may be necessary to look through several draft boards to locate the proper registration card.

In addition to the federal draft registration, the state of Connecticut conducted a military preparedness survey in February 1917. All males living in the state, as well as female nurses, were asked to fill out surveys. The information included name, address, occupation, age, height, weight, marital status, dependents, physical disability, and questions about various skills, such as horseback riding, wireless operation, navigation, and so forth. There are also three questions on citizenship: Are you a citizen of the United States? If not, have you taken out first papers? If not, what is your nationality? Another question asks about military service "in this or any other country." This question can lead to information in the Canadian Archives if the individual served in the military before emigrating.

These are just some of the ways to pinpoint your ancestor's place of origin. The more precise information you can glean from records in the United States the better off you will be when turning north to continue the search for your family. Search all the records and examine all the information with care, and hopefully you will be amply rewarded.

Major Nineteenth-Century Immigrant Sources at NEHGS
Gary Boyd Roberts

Photo of men in military uniform in an unidentified foreign country. (Mss.)

I'm not a specialist in the middle and late nineteenth century, but a few thoughts about sources used in our library every day may prove useful.

On our fourth floor, we have all New England and Canadian censuses before 1900 and some after. Likewise, we have all available vital records for New England and Canada, lacking only, among those recorded, Connecticut 1851–1900. Recent valuable acquisitions include the Boston Custom Passenger List (alphabetized), 1847–1891, and all county and local New England naturalization records, 1791–1906. I know very little about French Canada, but my colleagues Michael Leclerc, Jerry Anderson, and George Sanborn do, and one of them is usually available to patrons. For early Québec families, I often retrieve the volumes by Tanguay and its recent partial update and expansion by Jetté; we also have the 47 volumes of French-Canadian baptisms, marriages, and burials to 1765. I'm sometimes sent articles — or they are brought to my

Major Nineteenth-Century Immigrant Sources at NEHGS (cont.)

attention — covering French seigneurial ancestry and Capetian royal descents. These are a special interest of Professor Roger Lawrence, formerly of St. Anselm College in Manchester, N.H. I keep what is brought to my attention, but I'm not actively collecting such data. I eagerly await a volume by Professor Lawrence, and would be equally fascinated by a volume of conquistador Spanish noble and royal descents for early settlers of South America (one surprising discovery in Salt Lake City was a volume that translates as "ancestry of the liberator," and outlined royal and other Spanish ancestry for Simon Bolivar).

Several years ago the great Norwegian scholar Gerhard Naeseth came to Boston and lectured at NEHGS. Before his death a few years ago, he published his long-planned volume I of, in effect, a genealogical dictionary of Norwegians in America (covering those through 1850). Another NEHGS speaker was the late Rabbi Malcolm Stern, whose *First American Jewish families* consists of charts covering descendants to date of Jewish immigrants (mostly Sephardic, from Spain or Portugal) through 1840; I was especially pleased to note the inclusion of Judah Benjamin, Benjamin Cardozo, and Louis Brandeis. Robert Swearinga has compiled, among other works on the Dutch in America, *Dutch Immigrants in U.S. Ship Manifests, 1820–1880* (2 volumes).

Concerning immigration largely post-1840, *Famine Immigrants* (8 volumes, covering the Irish exodus, 1846–1851), *Germans to America* (73 volumes to date,

1840s, 1850–1890s), *Italians to America* (16 volumes to date, 1880–1901), and *Migration from the Russian Empire* (6 volumes to date, beginning with 1875, and covering largely Polish and/or Jewish immigrants) are all excerpted from the New York passenger lists 1820–1929 (the close of Ellis Island). These volumes have been published by either Scholarly Resources in Wilmington, Delaware, or Genealogical Publishing Company in Baltimore, in cooperation with the Balch Institute of Temple University in Philadelphia, where the National Archives has deposited the originals of nineteenth century passenger lists. These volumes list all immigrants from ports in their respective exit country (not all of that nationality) to New York City only — not Boston, Philadelphia, Baltimore, New Orleans, or any other major ports. Genealogical Publishing Co. earlier published lists of immigrants to Philadelphia in the decades immediately before 1820, New York 1820–1832, and Baltimore 1820–1837. A recent volume by Maureen Taylor covered nineteenth-century immigrants to Rhode Island ports. P. W. Filby's massive *Passenger and Immigration Lists Index,* 3 volumes (1981, with annual supplements since) in effect covers all colonial immigrants and many more pre-1820. As Bill Filby found or heard about more early American passenger lists, he encouraged their publication, and was thus responsible for some of the comprehensiveness of his own work. As these Port of New York post-1820 volumes appeared, they have, I believe, been included in the supplements, all published, as were the original 3 volumes, by Gale Research Company in Detroit. Also of interest are the eight volumes of *The Search for Missing Friends*, advertisements for missing relatives from *The Boston Pilot*, 1831– 1920, published by NEHGS 1989–1999. These volumes contain probably over 100,000 Irish place origins and are the single largest source for these clues, essential for further research in Ireland.

Finding Your Civil War Ancestors at NEHGS

David Allen Lambert

Clement Granet, 1st Lieut., Co. J. 58th Regiment, Mass. Volunteers (Levitt Family Papers Mss. 623)

If you suspect an ancestor served in the Civil War, you can find a wealth of material at the NEHGS Research Library that may tell you more about him. For the scope of this article I will concentrate on Civil War soldiers from New England regiments. When examining the pedigree charts of NEHGS patrons I often inquire if their relative served in the Civil War. Generally a Civil War soldier's year of birth would be between 1820 and 1847. Of course there are examples of veterans with earlier or later years of birth, but this seems to be the average range. While you may already know the residence of your ancestor, don't be too surprised if he did not enlist in his hometown. Recruits would often seek out bounty being paid by communities looking to fill their state regimental quota. For instance, you might have a farm boy from Barnstead, New Hampshire, coming down to serve in a regiment being raised in Amesbury, Massachusetts.

To begin your search for your Civil War ancestor at NEHGS, follow the steps outlined below. If you already know the regiment in which your ancestor served, then you can skip to step 2.

Step 1:

Begin by looking for your ancestor's name in a series of books, found on the sixth floor of our library, titled *The Roster of Union Soldiers 1861–1865* (Wilmington, N.C.: Broadfoot Publications, 1997) [REF E494/H49/1997]. The

---

Published online on *NewEnglandAncestors.org*, August 9, 2002.

New England states are contained in the following volumes: Connecticut (vol. 4); Maine (vol. 1); Massachusetts (vols. 2–3); New Hampshire (vol. 1); Rhode Island (vol. 4); and Vermont (vol. 2). We also have the complete series for all other states of both the Union and Confederate armies. These volumes are arranged by state, and list the soldiers alphabetically. This is a quick way to determine if your ancestor served from a particular state. It will identify the soldier as: "Lambert, David A., 12th [Mass.] Inf., Co. A." You will then need to determine if this soldier is in fact your ancestor.

Step 2:

Look for a detailed listing of the soldiers in your ancestor's regiment. For some states there are compiled lists of soldiers containing details such as age, residence, race, service dates, and occupation. This information should help you narrow down if you in fact have the correct veteran from the first step. The following is a listing of statewide compiled volumes of veterans.

Connecticut:

Connecticut Adjutant General's Office, *Catalogue of Connecticut Volunteer Organizations (Infantry, Cavalry, and Artillery) in the Service of the United States 1861–1865*. (Hartford, Conn.: Brown & Gross, 1869) [E499.3/C66/1869 also Loan].

Massachusetts:

Massachusetts Adjutant General's Office, *Massachusetts Soldiers, Sailors, and Marines in the Civil War*. (Norwood, Mass.: Norwood Press, 1931–37), 9 volumes [REF E513/M32/1931–1937 also Loan].

New Hampshire:

Augustus D. Ayling, *Revised Register of Soldiers and Sailors of New Hampshire in the War of the Rebellion* (Concord, N.H.: Ira C. Evans,1895) [REF E520.3/N55/1895 also Loan].

Rhode Island:

Names of Offices, Soldiers and Seamen in Rhode Island Regiments, of Belonging to the State of Rhode Island. (Providence, R.I.: Providence Press, 1869; reprinted Salem, Mass.: Higginson Book Co., 1998) [E528.3/R46/1869 also Loan].

Vermont:

Revised Roster of Vermont Volunteers and Lists of Vermonters Who Served in the Army and Navy of the United States During the War of the Rebellion (Montpelier, Vt., Watchman Publishing Co., 1892) [Rare Book E533.3/V53/1892].

You can also use published regimental histories to find information. NEHGS maintains a collection of all New England Civil War regimental histories on microfiche on the fourth floor [E49/C58/1991]. These often include post–Civil War information on the veteran and occasionally photographs. There are also some Civil War–era Adjutant General reports for the state of Maine with limited details.

Step 3:

If your ancestor died during the Civil War, it should be indicated in either a compiled state list and/or a regimental history. Another source to determine this is the Roll of Honor, which could also reveal his last resting place. The printed version of this multivolume set can be found behind the sixth-floor library reference desk [REF E494/U558/1994], or you can view the CD-ROM [REF E494/R64/1996] on the fourth floor. With this resource you can easily determine if your Union Civil War ancestor is interred in a National Cemetery in United States. A grave number is often associated with each listing, which will allow you to find the location of the grave when you visit the cemetery. Sometimes the remains of the veteran were returned back to their hometown for burial in a family or military plot. Perhaps you will want to examine the extensive collection of gravestone transcriptions kept in the NEHGS Manuscript Department.

Step 4:

If your ancestor survived the Civil War, and/or left a widow or dependant, you might want to check to see if he had a pension file. At NEHGS we maintain Internet access to some of the databases at the *Ancestry.com* website. You can easily search through the database and view an online image of the actual card from the NARA T-288 series for pensions (1861–1934). To order the original pension files you will need to request the NATF-85 form from the National Archives and Records Administration, 8th and Pennsylvania Ave. NW, Washington, DC 20408

The pension file of your ancestor will unlock a virtual time capsule of information on his life after the Civil War. It details everything from medical problems, employment history, and residences since the war. You will usually find original handwritten letters sent by your veteran ancestor, his widow, or individuals representing them. Sometimes letters are from immediate family, neighbors, co-workers, clergy, or employers. These letters usually deal with the verification of a medical problem of the pensioner or marital details of the widow.

You will also want to investigate the pensions of fellow veterans in your ancestor's unit. You will often find that veterans wrote to the pension office after being queried about the service of a fellow soldier in their unit. This process can be rather costly if performed via the mail. So you might wish to attend a future NEHGS tour to the National Archives in Washington, D.C., to examine the documents first hand.

Step 5:

NEHGS also has a wealth of vital records extending into the twentieth century for all New England states. Our collection of deeds and probate for most of the New England counties will also assist your search. Federal and state censuses for New England states are also valuable research tools. Especially helpful are the indexed 1890 Special Census of U.S. Veterans (which also lists veterans' widows); the 1865 Rhode Island State Census; and the 1910 federal census. The 1910 census indicated if a person was a Civil War veteran [Union/Confederate]. You should also check sources outside of NEHGS such as newspaper obituaries and records of the GAR (Grand Army of the Republic). Also check the local historical societies of the town in which your ancestor lived after the war for group photos of local veterans' gatherings.

NEHGS keeps a large collection of Civil War letters and diaries, some of which may relate to your ancestor's regiment. If you have original Civil War letters or diaries, consider donating them to the NEHGS Manuscript Department for safekeeping. If you prefer to keep the original, we would be glad to keep a copy of the item. The careful preservation methods employed by our archival staff guarantee that your original treasures will be safely preserved for future generations.

Appendices

Donating Books and Manuscripts

NEHGS encourages our members and friends to consider donating their genealogical materials. Books donated to NEHGS will be added to our Research or Circulating Libraries as new titles or replacement copies. If not currently needed in the collection, duplicate copies of books may be resold to benefit the NEHGS Book Preservation Fund.

Many researchers own unique manuscript items. These may include early diaries, correspondence, Bible records, deeds, family papers, charts, and unpublished works. Over more than 150 years, members' donations such as these have been the cornerstone of our world-class manuscript collection. Many researchers wish to plan for the eventual disposition of their family collections. NEHGS is the perfect place to preserve and protect your family treasures, and make them available to future generations of family history researchers.

For more information on making a donation of books, manuscripts, artwork, or other items to NEHGS, please contact Archivist Timothy Salls, by email at tsalls@nehgs.org or at 617-536-5740 ext. 232.

Maps of the Library

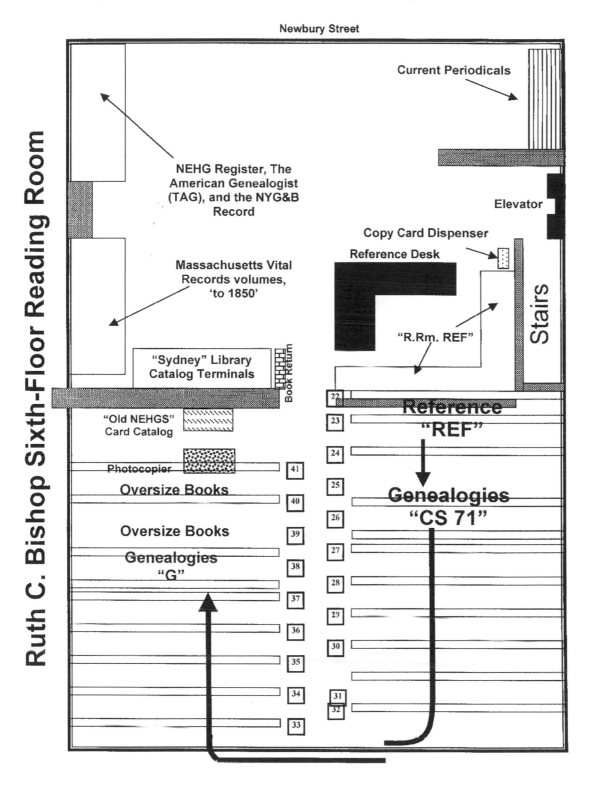

Newbury Street

Ruth C. Bishop Sixth-Floor Reading Room

Current Periodicals

NEHG Register, The
American Genealogist
(TAG), and the NYG&B
Record

Elevator

Copy Card Dispenser

Reference Desk

Massachusetts Vital
Records volumes,
'to 1850'

"R.Rm. REF"

Stairs

"Sydney" Library
Catalog Terminals

Book Return

22

Reference
"REF"

23

"Old NEHGS"
Card Catalog

24

Photocopier

41

25

Genealogies
"CS 71"

Oversize Books

40

26

Oversize Books

39

27

Genealogies
"G"

38

28

37

29

36

30

35

34

31

32

33

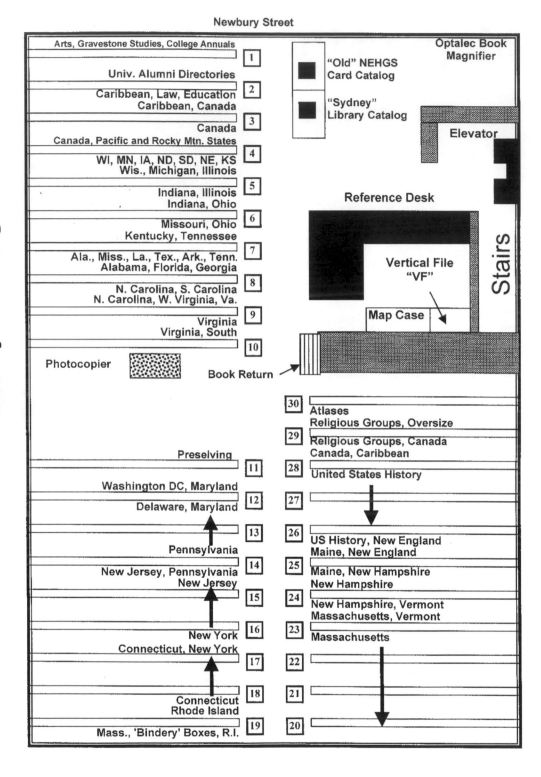

Fifth-Floor Local History Reading Room

Newbury Street

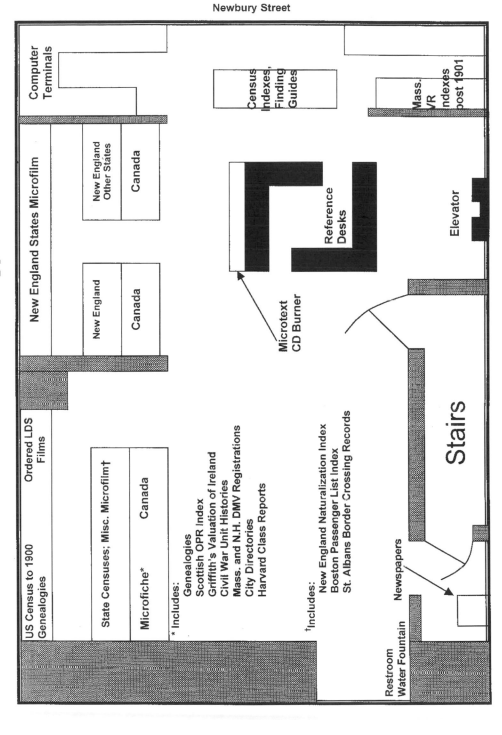

Dean C. and Roberta J. Smith
Fourth-Floor Technology Room

Computer Terminals

Census Indexes, Finding Guides

Mass. VR Indexes post 1901

New England States Microfilm

New England Other States

Canada

New England

Canada

Reference Desks

Elevator

Microtext CD Burner

Ordered LDS Films

US Census to 1900 Genealogies

State Censuses; Misc. Microfilm†

Microfiche*   Canada

* Includes:
    Genealogies
    Scottish OPR Index
    Griffith's Valuation of Ireland
    Civil War Unit Histories
    Mass. and N.H. DMV Registrations
    City Directories
    Harvard Class Reports

†Includes:
    New England Naturalization Index
    Boston Passenger List Index
    St. Albans Border Crossing Records

Stairs

Newspapers

Restroom Water Fountain

Newbury Street

First-Floor Treat Rotunda and Constance Wadley Fuller Reading Room

Bookstore

Huguenot Society of London Publications

Receptionist

Orientation Center

Fireplace

English Genealogy, Harleian Society Series, *The Genealogist*

London Parish Registers, English Counties (continued) B–Co

English Genealogy Index Library Series

Snack Room

Victoria County Histories of England

"Sydney" Library Catalog

English Counties La–Y

- England and Scottish Genealogy
- Irish Genealogy
- European Genealogy
- English History
- Scottish and Irish History
- International Oversize

Compact Shelving

English Counties (continued) Co–La

Parish Registers

International Reference

Treat Mss Collection Alcove

Computer Office

Index

This index includes subjects, collections, periodicals (if described), and other topics. It rarely includes specific places, names of authors, titles of books, or specific sources.